UNSTABLE MASKS

NEW SUNS:

RACE, GENDER, AND SEXUALITY IN THE SPECULATIVE

Susana M. Morris and Kinitra D. Brooks, Series Editors

# UNSTABLE MASKS

Whiteness and American Superhero Comics

Edited by Sean Guynes and Martin Lund

THE OHIO STATE UNIVERSITY PRESS
COLUMBUS

Copyright © 2020 by The Ohio State University.
All rights reserved.

Library of Congress Cataloging-in-Publication Data
Names: Guynes, Sean, editor. | Lund, Martin, editor.
Title: Unstable masks : whiteness and American superhero comics / edited by Sean Guynes and Martin Lund.
Other titles: New suns: race, gender, and sexuality in the speculative.
Description: Columbus : The Ohio State University Press, [2020] | Series: New suns: race, gender, and sexuality in the speculative | Includes bibliographical references and index. | Summary: "Contextualizes the history of race within comic books and the fundamental whiteness observed in American superhero narratives from the late 1930s to the present"—Provided by publisher.
Identifiers: LCCN 2019033331 (print) | LCCN 2019033332 (ebook) | ISBN 9780814214183 (cloth) | ISBN 0814214185 (cloth) | ISBN 9780814277508 (ebook) | ISBN 0814277500 (ebook)
Subjects: LCSH: Comic books, strips, etc.—United States—History and criticism. | Race awareness—United States—History and criticism. | Superheroes in literature.
Classification: LCC PN6725 .U485 2020 (print) | LCC PN6725 (ebook) | DDC 741.5/352—dc23
LC record available at https://lccn.loc.gov/2019033331
LC ebook record available at https://lccn.loc.gov/2019033332

Cover design by Black Kirby
Text design by Juliet Williams
Type set in Adobe Palatino

CONTENTS

| | | |
|---|---|---|
| *List of Illustrations* | | ix |
| *Foreword* | Unmasking Whiteness: Re-Spacing the Speculative in Superhero Comics | |
| | FREDERICK LUIS ALDAMA | xi |
| *Acknowledgments* | | xvii |
| Introduction | Not to Interpret, but to Abolish: Whiteness Studies and American Superhero Comics | |
| | SEAN GUYNES AND MARTIN LUND | 1 |

## PART I: OUTLINING SUPERHEROIC WHITENESS

| | | |
|---|---|---|
| Chapter 1 | Marked for Failure: Whiteness, Innocence, and Power in Defining Captain America | |
| | OSVALDO OYOLA | 19 |
| Chapter 2 | The Whiteness of the Whale and the Darkness of the Dinosaur: The Africanist Presence in Superhero Comics from *Black Lightning* to *Moon Girl* | |
| | ERIC BERLATSKY AND SIKA DAGBOVIE-MULLINS | 38 |
| Chapter 3 | "The Original Enchantment": Whiteness, Indigeneity, and Representational Logics in *The New Mutants* | |
| | JEREMY M. CARNES | 57 |

| Chapter 4 | Fearfully and Wonderfully Made: The Racial Politics of *Cloak and Dagger* | |
| --- | --- | --- |
| | OLIVIA HICKS | 72 |
| Chapter 5 | Worlds Collide: Whiteness, Integration, and Diversity in the DC/Milestone Crossover | |
| | SHAMIKA ANN MITCHELL | 90 |
| Chapter 6 | Whiteness and Superheroes in the Comix/Codices of Enrique Chagoya | |
| | JOSÉ ALANIZ | 103 |

## PART II: REACHING TOWARD WHITENESS

| Chapter 7 | Seeing White: Normalization and Domesticity in Vision's Cyborg Identity | |
| --- | --- | --- |
| | ESTHER DE DAUW | 127 |
| Chapter 8 | "Beware the Fanatic!": Jewishness, Whiteness, and Civil Rights in *X-Men* (1963–1970) | |
| | MARTIN LUND | 142 |
| Chapter 9 | Mutation, Racialization, Decimation: The X-Men as White Men | |
| | NEIL SHYMINSKY | 158 |
| Chapter 10 | White Plasticity and Black Possibility in Darwyn Cooke's *DC: The New Frontier* | |
| | SEAN GUYNES | 174 |

## PART III: WHITENESS BY A DIFFERENT COLOR

| Chapter 11 | White or Indian? Whiteness and Becoming the White Indian Comics Superhero | |
| --- | --- | --- |
| | YVONNE CHIREAU | 193 |
| Chapter 12 | "A True Son of K'un-Lun": The Awkward Racial Politics of White Martial Arts Superheroes in the 1970s | |
| | MATTHEW PUSTZ | 212 |
| Chapter 13 | The Whitest There Is at What I Do: Japanese Identity and the Unmarked Hero in *Wolverine* (1982) | |
| | ERIC SOBEL | 226 |

| | | |
|---|---|---|
| Chapter 14 | The Dark Knight: Whiteness, Appropriation, Colonization, and Batman in the *New 52* Era | |
| | JEFFREY A. BROWN | 242 |
| Afterword | Empowerment for Some, or Tentacle Sex for All | |
| | NOAH BERLATSKY | 258 |

*List of Contributors*   265

*Index*   269

ILLUSTRATIONS

FIGURE 1.1   White racial solidarity as a means to Hydra's end (*Captain America: Steve Rogers* #8). © Marvel Comics. Image presented under fair use legislation.   26

FIGURE 1.2   Right-wing talking points used by cable news pundits to discredit a black Captain America (*Captain America: Steve Rogers* #12). © Marvel Comics. Image presented under fair use legislation.   29

FIGURE 1.3   Protests against police violence (*Captain America: Sam Wilson* #20). © Marvel Comics. Image presented under fair use legislation.   30

FIGURE 1.4   Black martyrdom as a threat to whiteness (*Captain America: Sam Wilson* #14). © Marvel Comics. Image presented under fair use legislation.   32

FIGURE 1.5   Sam Wilson relinquishes the Captain America mantle, unintentionally reinforcing the constitutive whiteness of the role (*Captain America: Sam Wilson* #21). © Marvel Comics. Image presented under fair use legislation.   35

FIGURE 2.1   Tobias Whale hoses Black Lightning (*Black Lightning* #3). © DC Comics. Image presented under fair use legislation.   44

x • ILLUSTRATIONS

| FIGURE 2.2 | Superman comes for Black Lightning (*Black Lightning* #4). © DC Comics. Image presented under fair use legislation. | 45 |
| --- | --- | --- |
| FIGURE 2.3 | The Killer-Folk racialized through sartorial design (*Moon Girl and Devil Dinosaur* #2). © Marvel Comics. Image presented under fair use legislation. | 50 |
| FIGURE 2.4 | Lunella racialized and made savage (*Moon Girl and Devil Dinosaur* #8). © Marvel Comics. Image presented under fair use legislation. | 53 |
| FIGURE 4.1 | Religious imagery in the presentation of Dagger (*Cloak and Dagger: Shadows and Light*). © Marvel Comics. Image presented under fair use legislation. | 80 |
| FIGURE 4.2 | Left to right: Dagger presented as a madonna in Cloak's imagination (*Marvel Fanfare* #19). © Marvel Comics. Image presented under fair use legislation. | 81 |
| FIGURE 4.3 | Francesco Albani's *The Annunciation* (early 1630s). | 82 |
| FIGURE 6.1 | Superman in pilgrim guise versus Tlaloc (*Crossing*). Reprinted with the artist's permission. | 107 |
| FIGURE 6.2 | A superheroic battle in *Codex Espangliensis*. Reprinted with the artist's permission. | 115 |
| FIGURE 6.3 | Superman confronts the Mixtec (*Codex Espangliensis*). Reprinted with the artist's permission. | 117 |
| FIGURE 11.1 | Tomahawk as comics superhero (*Tomahawk* #68). © DC Comics. Image presented under fair use legislation. | 196 |
| FIGURE 11.2 | Injun Jones, blue-eyed Indian (*Blazing West* #1). © American Comics Group. Image presented under fair use legislation. | 199 |
| FIGURE 11.3 | Manzar, the white Indian chief (*Indians* #1). © Fiction House Publishing. Image presented under fair use legislation. | 201 |
| FIGURE 11.4 | David Brown, the Cheyenne-adopted Golden Warrior (*Indian Fighter* #2). © Youthful Magazines. Image presented under fair use legislation. | 202 |

FOREWORD

# UNMASKING WHITENESS

## Re-Spacing the Speculative in Superhero Comics

FREDERICK LUIS ALDAMA

WHEN STEVEN SPIELBERG'S much-hyped *Ready Player One* (2018) was released, it pulled in upwards of $566 million. Critics and cinemagoers celebrated its remarkable palimpsestic layers of pop culture, how technically Spielberg took the film entertainment industry to a new level, seamlessly integrating CGI sci-fi Otherworlds with the realism of a recognizable everyday life. It's true. The pop cultural references pop. There are no glitches in the post-production digital effects that might have one hesitate as we move back and forth between the virtual world of the Oasis and everyday life for people living in Columbus, Ohio, in 2044. However, few if any critics commented on how the film (and Ernest Cline, author of the book of the same title) reproduce the white-savior narrative. In fact, they not only reproduce it, they take it to a new level of affirmation by creating protagonist Wade Watts's avatar Parzival (Parzival, also known as Percival, was one of the legendary knights at King Arthur's Round Table) as *the one* who saves the day—and the planet along with it. It's 2018. You'd think that Spielberg (and Cline), along with his cadre of co-creators, would know better. It's not the case here. It's not the case in most pop cultural phenomena created today.

In film, TV, advertisements, literature, you name it, everywhere I turn I see white people. It's the social mirror that's become normalized. For many, it's become a comfortable everyday backdrop within a larger social canvas.

For many, it's simply there; they are habituated to it. It's like that picture on the wall in a bedroom or living room that one passes every day without notice.

Of course, for many others there's never any moment of habituation. From the moment one wakes to when one sleeps (and arguably even in sleep), whiteness actively puts into high relief one's own difference, whether a phenotypic, linguistic, cultural, or other difference, and does so constantly.

None of this is new, experientially or theoretically. What's important now is that we work not only to dishabituate whiteness but to trouble it by exploring and revealing how nonwhiteness interfaces with it. Sean Guynes and Martin Lund's volume here provides a road map for all of us—that is, to do the work to nuance our understanding of the making and consuming of cultural phenomena within this planetary ideological construct.

"Planetary" sounds rather bold and large. However, we have to keep in mind that while people of color *are* the planetary majority, because of capitalism's global barbarous practices—colonization, imperialism, neoliberalism—whiteness has become cemented and naturalized as the space of privilege and domination in law and social relations. In *White*, Richard Dyer put whiteness under the microscope; he denaturalized it as a seemingly invisible color, a canvas backdrop against which other ethnicities are measured, seen, evaluated, and examined.

In my work on Latinx pop culture, I seek to *dishabituate* whiteness by excavating the resplendent ways that Latinx creators distil and reconstruct the building blocks of reality to *make* new sensorially, cognitively, and emotively our understanding of intersectional identities. To this end, I'm singularly driven to understand how cultural phenomena by and about Latinxs operates in fractalizing, multi-refracting ways within and against whiteness.

Let me clarify. Every day, we see and experience whiteness as a space of privilege. This whiteness is invisible to many, and very visible to many more. It's an ideology that has thickened with misperceptions that have aligned skin hue with behavioral and personality type: light skin = good versus dark skin = bad. Within this binary, however, there are vectors moving along a spectrum from good/white to bad/dark. In my work on Latinx superheroes, we see this play out in the overwhelming reconstruction of superheroic Latinxs as more Caucasian featured than indigenous in our *mestizo* biological makeup. So, we have in the 1940s the *criollo*-identified Zorro superheroes like The Whip, and in the 2000s we have the same with Sam Alexander as the new Nova in Marvel's *Nova* (2013–2016). These are but a few examples of the many.

But let's unpack this a bit more. Here I want to bring to mind the issue of passing, racial passing in the distillation and reconstruction of Latinxs in cultural phenomena. Sam Alexander exemplifies the case for many other mainstreamed Latinx superheroes. To different degrees, creators may or may not provide some ethnoracial Latinx markers (name, cultural and family references, language), but it's always the Caucasian features that afford entry into the privileged world of whiteness—and with this the superheroic. This assumes that real, light-skinned Latinxs (the author of this foreword included) seek to *pass* into such spaces. The fact is, many light-skinned Latinxs who make up the building blocks of reality don't seek to pass as such; indeed, many choose to embrace Latinx markers that affirm ancestry, language, culture, and political activism generally and that trouble and curtail assumptions that Latinxs who can *pass* will do so. Here we might pause to ask: Where is the reconstruction of Sam Alexander as a light-skinned Latinx, one who we hope would announce his solidarity with his darker, more surveillanced brown and black brothers and sisters? We exist. We also need these characters to exist.

What I'm proposing is the idea that mainstream creators do the homework of *looking* carefully at the complexity of the building blocks of reality before they begin their distillation work. In *Blacker the Ink*, Frances Gateward and John Jennings analyze how willfully reconstructed storyworlds in comics can make visible the rich array of black identities and experience; they seek to demonstrate how these comics are "promising possible futures."[1] Importantly, this volume is published within the book series entitled "New Suns: Race, Gender, and Sexuality in the Speculative." Books in this series (and I sit on its editorial board) seek to enrich understanding about how speculative fiction (Afrofuturism, Latinxfuturism, ethnogothic, ethnosurrealism, and the like) can be a space for the articulating of otherwise unseen intersectional identities. Taking this volume as my springboard, what I'm proposing is less that they *speculate* and imagine something *not* present in our everyday, but that by willfully attending to reality, they can and will create cultural phenomena that will shake up the current space of the speculative in cultural phenomena—from comics to films to literature and the like.

All fiction is speculative. All fiction is relational. Its ontological reality is relational, and it can only be studied and understood as relational. In *The Crisis of European Sciences and Transcendental Phenomenology*, the German philosopher Edmund Husserl introduced the concept "lifeworld" (*Lebenswelt*)

---

1. Gateward and Jennings, "Introduction," 15.

to convey the idea of an all-shared human experience. The challenge for today's creators of fiction (comics, films, etc.) is to imagine a *Lebenswelt* that at once reflects the diversity of identity and that *troubles* the all-pervasive white/good versus dark/bad Manichean ideology. In so doing, it might also seek to create something that has yet to exist, a lifeworld with entirely new relationships among humans and between humans and nature as a whole and each one of its parts. It might depict new passionate minds and behaviors, where all humans, all animals, all plants, all mountains and rivers and valleys and seas are in a new lifeworld, a new *Lebenswelt,* a new shared experience of communion of fellow humans with their whole environment and with each other and with themselves.

The comic book (or other media text) will only work if creators willfully attend to the complexity of the building blocks of reality. In this way, cultural phenomena can unmask ideologies of whiteness as well as all categories that seek to fix gender, sexuality, and ethnicity. These more complexly built *Lebenswelten* can take us to other places—places not characterized by most fiction (speculative) works that are only extrapolations of today's capitalist barbarism. While solidly constructed from the building blocks of reality, their distillations can also take us into lifeworlds where we might experience with their characters what it means to create an entirely different and new and life-supportive *Lebenswelt*. In this way, creators can *willfully* shape fictions of existing and new ontological entities that unmask and *make* new (*enstrange*) readers' relationality to whiteness. The painting in the bedroom stands out again.

So, when I talk of speculative here, it's not in sense of creating new worlds that we don't see today. I mean speculative in the sense that we need to construct new worlds that *speculate* and radically revise the tradition of the fictional world-building activities that reproduce ideologies of whiteness. Put simply, the speculative that I'm talking about is actually the willful distillation and reconstruction of the *actual* building blocks of reality. In so doing, these lifeworlds will challenge the tradition of the speculative that's been white-focused and color-blind, a tradition whereby the majority of speculative world building only imagines these worlds as white; when characters of color are included, it's usually to highlight the naturalized space of white, male privilege—*Ready Player One* as a case in point.

It is only through art (films, comics, literature, and so on) in its myriad manifestations that we can get an inkling of what freedom really is and really must remain. It is only through willfully constructed cultural phenomena that we can surmise why it is essential for us to fight for and preserve the right to science, knowledge—the speculative—the right to all the refined (quintessence) movements of the mind, the right to invent tools that lead to systemic progress for all planetary flora and fauna.

Like all cultural creations, comic books are only bound by the materials they metabolize from the world and by the power of the brain to effect metabolism and make it yield a new product (artifact, action, thought) capable of activating the body's system of sense organs and the highly complex limbic system. This system's varied functions include inter alia the manifestation of affects, learning, long-term memory and consolidation of new memories, time perception, olfaction, posture and movement, decision making and motivation, reward and pleasure, and actions and motor behavior. Among the materials of the world that comic books have to contend with and metabolize, there is the persistent and even deadly racism growing among straight white (mostly men) in the US, that targets people of color and LGBTQ peoples. It has been well established that one of the factors responsible for this racism is fear, the fear many whites feel of losing social status and privilege linked in history to patriarchy, colonialism, and supreme military, economic, and political power.

But fear not only underlies racism, it also endorses political authoritarianism and the ideology of so-called white supremacy. In addition, fear can foster a certain delight in inflicting suffering. Here the number of targets becomes hugely wide: women (mainly black and brown workers); low-income Latinx and African Americans; bisexual, transgender, gay, and lesbian communities; the homeless; immigrants; and many other people considered unwelcome and disposable.

The warfare state, the state that maintains the country in permanent war against other countries and regions all over the world, the state that thrives and makes the whole economy thrive for a tiny minority by means of the arms industry and a permanent arms economy, is also the state of patriarchy and racism—both at home and abroad. In the US and everywhere, it is a state that wages war on the poor and underprivileged, war on immigrants, war on women, war on youth, war on children, war on gender minorities, war on ethnic minorities, war by the 1 percent against the 99 percent of our planetary population.

How could this not touch all creators and not be the subject matter of their art? The brutality of our everyday reality hits our senses and obsesses the mind. For us, the only danger is to trivialize, to transform our art into superficial, dumbing entertainment, as happens often in writings for Hollywood and mainstream comics that infantilize violence and turn our present predicaments into a spectacle of gratuitous cruelty and mechanical insensitivity, emptied of human and social responsibility. Today we see our silver screens becoming more and more an ever-expanding wasteland of white, straight male heroism.

This is to say, today's creators can do better. They can do the work to untether themselves from minds forged of this white/good versus dark/bad ideology. As the scholars in this volume attest, such creators can create comics that *see* the world as it is and then willfully distill and reconstruct this in ways that open eyes to new ways of perceiving, thinking, and feeling about the complex world we inhabit. As James Baldwin once wrote: "The world changes according to the way people see it, and if you alter, even by a millimeter, the way a person looks or people look at reality, then you can change it."[2]

## Bibliography

Dyer, Richard. *White*. London: Routledge, 1997.

Gateward, Frances, and John Jennings. "Introduction: The Sweeter the Christmas." In *Blacker the Ink: Constructions of Black Identity in Comics & Sequential Art*, edited by Frances Gateward and John Jennings, 1–17. New Brunswick, NJ: Rutgers University Press, 2015.

Husserl, Edmund. *The Crisis of European Sciences and Transcendental Phenomenology*. Evanston, IL: Northwestern University Press, 1970.

Romano, John. "James Baldwin Writing and Talking." *New York Times*, September 23, 1979, https://www.nytimes.com/1979/09/23/archives/james-baldwin-writing-and-talking-baldwin-baldwin-authors-query.html.

---

2. Quoted in Romano, "James Baldwin."

ACKNOWLEDGMENTS

MANY MINDS helped produce this book through labor that went largely unpaid (the shamefully expected norm in academia). We are grateful to all of our contributors, but we want to especially thank contingent faculty and graduate students for the efforts they put into producing this volume while coping with a hostile job market in an increasingly commodified neoliberal university system. We want to thank the editors of the New Suns series, Drs. Kinitra D. Brooks and Susana M. Morris, for including *Unstable Masks*; the editors at OSU Press, Kristen Elias Rowley and Ana Jimenez-Moreno, who walked us through the proposal and production processes; the anonymous peer reviewers for providing suggestions to better the book and for being as excited about the project as we are; and the artist duo Black Kirby, John Jennings and Stacey Robinson, for creating such a powerful cover. Big thanks to Frederick Luis Aldama and Noah Berlatsky, who penned the foreword and afterword, respectively.

We also want to acknowledge Noel Ignatiev and the collective of "race traitor" scholars who emerged in the 1990s around the (unfortunately short-lived) journal *Race Traitor*. Ignatiev's 1997 argument about whiteness studies—that "the point is not to interpret whiteness but abolish it"—was a driving force behind this book.

This volume is dedicated to the countless victims of whiteness across the centuries. It is beyond time to abolish whiteness and pay reparations for its crimes, both in the US and abroad. Thank you to all the comics scholars, fans, and creators who are bringing power to the page to help make this happen, to throw off the unstable mask of whiteness pulled tight over the superhero's face.

INTRODUCTION

# NOT TO INTERPRET, BUT TO ABOLISH

Whiteness Studies and American Superhero Comics

SEAN GUYNES AND MARTIN LUND

*Unstable Masks: Whiteness and American Superhero Comics* was born in the summer of 2016 amid the imminent (but, for many liberals, seemingly impossible) election of Donald Trump as the forty-fifth president of the United States. Trump's election and his deeply xenophobic, individualist, "America first" rhetoric emboldened American white nationalists to unmask and take up a new name, the "alt-right," that allowed them to claim their racism and white pride as a simply stated alternative to conservative politics as usual. While Trump ran on a largely incoherent platform of "making America great again," many—especially those for whom the experience of living in the US either was not yet, had rarely been, or only recently had become even remotely "great"—saw the rhetoric as little more than populist claptrap barely veiling the truth of its underlying racism. Indeed, three weeks after the election, writer and literary critic Toni Morrison unpacked Trump's platform to show plainly what he and those for whom he spoke were doing: They were making America white again after so many years of giving minimal concessions to the marginalized and oppressed, in order "to keep alive the perception of white superiority." White men and women, poor and wealthy, who voted for Trump, Morrison claimed, would rather "abandon their humanity out of fear of black men and women" than face "the true horror of lost status."[1] Despite much commentary about and out-

---

1. Morrison, "Making America White Again."

rage at the election results, none of this was new or unexpected. As Morrison stated so boldly twenty-four years earlier: "American means white."[2] Trump's ascendancy grew out of and continued a history of white privilege, of backlash against movements for social justice, and of conservative opposition to the expansion of equality in the US, all of which attempted unironically to defend the very statement Morrison used to diagnose the still thriving problem of Du Bois's color line.[3]

Let's be clear from the outset what we talk about when we talk about whiteness: It is not a phenotypical characteristic, an observable and unchangeable biological fact, nor is it a scientific designation, as the racialist term "Caucasian" would have us believe. Rather, whiteness is a set of malleable historically, culturally, and geographically situated values that join together various meanings of race, class, gender, sexuality, and other modes of being and belonging, and that establish a master category against which other hierarchies are developed. In the West, it is one of the key historical formations of power, surveillance, and control. Whiteness is not static, it is neither certain nor a given; it is made and remade and unmade as history and culture bend and shift and break. Throughout the long, winding history of whiteness, scientists and scholars (pseudo- and credible) have played an important role in the process through which it has been formed and lived under. So have governments and their agencies. And, crucially, so has popular culture.

As numerous critics and historians have demonstrated, from the Frankfurt School to the current renaissance in cultural studies, popular culture is an important field for the circulation of discourses of power. Popular culture has been crucial to the creation and structuring of hierarchies of race in the US, from the establishment and ordering of the color line to the whitening of once nonwhite or racially "in between" "white ethnics." The topic of race and popular culture has mostly been discussed in terms of nonwhite people, but as the growing field of whiteness studies has begun to show, focusing exclusively on people of color creates a blind spot in cultural analyses of power that reinforces the hegemonic status of whiteness as the ostensibly deracialized norm. From the creation of the first American superhero, Superman, in 1938 and onward, superheroes have been deeply informed and structured by notions and ideals of whiteness. The prominence of the white superhero—and, most commonly, of the white male superhero—in

---

2. Morrison, *Playing in the Dark*, 47.

3. For key discussions of backlash against strides for social justice, see Robin, *The Reactionary Mind*; Faludi, *Backlash* and *The Terror Dream*; Roediger, *How Race Survived*; Frye Jacobson, *Roots Too*.

American comic books and in the transmedial adaptation of their narratives throughout the twentieth and into the twenty-first century has transformed the white male body, and the boundaries of morality and justice that it polices and upholds, into a widely circulated visual lexicon of white (male) superiority. It is no surprise that the vast majority of the chapters in this volume emphasize the constitutive discourses of whiteness and masculinity in the narratives of American superhero comics' overwhelmingly male roster.

While it would seem self-evident, given the predominance of physically (and often mentally) superior white bodies in superhero narratives, that these stories are fantasies of white power, the relationship between whiteness and the American superhero has remained almost entirely unexplored. This is not to criticize comics scholars who have addressed issues of race (as opposed to the unmarked, and thus hegemonically nonracialized identity of whiteness), but simply to point out that while studies of representation and calls for greater diversity in superhero comics among scholars, critics, and fans are necessary, they largely address the symptoms, not the root causes from which the need for diverse superheroes (and creators) stems. The source of racial injustice in the field of superhero comics lies in the very fact that the superhero, as a generic figure and in many, if not most, of its specific manifestations, is a white male ideological formation nested in and supporting the discourses of power on which American society trades.

The aim of this book, then, is to address what we perceive as a critical lacuna in the fields of whiteness studies, comics studies, and superhero studies, building on earlier work on race in superhero comics but with the express intention of understanding the interstitial relationship among whiteness, American culture, and comic book superheroes. This book places the superhero at the center of a range of conversations about the history of whiteness in America, attending to key moments and movements in the development of the superhero genre, ranging from the relationship between white masculinity and the performance of Indianness (redfacing) in superhero and superhero-adjacent comics from the Golden Age to the present, to the phenomenon of white martial artist superheroes in the 1970s, and on to current debates about the configuration of whiteness, racial "inferiority," interracial relationships, and violence in comics like *Captain America*, *Wolverine*, *Cloak and Dagger*, and *Moon Girl and Devil Dinosaur*.

The chapters in this book bring together a range of scholars who demonstrate, historicize, and challenge the operations of whiteness in superhero comics. The authors look at superhero narratives as well as at the production, distribution, and audience and reception contexts of those narratives, highlighting the imbrication of forces that have helped to create, normalize, question, and even subvert American beliefs about whiteness and race. *Unstable Masks* considers the co-constitutive nature of identity, representation, narrative, production and consumption, and historical and cultural contexts in forging ideas about who gets to be American and who gets to be a superhero in the pages of comic books.

## Whiteness Studies and American Culture

The superhero champions a master narrative of whiteness. This narrative foregrounds the dialectical function of whiteness as simultaneously assimilationist and separationist. Since the beginning of the colonial age, and especially in the territories that became the US, whiteness has been used to strategically assimilate or separate, to incorporate, for example, formerly nonwhite Europeans (Jews, Slavs, Irish) into whiteness in order to arrange them against other not-as-yet or nonwhites, for example, Africans, Native Americans, Asians, mixed-race peoples, and so on. Historian Ronald Takaki gives an account of this process in his discussion of Bacon's Rebellion in 1676, when poor blacks and whites, indentured servants and slaves alike, joined together in rebellion against propertied white elites in Virginia. Takaki shows how, in the aftermath of the suppressed revolt, colonial authorities and wealthy landowners "reorganize[d] society on the basis of class *and* race" by turning to "Africa as their primary source of labor and to slavery as their main system of labor," in the process playing the grievances of poor whites against black slaves instead of against the landed elite.[4] As lawyer and legal scholar Michelle Alexander describes this pivotal moment in racial history, "deliberately and strategically, the planter class extended privileges to poor whites in an effort to drive a wedge between them and black slaves."[5] This strategy of division—this "racial bribe"—obscured potential ties of class solidarity between whites and nonwhites, co-opted and racialized long-held distinctions between civilization and barbarism, and laid the groundwork for what would, in decades and centuries to come, develop into a deeply ingrained conception of whiteness as "superior" and of any color as "inferior."[6] Under these conditions, whiteness has historically solicited assimilation from some while separating out and designating others as non-

---

4. Takaki, *A Different Mirror*, 60.
5. Alexander, *The New Jim Crow*, 25.
6. See, for example, Jackson, *Scandinavians in Chicago*; Frye Jacobson, *Whiteness of a Different Color and Roots Too*; Painter, *History of White People*; Roediger, *Wages of Whiteness, Working Toward Whiteness,* and *How Race Survived.*

white, in the process establishing a racialized regime of power that extends social control over those deemed both white and those marked as nonwhite.

The history and local dimensions of whiteness as a racialized regime of control mediating other forms of power, exploitation, and (imposed) difference has been the subject of an increasing body of scholarship known unsurprisingly as whiteness studies. One genealogy of whiteness studies sees its origin in the long history of intellectuals of color, from W. E. B. Du Bois to James Baldwin, addressing whiteness as the key problem structuring racial inequality and the color line. Particularly compelling in this tradition is African American novelist Richard Wright's *White Man, Listen!*, released in 1957 and later reissued as a mass market paperback in 1964, which challenged white readers to face the psychological effects of white supremacy on people of color the world over.[7] Analyses of race that attended to the place of whiteness in American culture and history appeared, in fits and starts, alongside the politically accented, radical work of black and ethnic studies scholars who found a place in the postwar and especially post-1960s US academy. Particularly notable is activist-writer Theodore W. Allen, whose work in the 1960s and 1970s pioneered the concept of whiteness or the "white race" as a formation for social control;[8] and in the 1980s, women's studies scholar Peggy McIntosh developed the now ubiquitous concept of "white privilege" in her working paper "White Privilege and Male Privilege" (1988). It was not until the early 1990s, in the midst of the "canon wars" and the push for a more diverse humanities, that whiteness studies emerged as an institutional force with the publication, in rapid succession, of historian David R. Roediger's *The Wages of Whiteness* (1991), Toni Morrison's *Playing in the Dark* (1992), sociologist Ruth Frankenberg's *White Women, Race Matters*, historian Noel Ignatiev's *How the Irish Became White* (1995), cultural theorist Mike Hill's critical reader *Whiteness* (1997), and film theorist Richard Dyer's *White* (1997), as well as the foundation of the controversial journal *Race Traitor* (1993–2005), edited by Ignatiev and legal scholar John Garvey, and featuring the slogan "treason to whiteness is loyalty to humanity."

From the mid-1990s onward studies of whiteness proliferated at a steady pace. The constructedness of race and of whiteness in particular, and the decisively ideological and material bases of the (constantly shifting) color line, have been definitively established. Each passing year sees the recovery

---

7. Wright, *White Man, Listen!* See also Roediger, *Black on White* for a collection of black intellectuals writing on whiteness.

8. Allen began publishing his historical research on the invention of whiteness in the 1960s, but it culminated in his meticulous, two-volume *The Invention of the White Race* (published in 1994 and 1997).

of yet more lost histories of race-making that deepen our understanding of the contours of racial domination and oppression, as well as of resistance against the hegemony of whiteness. Take, for example, recent work by legal historian James Q. Whitman, which shows how the "American model" of race law, from Jim Crow to the 1930s, formed the basis of Hitler's white supremacist legal system and by extension race laws worldwide.[9] Scholars of whiteness even, in some ways, predicted the "post-racial" moment that was supposedly signaled by Barack Obama's election in 2008, while also reining in the excesses of "post-racial" thought by vigorously questioning the public investment in the idea that race had lost its importance.[10] That race survived the "post-racial" and bore forth a new urgency for whiteness and critical race studies is self-evident from the vantage point of 2019. On the one hand, recent years have seen the formation of a resurgent, intersectional civil rights movement galvanized in the wake of George Zimmerman's 2013 acquittal for the murder of Trayvon Martin and coalescing following Michael Brown's 2014 murder in Ferguson, Missouri, as well as countless other instances of police brutality, inspiring the #BlackLivesMatter movement for black liberation and racial justice.[11] On the other hand, as already noted, the so-called alt-right has emerged from the fringes to become an influential public and political force, not least in the guise of movement figurehead Richard Spencer or former White House chief strategist and Breitbart News executive chairman Steve Bannon, or in the increasingly bold use of a racialized, white nationalist language by Donald Trump on social media and in speeches, where previously radical public statements of white pride and superiority were disassociated from the mainstream—even as liberals and conservatives, leftists and reactionaries alike maintain racially unjust policies that disproportionately benefit whites.

Thus, despite rumors of its demise, race-as-color retains its salience in the US to this day, although race-as-whiteness is becoming ever more talked

---

9. Whitman, *Hitler's American Model*; Kühl, *The Nazi Connection*.

10. Bonilla-Silva's *Racism without Racists* pioneered the study of the insipid racism of "post-racial" America; Roediger's *How Race Survived US History* offers a look at the many ways in which race as a social control mechanism mutated in key periods of social unrest, almost always to the benefit of whites and the detriment of blacks and other peoples of color.

11. Taylor's *From #BlackLivesMatter to Black Liberation* and Lebron's *The Making of Black Lives Matter* offer important historical and theoretical approaches to #BlackLivesMatter. Also of import to the larger colonial context of whiteness and its oppressive history was the #NoDAPL movement at Standing Rock in 2016–2017. Both movements are aspects of a larger, multipronged social justice movement against capitalism, racism, heteropatriarchy, and colonialism climaxing in the wake of Trump's presidential coup.

about, thanks no doubt to the pioneering work of the scholars mentioned here, and many others still. In fact, a growing number of people are becoming savvy readers of whiteness, able to identify and criticize the workings of "white privilege," for example, in their own lives (and those of friends and family), in the actions of public figures, especially politicians and celebrities, and in the media they consume. Literary critic Eleanor Courtemanche labels this new situation of engaged media criticism by educated youth—and particularly of the osmotic spread of once hefty concepts from feminist, queer, and cultural theory—"Cultural Studies 2.0."[12] In the era of Cultural Studies 2.0, *white privilege* is a widely understood term, and has become the basis for the proliferation of widespread, digitally mediated discussions about race and white people's complicity with racism *as a system of oppression* rather than as discrete instances, actions, or persons.

In an era that is alternatively criticized or praised as color-blind and post-racial, Americans are increasingly adept at seeing whiteness. Yet, in the academy, the influence of whiteness in many corners of American life and culture remains unstudied, even as the popular press and social media users write daily about issues of whiteness, race, and diversity in various popular culture texts. This is evident in popular criticism of the comics industry and especially in the fandoms surrounding mainstream superhero comics. But much of this popular criticism, while genuine and important, remains firmly rooted in the present racial formation of American superhero comics. With this book, we want not only to join that ongoing conversation but to supplement it with a longer historical view that recalls and reveals how the superhero got to where it is today.

## The Whiteness of the Superhero

Picture a superhero.

What comes immediately to mind?

Odds are that you are imagining a white man, perhaps even a specific white man with a name and origin story you've memorized or otherwise soaked up through your awareness of American popular culture tropes. This is only to be expected: The superhero is a white—and overwhelmingly cisgender, male, straight, and middle-class—ideological formation and has been so since its inception.

---

12. Courtemanche, "The Peculiar Success of Cultural Studies 2.0."

DC Comics's Superman is widely acknowledged as the prototypical American superhero. Created by Jerry Siegel and Joe Shuster, two young Jewish American men in Cleveland, Ohio, sometime in the early to mid-1930s and premiering in 1938, Superman is the product of a tense era in the history of whiteness. In the early twentieth century, Jewish Americans were feeling the simultaneous push and pull of Americanization: On the one hand, anti-Semitism in the US was at a historical fever pitch; on the other hand, Jewish Americans of (mostly) European descent, along with other groups now considered "white ethics," such as Italians, Greeks, and Slavs, were in the process of whitening. In early Superman comics, these tensions were dealt with in two ways, one "positive" and one "negative": While the vaguely ethnic Superman was a paragon of New Dealer ideology and of hyper-patriotism, his stories were larded with denigration and marginalization of women and people of color. Combined, this amounted to an argument for the Americanness of Jewish Americans and other white ethnic men.[13] As the model for countless imitators, Superman laid the groundwork for what would become the genre and field of the superhero in which, to this day, the implicit answer to the question of who gets to be a superhero remains: "the white heterosexual man."[14]

This is not to say that there are no, nor never were, superheroes of color, or female, queer, poor, or even disabled superheroes, for that matter. But it cannot be denied that, collectively, such superheroes are few and far between. As historian Mercedes Yanora points out, because black superheroes are inescapably expected to live up to the hypermasculine white ideal of the superhero, they are implicitly linked to "crime and therefore incapable of representing an altruistic crime-fighting" identity (while female superheroes are in a similar double bind because "acting too much like a man or woman would effectively undermine her credibility as both a desirable woman and legitimate superhero").[15]

When any character that deviates from the implicit white male norm is announced as the star of a forthcoming comic, especially one published by the "Big Two" of superhero comics, Marvel and DC, they are hailed as representatives of that entire demographic. On the flip side, when—almost invariably—they are cancelled on account of poor sales (or company reboots), or when their usefulness to the company's public image wears off and they are unceremoniously faded into the background, the demographic loses that tokenistic representation. As a result, characters of color are often assimi-

---

13. Lund, *Re-Constructing the Man of Steel*.
14. Yanora, "Marked by Foreign Policy," 117.
15. Yanora, "Marked by Foreign Policy," 116–17.

lated into the genre through submersion into the superhero "Melting Pot."[16] Long-running solo titles starring a nonwhite superhero—such as *Black Lightning* (1977–1978, 1995–1996), *Black Panther* (1977–1979, 1988, 1998–2003, 2005–2008, 2009–2010, 2016–), or the title characters of any Milestone Media comic (1993–1997)—are rare, and still rarer are those superheroes of color who have appeared regularly for decades; in most cases, though, the latter are sidekicks (Captain America's Falcon), members of a large superhero team (Storm, Sunfire, and Moonstar of the X-Men, Cyborg of the Teen Titans, Katana of the Outsiders), or new iterations of old characters (John Stewart, Simon Baz, and Jessica Cruz as Green Lanterns, Kamala Khan as Ms. Marvel, Ryan Choi as Atom, Jaime Reyes as Blue Beetle). In virtually every instance, they are written by white men. All of this has had the effect, over so many decades, of emphasizing that the superhero is, de facto, white. All else is an exception.

Still, in the academic study of superheroes, which has flowered since its meager beginnings in the 1990s, whiteness has remained nigh invisible. When the superhero has been analyzed as an entity, it has been through the lenses of mythology or form.[17] As race and ethnicity have come under the comics scholar's gaze, it has often been in the guise of marked differences from whiteness, for example through studies of representations of people of color and white ethnics. Cultural studies scholar Jeffrey A. Brown pioneered such critical scholarship with his book *Black Superheroes, Milestone Media, and Their Fans* (2000), which looked at the independent, black-owned superhero comics publisher that distributed through DC Comics between 1993 and 1997. Brown's study historicized the representation of blackness in superhero comics and popular culture, offering Milestone as an unprecedented case study. Since Brown's monograph, several books and edited collections have appeared on blackness in superhero comics, as well as on Latinxs, Native Americans, Asian Americans, Arab and Muslim Americans, and multiculturalism more generally—not to mention dozens of articles and book chapters.[18] In addition, there are many studies that read race as

---

16. See Lund and Lewis, "Whence the Muslim Superhero?," 6.

17. In this regard, perhaps the most influential and widely cited are Reynolds, *Super Heroes*; Klock, *How to Read Superhero Comics*; and Coogan, *Superhero*.

18. See, for example, Alaniz, *Death, Disability, and the Superhero*; Aldama, *Latinx Comic Book Storytelling*, *Latinx Superheroes*, *Multicultural Comics*, and *Your Brain on Latino Comics*; Aldama and González, *Graphic Borders*; Brown, *Black Superheroes*; carrington, *Speculative Blackness*, chaps. 3–4; Cocca, *Superwomen*; Fawaz, *The New Mutants*; Gateward and Jennings, eds., *The Blacker the Ink*; Howard and Jackson, *Black Comics*; Lewis and Lund, *Muslim Superheroes*; Nama, *Super Black*; Sheyahshe, *Native Americans in Comic Books*; Whaley, *Black Women in Sequence*.

an underlying structure for the genre, and while this is indisputably the case, as contributors argue in this book, these readings invariably trace an often tenuous metaphorical relationship between (white) superheroes and minority groups. This is especially the case with the so-called Jewish comics connection, or the idea that, as two scholars phrase it, "there is a tightly woven and indelible relation between Jewish identity and the genesis of the superhero."[19] Such scholarship attempts in large part to disavow superheroes' foundational whiteness by ascribing their Otherness, in relation to non-superpowered humans, to a supposed hidden Jewish identity or to an easily portable minority metaphor—in the case of the X-Men, for example, scholars have read mutants in the 1960s as black Americans and in the 1990s as victims of HIV/AIDS.[20]

Only a handful of studies have considered the underlying issue of the superhero's whiteness. Marc Singer has illustrated that most often the superhero genre's play with identity tends to uphold whiteness, even when paying "lip service" to diversity, although exceptions exist in which the same tropes are used to subvert hegemonic ideas of whiteness and race.[21] Film scholar Matthew Yockey has discussed the constitutive whiteness of Marvel's Fantastic Four.[22] Historian Neil Shyminsky has noted that, while using a language of difference and oppression to speak about "mutants," *X-Men* privileges white readers and invites them to appropriate discourses of marginalization, and thus, despite their often stated purpose of redressing inequality, they reinforce it.[23] Fellow historians Julian Chambliss and William Svitavsky have identified how the intersection of anxiety, identity, and culture informed the creation of the comic book superhero, in part by tracing the figure's genealogy to pulp fiction heroes with an emphasis on whiteness.[24] Sociologist Albert S. Fu has written about how fans policed white normativity and the color line when the idea of a black Spider-Man was first hypothetically raised and then realized in the early 2010s.[25] I (Martin)

---

19. Baskin and Omer-Sherman, introduction, xxiii. For similar claims, see Brod, *Superman Is Jewish?*; Fingeroth, *Disguised as Clark Kent*; Kaplan, *From Krakow to Krypton*; Weinstein, *Up, Up, and Oy Vey!*

20. Minority metaphor readings are occasionally productive. Useful criticism of the X-Men's metaphorical meanings include Darius, "*X-Men* Is Not an Allegory for Race"; Shyminsky, "Mutant Readers, Reading Mutants"; Lund, "The Mutant Problem"; and Guynes, "Fatal Attractions."

21. Singer, "'Black Skins' and White Masks," 118.

22. Yockey, "This Island Manhattan."

23. Shyminsky, "Mutant Readers, Reading Mutants."

24. Chambliss and Svitavsky, "From Pulp Hero to Superhero."

25. Fu, "Fear of a Black Spider-Man."

have, for example, addressed whiteness in relation to Superman's creation, as outlined above; in relation to the figuration of Marvel's New York City; and in relation to the Cold War imagination of US relations with Africa.[26] And through his popular criticism website *The Middle Spaces*, Osvaldo Oyola has deeply engaged the racial contours of superhero comics, especially the problems facing "diversity" in comics on account of the racist basis of the genre's ingrained whiteness.

This small body of work offers important case studies in the meanings and uses (by creators and readers) of whiteness in American superhero comics, largely tackling the major Marvel superheroes. But more is needed to address the range of issues, the many intersections of whiteness, its manifestations, and its implications for superhero comics, in order to further our account of the superhero—and, in doing so, to examine the racial dimensions exemplified by a genre often derided as mere power fantasy. While the rich archive of scholarship on superhero comics and the superhero figure across media demonstrates that there is certainly more to stories of superbeings than power fantasy, it cannot be doubted that power, especially the power wielded by white men, is fundamental to the genre's tropes and deeply intertwined with its eighty-year history.

Following the above discussion, it should be clear that when we speak of the "whiteness of the superhero," as every chapter in this book does, we are making a rhetorical claim similar to the one made by literary and black cultural studies scholar andré m. carrington about "the Whiteness of speculative fiction" (versus "the speculative fiction of Blackness").[27] Our claim that whiteness and the superhero are inextricably linked is not, as we have said, to deny the possibility and, indeed, the historical reality of the cultural figure's usage by people of color to create reflections of themselves in superhero comics. It is, rather, to recognize the historical imbrication of the superhero with the multiple discourses of whiteness circulating throughout the twentieth and twenty-first centuries in the US. Like the other genres constituting what science fiction scholar John Rieder calls the "mass cultural genre system"[28]—the sum of the relations between the uses of different genres by culture workers and media consumers within the material, economic, and political formations of late-stage capitalism—the superhero genre has historically been bound up with the logic of mass-market appeal that sees the majority of its audience as racially unmarked, and therefore white. In other

---

26. Lund, *Re-Constructing the Man of Steel*, "Introducing the Sensational Black Panther," and "'X Marks the Spot.'"

27. carrington, *Speculative Blackness*, 16–28.

28. Rieder, *Science Fiction and the Mass Cultural Genre System*.

words, superhero comics creators overwhelmingly, even if not consciously, assume white faces, bodies, and experiences to be the universal standards of American life.

Thus, when we and our contributors speak of the whiteness of the superhero and of superhero comics, we follow carrington in referring simultaneously to the "overrepresentation of White people among the ranks of" the genre's creators (writers, artists, and editors) and the "overrepresentation of White people's experiences within" superhero comics.[29] Moreover, just as carrington gestures to the "speculative fiction of blackness," reversing the semantic poles of the "whiteness of speculative fiction" and arguing compellingly that discourses of race and of blackness in particular operate much in the same way as the genre he discusses, so do we argue in the chiastic and claim that superhero comics assay whiteness as a superheroic power itself, as one of the constituent elements of identity and power that constitute the historical, narrative, material, and political dimensions of superhero comics and their generic extensions across other media via the mediating cultural figure of the superhero.

## Outlining Instability

As the above discussion of whiteness and its constituent place in American superhero comics makes clear, whiteness is only stable where its ability for social control is concerned. But the *look* of whiteness, of what and who counts as white, and of how whiteness makes its social, political, and even economic meanings known—these aspects of whiteness are far from static. The title of our book riffs on Frantz Fanon's *Black Skin, White Masks*, taking literally Fanon's conception of whiteness as a mask to be worn, an identity nonwhite people must perform in order to succeed in a white-dominated society, and equating it with the masks that are overwhelmingly associated with the sartorial design of the American comic book superhero, the mask that by and large abets the superhero's maintenance of the status quo. But the mask of whiteness, Fanon was aware, is unstable; its very presence is a violence, and a history of oppression roils beneath its surface. The mask changes and mutates to suit prevailing social niceties and market demands, yes, but it still pinches and squeezes in places: It hasn't always fit right on the ethnic white superhero; it fits uncomfortably on those deemed racially, sexually, or ably unfit to wear it; and sometimes it refuses to fit at all, acci-

---

29. carrington, *Speculative Blackness*, 16.

dentally, sometimes even apologetically, revealing its true color, the shifting hue and undulating face of its racial-power ideology.

The fourteen chapters in this collection parse the superhero genre's complex history and theorize its relation to American discourses of race, difference, and belonging in the context of the critical advancements made by whiteness studies. *Unstable Masks* is organized into three sections that group chapters thematically according to the ways in which they read or historicize the relationship of whiteness to the history or generic identity of the American superhero comics they take as case studies. Part I, "Outlining Superheroic Whiteness," establishes a baseline for thinking about whiteness as a problematic for the analysis and critique of American superhero comics. Next, part II, "Reaching toward Whiteness" looks at the instability and contingency of whiteness through investigations of how comics have framed or embodied negotiations about who gets to be white and what whiteness is in relation to other articulations of race and ethnicity. The chapters in the third and final part, "Whiteness by a Different Color," discuss issues of secret or secondary superheroic identity in terms of the fluidity and invisibility of whiteness and the privileges it affords.

Combined, these sections offer a challenge to the saying—most commonly articulated in Spider-Man comics, but common to many other figures as well—that with great power comes great responsibility, a claim that does not, and cannot, mean anything substantive so long as the superhero genre rests on white supremacy and white privilege. On the page, superheroes may be larger than life, but in reality they are often all too closely tied to the foundations of inequality and oppression in American life. Unlike in a superhero comic, then, the challenge offered here cannot be resolved neatly by the final page and it is not an undertaking that can be resolved by unilateral action; abolishing whiteness is a long-term project that can only be completed by ordinary people coming together to unmask those who claim to be their betters.

# Bibliography

Alaniz, José. *Death, Disability, and the Superhero: The Silver Age and Beyond.* Jackson: University Press of Mississippi, 2014.

Aldama, Frederick Luis. *Latinx Comic Book Storytelling.* San Diego: San Diego State University Press, 2016.

———. *Latinx Superheroes in Mainstream Comics.* Tucson: University of Arizona Press, 2017.

———. *Multicultural Comics: From Zap to Blue Beetle.* Austin: University of Texas Press, 2011.

———. *Your Brain on Latino Comics: From Gus Arriola to Los Bros Hernandez*. Austin: University of Texas Press, 2009.

Aldama, Frederick Luis, and Christopher González, eds. *Graphic Borders: Latino Comic Books Past, Present, and Future*. Austin: University of Texas Press, 2016.

Alexander, Michelle. *The New Jim Crow: Mass Incarceration in the Age of Colorblindness*. New York: New Press, 2010.

Allen, Theodore W. *The Invention of the White Race: Volume 1: Racial Oppression and Social Control*. 2nd ed. New York: Verso, 2012.

———. *The Invention of the White Race: Volume 2: The Origin of Racial Oppression in Anglo-America*. 2nd ed. New York: Verso, 2012.

Baskin, Samantha, and Ranen Omer-Sherman. Introduction to *The Jewish Graphic Novel: Critical Approaches*, edited by Samantha Baskin and Ranen Omer-Sherman, xv–xxvii. New Brunswick, NJ: Rutgers University Press, 2010.

Bonilla-Silva, Eduardo. *Racism without Racists: Color-Blind Racism and the Persistence of Racial Inequality in America*. Lanham, MD: Rowman & Littlefield, 2003.

Brod, Harry. *Superman Is Jewish? How Comic Book Superheroes Came to Serve Truth, Justice, and the Jewish-American Way*. New York: Free Press, 2012.

Brown, Jeffrey A. *Black Superheroes, Milestone Comics, and their Fans*. Jackson: University Press of Mississippi, 2000.

carrington, andré m. *Speculative Blackness: The Future of Race in Science Fiction*. Minneapolis: University of Minnesota Press, 2016.

Chambliss, Julian, and William Svitavsky. "From Pulp Hero to Superhero: Culture, Race, and Identity in American Popular Culture, 1900–1940." *Faculty Publications*, October 1, 2008, http://scholarship.rollins.edu/as_facpub/2.

Cocca, Carolyn, *Superwomen: Gender, Power, and Representation*. New York: Bloomsbury, 2016.

Coogan, Peter. *Superhero: The Secret Origin of a Genre*. Austin: MonkeyBrain, 2006.

Courtemanche, Eleanor. "The Peculiar Success of Cultural Studies 2.0." *Personal Brand*, September 1, 2016, https://eleanorcourtemanche.wordpress.com/2016/09/01/the-peculiar-success-of-cultural-studies-2-0/.

Darius, Julian. "X-Men Is Not an Allegory for Race." *Sequart*, September 25, 2002, http://sequart.org/magazine/3201/x-men-is-not-an-allegory-of-racial-tolerance/.

Dyer, Richard. *White: Essay on Race and Culture*. New York: Routledge, 1997.

Faludi, Susan. *Backlash: The Undeclared War against American Women*. New York: Three Rivers Press, 1991.

———. *The Terror Dream: Myth and Misogyny in an Insecure America*. New York: Picador, 2008.

Fawaz, Ramzi. *The New Mutants: Superheroes and the Radical Imagination of American Comic Books*. New York: New York University Press, 2016.

Fingeroth, Danny. *Disguised as Clark Kent: Jews, Comics, and the Creation of the Superhero*. New York: Continuum, 2007.

Frankenberg, Ruth. *White Women, Race Matters: The Social Construction of Whiteness*. Minneapolis: University of Minnesota Press, 1993.

Frye Jacobson, Matthew. *Roots Too: White Ethnic Revival in Post–Civil Rights America*. Cambridge, MA: Harvard University Press, 2008.

———. *Whiteness of a Different Color: European Immigrants and the Alchemy of Race*. Cambridge, MA: Harvard University Press, 1999.

Fu, Albert S. "Fear of a Black Spider-Man: Racebending and the Colour-Line in Superhero (Re)Casting." *Journal of Graphic Novels and Comics* 6, no. 3 (2015): 269–83.

Gateward, Frances, and John Jennings, eds. *The Blacker the Ink: Constructions of Black Identity in Comics and Sequential Art*. New Brunswick, NJ: Rutgers University Press, 2015.

Guynes, Sean. "Fatal Attractions: AIDS and American Superhero Comics, 1988–2014." *International Journal of Comic Art* 17, no. 2 (Fall/Winter 2015): 177–216.

Hill, Mike, ed. *Whiteness: A Critical Reader*. New York: New York University Press, 1997.

Howard, Sheena C., and Ronald L. Jackson II, eds. *Black Comics: The Politics of Race and Representation*. New York: Bloomsbury, 2013.

Ignatiev, Noel. *How the Irish Became White*. New York: Routledge, 2008.

Jackson, Erika K. *Scandinavians in Chicago: The Origins of White Privilege in Modern America*. Champaign: University of Illinois Press, 2019.

Kaplan, Arie. *From Krakow to Krypton: Jews and Comic Books*. Philadelphia: The Jewish Publication Society, 2008.

Klock, Geoff. *How to Read Superhero Comics and Why*. New York: Continuum, 2002.

Kühl, Stefan. *The Nazi Connection: Eugenics, American Racism, and German National Socialism*. New York: Oxford University Press, 2002.

Lebron, Christopher J. *The Making of Black Lives Matter: A Brief History of an Idea*. New York: Oxford University Press, 2017.

Lewis, A. David, and Martin Lund, eds. *Muslim Superheroes: Comics, Islam, and Representation*. Cambridge, MA: ILEX Foundation/Harvard University Press, 2017.

Lund, Martin. "'Introducing the Sensational Black Panther!' *Fantastic Four* #52–53, the Cold War, and Marvel's Imagined Africa." *The Comics Grid: Journal of Comics Scholarship* 6 (2016): 1–21.

———. "The Mutant Problem: *X-Men*, Confirmation Bias, and the Methodology of Comics and Identity." *European Journal of Comics Art* 10, no. 2 (2015). https://ejas.revues.org/10890.

———. *Re-Constructing the Man of Steel: Superman 1938–1941, Jewish American History, and the Invention of the Jewish-Comics Connection*. New York: Palgrave Macmillan, 2016.

———. "'X Marks the Spot': Urban Dystopia, Slum Voyeurism and Failures of Identity in *District X*." *Journal of Urban Cultural Studies* 2, no. 1–2 (2015): 34–56.

Lund, Martin, and A. David Lewis. "Whence the Muslim Superhero?" In *Muslim Superheroes: Comics, Islam, and Representation*, edited by A. David Lewis and Martin Lund, 1–19. Cambridge, MA: ILEX Foundation/Harvard University Press, 2017.

Morrison, Toni. "Making America White Again." *The New Yorker*, November 21, 2016, http://www.newyorker.com/magazine/2016/11/21/making-america-white-again.

———. *Playing in the Dark: Whiteness and the Literary Imagination*. Cambridge, MA: Harvard University Press, 1992.

Nama, Adilifu. *Super Black: American Pop Culture and Black Superheroes*. Austin: University of Texas Press, 2011.

Painter, Nell Irvin. *The History of White People*. New York: W. W. Norton, 2011.

Reynolds, Richard. *Super Heroes: A Modern Mythology*. Jackson: University Press of Mississippi, 1994.

Rieder, John. *Science Fiction and the Mass Cultural Genre System*. Middletown, CT: Wesleyan University Press, 2017.

Robin, Corey. *The Reactionary Mind: Conservatism from Edmund Burke to Sarah Palin*. New York: Oxford University Press, 2013.

Roediger, David R., ed. *Black on White: Black Writers on What It Means to Be White*. New York: Schocken, 1998.

Roediger, David R. *How Race Survived US History: From Settlement and Slavery to the Obama Phenomenon*. New York: Verso, 2010.

———. *The Wages of Whiteness: Race and the Making of Working Class America*. 2nd ed. New York: Verso, 2007.

———. *Working Toward Whiteness: How America's Immigrants Became White. The Strange Journey from Ellis Island to the Suburbs*. New York: Basic Books, 2005.

Sheyahshe, Michael A. *Native Americans in Comic Books: A Critical Study*. Jefferson, NC: McFarland, 2008.

Shyminsky, Neil. "Mutant Readers, Reading Mutants: Appropriation, Assimilation, and the X-Men." *International Journal of Comic Art* 8, no. 2 (Fall 2006): 387–405.

Singer, Marc. "'Black Skins' and White Masks: Comic Books and the Secret of Race." *African American Review* 36, no. 1 (Spring 2002): 107–19.

Takaki, Ronald T. *A Different Mirror: A History of Multicultural America*. New York: Little, Brown, and Co., 2008.

Taylor, Keeanga-Yamahtta. *From #BlackLivesMatter to Black Liberation*. Chicago: Haymarket, 2016.

Weinstein, Simcha. *Up, Up, and Oy Vey!: How Jewish History, Culture, and Values Shaped the Comic Book Superhero*. Baltimore: Leviathan Press, 2006.

Whaley, Deborah Elizabeth, *Black Women in Sequence: Re-Inking Comics, Graphic Novels, and Anime*. Seattle: University of Washington Press, 2015.

Whitman, James Q. *Hitler's American Model: The United States and the Making of Nazi Race Law*. Princeton, NJ: Princeton University Press, 2017.

Wright, Richard. *White Man, Listen!* New York: Doubleday, 1964.

Yanora, Mercedes. "Marked by Foreign Policy: Muslim Superheroes and Their Quest for Authenticity." In *Muslim Superheroes: Comics, Islam, and Representation*, edited by A. David Lewis and Martin Lund, 110–33. Cambridge, MA: ILEX Foundation / Harvard University Press, 2017.

Yockey, Mathew. "This Island Manhattan: New York City and the Space Race in *The Fantastic Four*." *Iowa Journal of Cultural Studies* 6 (Spring 2005): 58–79.

PART I

# Outlining Superheroic Whiteness

CHAPTER 1

# MARKED FOR FAILURE

Whiteness, Innocence, and Power in Defining Captain America

OSVALDO OYOLA

THE MANTLE of Captain America has passed from Steve Rogers—the puny, good-hearted 4-F would-be Nazi-fighter who received the "super-soldier formula" in 1941—to several other characters in the decades since *Captain America Comics* first appeared. In each case, whether the retconned commie-smashing Captain America of the 1950s, John Walker in the 1990s, or Bucky Barnes in the 2000s, the recipients have all been white. That is, until 2014, when Cap's former sidekick, African American Sam Wilson (the Falcon), took over for a de-powered Rogers. The original series to feature Sam Wilson as the new Captain America—Rick Remender and Stuart Immonen's *All-New Captain America* (2014–2015)—barely addressed race and the potential resistance within the world of the comics, among readership, and in the culture at large to the American icon being a black person. Nick Spencer and Daniel Acuña's *Captain America: Sam Wilson* (2015–2017), however, takes up that resistance, frequently echoing right-wing reaction to the election of Barack Obama in 2008 in depicting public backlash against Wilson. Read alongside its companion series, *Captain America: Steve Rogers* (2016), also by Spencer (with various artists), in which Rogers regains his powers, together the two series limn the complex oscillations between the color- and power-evasive discourse and race cognizance of whiteness in American racial politics.[1] Furthermore, these two series highlight how justice, heroism, and even

---

1. Frankenberg, *White Women, Race Matters*, 15.

19

humanity itself are defined by reference to whiteness, making it a constitutive aspect of Captain America in particular and of the American superhero more generally.

In *White Women, Race Matters*, Ruth Frankenberg describes three definitive "moments" in racial thinking in America: "racist essentialist," "color- and power-evasiveness" and "race cognizant reassertions and reorientations of race difference." Color- and power-evasiveness is a discourse built on assimilationist assumptions used to challenge essentialist ideas of race, but that value "colorblindness" and reject systemic disparities in racial experience. Race cognizance, on the other hand, "opposes both the first and second moments. For it articulates the new characterizations of race difference (including awareness of structural and institutional inequity . . .) that emerged out of [the] civil rights [movement]."[2] This third category is described by Frankenberg as one in which racial "difference signals autonomy of culture, values, aesthetic standards, and so on." Such an outlook, while a positive step toward awareness of positional differences operating in racialized social structures of the racially marginalized, can be (and has been) put to work as a structure to reinforce white supremacy. It provides a rhetoric for white racial cognizance that unroots it from its essentialist origins and equates any sense of loss of power to racial oppression on the scale of what black and brown people have suffered in America. In this context, the potential subtext that renders Captain America the agent of white American hegemony rises to the surface, even as its racialized outlook remains "power-evasive."

Race has always defined Captain America. As Toni Morrison asserts in her seminal work on whiteness and the literary imagination, *Playing in the Dark*, "American means white,"[3] and while his whiteness went unmarked for decades after the character's introduction in 1941, the inability to imagine a nonwhite Captain America until more than seventy years later reinforces the relationship between whiteness and the "truly American." This relationship was first made explicit in the comics through the 2003 miniseries *Truth: Red, White, and Black* by Robert Morales and Kyle Baker. The series imagines Tuskegee-like human experimentation on Black American soldiers in the effort to reproduce the lost super-soldier serum that granted Steve Rogers his strength, speed, and physical resilience. The vast majority of the subjects die horrible deaths due to the side effects of the proto-formulas, though one—Isaiah Bradley—survives the ordeal and ends up imprisoned

---

2. Frankenberg, *White Women, Race Matters*, 140.
3. Morrison, *Playing in the Dark*, 47.

for his efforts to embody the ideals Captain America was meant to represent. The story retcons the early history of Captain America to insert an originary moment that makes clear that the first, "real," Captain America was white and exceptional, and any others taking up the mantle are not only "fake" but expendable. Black bodies become the measure against which the exceptional quality of Steve Rogers is defined, and thus how Captain America becomes synonymous with whiteness.

In "American Truths: Blackness and the American Superhero," Consuela Francis suggests that rather than revise a history of whiteness to be more inclusive and highlight the toxic and violent treatment of African Americans in the guise of inclusivity and participation, *Truth* ultimately serves to marginalize Isaiah Bradley and the notion of the Black Captain America.[4] By story's end, Steve Rogers is placed back at the center of the "Captain America" narrative, and Bradley's saga becomes another way for the white Captain America to establish his magnanimity. While he seeks out the "Black Captain America" in order to make amends for Bradley's treatment, he never actually tries to hold the US government accountable for it. The story becomes another in a long line of unfortunate "past" occurrences that make Black Americans the subjects of sympathy and admiration for their resilience, without addressing underlying systemic formations that have repeatedly led to violent and discriminatory results.

The more recent black incarnation of Captain America reinforces Francis's point that "to place a black man in [Captain America's] uniform calls into question those virtues [Cap represents] and makes many things we would rather not see, such as the whiteness of American heroism, visible."[5] Furthermore, the new story's deep integration with current mainstream Marvel continuity demonstrates how the marketing demands and genre expectations of today's superhero comics cement the impossibility for such characters to actually accomplish something akin to racial parity and inclusivity. As James Lamb has written, the history and traditions of superhero comics inarguably establish whiteness as the core property required for their narratives to function. Not only are the most popular American superheroes all white, but it becomes impossible to imagine a positive reception to their autonomous choices in regard to their social and political world if Superman or Wonder Woman were black. Furthermore, Lamb asserts that extant black superheroes are "pale knockoffs of the White male power fantasies" that reinforce the centrality of whiteness, rather than actually valuing difference.[6]

---

4. Francis, "American Truths," 147.
5. Francis, "American Truths," 139.
6. Lamb, "Superman Is a White Boy."

Compounding this problem is the cyclical nostalgia of the genre, which makes the return and eminence of established white superheroes inevitable. Since superhero characters are multi-million-dollar corporate properties, in the words of Douglas Wolk, "significant lasting change is almost impossible to get past the marketing department."[7] As such, the whiteness of foundational characters in these shared universes is both ossified and perpetually emergent.

This cyclical focus on white characters means that from the introduction of Sam Wilson as the new Captain America, the inevitability of Steve Rogers's return and his readoption of the mantle of Captain America undermined the ability for Wilson to be the "real" Captain America. As such, when Steve Rogers regained his superpowers, his concurrent existence with his successor not only sped up the clock on Wilson abandoning the Captain America identity but also reinforced the idea of the "realness" of Captain America being tied to his race. With the white Captain America back, the black replacement is no longer needed, even if the white Cap asserts otherwise.[8] Here is a strong echo with the concluding events of *Truth*. Whiteness returns to the center of the narrative.

Increasing the problems of this recentering, Rogers's return is marked by a change in his character that remains a secret until the events of "Secret Empire," a company-wide summer 2017 crossover event. In the cosmic rewriting of reality that gives Rogers his powers back, his history has been changed and he is revealed to have been a secret agent of Hydra, one of Marvel's well-established evil organizations, all along. Recruited as a child in the Depression years before World War II, in this figuration he has always been dedicated to overthrowing the US government. While Hydra's history, both in terms of story-world narrative and publication, is too convoluted to recount here, its association with fictional Nazis like the Red Skull and Baron Wolfgang von Strucker, along with its iconography and vocabulary, squarely place it in the realm of white supremacist organizations. As such, Rogers's simultaneous embodying of American ideals and his performance of white race cognizance highlights how the two are imbricated, and provides a site for examining the slippage between color-and-power evasive discourse and race cognizance where whiteness and American identity converge.

What is meant to be shocking about this transformation of Captain America (called Hydra-Cap by fans), actually puts him in line with the ideology that undergirds American exceptionalism and much of both domes-

---

7. Wolk, *Reading Comics*, 102.
8. Spencer, Acuña, Unzueta, Yackey, and Caramagna, *Captain America: Sam Wilson*, vol. 1, #7.

tic and foreign policy: white supremacy. In "Southern Super Patriots and United States Nationalism," Brannon Costello explains how in a late 1980s *Captain America* storyline[9]—in which "well-intentioned, but reactionary and violent southerner, John Walker" takes the mantle of Captain America—a tension arises between idealized "American" values and the racial and political history of the American South. Costello writes, "the South functions as a place where the US imagines its un-American qualities are contained—a place a part of, and apart from, the rest of the nation."[10] The obfuscation of the complicity in racial discrimination, inequality, and violence of the northern and western US seeks to erase the degree to which what are considered "white southern" values are really American values in a different rhetorical frame. In one story of this arc, Walker abandons his African American sidekick to be lynched by white domestic terrorists—the Watchdogs—to keep them from discovering his identity. Costello notes that Walker's "chosen solidarity with whiteness . . . allows this southerner to be Captain America [and] allows his 'American' and 'southern' identities to coexist."[11] In other words, it is the callous devaluation of black life that allows Walker to complete his mission.

As a representative of a broader and "complete" America, Walker demonstrates how solidarity *across* race is frequently abandoned in the name of greater peace and stability among white people, regardless of the consequences for black and brown America. Costello describes Steve Rogers as unwilling "to ground . . . his [Captain America] identity in law and history," preferring to rely on the "timelessness" of American ideals. This is, however, a convenient dodge, because such a distinction erases how American law and history repeatedly reinforce a system of white supremacy that at best undermines the professed ideals that Captain America is meant to represent, and at worst demonstrates how those ideals are synonymous with it.[12]

This compartmentalization is not only a necessary component of being and believing in "Captain America" but is also a fundamental way in which American whiteness functions: through maintaining a space where white people can remain innocent of any responsibility for racial injustice. As Frankenberg reminds us, "white people have too often viewed themselves as nonracial or racially neutral."[13] The frequent invisibility of whiteness as a racial category allows white Americans to project that invisibility as ideal for

---

9. *Captain America*, vol. 1, #333–350 (1987–89).
10. Costello, "Southern Super Patriots," 63.
11. Costello, "Southern Super Patriots," 78.
12. Costello, "Southern Super Patriots," 69.
13. Frankenberg, *White Women, Race Matters*, 1.

other races. As Morrison explains, for white people, "the habit of ignoring race is understood to be a graceful, even generous, liberal gesture."[14] The very "non-racial" self-perception of whiteness allows it to imagine a lack of cross-racial cognizance as a positive value, while conveniently allowing for a form of generalized "white innocence" that always demands the benefit of the doubt and serves as an unnamed form of race cognizance. This undermines the radical potential of Captain America stories that address racial inequality, because whiteness can only be temporarily decentered. For example, as Francis explains in *Truth*, Steve Rogers "is allowed to remain innocent because [Bradley] is silenced, literally and figuratively."[15] The legacy of Captain America remains unstained by its complicity in the history of white power structures exploiting black bodies, through the erasure of that history. And, as I will argue when examining scenes from *Captain America: Sam Wilson*, Rogers benefits from whiteness as "a place from which white people look at [them]selves, at others, and at society,"[16] that allows for interpersonal relations to obviate deeply entrenched institutional racism.

This mediation functions on two levels in Nick Spencer's *Captain America* comic books: within the story-world, and on the meta-level, providing plausible relatability with Hydra-Cap for readers. It provides opportunities for readers to obviate any discomfort that might come along with identifying with the fascistic protagonist. In *Secret Empire*, Hydra operative Steve Rogers is consistently given an out, a layer of deniability that keeps the character innocent of direct violence and free of any explicit racial rhetoric, so as to not taint the character before his eventual absolution and return to the righteous superhero fold, as happens with every superhero that is written to "go bad." For example in *Captain America: Steve Rogers* #8, in a flashback to the revised reality that saw Rogers raised by Hydra operatives, he witnesses a pre-WWII meeting of high-ranking Hydra officials, including Nazi Baron Helmut Zemo XII, in which they decide for strategic reasons to align themselves with the Axis powers, rather than for explicit ideological ones.[17] This scene specifically distances an organization frequently aligned with racial supremacy and Nazism from such ideals in order to make Captain America's association with it more palatable. Hydra-Cap cannot be actually racist in this narrative, because the rhetoric of explicit racism is anathema to a hero in mainstream superhero comics, which would make redeeming the character difficult, if not impossible. That Captain America's would-be

---

14. Morrison, *Playing in the Dark*, 9.
15. Francis, "American Truths," 149.
16. Frankenberg, *White Women, Race Matters*, 1.
17. Spencer and Saiz, *Captain America: Steve Rogers*, vol. 1, #8.

allies express distaste for the "unsavory" aspects of their Axis cohort provides a layer of deniability, even as Hydra explicitly leverage their whiteness to make use of Nazi resources for their greater plan (see figure 1.1). It goes unspoken, but it is their whiteness (and Rogers's) that not only makes the alliance possible but its invisibilizing qualities allow them (and potentially white readers) to ignore the plight of Jews, Romani, the disabled, queer, and any other groups targeted by Nazism.[18]

This ethical leap over the concerns of nonwhite or otherwise marginalized Americans depicted in *Secret Empire* forms a pattern when considered in light of the aforementioned choices made by John Walker in the 1980s and in other Marvel comics.[19] It also echoes contemporary concerns in American politics regarding President Donald Trump's political base's acceptance of white nationalism through the "economic anxiety" driving their electoral choices, and the justifications for it evident in moderate apologia for and media obsession with the topic.[20] And yet in interviews about the *Secret Empire* event series, Spencer and then Marvel editor-in-chief Axel Alonso claim that "*Secret Empire* has little to do with contemporary political parallels,"[21] despite implicitly leaning on those parallels to make the story relatable. The claim suggests a plausible (but unlikely) innocence that signals race cognizance with what are often thought of as Marvel's core readers, white men.[22] In other words, *Secret Empire* oscillates between race neutrality and race cognizance, navigating the complex context of American racial discourse while also allowing editorial to retain deniability.

Distancing Hydra from Nazism through a reimagining of their relationship is a conscious effort by Marvel editorial and writer Nick Spencer to keep Captain America from being a literal Nazi. Such a narrative revision also attempts to obfuscate the fascistic impulses of the superhero genre[23] that might make a Hydra-aligned Cap still fall in line with many superheroic conventions despite now being one of the "bad guys." When interviewed by Christian Holub for *Entertainment Weekly* about *Secret Empire*, both Spencer and Alonso dodged the question of association with Nazism. Spencer reinforces both Hydra's age as an organization (thus predating

---

18. In another example of the narrative giving Rogers a buffer of innocence, just when he is about to kill a comatose colleague who can reveal his secret if he awakens, his family chooses to take him off life support. *Captain America: Steve Rogers*, vol. 1, #10.
19. See Oyola, "The Captain White America Needs," for other examples of performative racist ideology excused by other narrative circumstances.
20. McElwee and McDaniel, "Economic Anxiety."
21. Spencer and Alonso, "Secret Empire Creators."
22. MacDonald, "Marvel."
23. Berlatsky, "Superheroes Are about Fascism."

FIGURE 1.1. White racial solidarity as a means to Hydra's end (*Captain America: Steve Rogers* #8). © Marvel Comics. Image presented under fair use legislation.

Nazism), and their focus on their ideology of "strength at all costs." He also describes those who do not align with this ideology as "in a tough spot," downplaying the violent ways that Hydra's core values parallel Nazism, including euthanizing the weak or disabled and exiling, interning, or killing those marked as outsiders. This editorial concern is confirmed by a real-world reading of Wilson's actions as Captain America as anti-conservative and anti-American, as when Tucker Carlson of *Fox & Friends* objected to the tepid pro-immigrant storyline explored in the first issue of *Captain America: Sam Wilson*[24]—an objection that, ironically, reifies satirical conservative pundit TV talking heads within the narrative. Steve Rogers, despite his apparent shift in alliances, remains not only recognizable as Captain America but legible as a leader of the US because of his whiteness. As such, the story of his rise to power serves to mark whiteness as his primary asset and an "American" ideal. This is compounded by the concurrent attempts by Sam Wilson to fulfill the purported American ideals represented by the role, and his ultimate failure in the companion series.

In explicating the necessity of whiteness studies in literary analysis, Toni Morrison explains that when white American writers either address or ignore blackness as constitutive of American experience and foundational cultural meaning, it reveals "a powerful exploration of the fears and desires that reside in the writerly conscious."[25] As such, an examination of Captain America and his associated mythos reveals in multivalent ways how whiteness is encoded into the character, even when Captain America is temporarily black. Furthermore, in the case of *Captain America: Sam Wilson*, Spencer's

---

24. "Fox & Friends."
25. Morrison, *Playing in the Dark*, 17.

story reveals an anxiety that lingers under the surface of superhero comics and American society: that black and brown Americans' thirst for justice, equity, and social progress are incompatible with the dominant cultural framework as defined by perpetually evasive, but always influential, whiteness. Morrison's assertion that "American means white and [that] Africanist people struggle to make the term applicable to themselves"[26] is particularly relevant to Sam Wilson's adoption of the Captain America mantle. In superhero comics, Wilson's situation demonstrates that if "American means white," then only white can mean "American," making the "America" in the name "Captain America" a site of contention. In most of the stories in *Captain America: Sam Wilson*, Wilson's struggle to make "America" applicable to himself emerges from his difficulty getting white America to accept his social and political concerns—concerns clearly inspired by the current Black Lives Matter and pro-immigrant movements that define black and brown folks as deserving "American" rights—and the degree to which those concerns are considered divisive because they threaten to undermine white innocence.

Two events in *Captain America: Sam Wilson* best illuminate the oscillations between color- and power-evasive discourse and race cognizance through which whiteness functions to marginalize black lives and maintain power in American culture and politics. The first involves the aforementioned John Walker, and the second, Hydra-Cap's manipulation of racial politics to undermine Sam Wilson. In current comic book continuity, John Walker is USAgent. In this guise, he remains a violent, reactionary alternative to Steve Rogers. In *Captain America: Sam Wilson* #11, USAgent is recalled from disrupting a terrorist cell somewhere in the Middle East[27] by a cabal of corporate interests, right-wing cable news media, and a US senator. He is summoned to accomplish what the "number one trending topic on Twitter" has been asking of the new Captain America, to force him to "#givebacktheshield." The use of a viral hashtag reinforces American social media as a battleground for racial discourse in the US.

The cabal tries to convince John Walker to force Sam Wilson to give up the shield and return it to a repowered Steve Rogers, explaining that Rogers cannot ask for it back himself. As Paul Keane, CEO of Keane Industries

---

26. Morrison, *Playing in the Dark*, 47.
27. Spencer, Acuña, and Caramagna, *Captain America: Sam Wilson*, vol. 1, #11. The terrorist cell is a group of unnamed men (and one woman) with no dialogue. The undifferentiated brown men are depicted in a mix of Afghani pakols and Arabian keffiyeh (the woman is in a full burqa), reflecting a lack of concern with cultural and geographic specificity in relation to American whiteness.

(which profits from a privatized law enforcement initiative, Americops), explains, "A *white* Captain America telling a *black* Captain America to stand down? The liberal media would go nuts!" The implication here, as Costello suggests in his analysis of the original John Walker Captain America stories, is that Walker's Southern identity acts as an acceptable container for the antiblack sentiment that benefits Steve Rogers.[28] The focus on the optics of racial hierarchy underlines their cognizance of how whiteness functions in different power frameworks. Harry Hauser, a Marvel Universe cable news talking head, even adds (after going through a litany of Wilson's "unAmerican" activities; see figure 1.2) that Steve Rogers "has to remain above the fray," suggesting that ideals (as embodied by Captain America) must remain distinct from the active agents of the state (USAgent).

This buffer allows a color- and power-evasive discourse ("America" as an ideal) to exist simultaneously with coded race cognizance (Walker needs to help his fellow white man navigate an inconvenient racial morass). As Hari Ziyad contends, "Any utilization of racial power is never in the service of black liberation because blackness cannot wield it within a racial system."[29] The scene reveals this by depicting the paradox of how, through the lens of whiteness, the appearance of white power over black life translates into black power over white life, and thus a threat to the status quo.

In this case, as in the previous example involving John Walker, we see an intra-whiteness negotiation that overlooks black lives or agency as anything other than an obstacle to retaining power. Throughout *Captain America: Sam Wilson*, the impossibility of black liberation within the context of the superhero project due to the generic figure's constitutive whiteness becomes increasingly clear. The story suggests a strong understanding of the optics of race in American politics on the part of writer Nick Spencer, but the story never provides options other than "reasonable" acquiescence on the part of the poor black and brown citizens to the necessity of a white-serving semblance of law and order.[30] Violent disruption or even too effusive a protest is framed as always wrong, even as it depicts a decidedly corrupt legal, social, and economic system. Trapped between the impossibility of change without a collapse of the status quo, and how the status quo ungirds superheroic authority, Sam Wilson is depicted as increasingly confused and despondent. The story cannot present an understanding any deeper than what racial conflict *looks* like, because the comic book's visual focus remains structured by whiteness. The public assemblies of black and brown people depicted in

---

28. Costello, "Southern Super Patriots," 63.
29. Ziyad, "Playing 'Outside' in the Dark," 145.
30. Spencer, Acuña, and Caramagna, *Captain America: Sam Wilson*, vol. 1, #13.

**FIGURE 1.2.** Right-wing talking points used by cable news pundits to discredit a black Captain America (*Captain America: Steve Rogers* #12). © Marvel Comics. Image presented under fair use legislation.

the pages of *Captain America: Sam Wilson*, protesting or responding to police violence with thrown rocks and bottles and starting fires (see figure 1.3),[31] do not show a concern with black *lives*, but are a "representation of lawless violence," a situation to be avoided rather than embraced as a means for justice.[32]

Spencer's Sam Wilson story is a critical example of the fallacy of "both-sidesism," balancing the need to address oppression against the fear that he might appear partisan by expressing anger or frustration. Wilson's status as a black superhero is undermined by whiteness's demand that any expression of concern over the treatment of nonwhites include a disclaimer also expressing concern over maintaining the social structures that benefit the dominant culture. Failure to properly frame demands for justice may lead to accusations of "divisiveness," but *Captain America: Sam Wilson* makes clear that even respectability is insufficient as a shield against such accusations. At the end of issue #13, we discover that the white cabal's rhetoric required Steve Rogers's apparently reluctant co-signature to convince John Walker to act. Rogers describes Wilson's efforts to use his influence to protect those at the social margins as "out of control." He reiterates the notion that racial

---

31. Spencer, Renaud, and Caramagna, *Captain America: Sam Wilson*, vol. 1, #20.
32. Marriott, *Haunted Life*, 240.

FIGURE 1.3. Protests against police violence (*Captain America: Sam Wilson* #20). © Marvel Comics. Image presented under fair use legislation.

optics are a straitjacket to just action, that they are ultimately socially divisive.

"Divisive" is, of course, code for "dividing whites from power" and not actually a call for the positive value of cross-racial "togetherness." Any claim for racial justice that rejects white innocence is called "divisive." Examples of this rhetoric resounded among cable news pundits during Obama's tenure and in response to the demands of the Black Lives Matter movement, divorced from any cogent cultural analysis or sense of history. Consider Jeanine Pirro's 2014 claim on her Fox News show that "Americans, once hopeful that after electing the first African American president, the issue of race would be a thing of the past, are left with Barack Obama, who stokes the flames of racial hatred, resentment and divisiveness."[33] Here "Americans" must mean "white," given her claim. "Divisive" is a word used multiple times throughout Spencer's series by Wilson's opponents, but also by Wilson himself, when expressing fear over the consequences of taking political stances in the guise of Captain America.

Like Obama, Wilson's own race cognizance is limited by the very role of power he inhabits. As Kenneth Ghee points out, "most Black superheroes do not *explicitly* fight for Black cultural integrity or relevance."[34] Wilson might advocate for black people, but he is depicted as conflicted, and reluctant to actually *fight*. He responds to the urban conflict of a privatized police force—the Americops, accused of excessive force, selective enforce-

---

33. Pirro, "'You See Racism Everywhere.'"
34. Ghee, "'Will the Real Black Superheroes Please Stand Up?!,'" 232.

ment, racial profiling, and so on—by insisting on "talking it out," on being "reasonable." And, when a young black superhero called Rage, along with the poor brown and black communities policed by Americops, erupt, Wilson broadcasts a message expressing his wish that the problem with overpolicing could have been "talked through" and "settled ... the right way."[35] He is unable to effectively address these intractable problems because he is bound by his public blackness and unable to leverage the symbolic whiteness of the Captain America role in order to act decisively, even though the genre standards of superhero comics frequently call on protagonists to act with immediacy, unhampered by burdens of proof. In fact, later, even when proof of police misconduct emerges, it is insufficient to exonerate Rage of a crime he did not commit.[36] As Wilson asserts when faced with the fact that prosecuting corporate malfeasance could lead to national economic collapse, systemic corruption is "not something even Captain America can stop."[37] The serialized superhero genre needs the systemic limitations of justice that whiteness undergirds and that make black liberation impossible.

*Captain America: Sam Wilson* #14 most clearly demonstrates how Wilson is set up for failure from the moment he accepts the offer to become Captain America. While at the time of the offer, the story-world had not yet been altered to make Steve Rogers a lifelong agent of Hydra,[38] this circumstance becomes a metaphor for a turn of events against the black superhero. The Hydra-Cap shift demonstrates that even the well-intentioned white mentor can become the instrument of black failure. The issue concludes with the revelation that Wilson's latest in a long list of failures as Captain America (failing to stop the murder of a US senator) was manufactured by Steve Rogers in order to undermine his former sidekick. As Rogers explains to one of his co-conspirators, Sam Wilson alive as Captain America is more useful than Sam Wilson dead and a potential martyr (see figure 1.4). He highlights in this dialogue what Morrison asserts in *Playing in the Dark,* that whiteness *needs* blackness in order to define itself.[39]

By placing Wilson in a position of inevitable failure, Rogers signals to the American public the necessity and supremacy of whiteness. Rogers explains, "[Wilson] doesn't need my help courting controversy and getting mired

---

35. Spencer, Acuña, and Caramagna, *Captain America: Sam Wilson,* vol. 1, #13.
36. Spencer, Acuña, and Caramagna, *Captain America: Sam Wilson,* vol. 1, #11.
37. Spencer, Bennett, Brabo, Farjardo, and Caramagna, *Captain America: Sam Wilson,* vol. 1, #6.
38. See *Captain America,* vol. 7, #25.
39. Morrison, *Playing in the Dark,* 33.

FIGURE 1.4. Black martyrdom as a threat to whiteness (*Captain America: Sam Wilson* #14). © Marvel Comics. Image presented under fair use legislation.

in the corrupt politics around him—so let those forces tear him apart."[40] Rogers's words here echo Francis when she writes that "[comics] readers' assumption is that black equals political and that political equals bad."[41] In other words, by the very fact of his blackness Sam Wilson's being Captain America is "political," while the assumed default neutrality of "whiteness" in both superhero comics and American culture at large allows for even a character who wears an American flag on his chest to be "above politics" when white. Hydra-Cap performs his own kind of "race cognizance," taking advantage of how whiteness grants him a degree of political invisibility.

Despite a call among many academics for an increased awareness of and scholarship examining whiteness and its racial imagination, outside of the academy, white racial consciousness fosters racist/antiblack sentiments. The false equivalency of the interpersonal with the institutional and "the fallacious assumption that [the] functions [of whiteness and blackness] must parallel one another" allows individual white discontent to become racialized in ways that puts civil rights discourse to use in trying to maintain white

---

40. Spencer, Renaud, Rauch, and Caramagna, *Captain America: Sam Wilson*, vol. 1, #14.

41. Francis, "American Truths," 141.

power.[42] Hydra-Cap's cynical manipulations are potentially productive to us as readers because they make conscious the more frequently unconscious movement back and forth between the racially evasive and cognizant discourses of whiteness. They also allow for a retroactive reconsideration of the way the old Cap put his whiteness to use, even when ostensibly a "good guy."

Take, for example, the opening flashback in *Captain America: Sam Wilson* #12, which visually evokes the 1970s version of *Captain America* comics. Steve Rogers arrives at a local precinct to get Sam Wilson released, as the latter was mistaken for a criminal when trying to stop a C-list white villain from robbing a bank.[43] The scene highlights not only how blackness is read by law enforcement but how whiteness goes unmarked. While the comic narrative is sure to highlight the unfairness to black Wilson, no one mentions how a masked vigilante's intentions go unquestioned by virtue of his whiteness. Later, in issue #18, the necessity of whiteness in performing the role of Captain America is reinforced when Wilson arrives at a police precinct to deal with a falsely accused Rage, but is dismissed by a white officer.[44] In the flashback scene, Rogers is given access and Wilson his freedom by virtue of Rogers's reputation alone. Wilson, on the other hand, cannot attain the cultural cachet necessary to perform the usual duties of Captain America, or shift the social understandings of those duties, because the role only functions through its complicity with whiteness. Rogers has been unquestioningly benefitting from this even before the change to his reality. Whiteness remains unchanged, but reframes any superficial power it may cede as an unassailable new beginning, which then makes any potential progress that much more difficult and calls into question the very possibility of incremental equality.

Toni Morrison writes that "newness translates into 'innocence,'"[45] meaning that American literature relies on the purported ideals of the supposed new American beginning through its democratic experiment and resistance to Old World tyranny to shield itself from the history of racism, slavery, genocide, sexism, and capital that underwrites the American project. In the case of Hydra-Cap, however, this notion of "newness" is twisted even further, because if the "new" Steve Rogers is evil, then the "old" Steve Rogers must be good, and innocent in his maintenance of the status quo. In other words, in this case the "innocence" that comes with this "new" version of

---

42. Ziyad, "Playing 'Outside' in the Dark," 144.
43. Spencer, Acuña, and Caramagna, *Captain America: Sam Wilson*, vol. 1, #12.
44. Spencer, Acuña, and Caramagna, *Captain America: Sam Wilson*, vol. 1, #18.
45. Morrison, *Playing in the Dark*, 44.

Captain America is applied retroactively. When the American ideals the original Cap stands for are let off the hook, their fascistic underpinnings—whose acceptability the Hydra-Cap takes advantage of—become completely disconnected from history. The new Cap's fascism then seems *ex nihilo*, not the product of a structure of white supremacy. The fascist order that Hydra-Cap offers (and that in the *Secret Empire* series most of America seems to go along with) is acceptable *because* of his whiteness.

Ultimately, Sam Wilson's resignation as Captain America at the end of *Captain America: Sam Wilson* #21 does more than simply suggest the incompatibility of blackness with the role of "Captain America," it reinforces the degree to which whiteness and the frame of presumed innocence that comes with it is constitutive of the symbolic position. Whiteness is what allows Captain America to be "symbolic" as opposed to "political." Wilson's frequent claims throughout the series that he wanted to be "more than a symbol" also suggest that the series as a whole is the manifestation of Francis's assertion about *Truth*'s conclusions, that "while Marvel may have intended to deepen the mythology and complexity of Captain America by using race to disrupt the superhero narrative, [the effort] ultimately succeeds in demonstrating the genre's ideological limits."[46] When Wilson resigns, it is not his blackness that causes him to fail, but a deadly cocktail of intentional manipulation of toxic white identity politics mixed with whiteness's retreat from a recognition of its own racial identity when convenient to undergird narratives of personal responsibility, respectability, and individualism. Even in resigning, Wilson maintains his faith in the system and in Steve Rogers (see figure 1.5), insists on the inevitability of change, and admonishes young people to not "lose hope."[47]

Neither the character within the narrative nor the story's writer or editors can afford to radically split from the hypocritical ideology of American freedom and equality. In this light, *Captain America: Sam Wilson* can be read as a profound work of Afro-pessimist critique that challenges readers to acknowledge the deep antiblackness of imbricated material and cultural systems, including the industry that produced the comic itself. In catering to the constitutive whiteness of the superhero genre, Sam Wilson's narrative arc reifies the dreadful reality unveiled in *Captain America: Steve Rogers* and *Secret Empire* made possible by the genre's ultimate alliance with white power.

---

46. Francis, "American Truths," 151.

47. Spencer, Acuña, Rosenberg, and Caramagna, *Captain America: Sam Wilson*, vol. 1, #21.

**FIGURE 1.5.** Sam Wilson relinquishes the Captain America mantle, unintentionally reinforcing the constitutive whiteness of the role (*Captain America: Sam Wilson* #21). © Marvel Comics. Image presented under fair use legislation.

## Bibliography

Berlatsky, Noah. "Superheroes Are about Fascism." *The Hooded Utilitarian*, December 26, 2013, http://www.hoodedutilitarian.com/2013/12/superheroes-are-about-fascism/.

Costello, Brannon. "Southern Super Patriots and United States Nationalism." In *Comics and the U. S. South*, edited by Brannon Costello and Qiana J. Whitted, 62–88. Jackson: Mississippi University Press, 2012.

"Fox & Friends: Captain America Is Targeting Conservatives." *YouTube.com*, October 18, 2015, https://www.youtube.com/watch?v=5v46yDz7oX8&feature=youtu.be.

Francis, Consuela. "American Truths: Blackness and the American Superhero." In *The Blacker the Ink: Constructions of Black Identity in Comics & Sequential Art*, edited by Frances Gateward and John Jennings, 136–52. New Brunswick, NJ: Rutgers University Press, 2015.

Frankenberg, Ruth. *White Women, Race Matters: The Social Construction of Whiteness*. Minneapolis: Minnesota University Press, 1993.

Ghee, Kenneth. "'Will the Real Black Superheroes Please Stand Up?!': A Critical Analysis of the Mythological and Cultural Significance of Black Superheroes." In *Black Comics: Politics of Race and Representation*, edited by Sheena Howard and Ronald L. Jackson III, 223–37. London: Bloomsbury Academic, 2014.

Lamb, James. "Superman Is a White Boy." *Snoopy Jenkins,* March 27, 2014, https://snoopyjenkins.wordpress.com/2014/03/27/superman-is-a-white-boy/.

MacDonald, Heidi. "Marvel: Retailers and Readers 'Turning Their Nose Up' at Their More Diverse Titles - UPDATED." *The Comics Beat,* March 31, 2017, https://www.comicsbeat.com/marvel-retailers-and-readers-turning-their-nose-up-at-their-more-diverse-titles/.

Marriott, David. *Haunted Life: Visual Culture and Black Modernity.* New Brunswick, NJ: Rutgers University Press, 2007.

McElwee, Sean, and Jason McDaniel. "Economic Anxiety Didn't Make People Vote Trump, Racism Did." *The Nation,* May 8, 2017, https://www.thenation.com/article/economic-anxiety-didnt-make-people-vote-trump-racism-did/.

Morrison, Toni. *Playing in the Dark: Whiteness and the Literary Imagination.* Cambridge, MA: Harvard University Press, 1992.

Oyola, Osvaldo. "The Captain White America Needs." *The Middle Spaces,* November 3, 2015, https://themiddlespaces.com/2015/11/03/the-captain-white-america-needs/.

Pirro, Jeanine. "'You See Racism Everywhere': Judge Jeanine Slams Obama's Racial Bias." *Fox News.com,* December 7, 2014, http://insider.foxnews.com/2014/12/07/you-see-racism-everywhere-judge-jeanine-pirro-slams-president-obamas-racial-bias.

Spencer, Nick (writer), Daniel Acuña (artist), and Joe Caramagna (letterer). *Captain America: Sam Wilson,* vol. 1, #11. New York: Marvel, September 2016.

———. *Captain America: Sam Wilson,* vol. 1, #12. New York: Marvel, October 2016.

———. *Captain America: Sam Wilson,* vol. 1, #13. New York: Marvel, November 2016.

———. *Captain America: Sam Wilson,* vol. 1, #18. New York: Marvel, March 2017.

Spencer, Nick (writer), Daniel Acuña (artist), Rachelle Rosenberg (colorist), and Joe Caramagna (letterer). *Captain America: Sam Wilson,* vol. 1, #21. New York: Marvel, June 2017.

Spencer, Nick (writer), Paul Renaud (artist), and Joe Caramagna (letterer). *Captain America: Sam Wilson,* vol. 1, #20. New York: Marvel, May 2017.

Spencer, Nick (writer), Daniel Acuña (artist), Angel Unzueta (artist), Matt Yackey (colorist), and Joe Caramagna (letterer). *Captain America: Sam Wilson,* vol. 1, #7. New York: Marvel, May 2016.

Spencer, Nick, and Axel Alonso. "Secret Empire Creators Preview Captain America's Assault on the Marvel Universe." Interview by Christian Holub. *Entertainment Weekly,* April 7, 2017, http://ew.com/books/2017/04/07/secret-empire-creators-preview-captain-americas-assault-on-the-marvel-universe/.

Spencer, Nick (writer), Joe Bennett (artist), Belardina Brabo (inker), Ramulo Farjardo Jr. (colorist), and Joe Caramagna (letterer). *Captain America: Sam Wilson,* vol. 1, #6. New York: Marvel, April 2016.

Spencer, Nick (writer), Paul Renaud (artist), Jim Rauch (colorist), and Joe Caramagna (letterer). *Captain America: Sam Wilson,* vol. 1, #14. New York: Marvel, December 2016.

Spencer, Nick (writer), and Jesús Saiz (artist). *Captain America: Steve Rogers,* vol. 1, #8. New York: Marvel, February 2017.

Spencer, Nick (writer), and Jesús Saiz (artist, inker), Ro Stein (artist), Kevin Libranda (artist, inker), Ted Brandt (inker), Rachelle Rosenberg (inker), and Joe Caramagna (letterer). *Captain America: Steve Rogers*, vol. 1, #10. New York: Marvel, March 2017.

Wolk, Douglas. *Reading Comics: How Graphic Novels Work and What They Mean.* Cambridge, MA: Da Capo Press, 2007.

Ziyad, Hari. "Playing 'Outside' in the Dark: Blackness in a Postwhite World." *Critical Ethnic Studies* 3, no. 1 (2017): 143–61.

CHAPTER 2

# THE WHITENESS OF THE WHALE AND THE DARKNESS OF THE DINOSAUR

The Africanist Presence in Superhero Comics from *Black Lightning* to *Moon Girl*

ERIC BERLATSKY AND SIKA DAGBOVIE-MULLINS

In *Playing in the Dark,* Toni Morrison argues that traits associated with "American-ness" are actually only associated with *white* America and that these traits have always been defined through juxtaposition with an unacknowledged but inescapable "Africanist presence."[1] To take one example, in referring to eighteenth-century explorer William Dunbar's settling in the New World, Morrison articulates the way in which Dunbar's "authority and autonomy" emerge from his "absolute control" over his slaves, how his "civilized" identity can only be fully defined in the "raw, half-savage" New World, and how his "sense of freedom" can only be articulated in the context of enslaved blacks.[2] Morrison notes that for Dunbar, "[white] authority and absolute power become a romantic, conquering 'heroism' [and] virility."[3] Though the context is different, her observations apply to early superhero comics in which whiteness, heroism, virility, and "absolute power" become inextricable from the genre. As in the literature Morrison discusses, these comics often do not depict black heroes, but they are nevertheless defined by the "Africanist" historical presence. As Ramzi Fawaz notes, WWII-era superhero comics "associated justice with white figures of authority (and crimi-

---

1. Morrison, *Playing in the Dark,* 47.
2. Morrison, *Playing in the Dark,* 43.
3. Morrison, *Playing in the Dark,* 44.

nality with ethnic minorities, the disabled, and the mentally disturbed)."[4] That is, they operated within invidious racial stereotypes that remain with us and that manifest themselves in many ways, including in the mass incarceration of black men.

Despite his above statement in regard to early superhero comics, Fawaz devotes much of his book to the oppositional claim that postwar comics develop "an emergent identification between the superhero and marginalized figures, including racial minorities."[5] That is, Fawaz argues that "heroism" has been progressively uncoupled from whiteness over the past sixty-five years of superheroic representation, resisting the ways in which blackness initially served only as a binary counterpoint for whiteness and heroism. In this chapter, we argue that, while on a literal level Fawaz's optimism has validity (the numbers of superheroes of "other" races and genders has increased dramatically), Morrison's subterranean "Africanist presence" continues to recur in American superhero comics, building on the binaries of civilization/primitivism, freedom/incarceration, justice/criminality, and intelligence/ignorance defined in terms of racial difference, even in cases where the superhero is black. To show this, we look at two indicative case studies, one from early in the history of black superheroes, the first *Black Lightning* series (1977–1978), and the second, the contemporary *Moon Girl and Devil Dinosaur* (2016–2017). By exploring both early and recent versions of the "black superhero," we seek to highlight continuities and developments in the treatment of the symbology of the "Africanist presence" in superhero comics. In *Black Lightning*, we see an early effort to escape (stereo)typical associations with black and white through a practice of simple reversal. *Moon Girl and Devil Dinosaur* complicates the associations of the Africanist presence even further, investing its protagonist, Lunella Lafayette, with traits associated with both whiteness and blackness, a semiotic instability articulated most clearly when Lunella's consciousness switches bodies with that of her dinosaur companion, Devil. In both cases, and throughout the representational history of black superheroes, these comics struggle with overcoming the traditional tropes of the genre in order to shake free of long-held stereotypical associations. The variably successful attempts to do so reveal the resilience and persistence of the meanings of whiteness in contemporary America.

---

4. Fawaz, *New Mutants*, 174.
5. Fawaz, *New Mutants*, 174.

## "Justice, like lightning . . ."

The story of black superheroes is often, if problematically, said to begin with Marvel's introduction of Black Panther in *Fantastic Four*[6] #52–53 (1965). Panther, aka T'Challa, is the king of the fictional African nation of Wakanda and the forerunner of the trickle of black heroes to follow at Marvel and DC, including The Falcon (1969), John Stewart/Green Lantern (1971), Luke Cage (1972), Storm (1975) and Black Lightning (1977).[7] Even in T'Challa's earliest appearances, there are reversals and mixings of long-held semiotic associations of black and white. Certainly, creators Stan Lee and Jack Kirby take the opportunity to challenge some of the accepted wisdom about white superheroes and their opposition, as well as the relationship of the West to the "third world." Fawaz argues that "the Fantastic Four are forced to reevaluate their assumptions about Western technological supremacy" when they enter the Wakandan jungle and are confronted with machinery far beyond any seen in the West.[8]

On one level, then, *FF* #52–53 challenges simplistic binary divisions. Africa is not merely a land of "primitive" savagery that serves to define the civilized nature of the West. Rather, T'Challa serves as a (black) mirror image for the (white) Reed Richards/Mr. Fantastic. Both men are scientist/heroes with physical powers whose true talents lie in their scientific minds. At the same time, the story recirculates many stereotypical associations with Africa. The Wakandans wear animal pelts, are often partially naked, bear "primitive" weapons like spears, perform tribal dances, and are surrounded by a variety of jungle animals. Indeed, rather than building a conventional "Western" city from their technology, the Wakandans make a "man-made jungle" in which "flora . . . branches . . . flowers . . . and . . . boulders can be heard to hum with the steady pulse of computer dynamos."[9] Fawaz reads these details as "undermin[ing] the logic of . . . stereotype through a series of . . . reversals," first presenting the reader with what they expect (an actual

---

6. Hereafter FF.

7. For accounts of the early history of black superheroes, see Nama, *Super Black*; Brown, *Black Superheroes*, 15–26.

8. Fawaz, *New Mutants*, 117–18. For an opposed reading, see Lund, "Introducing . . ." Lund argues that the depiction of Africa in *FF* #52–53 is continuous with stereotypical Cold War representations of the period. Lund notes that in these comics, Africa functions simply as a site of struggle over natural resources (in this case Vibranium) between the US (represented by the FF) and the Soviets (represented by the villain, Klaw). Thus, Panther's eventual decision to ally himself (and his country's resources) with the FF and US is simply the "right" decision from a Western foreign policy point of view.

9. Lee and Kirby, "The Black Panther."

jungle) before revealing the "truth" of Wakanda's "advanced" society.[10] In truth, however, these depictions do not provide a univocal challenge to hegemonic discourse.

After all, readers of *FF* #52–53 are presented with a confusing mixture of familiar "primitivisms" alongside images of "civilization." While the reader marvels at Wakandan technology and T'Challa's genius, she also witnesses a "primitive" world of half-naked "natives," surrounded by animals, in a jungle both "natural" and synthetic. As a result, the "Africanist presence" that defines the West remains available to the reader even as stereotypical depictions are challenged. As andré m. carrington notes, Africa is often depicted in popular media as "outside of 'civilization'" and "outside of time," and though Wakanda does not completely fit this description, it leaves a significant trace of such depictions.[11]

Likewise, the white Fantastic Four (FF) are initially attacked by T'Challa, meaning he initially fulfills the role of the "black" criminal or villain.[12] Soon enough, the encounter turns into an equally familiar narrative, wherein superheroes fight one another as a case of mistaken identity, or as a "supreme test," putatively necessary before tackling the real enemy.[13] Again, however, the signifier "black" here fluctuates between criminality and heroism, just as it toggles between primitivism and civilization, as if the comic wishes to challenge typical meanings associated with blackness but cannot do so without first evoking, circulating, and perpetuating them.

In this regard, *Black Lightning*, DC's first series with a black superhero in the title role, is similar. Created by Tony Isabella, with art by Trevor von Eeden,[14] the short-lived series exhibits a fascination with the instability of signifiers, and particularly those linked to color or race. The first caption on

---

10. Fawaz, *New Mutants*, 118.

11. carrington, *Speculative Blackness*, 98–99.

12. Supervillains often include "Black" or "Dark," as part of their name to indicate their evil nature, even where race is not explicitly in play. Given these associations, it is interesting that so many early black heroes, like Black Panther and Black Lightning, also have "black" in their names.

13. Lee and Kirby, "The Way It Began."

14. Isabella, a white man, is credited as the sole creator of Black Lightning and has had legal disputes with DC as to who "owns" the character as intellectual property. Von Eeden, a black teen at the time, is typically credited simply as illustrator. The racial politics of the creation of Lightning, and the comics industry's treatment of black creators, is an important one, but not one we have the room to discuss here. *Moon Girl* is also scripted by white creators, Brandon Montclare and Amy Reeder, with art by a black woman, Natacha Bustos. Given Toni Morrison's interest in representations of blackness by white authors as a window into the (racist) unconscious of America, the racial identity of these comics creators has relevance to our theoretical framework.

the interior of *Black Lightning* #1 (mis)quotes eighteenth-century legislator Thomas Randolph: "Justice, like lightning, should ever appear to some men hope. And to other men fear!"[15] This "poem" is attributed to Lightning's alter ego, Jefferson Pierce, in the story-world. Randolph's actual lines (borrowed from a seventeenth-century play[16]) are "Justice, like lightning, ever should appear / To few men's ruin, but to all men's fear."[17] Pierce's adjustment of the line points to the importance of perspective, uncoupling "justice" from any kind of universal meaning. For Randolph, "justice" is *always* (for "all men") associated with "fear." For Pierce, justice is associated with "hope" for some, "fear" for others. Given the longstanding troubled relationship between the biased "justice system" and the African American community, it is hardly surprising that a poem (re)written by a black character sees the definition of "justice" as open to contestation.

The premise of slippery semiotics is also applied to race/color throughout *Black Lightning*, the archvillain of which is underworld kingpin Tobias Whale. Whale is not merely white but is hyperbolically so: huge, bald, and albino. Similarly, Lightning is, in some ways, hyperbolically black. Though schoolteacher Jefferson Pierce is already African American, to "become" Black Lightning, he dons not only a mask but also an afro wig, an affected urban dialect, and a shirt whose neckline plunges to his navel. As Blair Davis points out, the "afro-mask . . . serves to make an ethnic minority character 'more ethnic,'" or "blacker."[18] In addition to associating him (and similar characters, like Luke Cage) with 1970s blaxploitation cinema, Lightning's inconsistent "street" lingo ("cupcake," "lordy," "sucker") suggests that he not only looks "blacker" but that he (sometimes) sounds "blacker" too. Likewise, Lightning's costume exposes his chest in ways similar to other black heroes of the 1970s (Luke Cage, Falcon). As Davis observes, the exposure of black bodies links black superheroes to the history of slavery wherein the "public display and . . . literal commodification of the human body" was an inescapable dehumanizing reality, while the "need to 'look closely' at the chest, arms, and thighs of such slaves [is] uncannily paralleled in . . . many black superheroes."[19] Interestingly, even as Lightning's speech, wig, and exposed skin emphasize his blackness, they also indicate the constructed nature of race. If Pierce is already black, how can his clothing and

---

15. Isabella et al., *Black Lightning*. Our citations refer to the 2016 collected edition of the series.
16. Grosart, *Swetnam*, 52.
17. Wilstach, *A Dictionary of Similes*, 222.
18. Davis, "Bare Chests," 203.
19. Davis, "Bare Chests," 209–11.

speech make him more so? If blackness is "real," how can it be "put on" like a costume?

In this context, it is appropriate that Lightning's foe is a man who resembles a white whale, whom Lightning calls "Moby Dick" during one of their battles.[20] In Herman Melville's classic novel, the semiotic instability of whiteness is discussed in the chapter entitled "The Whiteness of the Whale." Therein, Ishmael first acknowledges the longstanding positive associations with whiteness, including "the majesty of Justice" and "divine spotlessness and power," while linking them to race by referring to "the white man['s] ideal mastership over every dusky tribe." Here, as in early superhero comics, power, justice, whiteness, and divinity are welded together. However, Ishmael then explains not these positive associations, but the "elusive" idea of whiteness, "which strikes more of panic to the soul."[21] Ishmael concludes by noting that whiteness is most troubling as the "absence of color" or the "colorless all-color of atheism," particularly as it relates to light, wherein other colors are actually nothing but "subtile deceits," without which "the palsied universe lied before us like a leper."[22]

Here, whiteness is revealed to be a symbol of the meaninglessness of the universe, a sentiment that seems at first blush to be only tangentially linked to race. However, in "Unspeakable Things Unspoken," Toni Morrison rejects efforts to deracialize *Moby-Dick*'s color imagery, focusing on "The Whiteness of the Whale" in the context of Melville's personal antipathy to slavery and belief in racial equality. For Morrison, Moby-Dick signifies the "ideology of whiteness" itself, and Melville articulates the belief that "it is white racial ideology that is savage" and "an inhuman idea," reversing stereotypical associations of blackness with savagery/animality and whiteness with civilization/humanity.[23]

The reversals Morrison cites are reflected in *Black Lightning* via the depiction of Tobias Whale. While often Whale is simply a stereotypical gangland boss, his violence is occasionally associated with his whiteness, particularly when Whale turns a fire hose on Lightning (see figure 2.1), "evok[ing] the imagery of civil rights advocates assaulted by water cannons and surrounded by white mobs."[24] Here, through the animalistic appearance and criminal behavior of Whale, it is suggested that the "ideology of whiteness"

---

20. Isabella et al., *Black Lightning*.
21. Melville, *Moby-Dick*, 993–94.
22. Melville, *Moby-Dick*, 996–1001.
23. Morrison, "Unspeakable Things Unspoken," 2309–10.
24. Nama, *Super Black*, 27.

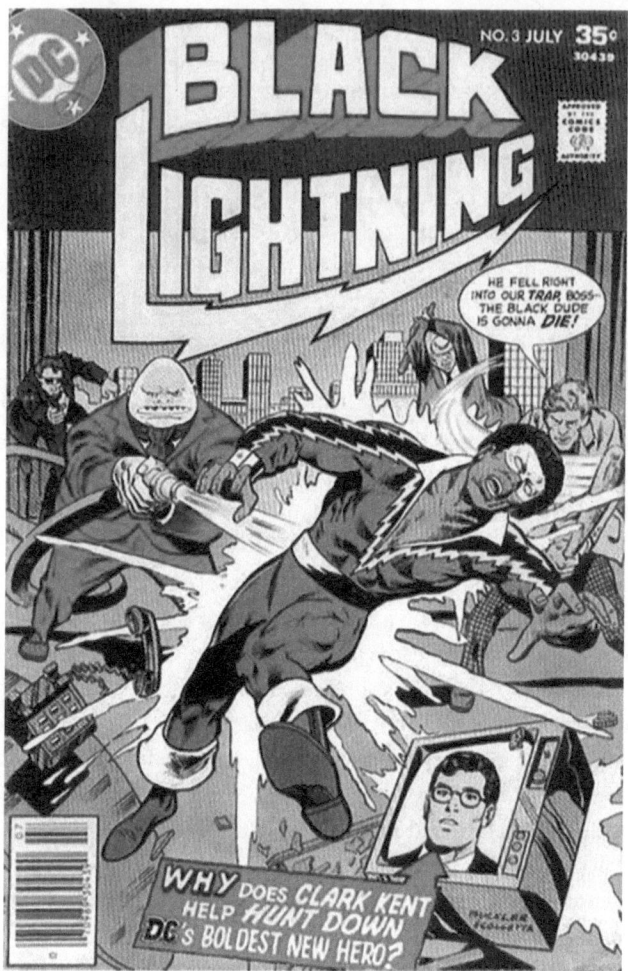

**FIGURE 2.1.** Tobias Whale hoses Black Lightning (*Black Lightning* #3). © DC Comics. Image presented under fair use legislation.

is "criminal" and "savage," whether wielded by a villain like Whale or by police enforcing the status quo.

A similar point is made in issues #4–5 via the appearance of Superman (see figure 2.2). Here, Lightning is framed for murder, leading Superman (like the FF with Black Panther) to mistake Lightning for a criminal.

On one level, again, this is simply a misunderstanding that allows fans to witness a battle between two favorite heroes. However, there is also a metatextual element at play, wherein Superman takes the place of an uninitiated reader, who attempts to understand the situation in terms of hegemonic discourse. Superman understands the situation as if he were in his own

FIGURE 2.2. Superman comes for Black Lightning (*Black Lightning* #4). © DC Comics. Image presented under fair use legislation.

comic, reading Lightning as the stereotypical black criminal. Even though color/race polarities are largely reversed in *Lightning,* Superman comes from the broader DC Universe (and the US), wherein black male criminality[25] is assumed, especially by supposed agents of justice and power.

Superman is just such an agent here, a fact emphasized by the passing mention that he is deputized as a policeman. Like the police, he stands for "truth, justice, and the American way," all three of which, as Morrison

---

25. For a historical overview of the association of American blackness and criminality, see Babb, *Whiteness Visible,* 79–86.

has argued, are linked to whiteness. Although this catchphrase nowhere mentions power explicitly, it too is linked with American whiteness and is embodied by Superman, who resides at the top of the DC Universe's power hierarchy.[26] Within this context, justice is not merely (as Pierce's poem suggests) a matter of perspective but is also defined by power. As in America itself, justice, morality, and ethics in superhero comics are simply matters of "might makes right" (or "white makes right"). When a superhero defeats a villain in physical struggle, the triumph of power serves as a tacit confirmation of his moral superiority. This dynamic must, of course, remain unspoken if the status quo is to remain uncontested. Likewise, in the vast majority of superhero comics through at least the mid-1960s, if a villain is apprehended robbing a bank, the reader is typically not encouraged to consider whether or not the current distribution of "authority and property rights" is actually just.[27] Rather, in impregnably circular logic, the superhero is just because he is protecting the status quo and the status quo is just because the superhero protects it. Likewise, white supremacy and white privilege are given tacit approval through their association with super "heroism." Superman's misrecognition of Lightning's criminality momentarily places this dynamic into question, as the reader cannot help but notice that Superman's brand of justice is actually an act of racial profiling and Lightning's crime a simple act of "superheroing while black," an uncomfortable reminder of the substantial flaws in America's actual justice system.

Superman's linkage to constituent conceptualizations of America and whiteness is, of course, ironic. Though in most iterations he is raised in the heartland of America by white adoptive parents, he is actually an alien from the planet Krypton and thus has no essential ties to America nor to any race. Phenotypically, however, Superman could not be whiter, a fact that confers him with the social power metaphorically embodied by his superpowers. Indeed, as Morrison's work implies, the whiteness/power/justice that Superman represents can only be defined in juxtaposition to an Africanist presence, embodied in the present case by Black Lightning. As Pierce says in the first issue of *Black Lightning*, "I'm no Superman, mac,"[28] meaning that in the logic of white America, Superman cannot be black. Eventually, Superman realizes that Lightning is no killer, allowing for the possibility that they are more alike than different and therefore not defined in binary opposition. It is at this moment, however, that Superman must inevitably depart. If blackness is to take on the meaning of heroic opposition to the corrupt ideol-

---

26. Reynolds, *Superheroes*, 40–41.
27. Uricchio and Pearson, "'I'm Not Fooled,'" 195.
28. Isabella et al., *Black Lightning*.

ogy of white supremacy, it cannot do so in a world wherein whiteness also (and always) means heroism, as it must where Superman is involved. Superman's intrusion, then, indicates just how difficult a dislodging of the association of "white" and "right" is in 1970s America—and largely remains today. Though Jefferson Pierce is born and raised in the American city of Metropolis and Kal-El is rocketed to Earth from another planet, it is Superman who is most immediately associated with America and justice, both through his phenotypic whiteness and the power that comes with it. Black Lightning, by contrast, is always moments away from being mistakenly apprehended as a criminal. Neither *Black Lightning*'s temporary reversal of color/racial polarities nor the self-conscious emphasis on the constructed nature of race can change that reality for long.

## White Moon, Dark Devil

Nearly forty years after Black Lightning's introduction, *Moon Girl and Devil Dinosaur* occupies a much more crowded marketplace of "diverse" superhero comics, but like its predecessor, it struggles to escape the racial polarity whereby a stereotypical "Africanist presence" serves to define a preferable whiteness. Rather than relying upon a *Lightning*-style reversal of racial/color signifiers, *Moon Girl* complicates the reader's experience by imbuing a single character with symbolic characteristics of both whiteness and blackness, allowing the binary juxtaposition to play out within her body and across her story, while also externalizing blackness in a number of ways. A loose sequel to Jack Kirby's 1978 *Devil Dinosaur* series featuring Moon-Boy, a "missing link" figure, and his red *Tyrannosaurus rex* partner, the contemporary version centers on a nine-year-old black girl named Lunella Lafayette.

Throughout the series, Lunella alternately represents both whiteness and blackness. On one hand, as a super-intellect and inventor who sports natural hair and wears nerdy round glasses and retro, knee-high socks, Luna presents as a preteen black hipster.[29] In this context, her scientific/magical abilities are an embodiment of "#BlackGirlMagic," "a term used to illustrate the universal awesomeness of black women. It's about celebrating anything we deem particularly dope, inspiring, or mind-blowing about ourselves."[30]

---

29. Lunella's clothing also associates her with whiteness. She is positioned as the typical "nerd" who is bullied for her intellect and appearance, repeating a familiar superhero trope.

30. Wilson, "The Meaning." One Amazon reviewer of *Moon Girl* even includes the hashtag at the end of her positive review: "Pretty cool to have a black girl super hero. #BlackGirlMagic."

Lunella is magical; she is Inhuman and later learns that her power is the ability to switch bodies with her dinosaur. Like Lightning's afro, Lunella's hair acts as an important signifier of "authentic" blackness. She wears several natural hairstyles, from the classic ponytail puff to afro puffs accompanied by a zigzag part, jumbo bead hair ties, or cornrows. Lunella's mother is also a naturalista who frequently wears headscarves, the quintessential accessory for natural hair. While it is true that natural hair is increasingly popular and thus viewed as less radical than it once was, black hair in its natural state remains political, regardless of wearers' intentions.[31] The Lafayette family, then, at least superficially resists the whitewashing otherwise common in the representation of superhero comics characters of color.

Despite nods to Lunella's racial and cultural identity, however, her race plays no significant role in the stories told in the first two volumes of *Moon Girl*. Aside from occasional cultural cues, she could easily be any race or ethnicity. Quotes taken from renowned scientists, inventors, and businesspeople that appear as epigraphs at the beginning of each issue speak to the ways in which Lunella comes to be associated with both whiteness and blackness. Epigraphs in volume 1 describe Lunella's role as child-scientist; epigraphs in volume 2 focus more on Lunella's strengths and challenges on her way to superherodom. The famous figures quoted in issues #7–12, for example, alternate between black and white (Dean Kamen, Ursula Burns, Isaac Newton, George Washington Carver, Rosaline Franklin, Katherine Johnson), as if she defies racial identification. Lunella's full name, superhero moniker, and nickname (Nella) also intimate shifting racial connotations. Images of the moon often connote whiteness (e.g., A. E. Housman's 1896 "White in the moon the long road lies"), and many consider the moon to be white (even though lunar soil is gray). Likewise, the moniker "Moon Girl" originally belonged to a white superheroine from the 1940s. Thus, Lunella's superheroic identity recalls both a white female character and Kirby's Moon-Boy, whose primitive, apelike features render him symbolically nonwhite.[32] Similarly, the name Luna/Nella recalls two famous black woman "firsts" whose identities symbolized racial mixture: Donyale Luna, the first internationally renowned African American fashion model, who, as Richard Powell notes, embraced "an unorthodox black identity" and "preferr[ed] to think of herself as 'multiracial'" in the 1960s, and Nella Larsen, a mixed-race Harlem Renaissance writer celebrated for being the first black woman creative writer to receive a Guggenheim Fellowship.[33]

---

31. See Mercer, *Welcome to the Jungle*, chap. 4.
32. See Cronin, *Was Superman a Spy?* for details on the original Moon Girl.
33. Powell, *Cutting a Figure*, 87, 111.

Despite Lunella's symbolic racial liminality, when she is placed within the comic's storyline involving Kirby-era beasts from the prehistoric Valley of the Flame (the "Killer-Folk" and Devil the dinosaur), she ironically and increasingly embodies whiteness. Morrison explains that the black presence has served multiple roles for white America, allowing the nation to contemplate freedom and power. She writes, "Through the simple expedient of demonizing and reifying the range of color on a palette, American Africanism makes it possible to say and not to say, to inscribe and erase, to escape and engage, to act out and act on, to historicize and render timeless. It provides a way of contemplating chaos and civilization, desire and fear, a mechanism for testing the problems and blessings of freedom."[34] The racialized Killer-Folk—a tribe of primitive humans who resemble apes—and Devil enter Luna's world via a vortex created by the "nightstone" and signify ("say," "inscribe," "engage," "act out") blackness without being black. Since Lunella is visibly black, despite the comic's narrative ambiguities regarding her race, the Killer-Folk substitute for what she is and is not, making their blackness unambiguous. When they first appear in the twenty-first century, the Killer-Folks' indigenous language evokes B-movie cavemanspeak ("OOH OOH OHH AH AH AH!").[35] The sounds they make (frequently "OOH" and "OOK") reflect a reductionist and simplistic approach to capturing what is translated as advanced speech in earlier scenes, when they are still in the "primitive" past. Considering the ways in which the Killer-Folk are already racialized (via their brown color and violent tendencies), the simple phonetic transcription of their language affirms Ella Shohat and Robert Stam's assertion that "the colonized are denied speech in a double sense, first in the idiomatic sense of not being allowed to speak and second in the more radical sense of not being recognized as capable of speech." Shohat and Stam maintain that in cinema, "linguistic discrimination and colonialist 'tact' go hand in hand with condescending characterization and distorted social portraiture."[36] This applies to the scene wherein the Killer-Folk enter a subway station and attack a group of subway riders in order to steal their clothes and fit in. In this scene, their ignorance regarding fashion serves to urbanize and racialize them, as their headgear includes a backward baseball cap, an upside-down purse worn as a hat, a tie worn as a headband, and headphones (see figure 2.3). Likewise, the only article of stolen clothing that appears ripped is a (white) woman's button-down shirt. Although this is ostensibly because the woman's shirt does not fit the larger Killer-Folk, it

---

34. Morrison, *Playing in the Dark*, 7.
35. Montclare, Reeder, and Bustos, "Old Dogs and New Tricks."
36. Shohat and Stam, *Unthinking Eurocentrism*, 192.

FIGURE 2.3. The Killer-Folk racialized through sartorial design (*Moon Girl and Devil Dinosaur* #2). © Marvel Comics. Image presented under fair use legislation.

also subtly indicates the underlying racial violence (and sexual threat) the tribe's name announces.

At this juncture, the Killer-Folk begin to speak stuttered and broken English, as if their new clothes complete their evolution from primitive humanoid to black. They spend the remainder of the volume as the Killer-Folk gang. When they find Lunella and the nightstone, one holds the stone, exclaiming "OOK!" while another tells her "SSSS . . . Stayyyyy heeerrrrrree . . . Y-You in trouble. And y-you not gonna like it."[37] Morrison's comments about African idiom apply here: "We need to explicate the ways in which specific themes, fears, forms of consciousness, and class relationships are embedded in the use of Africanist idiom: how the dialogue of black characters is construed as an alien, estranging dialect made deliberately unintelligible by spellings contrived to disfamiliarize it."[38] When the Killer-Folk

37. Montclare, Reeder, and Bustos, "Old Dogs and New Tricks."
38. Morrison, *Playing in the Dark*, 52.

become a gang ("caveman gangbangers"),[39] their language is more intelligible but also infantilizing: "Killer Folk good! New world bad. Different and sad and bad. But Killer Folk here."[40] One member trades his horn necklace for a real chain link and lock. When they attempt to collect "protection-money" from a local store, the same character wears his vest hoodie up (a hoodie that belonged to the only black subway rider depicted). Considering that "the racist implicit association that stains young Black men with the mark of the criminal is interwoven with this widely recognizable garment," it becomes obvious that the gang becomes symbolically associated with blackness.[41] Likewise, their blackness is immediately linked to criminality, as they throw up gang signs and a "KF" appears behind them in large yellow letters with a red background, initials that later also appear on their jackets. Ultimately, the Killer-Folk are explicitly criminals/gang members and implicitly black, and these identities become inextricable, as they are in much American public discourse.

While the Killer-Folk never stray from their racialized place, Lunella's growing relationship with Devil reverses her racial signification. While the relationship is initially tense and frustrating, she and Devil soon build a close, protective friendship. When Devil is defeated and handcuffed by Hulk, who hands him over to the police, she vows to "rescue my friend . . . and set him free."[42] She lives up to her word and they team up to take back the nightstone. Immediately after, Terrigen Mist appears and Lunella's transformation turns her into an egg ready to hatch. Devil brings her back to her lab (hidden in the basement of the school) and plays a parental role, incubating Lunella until she hatches. This moment cements Lunella's symbolic racial embodiment of blackness (in the white imagination)—as she is reborn as something other than human. In fact, as she hatches, she thinks, "The question isn't *where* am I . . . it's what am I?"[43] Lunella soon learns her terrigenesis has given her the power to switch minds with Devil. When her mind first inhabits Devil's body, all she can do is roar and growl, turning into a "shambling, rambling monster."[44] Meanwhile, when her body is inhabited by Devil's mind, Devil/Lunella attacks, sniffs, and snarls, and her classmates begin to think she is crazy. Lunella's merging with an animal recalls other black superheroines whom Jeffrey Brown maintains are constructed as

---

39. Montclare, Reeder, and Failla, "Growing Up Is Hard."
40. Montclare, Reeder, and Bustos, "Hulk + Devil = 'Nuff Said."
41. Jeffries, "'Where Ya At?,'" 320.
42. Montclare, Reeder, and Bustos, "Know How."
43. Montclare, Reeder, and Bustos, "Growing Up Is Hard."
44. Montclare, Reeder, and Bustos, "Switcheroo."

"metaphorically bestial."[45] Equating black people with animals has its roots in slave-era ideology and racial hierarchies, and Lunella's behavior brings to mind racist conflations of black people and beasts.

Lunella and Devil switch bodies three times; each time one of them confronts Mel-Varr (aka Kid Kree), a Kree boy who comes to Earth to apprehend Lunella for the Kree Empire because she seems like a "simple [Inhuman] target" and to impress his father.[46] Much to her annoyance, Mel-Varr soon falls in love with Lunella. He passes as a new student in Lunella's science class, using the name "Marvin Ellis." Upon learning that she will have to work with Marvin to head the class project in the "First® LEGO® League" competition, Lunella becomes furious, triggering her first body-switch with Devil. Recalling an earlier moment when the Killer-Folk smell Lunella's scent on her mother and attack her, Lunella charges at Melvin, sniffing him suspiciously before she is confronted by Coach Hrbek. Like the Killer-Folk when they first arrive in the twenty-first century, Lunella is unable to communicate while in Devil's body. According to Morrison, one strategy white writers use when confronting the black presence is "metaphysical condensation": "Collapsing persons into animals prevents human contact and exchange; equating speech with grunts or other animal sounds closes off the possibility of communication."[47] In contrast to when Lunella serves as the antithesis to the Killer-Folk's savagery, Lunella temporarily becomes the unintelligible savage during these mind-switching episodes, unable to communicate, to control her emotions, or to behave rationally (see figure 2.4). When positioned next to the dinosaur's darkness (as devil and beast), Lunella earlier embodies whiteness. As Morrison might note, her blackness is both "inscribe[d] and erase[d]" as her mind occupies Devil's body (and vice versa).[48] Here, she both is and is not the brute the dinosaur's behavior prompts others to think she is.

The second time Lunella switches bodies, Marvin joins her at the lunch table. Suddenly famished, she grabs his hot dog with her teeth and runs off. Lunella (in Devil's body) then arrives at the school just in time to find Devil (in her body), who jumps out of the window to join her. Marvin yells, "You can't—She's . . . She's mine," while Lunella and Devil vanish into

---

45. "Popular Black superheroines like Storm, Vixen, Pantha, and the Black Panther are explicitly associated with exoticized notions of Africa, nature, noble savagery and a variety of Dark Continent themes." Brown, "Panthers and Vixens," 134.

46. "Montclare, Reeder, and Bustos, "Growing Up Is Hard."

47. Morrison, *Playing in the Dark*, 68.

48. Morrison, *Playing in the Dark*, 7.

**FIGURE 2.4.** Lunella racialized and made savage (*Moon Girl and Devil Dinosaur* #8). © Marvel Comics. Image presented under fair use legislation.

the distance.⁴⁹ Mel-Varr's presumptive possession of Lunella on one level asserts the Kree Empire's proprietary rights over the Inhuman, whom the Kree regard as "traitors," but on another level, it speaks to Mel-Varr's personal sense of ownership over Lunella. Although Lunella spurns Mel-Varr's romantic advances, his possessiveness recalls white men's historical ownership over black women's bodies and the sexualized animalization of black women, particularly since he has already witnessed her (mind-switched) savage behavior twice.

Following Mel-Varr's departure, Lunella is greeted by the Totally Awesome Hulk (aka Amadeus Cho), who has come to test her intelligence. To Hulk's astonishment, she quickly and correctly solves the problem, leading him to pronounce, "I think this means you're the smartest person in the whole world."⁵⁰ While this declaration does not make Lunella white, it does

49. Montclare, Reeder, and Bustos, "Switcheroo."
50. Montclare, Reeder, and Bustos, "Unrequited."

symbolically return her closer to the whiteness she exhibits in early issues while arresting, at least temporarily, the vertiginous play of race, mind, body, and gender that dominates the series after she is "reborn" from her egg-like cocoon. The whiteness that attaches itself to Lunella through juxtaposition with Devil and the Killer-Folk threatens to dissolve when Lunella periodically becomes animal, primitive, inarticulate, male, and possessed. In this way, the comic literally plays out some of the symbolic and metaphorical ideas discussed in this chapter.

While there is little doubt that both *Black Lightning* and *Moon Girl* have the best of intentions in challenging stereotypical associations of racial blackness with darkness, primitivism, and criminality (while in so doing also challenging oppositional associations with whiteness), such associations are difficult, if not impossible, to remove entirely from our systems of signification. Just as Black Panther and Black Lightning are pulled back within the orbit of such representations, whether it be through a jungle setting or a battle with a white superhero (or villain), so too the jumbled set of associations that define Lunella cannot help but play off of, and at times be subsumed within, the animalistic and the primitive (not to mention the hypersexualized and the possessed). Even as Lunella is set apart from such images through her juxtaposition with the Killer-Folk and Devil in the early issues of *Moon Girl*, her mind-switching possession of/by Devil in the second volume literalizes the pull of such stereotypical representations, even as we, like Lunella, resist them.

In many ways, both *Black Lightning* and *Moon Girl* simply make use of a variety of common superhero clichés. Whether this be mind-switching or battles between heroes born of misunderstanding, these storylines are as old as superhero comics themselves. However, such common tropes take on new, and unstable, meanings when black heroes take on familiar roles. In these cases, superheroism's origins in an ideology of whiteness that deploys blackness as a defining antithesis destabilizes traditional meanings. Attaching a black character to stereotypically "white" traits can throw the entire signifying system off kilter, though in our examples the system (and racism itself) shows itself to be remarkably resilient. Rather than categorically reject stereotypes of primitivism, hypersexuality, and criminality, such stereotypes persistently reappear, attaching themselves to new objects, as if the Africanist presence is necessary to define heroism (and, as such, whiteness), even if that presence is not always and everywhere attached to black people. Lunella Lafayette, in particular, is a remarkably post-racial figure, as her adventures rarely if ever explicitly explore the vexed politics of race. Nevertheless, a history of pseudo-scientific racism attached to evolution, white male ownership of black women, and associations of black men with criminality are inscribed within its playful storytelling. In *Black Lighting*, Tobias Whale functions as an embodied symbol of the ways in which an ideology of whiteness continues to define, oppress, and oppose both black people and racial justice. The absence of such a singular symbol in *Moon Girl* does not prevent whiteness, as an ideology, from pervading its pages.

## Bibliography

Babb, Valerie. *Whiteness Visible: The Meaning of Whiteness in American Literature and Culture*. New York: New York University Press, 1998.

Brown, Jeffrey. *Black Superheroes, Milestone Comics, and Their Fans*. Jackson: University Press of Mississippi, 2001.

———. "Panthers and Vixens: Black Superheroines, Sexuality, and Stereotypes in Contemporary Comic Books." In *Black Comics: Politics of Race and Representation*, edited by Sheena Howard and Ronald L. Jackson II, 133–49. New York: Bloomsbury, 2013.

carrington, andré m. *Speculative Blackness: The Future of Race in Science Fiction*. Minneapolis: University of Minnesota Press, 2016.

Cronin, Brian. *Was Superman a Spy?: And Other Comic Book Legends Revealed*. New York: Plume, 2009.

Davis, Blair. "Bare Chests, Silver Tiaras, and Removable Afros: The Visual Design of Black Comic Book Superheroes." In *The Blacker the Ink: Constructions of Black Identity in Comics and Sequential Art*, edited by Frances Gateward and John Jennings, 193–212. New Brunswick, NJ: Rutgers University Press, 2015.

Fawaz, Ramzi. *The New Mutants: Superheroes and the Radical Imagination of American Comics*. New York: New York University Press, 2016.

Grosart, Alexander B., ed. *Swetnam: The Woman-Hater: Arraigned by Women*. Manchester, UK: Charles E. Simms, 1620.

Isabella, Tony (writer), Dennis O'Neil (writer), Trevor von Eeden (penciller), and Michael Netzer (penciller). *Black Lightning*. New York: DC Comics, 2016.

Jeffries, Michael. "'Where Ya At?' Hip-Hop's Political Locations in the Obama Era." In *The Cambridge Companion to Hip-Hop*, edited by Justin A. Williams, 314–26. Cambridge, UK: Cambridge University Press, 2015.

Kirby, Jack. *Devil Dinosaur*. New York: Marvel Comics, 2014.

Lee, Stan (writer), and Jack Kirby (penciller). "The Black Panther." *Fantastic Four* vol. 1, no. 52. New York: Marvel Comics, July 1966.

———. "The Way It Began." *Fantastic Four* vol. 1, no. 52. New York: Marvel Comics, August 1966.

Lund, Martin. "'Introducing the Sensational Black Panther!' *Fantastic Four* #52–53, the Cold War, and Marvel's Imagined Africa." *The Comics Grid: Journal of Comics Scholarship* 6, no. 1 (2016): 7.

Mercer, Kobena. *Welcome to the Jungle: New Positions in Black Cultural Studies*. New York: Routledge, 1994.

Melville, Herman. *Moby-Dick, or, The Whale* (1850). In *Herman Melville: Redburn, His First Voyage; White-Jacket, or The World in a Man-of-War; Moby-Dick, or, The Whale.* New York: The Library of America, 1983.

Montclare, Brandon (writer), Amy Reeder (writer), and Natacha Bustos (artist). "Hulk + Devil = 'Nuff Said." *Moon Girl and Devil Dinosaur* vol. 1, no. 4. New York: Marvel, February 2016.

———. "Know How." *Moon Girl and Devil Dinosaur* vol. 1, no. 5. New York: Marvel, March 2016.

———. "Old Dogs and New Tricks." *Moon Girl and Devil Dinosaur* vol. 1, no. 2. New York: Marvel, December 2015.

———. "Switcheroo." *Moon Girl and Devil Dinosaur* vol. 1, no. 8. New York: Marvel, June 2016.

———. "Unrequited." *Moon Girl and Devil Dinosaur* vol. 1, no. 12. New York: Marvel, October 2016.

Montclare, Brandon (writer), Amy Reeder (writer), and Marco Failla (artist). "Growing Up Is Hard." *Moon Girl and Devil Dinosaur* vol. 1, no. 7. New York: Marvel, May 2016.

Morrison, Toni. *Playing in the Dark: Whiteness and the Literary Imagination.* New York: Vintage, 1992.

———. "Unspeakable Things Unspoken: The Afro-American Presence in American Literature." In *The Norton Anthology of African American Literature,* 2nd ed., edited by Henry Louis Gates Jr. et al., 2299–322. New York: W. W. Norton, 2004.

Nama, Adilifu. *Super Black: American Pop Culture and Black Superheroes.* Austin: University of Texas Press, 2011.

Powell, Richard. *Cutting a Figure: Fashioning Black Portraiture.* Chicago: University of Chicago Press, 2008.

Reynolds, Richard. *Superheroes: A Modern Mythology.* Jackson: University Press of Mississippi, 1994.

Shohat, Ella, and Robert Stam. *Unthinking Eurocentrism: Multiculturalism and the Media.* New York: Routledge, 1994.

Uricchio, William, and Roberta Pearson. "'I'm Not Fooled by That Cheap Disguise.'" In *The Many Lives of the Batman: Critical Approaches to a Superhero and His Media,* edited by Roberta Pearson and William Uricchio, 182–213. New York: Routledge, 1991.

Wilson, Julie. "The Meaning of #BlackGirlMagic and How You Can Get Some Of It." *HuffingtonPost.com,* January 12, 2016.

Wilstach, Frank *A Dictionary of Similes.* Boston: Little Brown & Company, 1917.

CHAPTER 3

# "THE ORIGINAL ENCHANTMENT"

Whiteness, Indigeneity, and Representational Logics in *The New Mutants*

JEREMY M. CARNES

## Introduction

Since the first appearance of the X-Men in 1963, conversations surrounding the book and team have centered on issues of representation. Whether from readings of Xavier and Magneto as allegories for Martin Luther King Jr. and Malcolm X, embodying their disparate approaches to racial injustice and inequalities, or in readings of the connections between queer identity and mutant identity,[1] the X-Men have become a central locus for discussing the representation of oppressed or "minority" communities in comics among fans and in scholarly work alike. Yet, many scholars argue that the entire allegorical reading is problematic, at best, because mutantcy remains an invitation to a largely white, cisgender, heterosexual male audience to inhabit the marginalization of others.[2] Most scholars do agree that the use of the category "mutant" as an allegory for racial, ethnic, gender, or sexual difference in Silver Age X-Men stories quickly fell flat given the white, suburban cast of characters who failed to draw direct, purposeful associations between "mutant" and "Other" in any meaningful way. The original team of

---

1. See Darowski, *X-Men and the Mutant Metaphor*; Fawaz, *The New Mutants*.
2. See Lund, "The Mutant Problem"; Shyminsky, "Mutant Readers, Reading Mutants."

Scott Summers (Cyclops), Jean Grey (Marvel Girl), Hank McCoy (The Beast), Warren Worthington III (Angel), and Bobby Drake (Iceman) were not able to unsettle categorization or oppression, as might have been the hope. As Ramzi Fawaz notes, "In the case of the original X-Men, the failure to explicitly articulate mutation to race, gender, and sexuality evacuated the political purchase of the category by leaving it an empty placeholder for a variety of real-world difference."[3]

The rebranding of the team in 1975 as the "All-New, All Different X-Men" included the introduction of many new characters: the Canadian hothead, Logan (Wolverine); the blue-skinned, German Catholic, Kurt Wagner (Nightcrawler); the fun-loving Scotsman, Sean Cassidy (Banshee); the Kenyan street thief turned weather goddess, Ororo Munroe (Storm); and the short-tempered Apache, John Proudstar (Thunderbird). The inclusion of a variety of racial, ethnic, and gender identities made mutation one of many markers of difference readers could see in the X-Men. The diversification of the team did not go unnoticed by readers. As early as *The X-Men* #97, Marvel printed a letter from Tom Runningmouth, a self-identified American Indian, who writes, "I was proud to see one of my people, an American Indian—America's First Citizens—become a member."[4] However, the appearance of a Native character did not necessarily translate to a strong representation. Runningmouth's letter continues, "But to my dissatisfaction, in *X-Men* #94, you started to oppress him. But the clincher was in *X-Men* #95. You killed him. Why was he chosen? Why Thunderbird?" In response, Wein and Cockrum explain that "death . . . is a part of that reality" they strive to represent in their comics. Thunderbird had to die, they continue, "because he was the weakest potential character in the X-Men. He had no powers which weren't duplicated by other members of the team . . . and, harsh as it sounds, duplicated better." But worse than that, Cockrum and Wein note, the character "had nowhere to go. All he was, all he really ever could be, was a wisecracking, insolent, younger, not-as-interesting copy of Hawkeye the Marksman in the Avengers."[5]

Wein and Cockrum's efforts to explain the death of Thunderbird are mired in white settler colonial discourse regarding Native individuals.[6]

---

3. Fawaz, *The New Mutants*, 145.
4. Letter published in Claremont and Cockrum, "My Brother, My Enemy!"
5. Letter in Claremont and Cockrum, "My Brother, My Enemy!" It is also possible to read the hostility of Thunderbird in these early issues as connected to the visibility of the American Indian Movement (AIM) and the struggle for Native rights throughout the late 1960s and early 1970s.
6. I use the term "Native" here and throughout to mark indigenous individuals in both North and South America, while keeping the term divorced from problematic

Thunderbird must be killed because he is "the weakest" and "had nowhere to go." These phrases mirror ideas about Native individuals as being consistently stuck in the past, unable to adequately modernize. In reality, it turns out that Thunderbird had to die because Wein and Cockrum could not envision a Native character that existed in the present and that fit with a modern superhero team. Thunderbird is killed because of the dominant, settler colonial ideology from which, purposeful or not, Wein and Cockrum could not divorce themselves. Thus, Wein and Cockrum's rhetoric mirrors the settler colonial notion that "white Americans needed either to destroy Indians or to assimilate them into a white American world."[7] Because of stereotypical understandings of indigeneity embedded in white settler colonialism, the X-Men as a concept could not adequately accommodate a Native character.

This reading of Thunderbird outlines a dominant critical approach to representation in comics (and literary/artistic forms generally) that focuses primarily on the subjectivity of marginalized characters themselves. While this approach has been crucial to understanding the history of American comics, in this chapter I hope to expand the ways that we can approach representation by focusing less on indigenous characters themselves and more on indigeneity conceptually. Central to my argument is Jodi Byrd's (Chickasaw) notion of "representational logics," which names the process whereby "Indianness becomes a site through which U. S. empire orients and replicates itself by transforming those to be colonized into 'Indians' through continual reiterations of pioneer logics."[8] Thus, for Byrd, representational logics are made up of the various structures wherein indigeneity is made indigenous to a place and thus colonizable. In the course of this chapter, I expand upon Byrd to examine how representational logics of indigeneity in comics are consistently framed through markers of dominance, whether through race (whiteness), sexuality (heterosexuality), or gender (maleness). In exploring Chris Claremont's X-Men spinoff series *The New Mutants* (1982–1991), I focus on how indigeneity is always marked through the representational logics of settler colonialism and the embedded markers of racial dominance (whiteness).

---

national imagery with the added "American." I occasionally (synonymously) use "indigenous" as an even broader, global term.

7. Deloria, *Playing Indian*, 4.

8. Byrd, *The Transit of Empire*, xiii. I am using "representation" in relation to the appearance of marginalized characters in the comics, while "representational logics" is more broadly about the ways in which these comics are continually influenced by structures of settler colonialism that affect the understanding of indigeneity itself.

## *The New Mutants* on the Block

With the "All-New, All-Different X-Men" becoming an industry best seller under the guidance of writer Chris Claremont and artists Dave Cockrum and John Byrne, most notably, Claremont and Marvel editors expanded Marvel's mutant world with a new and similarly diverse team of younger mutants in 1982's *Marvel Graphic Novel #4: The New Mutants*. In the graphic novel we encounter teenage mutants as their powers manifest: Rahne Sinclair (Wolfsbane), with the ability to transform into a wolf or various stages between human and wolf; Roberto Da Costa (Sunspot), who can absorb and channel solar power into superhuman strength; Sam Guthrie (Cannonball), who blasts around at jet-like speeds while encased in a protective forcefield; Xi'an Coy Mahn (Karma), with the ability to possess those around her; and Danielle "Dani" Moonstar (Psyche/Mirage), who can psychically project people's greatest fears or desires into seemingly physical forms.

Dani is a young Cheyenne woman who grew up in the mountains of Colorado with her grandfather, Black Eagle, a friend of Professor Xavier. From the outset of her appearance, she struggles with the opposition of whiteness and indigeneity. She first refuses to attend Xavier's school, questioning her grandfather, "A white!?! You would send me to an Anglo?!?" Working with Xavier and the New Mutants "seems to her a form of selling out to white culture."[9] However, after the death of her grandfather, she joins Xavier, though she pushes against his expectations at the conclusion of the graphic novel by changing her outfit to show more of a connection to her Cheyenne heritage (albeit through the stereotypical use of a turquoise belt). She argues, "I am Cheyenne. Nothing—no one—will ever make me forget or abandon my heritage. I'm also an individual, professor. You say we must wear these clothes—I will do as you ask, but in my own manner. If that bothers you, I can leave."[10] We see the beginning here of Dani working through what Fawaz calls "her dual identity as both a member of the New Mutants and the Cheyenne."[11] Dani, in opposition to Thunderbird, is a character for whom indigeneity remains central and is not discounted or erased by membership in a superhero team.

In many ways, then, Dani's story is about making sense of her own indigeneity in relation to whiteness and to white individuals. Dani, as one of the first nuanced examples of indigeneity in mainstream comics writ-

---

9. Fawaz, *The New Mutants*, 249.
10. Claremont and McLeod, *Marvel Graphic Novel #4*.
11. Fawaz, *The New Mutants*, 258.

ten by white creators, stands in a liminal space in the first twenty issues of the homonymous continuing series that followed the graphic novel, where she "gain[s] the confidence to see that the two aspects of her personal history could sustain one another rather than exist in contradiction."[12] Dani can wholeheartedly support the mission of the New Mutants without turning her back on the history of her people and on her own personal Cheyenne identity. Further, the personal relationships with her diverse teammates form the bedrock of her developing understanding of the complex relationship between whiteness and indigeneity. In more than one story, the personal relationships between the members of the New Mutants help them to defeat various enemies, most notably for Dani, the Demon Bear.

Yet, it is not just Dani's story and representation, but also the secondary characters and locations that form the backdrop to their pursuits of mutant and other identities, that distinctly highlight the ways representational logics are filtered through markers of gender, racial, and colonial dominance in this series.[13] Imagined cultures like the Nova Romans and characters like Tom Corsi and Sharon Friedlander mark *The New Mutants* itself as caught between two contradictory discourses. On the one hand is a liberatory discourse that understands personal relationships as a foundation for breaking down white imperial systems, as embodied in the relationships between the members of the New Mutants themselves. On the other hand, *The New Mutants* (re)produces a settler colonial rhetoric that makes whiteness a racially blank signifier capable of co-opting discourses of oppression, racism, and settler practices with regard to land. Thus, precisely because indigeneity in *The New Mutants* is designated in relation to markers of racial dominance (whiteness), the series stands on the line between liberation and oppression—a line that, perhaps unsurprisingly, is imperceptibly fine. The remainder of this chapter explores two main story arcs of *The New Mutants*, the Nova Roma arc and "The Demon Bear Saga," to examine how the representational logics complicate the series's liberatory discourse. Both arcs highlight the particular ways whiteness is used to frame indigenous ontologies of white possession and race shifting.

---

12. Fawaz, *The New Mutants*, 258.

13. Dani Moonstar is not an unproblematic representation of Native identity. She is stereotypically able to commune with animals and wears stereotypical clothing. Yet, her struggles with identity present a more complex representation of indigeneity than mainstream comics had seen to this point.

## White Possession in New Rome

In *The New Mutants* #7–#11 (September 1983–January 1984), the team joins Roberto's mother, Nina Da Costa, on an archaeological journey to the Madería—the headwaters of the Amazon. After some run-ins with various henchmen hired by the Hellfire Club, the New Mutants are captured by the "4th maniple, 1st cohort, Thunderclap Legion" from an ancient Roman colony called Nova Roma.[14] This colony has remained hidden from the larger global population, and thus remained, in practice and appearance, an imperial city of the ancient Roman Empire. The concealment of the area is what attracts the Hellfire Club, led by Sebastian Shaw and Emmanuel Da Costa, Roberto's father and Nina's husband, to want to enter this "uncharted, unexplored, virtually inaccessible" territory.[15] In Nova Roma, the New Mutants meet Amara Aquilla, daughter of Lucius Aquilla, first senator of Nova Roma. When the New Mutants first meet her, Amara has disguised herself as one of the brown-skinned, black-haired Inca warrior women that live in areas surrounding Nova Roma. After a battle in the arena for the entertainment of the citizens of Nova Roma and the near murder of Roberto, the New Mutants find themselves facing off against the Black Priestess, Selene, a vampire priestess who hopes to continue ruling Nova Roma from the shadows as she has done up to this point. It is against Selene that Amara's mutant powers manifest; she becomes Magma, able to control the molten core of the Earth, thus giving her command over flame and earthquakes in various plot-reliant ways. With the help of Magma, the New Mutants defeat Selene and bury her in a tomb of molten lava.

Amara's disguise is particularly relevant to the representational logics at play in the Nova Roma story arc. Her Inca warrior outfit is motivated by a desire to keep herself safe from the Black Priestess who, the story reveals, killed Amara's mother. Further, the other Inca warriors encountered in the story are also young girls sent into hiding from the Black Priestess. Thus, there are no actual Inca people in the story. In fact, Inca "identity" appears only as a disguise, a tool used by white characters to legitimize their claim to Nova Roma and the land that it rests on. Such a practice is what Aileen Moreton-Robinson (Geonpul) has called "white possession." Moreton-Robinson outlines the ways in which whiteness becomes the primary marker through which "possessive logics" are operationalized. She explains that possessive logics are "a mode of rationalization, rather than a set of positions that produce a more or less inevitable answer, that is under-

---

14. Claremont and Cockrum, "The Road to . . . Rome?"
15. Claremont and Cockrum, "The Road to . . . Rome?"

pinned by an excessive desire to invest in reproducing and reaffirming the nation-state's ownership, control, and domination." Further, she notes that "race indelibly marks the law's possessiveness."[16] Thus, white possession of the nation, land, industrial capital, and—evident in the case of the Nova Roma storyline—colony is based in the whiteness of dominant communities. Racial difference marks "them" apart from "us" and thus indicates "their" unworthiness to maintain control over not only the land, but everything that was built upon or extracted from it. And while whiteness is used to operationalize white settler colonial tactics of possession, it also "disavows colonization . . . tied to the appropriation of Native American lands" through the creation of a white identity that works to disconnect itself from the history and practices of dispossession, slavery, and migration.[17] White possession is doubly valent in its role as a tactic of settler colonialism: first as a "hypervisual" marker to separate savage and civilized, and second as the central node in a multicultural network focused on diverting attention from the role of whiteness in colonization and oppression.

Throughout this arc, Nova Roma and its inhabitants exemplify white possessive logics. The power and positioning of Nova Roma is continually constituted throughout the series by discussions embedded in a settler colonial practice of indigenizing whiteness. Shortly after the New Mutants meet Amara, for example, she is revealed to be a white-skinned, blond-haired citizen of Nova Roma, rather than the dark-skinned Inca warrior she initially seemed. Amara's Inca disguise is premised on a racialized understanding of indigeneity—marked by the brown pigment on her skin that easily washes away in the Amazon river;[18] the associations here, as elsewhere, between "playing Indian" and blackface are nearly impossible to miss. While indigenous claims to sovereignty have been and continue to be based in claims of tribal citizenship, from a dominant, white perspective, indigeneity is designated specifically by racial markers of difference. As Kim Tallbear (Sisseton Wahpeton Oyate) notes, "race has also been imposed on us. Race politics over the centuries . . . have conditioned our experiences and opportunities [and] impinged our ability as indigenous peoples to exercise self-government."[19] The racialization of indigeneity is "predicated on the logics of possession" precisely because racializing indigeneity strips indigenous communities of their land through dehumanizing methods both symbolic and tangible. As Moreton-Robinson explains, colonial "territory has been marked by and through violence and race. Racism is thus inextricably tied

---

16. Moreton-Robinson, *The White Possessive*, xii.
17. Moreton-Robinson, *The White Possessive*, xx.
18. Claremont and Cockrum, "The Road to . . . Rome?"
19. Tallbear, *Native American DNA*, 32.

to the theft and appropriation of Indigenous lands."[20] Racialization divorces indigeneity from tribal sovereignty and subsumes Natives under multicultural understandings of racial integration and inclusion. Thus, Amara's "playing Indian" is embedded in symbolic practices that dehumanize indigenous peoples and delegitimize claims to land rights, self-determination, and sovereignty.

While racializing indigeneity delegitimizes Native identity, it simultaneously legitimizes white colonial power. In the New Mutants' first extended conversation with Amara, she explains to them, "We are not all Roman. Much of the city is descended from the Incas who fled here centuries ago, when their own land was conquered."[21] The possessive logics of this region of South America become embroiled in analogous versions of US assertions to indigenous ancestry. The Nova Romans' claims to indigenous ancestry and thus of autochthonous ties to the land create a cultural-historical "connection" to the place while also producing an apparent legitimizing legal claim to its ownership and subsequent use, development, or extraction of resources. As Philip J. Deloria (Dakota) argues about the practice of "playing Indian," "Americans wanted to feel a natural affinity with the continent, and it was Indians who could teach them such aboriginal closeness."[22] Both Amara's claims to Inca ancestry and her practice of disguising herself and the other young women as Inca warriors highlights the ways in which indigeneity as a marker of differences is always constituted through the way white characters make use of it in the story. In many ways, Amara is simultaneously claiming indigeneity while also exploiting it to write Nova Roma as white.

The double valence of white possession is also visible in New Rome itself, primarily through differences in political organization. Amara explains the political struggle in New Rome caused by what Claremont frames as opposing Inca and Roman political structures: "Nova Roma is a republic but the Incas were an absolute monarchy. A faction has arisen seeking to transform Rome into the same kind of imperial state. I am part of the opposition to that party."[23] The rhetoric Amara uses, paired with the creation of an "us" versus "them" mentality in her act of "playing Indian," further racializes and differentiates Nova Romans and Incas. Nova Romans are the "civilized" republic that respects its citizens, unlike the "absolute monarchy" that here seems "savage" or "backwards." However, Amara's use of the past tense "were"

---

20. Moreton-Robinson, *The White Possessive*, xiii.
21. Claremont and Cockrum, "Arena."
22. Deloria, *Playing Indian*, 5.
23. Claremont and Cockrum, "Arena."

marks the Inca monarchy as a political practice placed firmly in the past. As such, her past tense verb also designates Incas as a constituent of the multicultural Nova Roman republic, since they no longer practice monarchy. Finally, her description of the pre-contact Inca polity as an "imperial state" diverts attention from the role whiteness played in the colonization of Inca by Spaniards in the 16th century. In the same way that framing colonization through beneficiary rhetoric focused on "helping" the "savage" Natives to "civilize," as we see implicitly in the practice of "playing Indian," drawing associations between imperialism and indigeneity divorces whiteness (Nova Roma) from imperialism and makes the "backwards" practices of indigenous communities as themselves the cause of white settler colonialism.

The Nova Roma arc highlights the way in which indigeneity, especially when divorced from the primary Native character, Dani Moonstar, is always understood in relation to whiteness. The colonial structures at the heart of New Rome seek to constantly lessen indigeneity in terms of whiteness, while also using that same indigeneity to legitimize white ownership and control of the land. White possession thus marks indigeneity in terms of whiteness; it clearly highlights the dialectical relationship between the two. Claremont's creation of Nova Roma in the Amazon is only possible, whether purposefully or not, through practices of settler colonialism that are founded on the logics of white possession. Some might see the practice of "playing Indian" and the logics of white possession as a precursor to a more dramatic and more violent racial shift and attack on indigenous sovereignty, which appears later in *The New Mutants*.

## Race Shifting Out of the Badlands

"The Demon Bear Saga" introduced artist Bill Sienkiewicz to *The New Mutants*, and immediately his art opened the series to new narrative possibilities. Beginning in issue #18 (August 1984), Dani decides that she must face the Demon Bear that has been haunting her nightmares since she was a child. She does so, and for a moment, the battle seems to swing in her favor. But the issue ends with the other New Mutants finding Dani's bloody, mutilated body at the base of a large, snow-covered tree.[24] With Dani in the hospital, the New Mutants confront the Demon Bear and, in the battle, experience "a moment of absolute madness—of their universe, the proper order of things, being turned upside-down, inside-out—followed

---

24. Claremont and Sienkiewicz, "Death-Hunt."

by blessed oblivion."[25] Upon waking, Illyana (Magik) realizes that the bear has transported them to his turf, the Badlands. There, in "a virgin America, untouched by the white invaders from across the sea," the team fights both the Demon Bear and its henchmen, indigenized versions of the police officer and nurse—Tom Corsi and Sharon Friedlander—from the hospital where Dani is recovering. With the help of the other New Mutants and her Soulsword, Illyana kills the bear after she learns that Dani was not bound to defeat it alone. The power to defeat the Demon Bear rested in the combined efforts of the New Mutants.[26]

Ramzi Fawaz reads "The Demon Bear Saga" as indicative of the team's need to view the world through multiple perspectives. He writes, "The central thematic . . . lay not in an image of the harmony of all things but in each teammate's development of a faculty of radical imagination, the ability to see from each other's viewpoints as they faced a shared threat from competing perspectives."[27] For Fawaz, facing the Demon Bear means that the New Mutants must face the horrors of colonialism and the genocide of Native peoples that it represents. The bear's presence is synonymous with the act of colonization itself, a suggestion made most evident in the map reproduced throughout *The New Mutants* #20 (October 1984) that depicts "areas of land consumed by Demon-Bear's shadow."[28] The New Mutants must, in the end, face the bear in a landscape that is being rapidly corrupted by the Demon Bear's power, an analogue to the corruption of white settler colonialism across contemporary North America.

Fawaz further explains that the showdown with the Demon Bear brings the New Mutants into solidarity with one another. For Fawaz, the Demon Bear embodies the past horrors each member of the New Mutants faced "in the form of the foundational indigenous trauma, the genocide of Native American peoples."[29] This resonance marks indigeneity as a category that allows *The New Mutants* "to question the very nature of original belonging to any group, land, history or political vision." Such an approach makes indigeneity a categorical path toward liberatory freedom for many of the New Mutants, though in "The Demon Bear Saga" it is still Dani, the only actual indigenous character, who carries physical wounds that also signify the violence of white settler colonialism on indigeneity. Fawaz's reading highlights the positionality of *The New Mutants* between the liberatory, radical readings

---

25. Claremont and Sienkiewicz, "Siege."
26. Claremont and Sienkiewicz, "Badlands."
27. Fawaz, *The New Mutants*, 256.
28. Claremont and Sienkiewicz, "Badlands."
29. Fawaz, *The New Mutants*, 261.

that question traditions embedded in the past and the dominant colonial discourse that reifies white supremacy, even under the façade of indigenous inclusion. In "The Demon Bear Saga," this latter discourse is clearest in a reading of Corsi and Friedlander, the policeman and nurse, who are markedly absent from Fawaz's discussion.

Corsi and Friedlander first appear in *The New Mutants* #19 after Dani has been taken to the hospital to treat her life-threatening wounds from her battle with the Demon Bear. Corsi is a night guard in the hospital and Friedlander is one of the night nurses. Shortly after Corsi sees Rahne in a transitional stage between human and wolf, which he blames on the fact that "these lights are too blasted low, an' I'm too blasted tired," he goes to speak with Friedlander. In the middle of Corsi working up the courage to ask Friedlander on a date, they hear a low growl in the hallway and come face-to-face with the Demon Bear. They disappear and the rest of the New Mutants only find a large bloodstain. They return at the very end of issue #19, after the bear has transported them and the New Mutants to the "badlands." However, it is at the beginning of the final issue in the arc that the Demon Bear strikes on Corsi and Friedlander again, "its claws doing no harm to the bodies of its helpless captives . . . only to their souls."[30] The demonic, and visually indigenized, representation of Corsi and Friedlander—along with their eventual full transformation into indigenous characters—complicate the liberatory reading of indigeneity offered by Fawaz by drawing analogies to issues of race shifting and, relatedly, the practice of "going Native."

In her book *Becoming Indian*, anthropologist Circe Sturm defines "race shifting" as a practice whereby white individuals claim Native identities as their own, much like Amara's claiming of Inca ancestry for the Nova Romans. Kim Tallbear associates "race shifting" with the ways in which whites often claim indigeneity through DNA testing or blood quantum self-definitions.[31] Race shifting, then, highlights the apparent racelessness of whiteness; that is, whiteness operates as a racially blank canvas that can adopt racial identities as necessary to maintain control in colonial spaces. Shari Huhndorf refers to this as "going native," which, like Deloria's "playing Indian," "articulates and attempts to resolve widespread ambivalence about modernity as well as anxieties about the terrible violence marking the nation's origins."[32] Yet,

---

30. Claremont and Sienkiewicz, "Badlands," 4.
31. Tallbear, *Native American DNA*, 133. Blood quantum is the defining of indigenous peoples based on ancestry, dividing Indian and non-Indian peoples by amounts of "Indian blood" in their lineage.
32. Huhndorf, *Going Native*, 2.

both going Native and race shifting introduce another facet to the relationship between whiteness and indigeneity, embodied in the sustained practice of claiming, acting, and trying to appear "Native." While "playing Indian" is momentary, going Native and race shifting are continuous practices that consistently rely on the mutability of whiteness and the subalternity of indigeneity. As such, Corsi's and Friedlander's initial transformation into indigenized demonic minions and their subsequent, and lasting, transformation into nondescript indigenous beings both highlight how indigeneity is still subsumed under conversations of "savage" and "civilized," and thus "traditional" or "modern," and how the racialization of indigeneity glosses tribal difference in an effort to incorporate indigeneity into discourses of American multiculturalism and inclusion.

After being transformed, Corsi and Friedlander "go native" to the point of "savagery." The fringe, loincloths, and arm bracelets all signify broad, stereotypical understandings of Native clothing, divorced from specific tribal contexts. Further, their masklike faces simultaneously imply equally decontextualized indigenous ceremonial masks while also depicting frightening, wild visages. As maker of these demon underlings and embodiment of the horrors of colonialism, the Demon Bear writes indigeneity as "savage" on the bodies of Corsi and Friedlander. In the "badlands," a landscape that analogously repeats white colonial spread in the US, marking indigeneity as "savage" coincides with practices of settler colonialism. Their later appearance as Native characters, now at least shorn from the stereotypes suggested by their clothing and crazed looks, brings their identities closer to the noble savage portrayal, which "conflates an urge to idealize and desire Indians and a need to dispossess them."[33] In the span of a single issue, Corsi and Friedlander show the varying approaches to going Native from a dominant, white perspective: the negative form of "savage" and the positive "noble savage."

Corsi's and Friedlander's race shifting, their process of going Native, comes at the hands of the embodiment of white settler colonial power. The Demon Bear uses its power of corruption, that is, its power of settler colonialism, to rewrite whiteness as indigenous and to dispel indigeneity itself. After all, we learn at the end of the arc that the Demon Bear is made up of the imprisoned souls of Dani's parents. Dani's father, William Lonestar, explains to her, "We weren't killed, but enslaved—transformed into the Demon Bear you fought, a foul corruption of our sacred symbol."[34] Here,

---

33. Deloria, *Playing Indian*, 4.
34. Claremont and Sienkiewicz, "Badlands," 23.

*The New Mutants* foregrounds the issues of settler colonial co-optation of indigeneity. Their imprisonment in the bear mirrors the continued oppression of Native communities across the US through white settler colonialism. Furthermore, these representational logics, which here end up marking indigeneity as a threat in the body of the Demon Bear, also make indigenous people the cause of their own colonization. Whiteness is then formulated as the savior from the dangers indigenous peoples pose to themselves and to others, like Corsi and Friedlander, whose transformation could have also come at the hands of indigenous peoples.

However, simultaneously, we see the now-changed bodies of Corsi and Friedlander; as Rahne explains, "They're still red Indians!" Lonestar notes, "Their bodies were reshaped before they were possessed. You drove out their demonic natures, but that didn't affect the original enchantment. It's kind of a vicious reminder that, while you defeated the bear, you've a long way to go before challenging the evil that spawned it."[35] In one way, Lonestar's description mirrors decolonial rhetoric working to challenge and deconstruct white settler colonial power. Yet, in the same instance, the series writes over the complex identity marker of indigeneity, again making it simply a racial marker. The darker skin and black hair are what make Corsi and Friedlander "red Indians" here, rather than anything related to cultural practice or tribal citizenship. They are both marked as Native without traditional tribal affiliations. Thus, while the end of "The Demon Bear Saga" works to foreground conversations about struggles in decolonial futures, it does so while still mired in white settler colonial understandings of indigeneity and Native communities. Again, the appearance of Native-ness is always defined in terms of the whiteness continually co-opting and reformulating it, here visible in the lasting "curse" on the bodies of Corsi and Friedlander.

## Coda

What both arcs make clear, then, is that representational logics are not marked by responsible and nuanced approaches to a variety of ethnic, racial, or indigenous backgrounds. Rather, representational logics are always constituted by and in whiteness. *The New Mutants* stands on the line between two ways of thinking about Native representation—as liberatory and radical, or as continually mired in issues of settler colonial ideology. In effect, the series is largely defined not by its radicalness or its coloniality, but by the

---

35. Claremont and Sienkiewicz, "Badlands," 21.

dialectic of the two. In it we can see the push and pull between decolonial rhetorics and the colonial structures we are continually working to deconstruct. It is precisely in exploring this liminal space between liberatory and colonial in a single series that we can better understand the ways in which cultural productions, like *The New Mutants*, can help us to distinguish how complex colonial foundations can still appear beneath the articulations of decolonial futures.

In comics studies and literary studies more broadly, we need to widen our field of view when analyzing representations of non-hegemonic identity formations because, especially in terms of indigeneity, the power of whiteness is an embedded practice of settler colonialism that affects all characters and skews even seemingly progressive representations. The appearance of a nuanced character like Dani does not disassemble the representational logics of settler colonial tactics. Rather, whiteness continues to oppress and dispossess, even in the background. Liberatory articulations, as important as they are, do not always "affect the original enchantment" of white settler colonialism. In many instances, the two "enchantments" coexist.

## Bibliography

Byrd, Jodi. *The Transit of Empire: Indigenous Critiques of Colonialism*. Minneapolis: University of Minnesota Press, 2011.

Claremont, Chris (writer), and Dave Cockrum (penciller). "Arena." *The New Mutants* #9. Marvel, November 1983.

———. "My Brother, My Enemy!" *The X-Men* #98. Marvel, February 1976.

———. "The Road to . . . Rome?" *The New Mutants* #8. Marvel, October 1983.

Claremont, Chris (writer), and Bob McLeod (penciller). *Marvel Graphic Novel #4: The New Mutants*. New York: Marvel, 1982.

Claremont, Chris (writer), and Bill Sienkiewicz (penciller). "Badlands." *The New Mutants* #20. Marvel, October 1984.

———. "Death-Hunt." *The New Mutants* #18. Marvel, August 1984.

———. "Siege." *The New Mutants* #19. Marvel, September 1984.

Darowski, Joseph J. *X-Men and the Mutant Metaphor: Race and Gender in the Comic Books*. Lanham, MD: Rowman & Littlefield, 2014.

Deloria, Philip J. *Playing Indian*. New Haven, CT: Yale University Press, 1998.

Fawaz, Ramzi. *The New Mutants: Superheroes and the Radical Imagination of American Comics*. New York: New York University Press, 2016.

Huhndorf, Shari. *Going Native: Indians in the American Cultural Imagination*. Ithaca, NY: Cornell University Press, 2001.

Lund, Martin. "The Mutant Problem: *X-Men*, Confirmation Bias, and the Methodology of Comics and Identity." *European Journal of Comics Art* 10, no. 2 (2015). https://ejas.revues.org/10890.

Moreton-Robinson, Aileen. *The White Possessive: Property, Power, and Indigenous Sovereignty*. Minneapolis: University of Minnesota Press, 2015.

Shyminsky, Neil. "Mutant Readers, Reading Mutants: Appropriation, Assimilation, and the X-Men." *International Journal of Comic Art* 8, no. 2 (Fall 2006): 387–405.

Sturm, Circe. *Becoming Indian: The Struggle over Cherokee Identity in the Twenty-First Century*. Santa Fe: School for Advanced Research Press, 2011.

Tallbear, Kim. *Native American DNA: Tribal Belonging and the False Promise of Genetic Science*. Minneapolis: University of Minnesota Press, 2013.

CHAPTER 4

# FEARFULLY AND WONDERFULLY MADE

## The Racial Politics of *Cloak and Dagger*

OLIVIA HICKS

"THE DARKNESS and the light are both alike . . . I am fearfully and wonderfully made." So begins the 1983 miniseries *Cloak and Dagger*. The quote, from Psalm 139, also appears in the pair's ongoing 1985–1987 series, and sets out the racially charged aspirations of the characters: On the one hand, co-creator and writer Bill Mantlo tries to present whiteness and blackness as symbiotic, with the propensity for both good and evil. The world Cloak and Dagger live in, like many an ethnically diverse team in popular culture, is superficially post-racial—Cloak, a black man, is able to befriend Dagger, a white woman, and the two live reasonably harmoniously together. However, Cloak and Dagger's burning obsession is to destroy the drug trade, and this invocation of the War on Drugs situates the comic not in some postracial utopia, but firmly in the racialized landscape of Reagan's America. The comic performs several such sleights of hand through ongoing discrepancies between what the characters and (third-person) narration say and how the characters act, creating inconsistencies between the narrative and political subconscious. It is here where the construction of Dagger's whiteness, and the privileges it affords her, is laid bare. This chapter explores how Dagger's whiteness is constructed in three modes: First, how her whiteness is contrasted against Cloak's blackness; second, her construction as the ideal of white femininity, and how Cloak problematizes this; and finally, how her whiteness is contrasted with that of the white drugs (heroin and cocaine) that she and Cloak have vowed to destroy.

With the exception of a few appearances in *Peter Parker, The Spectacular Spider-Man* and *The New Mutants*, which were scripted by Al Milgrom and Chris Claremont, respectively, Mantlo wrote Cloak and Dagger from their initial appearance in *Spectacular Spider-Man* #64 (March 1982), through their 1983 miniseries, their 1985 ongoing series, and up to issue #6 of *Strange Tales* (September 1987), when he left the title due to disagreements with Marvel over the choice of artist.[1] In addition to this he penned two Marvel graphic novels starring the duo: *Predator and Prey* (1988) and *Shelter from the Storm* (1989). It is Mantlo's vision of Cloak and Dagger that this chapter discusses. Describing the conception of the characters to Marvel's promotional magazine *Marvel Age*, Mantlo wrote: "I went on long excursions with my typewriter. One of those excursions was by ferry to Ellis Island, a national park nestled in the Hudson River, a place dubbed the 'Island of Tears' by the countless immigrants who passed through it on their way to citizenship in America. The place haunted me. . . . Not long after, Cloak and Dagger came to me."[2] Mantlo's anecdote places Cloak and Dagger firmly within American narratives of ethnicity and whiteness.

Mantlo crafted Cloak and Dagger as street-level antiheroes in the vein of the Punisher. Rather than focusing their considerable powers on supervillains, Cloak and Dagger spent their energies on obliterating the drug trade and the "Mob." They occasionally squared off against Silvermane, Kingpin, or, on one occasion, Doctor Doom, but their quest to end the drug trade and thus protect other teenage runaways was the pair's overriding obsession. Cloak and Dagger were timely characters. In the comics industry, "'gritty urban' material" was gaining popularity, exemplified in the success of Frank Miller's *Daredevil* run.[3] Miller used superheroes to examine the troubled undercurrent of Reagan's America, turning them into "a force for ruthless morality in a corrupt society that feared and despised them. Theirs was a seemingly impossible task that no sane individual would undertake."[4]

Cloak and Dagger's seemingly impossible task of thwarting the drug trade may have alienated them from society, the law, and their superheroic peers, but it also aligned them with the policies of Ronald Reagan. Elected in 1981, Reagan quickly reignited Richard Nixon's War on Drugs, an initiative that accelerated the drug trade. In 1982, for example, Florida began to issue

---

1. Yurkovich and Mantlo, *Mantlo*, 57.
2. Mantlo, Milgrom, Hannigan, Leonardi et al., *Cloak and Dagger: Shadows and Light*, 416.
3. Howe, *Marvel Comics*, 247.
4. Wright, *Comic Book Nation*, 266.

identical mandatory prison sentences for both marijuana and cocaine, causing the amount of high-purity cocaine being smuggled into the US to drastically increase, which then led to plummeting cocaine prices. In 1983 crack cocaine reached the US, and by 1986, 5,000 Americans daily were trying cocaine for the first time.[5] In addition to this, the War on Drugs directly led to the mass incarceration of America's black male population.[6] The series's construction of whiteness, blackness, and the superhero is haunted, then, not merely by the immigrants of Ellis Island, but also by the highly racialized drug crisis of the 1980s.

## Angel of Light and Demon of Darkness: Cloak and Dagger's Ethnic (Super) Identities

In issue #4 of the miniseries, we learn that Tandy Bowen (Dagger) and Tyrone Johnson (Cloak) are two runaway teens from vastly different parts of America. Tandy, from Shaker Heights, Ohio, is the wealthy daughter of a frequently absent actress. Her biological father left the family to find himself in India. Her stepfather, a kindly comic-book artist, is unable to connect with her. Tandy devotes herself to ballet, but struggles to be taken seriously by her teacher because of her mother's fame. When her boyfriend Rob leaves for college, Tandy decides to run away to New York, feeling "empty, alone and unloved."[7] Tyrone, on the other hand, is from a poor South Boston neighborhood. He has loving parents and a relatively large friend group, and he is a basketball champion. However, when he and his best friend Billy witness two thieves murder a shopkeeper, they become the victims of racial profiling. The police, assuming Billy is the murderer, fatally shoot him as he flees the scene. Tyrone, who suffers from a debilitating stutter, is unable to convince the police in time that Billy is innocent. He too flees to New York, not only because he blames himself for his friend's murder, but because he is wanted by the law in connection with the shopkeeper's death.

Tyrone and Tandy meet when he saves her from an attempted mugging. They establish an alliance but are abducted by petty criminals and taken to Ellis Island, where, with a group of other runaways, they become test subjects for a new drug. The new synthetic drug—a proposed alternative to heroin—kills the others, but Tandy and Tyrone manage to escape and find themselves in the possession of superpowers. Tandy receives an

---

5. Davenport-Hines, *Pursuit of Oblivion*, 437–39.
6. Alexander, *The New Jim Crow*, 6.
7. Mantlo, Milgrom, Hannigan, Leonardi et al., *Cloak and Dagger: Shadows and Light*, 198.

excess of the living light that dwells within all people, and is able to manifest this light in the form of daggers, which have the power to kill, stupefy, or cleanse her targets of their addictions. Tyrone loses his physical body, but gains instead a dimension of darkness, which takes a roughly human form and is contained within his cloak. His new, incorporeal "body" can hold and consume people and objects, and any human not protected by Dagger's presence is doomed to face their worst fears and nightmares within Cloak's darkness. Echoing the addictive qualities of drugs, Cloak's darkness needs a constant supply of Dagger's light in order to appease its hunger for the living, and Dagger needs to feed her excess light to Cloak or she falls into an incapacitating fever. Mantlo establishes their powers as symbiotic; Cloak and Dagger need each other, not only to effectively dispense justice but also to function long term.

But where do these powers come from? In essence, the drugs amplify their ethnic identities. Dagger becomes "the angel of light," and Cloak becomes "the demon of darkness."[8] Their superpowers, just like their prior lives, are racialized. The differences between Cloak's and Dagger's background stories are vast. Dagger's problems are comparably insignificant. She feels unloved, even though she has a stepfather who loves and cares for her. She feels underappreciated by her ballet teacher, and yet she has won the lead in the troupe's performance of Swan Lake. She lives in a mansion in a wealthy suburb. Tyrone, on the other hand, has a speech impediment, is impoverished, has seen his best friend shot before his eyes, and is wanted for murder. And yet Dagger feels that her story is as tragic as Cloak's. The comic confirms its own narrative bias by giving five pages of storytelling to Dagger's background as opposed to Cloak's four. The text suggests that Dagger's problems are not equal to Cloak's; hers are *more* important and deserving of our attention and empathy. The differences in their backstories are stark, and yet the biggest difference is glossed over: race. We are told that Dagger is from a wealthy neighborhood, and Cloak is "a poor black boy from south Boston" (there is no corresponding comment in Dagger's story about her whiteness). But the comic goes further: Dagger's neighborhood is overwhelmingly white (there is only one nonwhite person depicted in her flashback; they do not receive a line), and Cloak's is overwhelmingly black (there are three white people in his flashback, the murdered shopkeeper and two policemen).[9] Born into their respective circumstances, Cloak's and

---

8. Mantlo, Leonardi, Shoemaker, Silvestri et al., *Cloak and Dagger: Lost and Found*, 33.
9. Mantlo, Milgrom, Hannigan, Leonardi et al., *Cloak and Dagger: Shadows and Light*, 200.

Dagger's experiences of blackness and whiteness are predestined and predetermine their superpowers.

At the behest of characters such as Spider-Man, the duo move away from their original mission to execute drug dealers and members of the Mob, and position themselves instead as moral saviors. They decide to use the threat of Cloak's super-blackness to "turn evildoers towards [Dagger's] light and salvation."[10] This development in the duo's crime-fighting practice is part of Mantlo's attempt to depict the characters' powers as capable of good or ill, without a particular moral predilection. And yet, Dagger's powers literalize whiteness as a purifying light, while Cloak's powers are steeped in pitch-black darkness and are terrifying. In *Predator and Prey* it is revealed that Cloak's body is a gateway that leads to a demon called Predator, and the comic forsakes its race-neutral stance to emphasize the horror that resides within his blackness. Predator tells us, "Cloak [fed] the living light of his world to the ultimate evil *dwelling* inside *him. Me!*"[11] As seen in the embodiment of their powers, the comic proposes that while white people and black people can work together harmoniously, there is something elevating and purifying about whiteness, something demonic and fearful about blackness. Whiteness is salvation, blackness damnation.

Both the 1983 miniseries and the 1985 ongoing series are keen to emphasize that blackness needs, even feeds on, whiteness. While Cloak feeds off the inner light of the common criminals who fall into his "body," the only light that can sustain him in any real way is Dagger's: "Without your light to sustain me," he tells Dagger, "the darkness within me could rise up to consume every living thing on this Earth."[12] To put the sexual connotations momentarily aside, sustaining Cloak is Dagger's version of the White Man's Burden. The comics detail at length how badly Cloak needs Dagger. Two issues of the 1983 miniseries, for example, open with splash pages detailing Cloak's hunger for her light. Issue #2 refers to this craving as a "Bellyful of Blues!," referencing the blues' ties to black cultural production and compounding Cloak's "obscene appetite"[13] for Dagger with race.[14] The entirety of issue #3 is devoted to this hunger, as Cloak, refusing to feed on Dagger, hides from her, so that she cannot give him any of her light. Dagger, for her part, attempts to sustain Cloak from afar, by sending her light out into the

---

10. Mantlo, Leonardi, Shoemaker, Silvestri et al., *Cloak and Dagger: Lost and Found*, 130.
11. Mantlo, Stroman, and Williamson, *Cloak and Dagger: Predator and Prey*, 21.
12. Mantlo, Milgrom, Hannigan, Leonardi et al., *Cloak and Dagger: Shadows and Light*, 254.
13. Mantlo, Milgrom, Hannigan, Leonardi et al., *Cloak and Dagger: Shadows and Light*, 145.
14. Mantlo, Milgrom, Hannigan, Leonardi et al., *Cloak and Dagger: Shadows and Light*, 144.

city in the hope of it finding him—a performance of martyred, selfless femininity that weakens her so much that she is rushed to the hospital. Eventually the two reunite and Cloak can feed on Dagger's light once more.

The importance of using Cloak's hunger as the driving motive for their continued partnership is that it obscures Dagger's own, similar needs. Dagger, too, cannot live without Cloak, and yet her need is addressed only sparingly, in the Marvel graphic novels and in *Marvel Fanfare* #19 (1983). In *Marvel Fanfare* #19, Dagger, bored with their mission, decides to leave Cloak and go out dancing. Without Cloak to siphon off the light within her, she is unable to control it and falls into a feverish delirium. In her weakened state she is abducted by the Mob, but when she is menaced the light grows into a "fiery fury."[15] By the time Cloak finds her, she has "become our lady of light, an avenging angel dancing like some deity of destruction over the bodies she's strewn across the floor."[16] Cloak, tellingly, is unsurprised that Dagger has lost control of her powers: "Now he *knows* what he has suspected all along. Dagger hungers, too. Her light disrupts the living as eagerly as his darkness consumes them."[17] The story ends with Cloak comforting the inconsolable Dagger: "Cloak cries too, knowing that when Dagger recovers, she will try again to reach for innocence, try again . . . and fail."[18]

Dagger showcases the paradoxical and parasitic nature of American whiteness that has historically profited from black labor, and yet disavows this historical subjugation in accounts of white America's economic success.[19] Although she needs Cloak, profits from his presence, and can only exercise her privileged superpowers with Cloak's facilitation, she is able to disavow for much of their adventures that he provides her with anything at all. Instead, the comic emphasizes Cloak's debt to her. Dagger's perception of their relationship is echoed in the narration, establishing the narrator not as an objective voice, but as a subjective mediator of the comic's racial ideology. When, in the ongoing series, Father Francis, a Catholic priest who shelters Cloak and Dagger, attempts to convince her to live a normal life, the comic continues to focus on how Cloak will deal with her loss; it doesn't consider that Dagger physically cannot live without him and that the possibility of a return to "normal" life is nothing short of a delusion. Furthermore, Dagger is tied to Cloak in another, crucial way. Cloak's black-

---

15. Mantlo, Milgrom, Hannigan, Leonardi et al., *Cloak and Dagger: Shadows and Light*, 344.
16. Mantlo, Milgrom, Hannigan, Leonardi et al., *Cloak and Dagger: Shadows and Light*, 347.
17. Mantlo, Milgrom, Hannigan, Leonardi et al., *Cloak and Dagger: Shadows and Light*, 347.
18. Mantlo, Milgrom, Hannigan, Leonardi et al., *Cloak and Dagger: Shadows and Light*, 348.
19. Loury, "An American Tragedy"; Horsey, "History of Economic Exploitation."

ness is essential to the text because it is from his Othering, the horror of his (black) (non)body, and the inner demons that inhabit both his cloak and his thoughts that we are to appreciate the physical beauty, racialized innocence, and gendered magnetism of Dagger. Calquing a classic motif of American literature, Cloak is a necessary contrast for Dagger. As author Toni Morrison argues, "Africanism, deployed as rawness and savagery, . . . provided the staging ground and arena for the elaboration of the quintessential American identity."[20] Without Cloak, Dagger cannot be the epitome of virginal, innocent whiteness.

## All the Power and Purity of Their Mistress's Soul: Dagger's Super-White Femininity

Mantlo's run on *Cloak and Dagger* is inordinately concerned with Dagger's embodiment of virginal whiteness. She is a vision of white femininity exaggerated to superpower status: "Her *daggers of light* fly . . . embodying all the power and purity of their mistress' soul!"[21] Historically, geographer and historian Alastair Bonnett argues, "the fetishisation of whiteness is organised around the figure of the white woman."[22] When Spider-Man sees Dagger for the first time, he describes her as "a girl—all in white—more beautiful than anyone I've ever seen!," conflating Dagger's attractiveness with her whiteness.[23] In addition to this, religious imagery is used in a heavy-handed manner throughout Mantlo's run on *Cloak and Dagger* to present Dagger as a virginal figure, akin to the Madonna. The visual alignment of Dagger with the Virgin Mary is crucial. As film historian Richard Dyer notes, "The Virgin Mary is the supreme exemplar of . . . feminine whiteness."[24] In issue #1 of the miniseries, Dagger is revealed to Father Francis for the first time, perched on an altar and glowing in the dark. Artist Rick Leonardi depicts her as beautiful, full of religious import, miraculous; she has appeared magically in the church due to Cloak's teleportation powers (see figure 4.1).[25] In Cloak's imagination, she is similarly presented with heavy religious iconography; her face looks upward toward salvation—her hands stretch down and out

---

20. Morrison, *Playing in the Dark*, 44.
21. Mantlo, Leonardi, Shoemaker, Silvestri et al., *Cloak and Dagger: Lost and Found*, 97.
22. Bonnett, *White Identities*, 25.
23. Mantlo, Milgrom, Hannigan, Leonardi et al., *Cloak and Dagger: Shadows and Light*, 7.
24. Dyer, *White*, 74.
25. Mantlo, Milgrom, Hannigan, Leonardi et al., *Cloak and Dagger: Shadows and Light*, 121.

in a gesture of openness and reception, echoing images of the Annunciation and the Immaculate Conception (see figures 4.2 and 4.3).[26] In another flight of fancy from Cloak, he imagines a stained-glass window of Santa Angela (drawn as a nun) morph into Dagger.[27] If she is not the Virgin Mary, she is at the very least a chaste saint.

The juxtaposition of Dagger with the Virgin Mary highlights one of the crucial components of her super-whiteness: Dagger's innocence and purity, which in the Virgin Mary is emphasized as chastity. As mythographer Marina Warner notes, "The virgin body was natural and integral, and as such the foremost image of purity."[28] Though not part of her power-set, the comics stress Dagger's innocence and childlike nature on multiple occasions: "She's so young, so innocent!," "When Dagger recovers she will try again to reach for innocence," "this child of light," "a lamb lost in the wilderness."[29] This innocence differentiates her from Cloak. In issue #5 of the ongoing series, while investigating crooked police, Dagger comments, "I never would have believed that policemen could break the law! Where I was raised you were taught that the police were your friends!" Cloak, who witnessed his friend's death at the hands of white policemen, can only reply, "You are far too naïve, Dagger."[30] Dagger's supposed innocence is used to justify the attempts of various white men to "save" her from Cloak and return her home. These attempts to save the beautiful white girl from a black boy have significant racial overtones. As Father Francis drives Dagger to a reunion with her mother, for example, he thinks, "[Dagger] isn't a child of the streets like you [Cloak]! She's a nice kid from a nice neighborhood who's just not equipped to deal with the horror your existences have become."[31] And yet Dagger's innocence is inherently artificial: In her origin story, detailed in issue #4 of the miniseries, we are explicitly shown that Dagger's "nice neighborhood" is a sordid, insincere world. Dagger is subjected to lying, artifice, abandonment, and people (such as Rob, the neighborhood lothario) sexualizing and objectifying her: "I couldn't fault *Rob Daltry* for his insincerity," she tells us. "After

---

26. Mantlo, Milgrom, Hannigan, Leonardi et al., *Cloak and Dagger: Shadows and Light*, 336.
27. Mantlo, Milgrom, Hannigan, Leonardi et al., *Cloak and Dagger: Shadows and Light*, 186.
28. Warner, *Alone of All Her Sex*, 73–74.
29. Mantlo, Milgrom, Hannigan, Leonardi et al., *Cloak and Dagger: Shadows and Light*, 35, 348; Mantlo, Leonardi, Shoemaker, Silvestri et al., *Cloak and Dagger: Lost and Found*, 136, 203.
30. Mantlo, Leonardi, Shoemaker, Silvestri et al., *Cloak and Dagger: Lost and Found*, 115.
31. Mantlo, Leonardi, Shoemaker, Silvestri et al., *Cloak and Dagger: Lost and Found*, 33. Father Francis's labeling of Cloak as a "child of the streets" is erroneous. Issue #4 of the miniseries tells us that until his friend's murder, he lived happily with his family.

**FIGURE 4.1.** Religious imagery in the presentation of Dagger (*Cloak and Dagger: Shadows and Light*). © Marvel Comics. Image presented under fair use legislation.

all, in *my* neighborhood, *lies* were the only things that came cheap!"[32] From this, it is clear that Dagger's post-transformation "innocence," where she is continually shocked by humanity, has been manufactured by the drugs. Her innocence is simply another of the superpowers of white femininity that has been bestowed upon her.

Through the comic's artifice we come to understand that Dagger's whiteness—in fact, whiteness itself—is a construct, rather than natural. But

---

32. Mantlo, Milgrom, Hannigan, Leonardi et al., *Cloak and Dagger: Shadows and Light*, 197.

it is not a stable construct. The purity of Dagger's whiteness is constantly negotiated through reference to Cloak's blackness. Cloak is, of course, in love with Dagger, because it is common-sense in racist white fantasies that white women exert an undeniable magnetism over black men. In these narratives, white women represent whiteness at its zenith; they are the "carriers of the white race" and thus are inherently attractive to nonwhites.[33] In addition to this, African American men have been historically constructed within American racist discourses as a "sexual aggressors or as 'supersexual' beings."[34] Journalist and critic Robert Jones Jr., in his discussion of DC Comics's Cyborg, argues that the removal of his genitals in the New 52 (2011–2016) *Justice League* is crucial to allaying the sexual threat of a superpowered black man: "Thus, it's safe for him to be around Wonder Woman."[35] Technically,

FIGURE 4.2. Left to right: Dagger presented as a madonna in Cloak's imagination (*Marvel Fanfare* #19). © Marvel Comics. Image presented under fair use legislation.

Cloak has no body, and so his sexuality should be similarly castrated. And yet, the symbiotic nature of Cloak's and Dagger's powers restores the sexual connotations of their partnership. His blackness feeds on her purity; he feeds on white femininity. Mantlo makes the connections clear in the first issue of the ongoing series, where he describes the demonic presence within

---

33. Bonnett, *White Identities*, 24.
34. Frankenberg, *White Women, Race Matters*, 77.
35. Jones, "Humanity Not Included."

**FIGURE 4.3.** Francesco Albani's *The Annunciation* (early 1630s).

Cloak as "ravenous, human-hungry . . . yet something which would forego all other substance if it could but feast on Dagger's light."[36]

For Cloak, Dagger's light has a sexual dimension. Whereas the daggers of light paralyze friend and foe alike (even Spider-Man is not immune), they have a radically different effect on Cloak: "Light penetrates the darkness that is Cloak . . . and his cry is one of sheer unbridled joy!"[37] In the first issue of the miniseries, Cloak, who has been watching Dagger fight to protect

---

36. Mantlo, Leonardi, Shoemaker, Silvestri et al., *Cloak and Dagger: Lost and Found*, 25.
37. Mantlo, Milgrom, Hannigan, Leonardi et al., *Cloak and Dagger: Shadows and Light*, 114.

two teenage runaways, tells her: "Dagger, your light brings me a pleasure ... that is almost unbearable."[38] One of the runaways is accidentally killed in the battle, and the issue ends with Cloak comforting Dagger in the Holy Ghost Church, the pair's base. As Father Francis watches, the two disappear entirely into each other; the light and the darkness "become one."[39] If merely watching Dagger's light brings Cloak an unbearable pleasure, the act of her body becoming pure light and being subsumed within his has clear sexual connotations.[40]

This relationship threatens to destabilize Dagger's super-white femininity and constructed purity. Sociologist Ruth Frankenberg noted that white women who date, sleep with, or marry black men are depicted in American culture as "'loose,' sexually unsuccessful, or (at the least negative) sexually radical."[41] The subversive element of Dagger's sexuality is further emphasized in *Shelter from the Storm*, where a grotesque being called Cadaver feeds off Dagger's light after promising that it will be "the *best* you ever had!"[42] The narration further heightens the sexual nature of the act while drawing an analogy between Cloak and Cadaver: "As Cadaver's finger-extensors caress her flesh . . . Dagger does indeed feel a momentary cooling, an easing of the inferno raging inside her. She has known such pleasure before . . . when Cloak would drain the fires that threatened to consume her to feed himself."[43] This is one of the rare occasions Mantlo makes explicit that the sexual aspect of Cloak and Dagger's partnership is reciprocated and enjoyed by Dagger. The sexual appeal of Cloak to Dagger threatens to destabilize her super-white femininity entirely. So, as white men have positioned themselves as the protectors of white women's sexuality, a variety of self-appointed white male saviors, including Spider-Man and Father Francis, attempt to convince her to leave Cloak and her super-career and return home.[44]

Mantlo was writing *Cloak and Dagger* in a period of increased public backlash against the feminist gains of the 1970s. As feminist writer Susan Faludi details, women who pursued careers in the 1980s were regularly characterized as depressed, stressed, unfeminine and man-hungry or, alter-

---

38. Mantlo, Milgrom, Hannigan, Leonardi et al., *Cloak and Dagger: Shadows and Light*, 138.
39. Mantlo, Milgrom, Hannigan, Leonardi et al., *Cloak and Dagger: Shadows and Light*, 140.
40. Although it is beyond the scope of this chapter, it is also worth noting that their relationship has clear queer connotations; the nature of their powers masculinizes Dagger and feminizes Cloak to create an inversion of heterosexual sexual imagery.
41. Frankenberg, *White Women, Race Matters*, 77.
42. Mantlo, Velluto, Farmer, and Michel, *Power Pack & Cloak and Dagger*, 46.
43. Mantlo, Velluto, Farmer, and Michel, *Power Pack & Cloak and Dagger*, 46–47.
44. Frankenberg, *White Women, Race Matters*, 76.

natively, as something to be pitied or villainized.⁴⁵ This attitude is echoed in the 1985 ongoing series: Dagger's mother is frequently away from home working on films and cheerfully fraternizes with drug abusers who threaten to sexually assault her daughter. Faludi observes that women were encouraged by the media in the 1980s to re-embrace their "true" calling as mothers, wives, housewives, and "New Traditionalists," who supposedly "gladly retreat to her domestic shell."⁴⁶ This desire for women to be inactive in public spheres has particular connotations for the vision of white femininity forged in imperialist fantasies. As Dyer notes, "Because of [women's] social marginality, and because, when they do anything, they do harm, the only honorable position for them, the only white position is that of doing nothing."⁴⁷ Thus white men must make a concerted, ritualistic effort to remove Dagger from the field of competition, of doing, and resituate her in the home, as is appropriate for a beacon of super-white femininity. Cloak, then, presents two significant threats to Dagger's white femininity that the narrative struggles to resolve: her constant black male companionship and her (white) female agency and action.

Thus, in order to retain her position as an ideal of white femininity, which calls for a supposedly civilized passivity, Dagger constantly struggles against her quest. For Dagger the mission is not a calling but a tiresome burden that keeps her away from what she truly desires: normalcy. She is aware that her mission threatens her purity, and thus her whiteness and her superpowers: "Our mission is making us *monsters!*" she notes, and elsewhere, "The act of becoming judge, jury and executioner to those we punish has surely stained *my* soul black as night!"⁴⁸ Alas for Dagger, the superhero genre's focus on action means that her quest for normalcy must be continuously delayed as she and Cloak pursue their heroic quest. After all, America needs them.

## A Blanket of White Powder as Soft as Snow: Drugs and Dagger

Unsurprisingly, Cloak and Dagger's mission is inherently rooted in ideas of preserving American whiteness. For white men, Dyer argues, the built

---

45. Faludi, *Backlash*, ix–xi.
46. Faludi, *Backlash*, 56.
47. Dyer, *White*, 205–6.
48. Mantlo, Leonardi, Shoemaker, Silvestri et al., *Cloak and Dagger: Lost and Found*, 26, 59.

body is necessary to resist the "horror of femininity and non-whiteness."[49] Crucially, it is also intertwined with ideas of imperial enterprise: The white man has landscaped his body and brought it under control, just as nonwhite people and their land must be brought under control.[50] Like most female superheroes, Dagger walks a tightrope between grasping for this hypermasculine ideal or resigning herself to feminine inactivity. In Dagger's dealings with Cloak, in the way the comic describes her daggers of light penetrating his darkness to bring him joy, and in the phallic motif of the dagger symbol cut into her costume, it is clear that Dagger is partially coded masculine. And yet she is depicted with a lithe, slight, graceful figure. She is not drawn muscular, nor is she seen to rigorously work to build her body following her transformation into Dagger. Film scholar Yvonne Tasker argues that female bodybuilders, the exemplar of the built feminine body, merely "serve to emphasize the arbitrary qualities of [muscles as] symbols of manual labor and physical power," and so the artists abstain from providing Dagger with an overly defined muscular body.[51]

Trapped, as a white superheroine, in the gendered double bind of the superhero genre, the body Dagger works to vigorously defend is that of American whiteness, exemplified in the location of her superheroic rebirth: Ellis Island. Ellis Island was the first port of call for many immigrants travelling to the US in the nineteenth and twentieth centuries. Although European immigrants were, for the most part, phenotypically "white," not all forms of whiteness were desirable: Bonnett argues that "whiteness was initially denied to those European immigrant groups (such as the Irish and Italians) who were socially and economically excluded from the Anglo-American elite."[52] Initially, ethnic white immigrants threatened the purity of the Anglo-Americans. However, in response to the civil rights movement, American ideas of whiteness began to change. Rather than striving to become a homogenized, Anglo-American form of white, the descendants of immigrants began to consciously celebrate those ethnic identities that differentiated them from the white "norm." Historian Matthew Frye Jacobson argues that these new forms of ethnic whiteness are explicitly informed by the (white) immigrant experience immortalized in Ellis Island, celebrating a narrative wherein the European immigrant is assimilated into American

---

49. Dyer, *White*, 153.
50. Dyer, *White*, 164–65.
51. Tasker, *Spectacular Bodies*, 142.
52. Bonnett, *White Identities*, 22.

society, and yet retains some of their particular ethnic identity.[53] Cloak and Dagger reside in a world full of these ethnic white identities; their supporting cast is rounded out by Francis Delgado and Brigid O'Reilly, and minor characters are called Falcone, Mazzilli, Cleary, and Carlotti. However, the Mob, arguably Cloak and Dagger's most important antagonists, are explicitly presented as Italian American, and are importing heroin (a white drug) from Italy.

Therefore, although there is an abundance of white ethnic identities in Cloak and Dagger's world, there still exists a hierarchy, in which some forms of whiteness are undesirable.[54] Dagger, vaguely ethnic (Bowen is a name of Welsh origin, and she is Catholic), but mostly presenting a homogenized Anglo-American whiteness, represents the ideal and thus possesses moral authority, whereas those immigrants who do not conform themselves to American society and remain committed to their own, separate community, with their own set of rules and morals (in this case, the Italian American "Family"), represent a treacherous form of whiteness, which, like heroin and cocaine, will weaken and poison American society. The Mob, like the white male villains of popular contemporary films *Mississippi Burning* (1988), *The Accused* (1988), and *The Casualties of War* (1989), have, according to scholar Susan Jeffords, taken "into their own hands the definitions of social law, community, and justice," and thus have betrayed the American body.[55]

The War on Drugs, initiated by Nixon, was more concerned with foreign drugs coming in and penetrating the American body than with addressing American-made narcotics.[56] The forces of nonwhiteness are constantly trying to enter Cloak and Dagger's America, requiring the two to be ever vigilant. They rarely sleep or rest in their mission. The increased "purity" of the drugs is a mockery of the authentic white purity that Dagger, as a white woman, exemplifies. A major arc of the *Cloak and Dagger* ongoing series details gangsters' attempts to smuggle dope into the country hidden in statues of Saint Angela, tellingly imported from Italy. This is a direct challenge to Dagger's white purity. After successfully foiling the attempt to smuggle drugs within religious symbols of female purity, Cloak and Dagger realize that they need to hit drug smuggling where it originates: "we [will]

---

53. Jacobson, *Roots Too*, 7, 95.
54. Mantlo, Milgrom, Hannigan, Leonardi et al., *Cloak and Dagger: Shadows and Light*, 416.
55. Jeffords, *Hard Bodies*, 138.
56. Davenport-Hines, *Pursuit of Oblivion*, 421–22.

follow the drug-trail back to its source . . . and eradicate it there!"[57] The rest of the series details the duo's efforts to squash the drug trade abroad, mimicking the transnational efforts of America's Drug Enforcement Administration. Echoing the correlation between building a muscular white body and successfully pursuing imperial enterprise, Cloak and Dagger have moved from policing the body of white America to enforcing American ideals of justice and morality abroad.

## Coda

Although it pays lip service to ideas of diversity and a post-race America, Mantlo's run on *Cloak and Dagger* is in many ways a love letter to white imperialist fantasies and Reaganism. With the tamed Cloak in tow, Dagger is able, by virtue of her virtue, to uplift modern, broken America, defending its body from threatening forms of nonwhiteness and expanding the American vision abroad. Cloak, for his part, showcases how difficult the position of a black superhero is in a genre based on white imperialist fantasies.[58] In a genre that is obsessed with bodies, he is denied one, and he is demonized for partnering with a white woman. Even as the comics seek to exalt Dagger, her partnership with Cloak strains her pure and virginal image and ends up throwing light on the instability of her whiteness. Underneath her blinding veneer, Dagger's constructed whiteness groans under an artifice that the comic fails to naturalize, showing us instead a series of revisions and omissions that reveal how belabored the ideals of white imperialist femininity are.

---

57. Mantlo, Leonardi, Shoemaker, Silvestri et al., *Cloak and Dagger: Lost and Found*, 146.

58. A more detailed examination of Cloak can be found in Nama, *Super Black*, 81–88. For a discussion of imperialism and the superhero genre, see Hack, "Weakness Is a Crime."

## Bibliography

Alexander, Michelle. *The New Jim Crow: Mass Incarceration in the Age of Colorblindness*. New York: The New Press, 2012.

Bonnett, Alastair. *White Identities: Historical and International Perspectives*. Harlow, Essex: Prentice Hall, 2000.

Davenport-Hines, Richard. *The Pursuit of Oblivion: A Global History of Narcotics*. London: W. W. Norton, 2001.

Dyer, Richard. *White*. London: Routledge, 1997.

Faludi, Susan. *Backlash: The Undeclared War against American Women*. New York: Crown Publishers, 1991.

Frankenberg, Ruth. *White Women, Race Matters: The Social Construction of Whiteness*. Minneapolis: University of Minnesota Press, 1993.

Hack, Brian E. "Weakness Is a Crime: Captain America and the Eugenic Ideal in Early Twentieth Century America." In *Captain America and the Struggle of the Superhero: Critical Essays*, edited by Robert G. Weiner, 79–89. London: McFarland, 2009.

Horsey, Davis. "History of Economic Exploitation Still Hinders Black Americans." *Los Angeles Times*, September 9, 2014, http://www.latimes.com/opinion/topoftheticket/la-na-tt-history-hinders-black-americans-20140908-story.html.

Howe, Sean. *Marvel Comics: The Untold Story*. New York: Harper Perennial, 2012.

Jacobson, Matthew Frye. *Roots Too*. Cambridge, MA: Harvard University Press, 2006.

Jeffords, Susan. *Hard Bodies: Hollywood Masculinity in the Reagan Era*. New Brunswick, NJ: Rutgers University Press, 1994.

Jones, Robert, Jr. "Humanity Not Included: DC's Cyborg and the Mechanization of the Black Body." *The Middle Spaces*, March 31, 2015, https://themiddlespaces.com/2015/03/31/humanity-not-included/.

Loury, Glenn C. "An American Tragedy: The Legacy of Slavery Lingers in Our Cities' Ghettos." *Brookings*, March 1, 1998, https://www.brookings.edu/articles/an-american-tragedy-the-legacy-of-slavery-lingers-in-our-cities-ghettos/.

Mantlo, Bill, Rick Leonardi, Terry Shoemaker, Marc Silvestri, Mike Mignola, Arthur Adams, Terry Austin et al., *Cloak and Dagger: Lost and Found*. New York: Marvel Comics, 2017.

Mantlo, Bill, Al Milgrom, Chris Claremont, Ed Hannigan, Rick Leonardi, Ron Frenz, Terry Austin et al., *Cloak and Dagger: Shadows and Light*. New York: Marvel Comics, 2017.

Mantlo, Bill, Larry Stroman, and Al Williamson. *Cloak and Dagger: Predator and Prey*. New York: Marvel Comics, 1988.

Mantlo, Bill, Sal Velluto, Mark Farmer, and Julie Michel. *Power Pack & Cloak and Dagger: Shelter from the Storm*. New York: Marvel Comics, 1989.

Morrison, Toni. *Playing in the Dark: Whiteness and the Literary Imagination*. New York: Vintage Books, 1993.

Nama, Adilifu. *Super Black: American Pop Culture and Black Superheroes*. Austin: University of Texas Press, 2011.

Tasker, Yvonne, *Spectacular Bodies: Gender, Genre and the Action Cinema.* London: Routledge, 1993.

Warner, Marina. *Alone of All Her Sex: The Myth and the Cult of the Virgin Mary.* London: Weidenfeld & Nicolson, 1976.

Wright, Bradford W. *Comic Book Nation: The Transformation of Youth Culture in America.* Baltimore: The John Hopkins University Press, 2001.

Yurkovich, David, and Michael Mantlo. *Mantlo: A Life in Comics.* Cannery Village, DE: Sleeping Giant Comics, 2014.

CHAPTER 5

# WORLDS COLLIDE

Whiteness, Integration, and Diversity in the DC/Milestone Crossover

SHAMIKA ANN MITCHELL

### First Encounters

DC Comics and Milestone Media's intercompany crossover event "Worlds Collide" (July–August 1994) is rife with apocalyptic bedlam and unbridled optimism. In the event, DC characters like Superman, Superboy, and Steel of Metropolis are juxtaposed with their more obscure Milestone counterparts, Icon, Rocket, Hardware, Static, and the Blood Syndicate of Dakota, who in their juxtaposition also stage an encounter between the largely white universe of DC Comics and the more diverse world of Milestone. The latter was introduced by the black-owned company that debuted the year prior, in June 1993. Though independent, Milestone comics were distributed through DC; their main mission was to incorporate and promote multiculturalism in comics. The fourteen-issue story arc of "Worlds Collide" played out across *Icon, Hardware, Superboy, Steel, Superman: The Man of Steel, Blood Syndicate, Static,* and the event-specific one-shot *Worlds Collide.*

Throughout the crossover, the DC and Milestone universes are thrust together, causing calamity and chaos in the cities of Metropolis (DC) and Dakota (Milestone). The event uses these cities to blur the lines between real/imaginary and utopia/dystopia through means that echo real-world societal structures and paradigms; it juxtaposes Metropolis and Dakota as two distinct images—one a white urbanism and one an urbanism of color—to represent racialized understandings of the urban, as seen through the racist eyes of the event's supervillain antagonist, Rift. The convergence of Metropolis and Dakota in "Worlds Collide" allows readers to explore these juxtapositions within specific sociohistorical contexts: Whiteness, ethnoracial identity, and diversity are central to the event's conflicts. As I argue in this chapter, the amalgamation of DC's long-established universe and Milestone's fresh, new one—and the disruption it causes—are a commentary on integration, diversity, and multiculturalism in the mid-1990s.

Just prior to the "Worlds Collide" event, Metropolis and Dakota are both in states of chaos following recent in-universe catastrophes. There are repeated references to Lex Luthor's attack on Metropolis, the plot of summer 1994's "The Fall of Metropolis" storyline, which led to the city's destruction. In *Superman: The Man of Steel* #34, aptly titled "War," Metropolis is laid to waste while battle erupts between four groups: the Underworlders (clone metahumans created by Project Cadmus), LexCorp robot mercenaries, the Special Crime Unit (Metropolis's elite police), and Project Cadmus's private militia. In the "Worlds Collide" series premier issue, *Superman: The Man of Steel* #35, Superman observes: "Metropolis . . . What's left of it . . . is slowly losing to entropy."[1] After the Milestone character Hardware's dimensional leap to Metropolis, he comments: "Far as I can tell, 'Metropolis' looks to be a bigger hellhole than Paris Island. There must have been some kind of war here."[2] Milestone's Dakota is a city where the poorest section, Paris Island, is isolated because the bridge was blown up during the Big Bang, a governmental mutagenic chemical attack. "Worlds Collide" introduces Dakota post–Big Bang, which gave its few survivors ("Bang Babies") superpowers. During "Worlds Collide," the worlds of Metropolis and Dakota intersect. From a symbolic standpoint, this is an allegory of integration, in which the pervasive whiteness of DC encounters the marked multiculturalism of Milestone.

The amalgamation of Dakota and Metropolis prompts characters on both sides to wonder which world is "real," so that the split between dream world and real world marks a key theme throughout "Worlds Collide." Dakota's characters recognize Metropolis and Superman as fictional entities in comic books, while the situation of Dakota is summarized nicely by Rift, who muses, "Is it a city of dreams or shattered dreams?"[3] Despite the personal and political challenges raised between characters who hail from

---

1. Simonson, Bogdanove, and Janke, "Afterburn," 6.
2. McDuffie, Cowan, Birch, and Rollins, "No Rest for the Weary," 16.
3. Kesel, Grummett, and Hazlewood, "Menace 2 Societies!," 19.

Metropolis and Dakota, they must collaborate in order to thwart the greater threat of annihilation. In an interesting shift, Superman and Superboy are the only white heroes featured in the crossover, but there are several white villains: Paul Westfield or Cadmus, Luthor, Alva, and most notably, Rift. Of the fourteen "Worlds Collide" issues, Superman is either featured or mentioned in eleven and Superboy is featured in eight, whereas Icon appears in seven, including one fleeting, unflattering reference. In comparison to Icon, whose plot contributions are more often than not insignificant, Superman and Superboy play central roles and have greater visibility, despite the fact that Icon and Superman are superficially as important to stopping Rift and saving both worlds.

## Continuity Problems: Is Coexistence Futile?

The primary conflict in "Worlds Collide" centers on white Dakota native Fred Bentson, who unknowingly teleports between Dakota and Metropolis when he sleeps. In his attempt to cure what he believes to be insomnia, he joins sleep studies sponsored by Alva Technologies in Dakota and Manuel Cabral (the villain Hazard) in Metropolis. During his intake interview, he explains:

> As long as I can remember, I've lived two lives. I go to work in Dakota every day, go home to bed at night and the second I fall asleep I wake up and it's morning again. Only I'm in another city called Metropolis. I go to work there all day, go home, go to sleep and instantly wake up the next morning here in Dakota. . . . Now I think I am crazy.[4]

In the course of these studies, scientists perfidiously experiment on Bentson and attempt to exploit the transdimensional portal he opens. Newly cognizant of the scientists' schemes, Bentson creates his seemingly omnipotent alter ego, Rift, from his subconscious. He declares his autonomy and sovereignty:

> I'm *nobody's* puppet. You're all *my* dreams. *My* creations. I was *afraid* of my power. Well I'm not anymore! *I'm* the one who's *real*. *I'm* the one with the

---

4. McDuffie, Cowan, Birch, and Rollins, "No Rest for the Weary," 4.

power. I *am* the power. I *am*. . . . Fool. *Understand* me. Fred Bentson is no more. Fantasy is *reality*. The word is made flesh. I am *Rift!*[5]

To prove his power, Rift merges Dakota and Metropolis. After converging these worlds, Rift repeatedly mentions the superfluousness of characters and settings, or what he calls "continuity problems," that appear redundant.[6] Rift notes to each universe's flagship superheroes, "I've had second thoughts, you see. I don't want to erase Dakota yet. Still, as Metropolis and Paris Island were equivalent, so you, Superman, and Icon, are equivalent." Imagining himself as their creator, he tells them, "I've given you and Icon similar powers."[7] Although they differ considerably, Clark Kent/Superman being the image of the white, all-American man and Augustus Freeman IV/ Icon the upwardly mobile black man, Rift asserts that their similarity makes them redundant.

Icon and Superman are the ultimate protectors of their cities, and Rift questions whether they can coexist now that Metropolis and Dakota have merged. As part of his "continuity problems" analysis, Rift points out a contentious judgment often leveled at Icon by critics. According to writer and creator Dwayne McDuffie, Icon is "the African American answer to Superman,"[8] but he is not a duplicate figure. Still, during Milestone's tenure in the mid-1990s, there were disagreements about Icon's characterization. Jeffrey Brown writes about the criticism Milestone received. The comment that the new character was "Superman in blackface"

> was initially heard quite a lot in reference to Milestone's most conventionally superheroic series Icon. The parallels between the two characters are undeniable. . . . They wear similar costumes and possess almost identical powers. At first glance the only difference seems to be the color of their skins. But it is the marked similarities between Superman and Icon, the degree of conformity to the well-established superhero genre, that allows the series to explore how conventional heroism might differ from a minority perspective.[9]

Icon and Superman are mostly characterized in similar ways in "Worlds Collide." The alien status of both makes them observers and protectors of

---

5. Washington et al., "How Can You Be in Two Places at Once," 26–28.
6. McDuffie, Cowan, and Rollins, "You Shouldn't, a Bit Fish," 3.
7. Simonson, Bogdanove, and Janke, "A Rift in Reality," 11, 13.
8. "Dwayne McDuffie and Milestone Media's Impact."
9. Brown, *Black Superheroes*, 49.

humanity. However similar the basic structures of their stories are, their most remarkable difference is their journeys to and in America.

Recognizing criticisms levied at their company and characters, Milestone creators transposed readers' skepticism into Rift's story, ultimately forcing Icon and Superman to resolve the meaning of their existence and to advocate for the lives in both universes. Although they prevail and their worlds ultimately diverge at the end of the series, Rift argues that Metropolis and Dakota cannot coexist, claiming "two worlds are too many."[10] During Rift's confrontation with Superman and Icon, he comments: "Perhaps neither myth can win out because both are necessary. Perhaps each myth is incomplete without the other."[11] Each city is a reflection of the other; Metropolis's Suicide Slum, for example, is a visible reminder of Superman's inability to save those most in need, whereas Paris Island is the section of Dakota that Icon disregarded. The inequalities in both cities are a constant reminder of each hero's duties and shortcomings. And yet the constant reminders of Dakota's subtle difference remain: In *Worlds Collide* #1, for example, Superboy refers to Icon as a "wannabe Superman" and calls Dakota "a podunk town."[12]

As the villain mediating the racialized conflict of the two companies, their characters, and their cities, Rift promotes an elitist, bigoted ideology that vulnerable, poor people are disposable, and diversity is unfavorable. Thus, he regards his destruction of Paris Island as an act of mercy. And now that Metropolis is a fallen city, he also contemplates destroying it: "Paris Island was a *slum!* A poverty-stricken eyesore! [. . .] Metropolis is rubble now . . . even worse than Paris Island. It's trash. I'm not sure this world needs Metropolis either."[13] Although Rift initially thought he imagined both worlds, he eventually concludes that Dakota is the manifestation of his nightmares. Despite Rift's many threats, he hesitates to destroy Metropolis, but he unconcernedly annihilates Paris Island without warning.[14] Despite being a Dakota native and leading identical lives in both cities, Bentson has a stronger affinity for Metropolis, which he considers his home.[15] Bentson lacks any affinity for Dakota; when conflict ensues, he teleports Superboy, Hardware, and Rocket with him to Metropolis, saying, "I forgot Metropo-

---

10. Kesel, Grummett, and Hazlewood, "Menace 2 Societies!," 13.
11. McDuffie, Bright, and Gustovich, "Ain't No Such Thing as Superman," 30.
12. Washington et. al, "How Can You Be in Two Places at Once," 8–9.
13. Simonson, Bogdanove, and Janke, "A Rift in Reality," 7–8.
14. Washington et al., "How Can You Be in Two Places at Once," 39.
15. Simonson, Batista, and Faber, "Collision Course," 12.

lis was like this now. I just wanted to go home."[16] Metropolis seems to be a safe space for the white Bentson, where he has developed personal relationships and is happy. Bentson considers Steel to be his friend,[17] and as Rift, he expresses care and concern for Lois Lane.[18] However, he has only contempt for Dakotans. The idealized whiteness of Metropolis seems the only explanation for Rift's avoidance of destroying it. Rift rationalizes his destruction of Paris Island, saying, "I would never have destroyed them had they been real. The island was a figment of my own imagination," and even after Superman argues the legitimacy of Paris Island, Rift retorts, "So now I know that what's real doesn't matter! The only thing that matters is what I say matters!"[19] The context and subtext of this phrasing is significant. Rift views Metropolis, a world of predominantly white heroes, as reality, and Paris Island, a place without white heroes, as disposable.

Rift's binary imagining of Metropolis and Dakota plays out in the encounter between the superheroes from the respective cities, and they accuse each other of being products of Rift's imagination. When Rift merges Dakota and Metropolis, it is unclear what will remain after the "continuity problems" are resolved. Superman proclaims his own validity without affirmation from Rift. However, when Superman says to Icon, "I'm confident that I'm real, Icon. What if Rift created you?," Icon does not respond.[20] Icon, then, faces the dilemma of black consciousness, in which he can proclaim his existence, but it is meaningless unless it is acknowledged by whiteness, in this instance represented by Superman and Rift, who insists that Dakota is imaginary. Despite the efforts of Static, Rocket, and Icon to safeguard and improve the city, Rift disregards their proclamations of selfhood. In this exchange, the matter of black self-determination becomes the focus. The Dakotaverse requires white recognition—and, in the case of the comics market, saleability to a largely white audience—to exist *at all*, which is why Rift cavalierly eliminates Paris Island. Rift's efforts to erase the binary between prosperity and poverty, white and nonwhite, Metropolis and Dakota, destabilizes and endangers both cities in the course of "Worlds Collide." Diversity and multiculturalism are unwelcome in Rift's new society, because his Eurocentric ideology requires the eradication of difference.

---

16. Simonson, Batista, and Faber, "Collision Course," 12.
17. Simonson, Batista, and Faber, "Collision Course," 17.
18. Simonson, Bogdanove, and Janke, "A Rift in Reality," 21.
19. Simonson, Bogdanove, and Janke, "A Rift in Reality," 7, 21–22.
20. McDuffie, Cowan, and Rollins, "After Worlds Collide," 32.

## Utopian Visions: Whiteness and Wonderment

Rift is seduced by the utopian myth of a city that symbolizes modernity and progress; in line with this myth, he creates a new world where he is supreme and only the well-bred elites thrive.[21] In the thirteenth "Worlds Collide" installment, Rift expresses his commitment to homogeneity and white supremacy by condemning Blood Syndicate's diversity. The infamous Blood Syndicate are "Bang Baby" vigilante antiheroes whose exploits mostly go unchecked by Dakota authorities, though they have occasional run-ins and crossover storylines with Icon and Static. When Rift appears, they join forces with others to fight for Dakota and Paris Island. But the Blood Syndicate's multiculturalism is strictly forbidden in Rift's new utopian vision; he refers to their diversity as "unstable" and admonishes them to "conform, and perhaps acquire some better breeding."[22] To underscore this, Rift hypnotizes the Blood Syndicate and teleports them to a different dimension in which explicit Euro-American white supremacy is championed as a sign of modernity, and colonization and genocide are lauded as progress—a world not unlike many readers' worlds, yet rendered dystopian through the Blood Syndicate members' experiences.

Rift's perspective here directly echoes a white supremacist rationale to aspire toward whiteness as a symbol of social progress. Rift repeatedly attempts to psychologically recondition the Blood Syndicate by teleporting them into various scenarios. In one instance, he transports them into a classroom setting, saying, "That's all you need. A proper education and the proper breeding. You'll be so much happier then." The proper education Rift extols is rife with a Eurocentric, racist, imperialistic world view. Rift changes the Blood Syndicate's appearances and mannerisms to reflect a Eurocentric standard. While Rift prattles on in his lecture, praising Christopher Columbus as "intelligent and well bred," "culturally superior," he also shames the Blood Syndicate for being different. In a humorous twist, when Blood Syndicate member Hannibal is questioned about Columbus, his response is, "*&%# Columbus and *&%# you!"[23] Their resistance to whiteness psychically frees them from Rift's mind control, and they return to the world. Despite this, Rift neutralizes the Blood Syndicate and declares,

---

21. Velez, Chriscross, Quijano, and Rollins, "Mirror Faces Mirror."
22. Velez, Chriscross, Quijano, and Rollins, "Mirror Faces Mirror."
23. Velez, Chriscross, Quijano, and Rollins, "Mirror Faces Mirror."

> You really just don't fit in. You're too much trouble and you'll have to go. [. . .] I have work to do. I have a world to fix. Let's see . . . a world without troubles. A clean, efficient and sparkling world. Something fun. Maybe something in a futuristic motif. Something without the troubles of the old world.[24]

Rift resents their rebellion and desires to cleanse his new world of the old world's problems. His plan to sanitize society requires genocide; the cleansing of stains, especially poverty and racial difference, indicates his desire for a pure white space. All of Rift's utopic characterizations are evocations of a desire for whiteness—a place without the blemishes or blight of marked racial difference.

Dakota and Paris Island represent the troubles of racial difference Rift wants to abolish. Other Milestone heroes who appear in "Worlds Collide" include Hardware, Icon's sidekick Rocket, and Static, a "Bang Baby" with electromagnetic powers. All three Dakotan heroes are African American and the latter two come from poor and working-class families. Static, for example, is unable to escape the poverty that pervades the city; he attends public school, works an after-school job, and rarely sees his parents, but he still finds time for superheroics, homework, and teenage quandaries. Rocket, too, struggles with teenage issues while also worrying about crime and poverty in her community. She is pregnant,[25] but she still wants to be Icon's sidekick so that her child will live in a safer Dakota. Her optimism inspires both Icon and Static, and her decision to maintain her pregnancy is an indication of her duty to make the city a better place; having an abortion would mean that she has given up hope. Rocket's persistence is essential to Icon's story arc; without her urging, he would not put his abilities to greater use.

Milestone's Dakota offers a dystopian, desolate landscape that is not much different from the urban blight experience throughout America's cities and especially in the classed and racialized areas known as the "inner city." Still, as Scott Bukatman writes, "American superheroes encapsulated and embodied the same utopian aspirations of modernity as the cities themselves,"[26] and the heroes in "World's Collide" are no different in this matter; the residents of Dakota and Metropolis view their heroes—namely, Icon and Superman—as symbols of protection. Although they are considered saviors, Superman openly embraces this role, while Icon initially avoids it. Even when he admits his social responsibility, Icon does not view his role

---

24. Velez, Chriscross, Quijano, and Rollins, "Mirror Faces Mirror."
25. McDuffie, Bright, and Gustovich, "Living in a Dream World," 29.
26. Bukatman, "A Song of the Urban Superhero," 170.

as that of a savior, saying to the Blood Syndicate, "I have not come here to save you. That isn't my place."[27] Instead, Icon espouses ideals of social uplift and internalized empowerment that have held a prominent place in black political thought since the turn-of-the-century conflict between Booker T. Washington and W. E. B. Du Bois. Icon takes to superheroics not just to save, but to inspire people to uplift themselves.[28] Augustus is a wealthy black professional and intellectual, which breaks from the stereotypical representation of blackness in comics. Icon's blackness and conservatism are the counterpart to Superman's liberal whiteness. "Ironically," writes Jeffrey Brown, "this attention to social injustices is also depicted as one of the reasons why Icon is in fact more conservative than Superman."[29] Of course, whatever the criticisms, Icon's conservative politics do not and should not delegitimize his character as a representation of blackness, especially given the multiplicity of ways in which Superman's whiteness operates.

As Jamie Egolf argues, "Superman and his alter ego Clark Kent together form a mythic, archetypal image" of American white masculinity, upward mobility, and individuality.[30] Superman's whiteness protects him and enables his free and unfettered assimilation into American society, whereas Icon's blackness marks him as lower caste, and he is forced into slavery when he first arrives on Earth in 1839. Both characters are upwardly mobile, but their origin stories of immigration to the US are intrinsically affected by their race. Superman and Icon are aliens passing as humans—Clark and Augustus, respectively—but their human experiences are remarkably different. As Clark Kent, the alien from Krypton assimilates into white American society in comics published at a time when black readers experienced explicitly racist laws and policies under Jim Crow. Although not human, he became an icon for the people of Metropolis and the real-world US. Since his debut, Superman's whiteness has granted him access into readers' homes and hearts, and it is absolutely Icon's blackness that in the same period in twentieth-century history would have prevented him from receiving enthusiastic reception, if black superheroes had appeared in the late 1930s;[31] it is the blackness of various black superheroes written since the 1960s that has, with few exceptions, kept them out of mainstream consciousness.

Superman's whiteness is what makes him a saleable mainstream character. In fact, initially, Clark's very earthly existence was dependent upon

---

27. McDuffie and Bright, *Icon*, 142.
28. McDuffie and Bright, *Icon*, 75.
29. Brown, *Black Superheroes*, 49.
30. Egolf, "Dreaming Superman," 142.
31. See Sean Guynes-Vishniac's chapter in this volume.

his access to whiteness. If he were not white, his parents could not have adopted him or passed him off as their biological child. During Rift's explanation of "continuity problems" in *Icon* #16, he provides a character synopsis for Superman:

> Your parents adopted you. In turn, you adopted their values. As Superman, you shared the special gifts that were your birthright with your adoptive land. You are the personification of the American Dream and not incidentally, the greatest hero this planet has ever seen.[32]

Clark always lived in a world where only or predominantly white people existed; the obvious absence of racial diversity is a direct allusion to legalized and socialized racial segregation that has played out at all levels of US society for centuries. Segregation and discrimination in the US were not legally outlawed until the Civil Rights Act of 1964; therefore, from a historical viewpoint, it is unsurprising that Superman and Metropolis do not show visible signs of integration until well after this date. In essence, then, Clark *has to be white* for there to be a story that would appeal to a broad audience. By the 1990s, *Superman: The Man of Steel*, which links directly into "Worlds Collide," had sprinklings of racial and class integration, but instances were often limited to stock or background characters who lacked development or even names.

## Worlds Collide: Whose World Is This?

Whatever Rift imagines becomes manifest, and the utopian world he envisions represents his truth: a whitewashed society. This futuristic world looks surreal: The architecture, technology, and flying vehicles are a nostalgic take on modernity and comics history. Superboy, Static, and Rocket are transported to Rift's new dimension, and their appearances are transformed into superhero costumes that reflect Silver Age aesthetics. Rocket's hair is bobbed and she wears a minidress, while Superboy dons a leotard, cape, and perfectly sculpted coif. Static, who wears a mask, leotard, and cape, comments on their dimensional shift, "Rift's playing continuity games again—uh, Superboy. He put everything into the future. . . . We're supposed to be the League of Superteens, like back in the fifties."[33] Rocket observes

---

32. McDuffie, Bright, and Gustovich, "Ain't No Such Thing as Superman," 4.
33. McDuffie, Cowan, and Rollins, "After Worlds Collide," 4.

that the new city "looks like the Jetsons," especially since they are housed in a building shaped like a giant rocket.[34] Now that dimensions have combined, Rift's futuristic fantasy unfolds; meanwhile, everyone debates the question of reality.

Who is real? How can one verify their existence? The encounters between the Dakotans and Metropolisians seem authentic, but only Rift has control over this. During her conversation with Static, Rocket asserts, "Look, Superboy isn't real. But Dakota is. We are."[35] Rocket's affirmation is a manifestation of subjectivity; she is real because she says she is, regardless of Rift's agenda. With Rift still in pursuit of their annihilation, their battle for existence continues. Once Icon and Superman ensnare Rift in a dimensional portal, their worlds separate and time reverses, undoing all of Rift's damage. Superman, Steel, and Superboy are teleported back to the Metropolis that was demolished by previous attacks. As Steel and Superboy lament the loss of the Dakotans, Superman points out, "Rift was real enough, but he's gone now, and so are all of his creations."[36] Even Superman cannot believe in the reality of a universe where superheroes are as diverse as Dakota's.

Subduing Rift, and not destroying him, suggests that his ideology cannot be destroyed. When they return to Dakota, Icon gives full credit to Superman, Superboy, and Steel, saying to Static, "The example they set, the courage they showed were real. Real enough to save us all from Rift."[37] Icon's acknowledgment of the DC superheroes as Dakota's saviors is problematic, and affirms the centering of Superman (and to lesser extent Superboy) as the hero protagonist. Brown writes: "Even when diversity and issues of discrimination do take center stage within the superhero genre, the white male hero serves as an anchoring point."[38] At no point is it noted that Static's energy charge is the only reason the dimensional portal has enough power to trap Rift, or that Hardware and Steel used their technological genius to build the machine itself. A host of other Dakotans also contributed to stopping Rift; yet, Icon's final statement draws attention to Superman, who is a fictional character in Dakota, and to Superboy and Steel. Icon's statement positions the racially diverse superheroes of the Milestone universe as spectators in the fight for their own freedom. Even in multicultural Dakota, whiteness is centered and prioritized.

---

34. McDuffie, Cowan, and Rollins, "After Worlds Collide," 4
35. McDuffie, Cowan, and Rollins, "After Worlds Collide," 19.
36. McDuffie, Cowan, and Rollins, "After Worlds Collide," 45.
37. Wright, *Comic Book Nation*, 46–47.
38. Brown, *Black Superheroes*, 112.

## Coda: Then and Now

"Worlds Collide" is both timely and symbolic of late twentieth-century optimism for inclusive social progress. The urban, multicultural approach that Milestone took was a response to the lack of diversity in the comics industry: Before the 1990s, DC Comics had on occasion made gestures to promote a progressive view and to include a range of racial differences. The representation of multiculturalism in Metropolis had made some progress by the time "Worlds Collide" was published, although nonwhite, non-middle-class residents were mostly relegated to Suicide Slum, while ethnoracial and class diversity was the norm in Dakota. That a diverse cast of heroes and antiheroes join forces in "Worlds Collide" to defeat Rift is a not-so-subtle statement about the values of diversity and collaboration. Everyone's talents are needed to stop the end of the world because Superman and Icon cannot handle the task alone; Superboy, Static, Hardware, Steel, the Blood Syndicate, Rocket, and others make meaningful contributions.

Milestone's efforts to establish a multicultural world (Dakota) in which people form a community, share a struggle, and are fully developed as characters was as noteworthy in 1994 as it remains now, in a period when black comics creators and characters still struggle to find a place. Take, for example, New York Comic Con's #BlackHeroesMatter panel in 2017, where various panelists spoke about the hostility they faced for promoting multiculturalism in comics; the animus aimed at these artists, including threats, resonate in Rift's judgment of Paris Island and the Blood Syndicate as unfit and disposable. Perhaps the somewhat dystopic existence of Dakota is symbolic of the tenuous existence of people of color in a world governed by whiteness, and for whom the hope represented by superheroes like Milestone's still seems a luxury.

## Bibliography

Brown, Jeffrey. *Black Superheroes, Milestone Comics, and Their Fans.* Jackson: University Press of Mississippi, 2000.

———. "Comic Book Masculinity." In *The Superhero Reader*, edited by Charles Hatfield, Jeet Heer, and Kent Worcester, 269–78. Jackson: University Press of Mississippi, 2001.

Bukatman, Scott. "A Song of the Urban Superhero." In *The Superhero Reader*, edited by Charles Hatfield, Jeet Heer, and Kent Worcester, 170–98. Jackson: University Press of Mississippi, 2001.

"Dwayne McDuffie and Milestone Media's Impact on the Superhero Genre." *Milestone Media*, June 12, 2018, http://milestone.media/dwayne-mcduffie-and-milestone-medias-impact-on-the-superhero-genre.

Egolf, Jamie. "Dreaming Superman: Exploring the Action of the Superhero(ine) in Dreams, Myth, and Culture." In *Super/Heroes: From Hercules to Superman*, edited by Wendy Haslem, Angela Ndalianis, and Chris Mackie, 139–52. Washington, DC: New Academia Publishing, 2007.

Kesel, Karl (writer), Tom Grummett (penciller), and Doug Hazlewood (inker). "Menace 2 Societies!" *Superboy* #7. New York: DC Comics, July 1994.

McDuffie, Dwayne (writer), and M. D. Bright (penciller). *Icon: A Hero's Welcome*. New York: Milestone Media, 1996.

McDuffie, Dwayne (writer), M. D. Bright (penciller), and Mike Gustovich (inker). "Ain't No Such Thing as Superman." *Icon* #16. New York: Milestone Media, August 1994.

———. "Living in a Dream World" *Icon* #15. New York: Milestone Media, July 1994.

McDuffie, Dwayne (writer), Denys Cowan (penciller), J. J. Birch (penciller and inker), and Prentis Rollins (inker). "No Rest for the Weary." *Hardware* #17. New York: Milestone Media, July 1994.

McDuffie, Dwayne (writer), Denys Cowan (penciller), and Prentis Rollins (inker). "After Worlds Collide." *Static* #14. New York: Milestone Media, August 1994.

———. "You Shouldn't, a Bit Fish." *Hardware* #18. New York: Milestone Media, August 1994.

Simonson, Louise (writer), Chris Batista (penciller), and Rich Faber (inker). "Collision Course." *Steel* #6. New York: DC Comics, July 1994.

Simonson, Louise (writer), Chris Batista (penciller), Humberto Ramos (penciller), Rich Faber (inker), and Stan Woch (inker). "Worlds Collide." *Steel* #7. New York: DC Comics, August 1994.

Simonson, Louise (writer), Jon Bogdanove (penciller), and Dennis Janke (inker). "Afterburn." *Superman: The Man of Steel* #35. New York: DC Comics, July 1994.

———. "A Rift in Reality." *Superman: The Man of Steel* #36. New York: DC Comics, August 1994.

Velez, Ivan Jr. (writer, penciller), Chriscross (penciller), Rober Quijano (inker), and Prentis Rollins (inker). "Mirror Faces Mirror." *Blood Syndicate* #17. New York: Milestone Media, August 1994.

Washington, Robert L. III (writer), Dwayne McDuffie (writer), Ivan Velez Jr. (writer), John Paul Leon (penciller), Chriscross (penciller), M. D. Bright (penciller), Chris Batista (penciller), Tom Grummett (penciller), Denys Cowan (penciller), Rober Quijano (inker), Bobby Rae (inker), Art Nichols (inker), Romeo Tanghal (inker), and Prentis Rollins (inker). "How Can You Be in Two Places at Once, When You're Not Anywhere at All?" *Worlds Collide* #1. New York: DC Comics / Milestone Media, July 1994.

Wright, Bradford W. *Comic Book Nation: The Transformation of Youth Culture in America*. Baltimore: Johns Hopkins University Press, 2001.

CHAPTER 6

# WHITENESS AND SUPERHEROES IN THE COMIX/CODICES OF ENRIQUE CHAGOYA

JOSÉ ALANIZ

THE CHICANX performance troupe Culture Clash, formed by members of the San Francisco arts collective Galería de la Raza in the 1980s, featured such stock characters as Orange Man, Bus Boy Man, and Leafblower Man, who trafficked in familiar American superhero iconography for their biting satire. Both silly and trenchant—"with the amazing ability to balance a load of heavy restaurant dishes and live on lousy tips!"[1]—Culture Clash's televised *Mex-Men* skit incorporated the superhero figure's visual tropes and narrative clichés into a critical hybrid vision.

Theirs was not a casual choice of figure.

The recycling, repurposing, and (re)mixing of mainstream visual culture (including the superhero) forms a pillar of Chicanx artistic practice, with the *Mex-Men* a particularly vibrant example. As noted by Chicanx studies scholar Carl Gutiérrez-Jones:

> In Chicano art, one finds complex processes of hybridization, both thematic and stylistic, that are self-consciously structured to comment on experiences of trauma, as well as on the interpretive conventions attached to these events. As works in the Chicano context demonstrate, these con-

---

1. "Culture Clash Chicano Superheroes."

ventions have symbolic and material consequences that significantly shape communities.²

The curator and author Terezita Romo has called this process a "bicultural aesthetic synthesis" of Mexican heritage and American art.³

All the same, the superhero and its reappropriations in painting, graphics, prints, record covers, playing cards, other ephemera, and diverse publications of the Chicanismo era (roughly the 1960s to the 1980s), by art collectives such as Mechanismo, Self-Help Graphics & Art, Los Four, the Royal Chicano Airforce, and others, remains an understudied aspect of Chicanx art and its sociopolitical context. This was highly politicized art, made to assail the status quo of ethnicity and class in America and to cheer on a social revolution; in this struggle, the superhero took on various guises and served as a symbol of empowerment, but also as an implement for critique—not only of the dominant white culture, but also of hypermasculinity across color lines.

Since their 1938 appearance in the person of Superman, superheroes have come to represent the exuberant optimism as well as latent violence of mainstream America. But as seen in Chicanx art, the superhero's very ubiquity and recognizability has also made it available to ethnic minorities and other marginalized groups—a compelling figure to co-opt, subvert, and, as Robert Neustadt wrote of the performance artist Guillermo Gómez-Peña, "contest the vulgar images with which hegemonic culture stereotypes minority 'others.'"⁴ In sum, Mexican American artists—caught between two national cultures, resisting and celebrating both—adapted, reimagined, exploded, and redirected US superhero iconography toward new ideological ends during the struggle for self-determination in the 1960s and 1970s, laying the political groundwork for Culture Clash and other later groups in the 1980s and beyond.

The invocation of the superhero by Mexican American artists in the Chicanismo era and after functions as a sort of "cross-dressing" and "crossing-over": polysemous, polymorphous, transcultural—"xicanosmotic," in William Nericcio's phrasing. Whether in Yolanda M. López's 1978 *Portrait of the Artist as Guadalupe* (with its echoes of Wonder Woman) or in various works incorporating Marvel and DC characters by Mel Casas; whether inspired by Mexican figures such as Chespirito's El Chapulín Colorado, the Pachuco, Zoot Suiter, Gangbanger, Aztec warrior, or lucha libre's El Santo, or

---

2. Gutiérrez-Jones, "Humor, Literacy," 116.
3. Quoted in Noriega, "The City of Dreams."
4. Gómez-Peña, "Texts," 131.

indeed by mainstream US creations such as Superman and Captain America; whether parodied, lionized, or rendered in ambiguous shades, the superhero in Chicanx art participates in what Adela C. Licona calls "third-space (B)orderland rhetorics" that rupture representational structures and "prove discursively disobedient to the confines of phallogocentrism and its colonizing effects."[5] Inspiring and absurd, superheroes as depicted by Chicanx artists incarnate Gloria Anzaldúa's "border consciousness," the space of ambivalence created by a clash of cultures.

As examined in this chapter, the paintings, prints, and codices of US-based Mexican artist Enrique Chagoya[6] (director of Galería de la Raza from 1986 to 1990) starkly visualize that transhistorical space of ambivalence. They stand out for their inventive pastiche of preexisting superhero imagery as a means of reimagining the conquest and colonizing of the Americas, their *détournement* of mass culture iconography in the service of redressing racial wrongs, and their tragicomic vision of whiteness confronting its ghostly, vengeful other.

## Chagoya's "Visual Density"

A Mexico City native, Chagoya (b. 1953) studied economics at the Universidad Nacional Autonoma de México and worked on rural development projects in Veracruz before moving to the US in 1977. He initially sought to unionize farmworker and migrant communities in Texas before returning to his early interest in art, attending the San Francisco Art Institute and in 1987 earning an MFA from the University of California at Berkeley. Today he teaches art at Stanford.

Chagoya's multimedia practice bears the stamp of many influences, from Francisco Goya and Giambattista Piranesi to Mexican caricaturist and printmaker José Guadalupe Posada, as well as the postmodern assemblagists Bruce Conner and Ed and Nancy Keinholz. He has also noted the strong impression made by the historian Miguel León-Portilla, director of Mexico City's Instituto Indigenista Interamericano and author of *Visión de los Vencidos* (translated as *The Broken Spears: The Aztec Account of the Conquest of Mexico*), which describes the lost world of pre-Columbian Mexica peoples in

---

5. Licona, "(B)orderlands," 106.
6. Chagoya does not self-identify as Chicano, though his directorship of Galería de la Raza and collaborations with Guillermo Gómez-Peña clearly place him in overlapping orbit with the Chicanx art movement.

their own words.[7] A second major thread in his work dates to the *Manifesto Antropofágico*, a 1928 call to arms by Brazilian artist Tarsila do Amaral and poet Oswald de Andrade. In brief, the manifesto called for a form of anti-colonialist "reverse cannibalism," a "cannibalizing the cannibalizers" stance to appropriate European art and culture as a form of indigenous opposition to the historical sacking of Latin America.[8]

From the mid-1980s, Chagoya's drawings and prints begin to utilize Mexican, European, and US popular culture figures such as Donald Duck and Mickey Mouse, recalling the work of Rubén Ortiz Torres, Rupert Garcia, and Roger Shimamura. The appropriation does more than decenter the hegemonic icon; as Dana Leibsohn argues, Chagoya's "cannibalistic" images go so far as to "reverse, if not overturn, the direction of influence in Western art."[9] The artist himself terms his method "reverse anthropology."[10]

Perhaps none other of Chagoya's paintings make the link between the costumed hero and the historical oppression of nonwhite peoples so explicit as *Crossing* (1994), which depicts Superman (as rendered by original artist Joe Shuster) in the guise of a pilgrim confronting the Aztec rain god Tlaloc,[11] rendering a moment of border policing as a slugfest between superbeings (see figure 6.1). This and similar conscriptions of the superhero reflect not only what journalist Scott Cunningham in 1993 deemed a "new undercurrent in cartoon-influenced painting" in Chicanx art that "returns to the traditions of the comics themselves, creating popular art with a whole range of ideas and emotions beyond the limited constraints of Pop art."[12] They also advance Chagoya's intensely ironic view of history derived from disparate elements: pre-Columbian art, modern advertising, European classics, and comics, all of which create a "visual density, a richness of color, and a certain rhythm of comedy and tragedy in his work."[13]

*Uprising of the Spirit* (1994) exemplifies both Chagoya's "visual density" and his tragicomic vision. The painting accesses at least four iconographic/ideological regimes: a smiling Superman in flight; a portrait of King Nezahualcoyotl, Aztec king of Texcoco, recorded in the sixteenth-century *Codex Ixtlilxochitl*; the 1598 Bartolemé de las Casas print *Massacre of Queen Anacaona and her Subjects*, on a Spanish massacre of natives; and El Lissitzky's

---

7. Watkin, "Utopian Cannibal," 23–24.
8. Watkin, "Utopian Cannibal," 9.
9. Leibsohn, "Seeing," 389.
10. Hickson, "Borderlandia," 15.
11. A visual quotation from the sixteenth-century *Codex Ixtlilxochitl*.
12. Cunningham, "From Pop back to Popular," 46.
13. Watkin, "Utopian Cannibal," 15.

FIGURE 6.1. Superman in pilgrim guise versus Tlaloc (*Crossing*). Reprinted with the artist's permission.

Soviet propaganda poster *Beat the Whites with the Red Wedge* (1919). In her reading of Chagoya's "biting political metacommentary," Leibsohn relates the ambiguous setting of the painting to *nepantla*,[14] "the middle space of the Aztec world," noting that the visual composition "transports these images across time and space to occupy a single site in the present ... underscor[ing] the privilege of twenty-first-century viewership: it is before contemporary eyes that these figures of such disparate histories clash."[15] The ambivalent "empty" background enacts Licona's "third-space (B)orderland rhetorics," where these wildly incongruous representations meet.

But the discolored void against which the Man of Steel and Aztec ruler contend recalls yet another ethereal space of possibility: the Phantom Zone, an interdimensional prison that has formed part of the Superman mythos since 1961. Here, too, insubstantial figures remain trapped in a timeless, frozen, eternal now. Further on, Leibsohn interprets the yellow beams emanating from the Last Son of Krypton's eyes as a sort of imperial X-ray vision

---

14. Constance Cortez sees the Aztec concept of *nepantla* as "a site of transformation, but one where the result of transformation is always secondary to the act. It is the place where transformation is possible, but more importantly, it is the magic and the potential for magic within that place." "The New Aztlan," 367.

15. Leibsohn, "Seeing," 389.

that "motivates and fissures modern encounters with the colonial past."[16] But perhaps just as plausibly (and more chillingly), we could gloss the beams as Superman's heat vision. He thus turns his gaze upon Texcoco not to examine but to annihilate. Given that the superhero seems to soar out of the *Massacre* print/panel, the strong implication is that he himself slaughtered the natives and set the village on fire with his eyes (and looks pretty happy about it).

I offer these readings of *Uprising of the Spirit* not to supplant other approaches, but to complement them. A comics history/superhero studies lens seems more than apt for analyzing Chagoya's work, given the additional layers of meaning it reveals—layers that scholars have traditionally ignored. Moreover, it feels incumbent upon me to point out that Leibsohn, an art historian, begins her article with the descriptor "Superman, of Marvel comic fame" and describes *Uprising* as staging a battle "through the juxtaposition of 1950s comics artistry and images extracted from sixteenth-century colonial manuscripts."[17] Superman was never published by Marvel, but by what is today known as DC Comics, while the specific Superman portrait Chagoya quotes is a 1976 version of the hero by US artist Ross Andru.[18]

In what follows, I examine Chagoya's transgressive conceptualist codices of the 1990s, which follow in the tradition of *Uprising of the Spirit*, as his fullest elaboration of how the superhero figure, far from merely serving as a generic marker for and defender of mass white American culture, here informs and deepens the artist's sardonic vision of race and history.

## The Codex

Rhetoric scholar Franny Howes describes pre-Columbian codices as pictographic "rhetorical practices" chronicling the myth and history of the Aztec and other peoples of the so-called New World before and after the Spanish Conquest.[19] Though derided by the invading Europeans as nonliterate, these texts were produced by highly trained artist/scribe/philosophers named *tlacuiloque*, using a sophisticated combination of hieroglyphs and partly phonetic ideographs, as demonstrated by León-Portilla and other scholars.[20] Their full meaning eludes those who study them to this day.

---

16. Leibsohn, "Seeing," 390.
17. Leibsohn, "Seeing," 389.
18. Conway and Andru, "Superman vs. The Amazing Spider-Man," 9.
19. Howes, "Imagining a Multiplicity."
20. Elizabeth Boone calls the codex "a graphic system that keeps and conveys knowledge" Quoted in Loria, "Painted," 56.

Though infamously brought under the umbrella of comics by Scott McCloud,[21] the Mesoamerican codex did not function as a purely graphic narrative form. Rather, it served as a mnemonic for performance, a pictoscript whose gaps the viewer/reader/listener imaginatively inhabited. No more than thirty precontact codices survived the destruction and Christianization of the Conquest; they, along with other remnants of precontact culture, have come to embody the lost history of many indigenous peoples. As such, they have taken on a quasi-nationalist role in Latinx cultures.

A 1992 Mexican Museum traveling exhibit, *Chicano Codex: Encountering Art of the Americas,* poignantly noted their significance to Chicanx artists by showcasing twenty-six newly produced codices that sought together to "symbolically gather the dispersed and destroyed pre-Hispanic picture books."[22] As participating artist/poet Cherríe Moraga put it in the show's catalog, "Our codices are a record of remembering. After five centuries of erasure, memories remain opaque. We sense them intuitively like an 'internal feather,' always present, always hidden."[23] Erasure and loss attend the pre-Columbian codices; Chagoya similarly mourned their mass destruction in the wake of the Spanish conquest, seeing in it the routine overwriting of history by the powerful. He personally witnessed a similar process as a young man, during the June 10, 1971, "Halconazo," during which a paramilitary squad repressed a student demonstration in Mexico City, resulting in an estimated 100 deaths. As he told an interviewer, "When I arrived home, there was nothing in the news except saying that there was a fight among students, and that there were about four people killed. You knew that the reality was a different reality. That was my first lesson in how society works, and how the politics of the state—at least in Mexico—works."[24]

Chagoya's own codices, then, like those of the *Chicano Codex* show, would function in the first instance as a recuperative act. Produced in collaboration with master printers, on traditional *amatl* paper (made from wild fig bark) in a folding accordion style that extends up to thirty feet, these forged "picture-books" create their own mirror-histories through "reverse anthropological" visual appropriation, flouting chronology, topography, and high/low cultural distinctions. Crucially as well, like the pre-Columbian works they reference and parody, the codices present "laconic texts" not intended as linear, coherent, self-sustaining narratives. "In my codex book concept," Chagoya stated, "I have decided that I am entitled to my own ideologi-

---

21. McCloud, *Understanding Comics,* 10–15. McCloud's influence here is discussed by, among others, Loria, "Painted," 58; Storr, "Strategies," 31.
22. Sanchez-Tranquilino, foreword, 3.
23. Moraga, "Codex Xeri," 21.
24. Karlstrom, "Oral Interview."

cal construct. I tell the stories of cultural hybrids, of political collisions of universal consequences."[25] Launched in 1992—500 years after the catalytic "discovery" of the Americas—Chagoya's codex practice now encompasses some twenty-five works.[26] As argued by Howes, they serve as "a massive act of memory, reaching into both American popular cultural imagery and indigenous imagery to invent a way to represent the ongoing struggles of colonialism in a way that is both new and old."[27] A mash-up of indigenous papermaking methods and modern laser-printing, they tell fractured tales of cultural collision and (not incidentally) superheroic apocalypse.

*Tales from the Conquest/Codex* (1992) typifies Chagoya's conceptualist approach. Its second screen, or page, overlays a panel of Superman in flight over page 29 of the *Codex Borgia*, among the few surviving precontact codices. This particular page bears a multivalent "border consciousness": Unusually for this work, it shifts the orientation of the pages; depicts an enclosure made up of an Aztec death goddess, wind figures, and a representation of Tlazoteotl, goddess of sin and midwifery; and initiates a long semi-narrative journey sequence filled with poorly understood ritualistic details.[28] The Superman portrait, in which the hero exclaims, "It's a *dimensional bridge*—and I'm *crossing it!—Right now!*"[29] is misidentified by journalist Sarah Kirk Hanley as "a panel from an early Superman comic book,"[30] though many comics scholars will recognize it from *Forever People* #1 (Mar. 1971), published more than three decades after Superman's debut.[31] Moreover, the image hails from a transitional moment in the history of superheroes: It counts among the first published pieces by seminal artist Jack Kirby after his departure from Marvel, where his 1960s innovations had virtually defined the genre's so-called Silver Age. The panel even carries with it a bit of controversy: Kirby's drawings, over his objections, were reworked by veteran Superman artist Al Plastino to better conform to the DC house style.[32] Chagoya's pastiche codex screen, then, enacts themes of trespassing, intrusion, overstepping, mutation—but also of beginnings, cross-pollination, new life. The latter are multiply connoted by Tlazoteotl; the void-like enclosure that recalls a birth canal; the New Genesis "Boom Tube" Superman is

---

25. Chagoya, "Imagery."
26. Hickson, "Borderlandia," 6.
27. Howes, "Imagining a Multiplicity."
28. Díaz and Rodgers, *The Codex Borgia*, xxiii.
29. Chagoya, *Tales from the Conquest Codex*.
30. Hanley, "Visual Culture," 4.
31. Kirby, "The Forever People," 253.
32. Evanier, "Jack Kirby's Superman."

trying to fly through, ditto; and the several tiny "duplicate" Supermen at bottom left.[33]

Screen five of the same work likewise superimposes costumed crusaders over the *Codex Borgia*, in this case Wonder Woman and Batman at extreme left and Superman at extreme right. They seem to float over the codex's plate (or two-page spread) 56, a double portrait of the god of life, Quetzalcóatl, and the god of death, Mictlantecuhtli, bordered by a 260-day ritual calendar.[34] Only Wonder Woman physically interacts with the deities, punching Mictlantecuhtli in the teeth, just as she does the similarly dome-pated villain Mongul in the story from which Chagoya took her image, Alan Moore and Dave Gibbons's *Superman Annual* #11.[35] The running Batman, meanwhile, originally appeared in *Action Comics* #241,[36] in which the Dark Knight rushes to help a Kryptonite-stricken Man of Steel. Superman himself stands across the expanse, on the far side of the Aztec gods, looking at the others and declaring, "*Hey! Hold on!* I've got a *million* questions!" The outcry points to the irreducible ambiguity of the pre-Columbian codices, while the visual/verbal tension of Superman's portrait extends the page's theme of duality—life/death, man/woman, action/stasis, superhero/secret identity, and so on—in idiosyncratically comics-like fashion: The dialogue comes from *Forever People*,[37] but the pose from *Superman* #247.[38] In addition, the stance originates in a particularly dramatic point in the *Superman* story scripted by Elliot Maggin with art by Curt Swan and Murphy Anderson, when the intergalactic Oans pronounce Superman "*guilty . . . guilty of crimes against humanity!*"[39] All these elements together thus underscore the binary ideology of colonialist repression—"active" agent and "passive" receiver—while implicating superheroes as emblems and agents of same.

But more than that, Chagoya's codex rhetorics, as noted by Damián Baca, "propose a detour, a revision or creolization of dominant assimilation narratives, of taking them in a plurality of directions, toward new ways of reading."[40] Such a "plurality of directions," as I see it, springs from the inherent aesthetic violence sparked by the juxtaposition of such contrastive visual components; the codices hardly fit the description of a "seamless montage

---

33. Chagoya quotes these from Moore and Gibbons, "For The Man Who Has Everything," 309.
34. Díaz and Rodgers, *The Codex Borgia*, xxviii.
35. Moore and Gibbons, "For the Man Who Has Everything," 284.
36. Coleman and Boring, "The Super Key to Fort Superman," 112.
37. Kirby, "Forever People," 252.
38. Maggin and Swan, "Must There Be a Superman?" 255.
39. Maggin and Swan, "Must There Be a Superman?" 255.
40. Baca, *Mestiz@ Scripts*, 83.

of heterochronic signs" attributed to them by Jennifer González.[41] The many critical references to "conflict" and "collision" in Chagoya's codex oeuvre,[42] in fact, recall the early Soviet filmmaker and film theorist Sergei Eisenstein's concept of cinematic montage as fundamentally built on the "conflict" and "collision" of elements, from which *"arises* a concept."[43]

> Note how the artist/neo-*tlacuilo* describes his intended effect in uncannily similar terms: What you see in some of my codices is this kind of influencing of each other, but the influence happens not in the book itself, because every character, every symbolic element is very distinctive. It's not like I have a Superman with feathers or anything like that. Maybe I should. But no, Superman is still Superman in my codices; or the pre-Columbian characters or the Catholic characters, but by the interactions I make between all these very different symbolic elements, I hope I will be able to create a third element in the minds of the people. That's where the mixture of ideas and cultures, hopefully, takes place.[44]

Chagoya's most fully realized comics/codex vision of history—a "third element" sparked by clashing worlds—would in truth have conflict, violence, colonialist slaughter at its core.

## *Codex Espangliensis*

In 1998, Chagoya collaborated with Chicano performance artist Guillermo Gómez-Peña and printer Felicia Rice on *Codex Espangliensis: From Columbus to the Border Patrol*,[45] a bravura conceptualist accordion book expandable to over twenty-one feet, which Gómez-Peña describes as a "post-Columbian Spanglish comix/codex" positing an alternate history in which an Aztec sailor named Europzin Tezpoca and other Aztecs colonize Europe, "cannibalizing the cannibalizers," massacring superheroes and cartoon characters along the way.[46] That recounting, of course, utterly fails to capture the opus's

---

41. González, "*Codex Espangliensis*."
42. "Iconic intercultural collision": Torres, "Enrique Chagoya," 389. "Collisions he constructs between ancient and modern historical visions": Leibsohn, "Seeing," 389; "A revealing clash of titans . . . Superman faces the Mexica king in a grudge match": Schmidt, "Superman vs. The Mexica."
43. Eisenstein, *Film Form*, 37.
44. Karlstrom, "Oral Interview."
45. "Espangliensis" is faux Latin for "Spanglish."
46. Gómez-Peña, "Texts."

dementedly anarchic, Monty Pythonesque excess, blending José Guadalupe Posada caricatures, pre- and postcontact codex imagery, comics and cartoon quotations, European prints, advertising, propaganda, collage, woodblock prints, religious iconography, and many other visual facets with excerpts from Gómez-Peña's performance pieces "Free Trade Art" and "Chicanost: Radio Nuevo Orden" in vertiginously varying typographical styles.

The book can open left to right or the reverse, and one may read its panels right to left, or indeed in any order, so as to experience what Jennifer González calls "the dissonance of bi-cultural literacy" directly tied to its grand narrative-inverting mission:

> In tales that unfold in poetic Spanglish and an elaborate pictography, the artists reveal history as anything but a coherent, linear narrative that leads step by step to the inevitable present. Instead, they offer an unfinished, catalectic text in which history must be read forward and backward, in fragments and in recurring episodes, in the changes in language that allow systems of power to remain unchanged—in short, as history itself tends to unfold.[47]

Such a fragmented, epic/parodic approach is suffused, as noted, by reminders of hemispheric genocide at every turn. Each page is saturated with blood, in drop, fingerprint, and splatter motifs used to "not only comment on the violence of the original conquest but also to draw attention to the violence that globalization and transnationalism, as represented by American pop-culture icons such as Mickey Mouse and Spiderman, are inflicting upon modern-day 'natives.'"[48] In this scheme, superheroes as stand-ins for US hegemony cannot but "join in a visual history of political oppression and exploitation that is both violent and seductive."[49] Rather than presenting a comprehensive account of Chagoya's superhero imagery in *Codex Espangliensis*, I will focus on some prominent examples.

Reading the book from right to left, the fourteenth plate depicts Superman and Wonder Woman in battle with King Nezahualcoyotl, the same *Codex Ixtlilxochitl* portrait used in *Uprising of the Spirit*. Here, however, the king has a new identity; as the accompanying Gómez-Peña-penned text explains, in 1492 the Aztec Europzin Tezpoca sailed east and discovered a new continent, which he named after himself. Thenceforth, "omni-potent Aztecs began the conquest of Europzin in the name of thy father, Tezcatli-

---

47. González, introduction.
48. Loria, "Painted," 62.
49. González, introduction.

poca, lord of cross-cultural misunderstandings."[50] The conqueror's immense size signals his prowess—he dwarfs the superheroes, easily swatting Superman aside with his shield. A reeling last son of Krypton cries out, "Whoof! No good!" as the same image of Wonder Woman seen in *Tales from the Conquest/Codex II* flies on, right arm outstretched in a fist, straight at the invader's bloodied head (see figure 6.2). In this new New World, the white heroes have perversely become the natives, the Amerindians the despoilers. As curator Mel Watkin puts it, Chagoya "juxtaposes images in absurd ways, going against known facts and historical chronology in order to *intentionally* play with meaning and context."[51]

More specifically given the pop culture figures press-ganged for the task, *Codex Espangliensis* refracts the "imaginary tale"/multiverse model of continuity prevalent in superhero narratives since the early 1960s. On such "alternate Earths," explains comics scholar Karin Kukkonen, "fully parallel, equally actualized realities" offer "counterfactual scenarios involving alternative developments of the story of a known superhero."[52] But of course, superhero comics get much weirder than that. As media studies scholar Andrew J. Friedenthal elaborates, even *within* "official" storylines, the narrative revamping of the retcon or "retroactive continuity" "deliberately alter[s] the history of that narrative/world such that, going forward, future stories reflect this *new* history, completely ignoring the old as if it never happened."[53] Retcons, which have grown more frequent in the last three decades, tend to divide creators and fans, but their proponents, significantly, market them as "improvements" to the status quo. DC writer/editor Marv Wolfman even called the paradigmatic massive continuity house-cleaning maxi-series *Crisis on Infinite Earths* (1985–1986) "corrective history."[54] Retcons, routine resurrections from death, parallel dimensions, and so on, have led critics like Sam Leith to declare, "The world of mainstream superhero comics, then, is one of infinite plasticity in terms of events."[55] Chagoya and his collaborators' invocation of the superhero thus feeds into their parodic blurring of distinctions between truth/untruth, life/death, white/nonwhite, and numerous other such "historical" binaries. It also relates to what postcolonial studies scholar José Rabasa calls the non-European "elsewheres" of

50. Chagoya and Gómez-Peña, *Codex Espangliensis*.
51. Watkin, "Utopian Cannibal," 15.
52. Kukkonen, "Navigating Infinite Earths," 40, 41.
53. Friedenthal, *Retcon Game*, 7.
54. Quoted in Friedenthal, *Retcon Game*, 89.
55. Leith, "One of These Comic Heroes."

**FIGURE 6.2.** A superheroic battle in *Codex Espangliensis*. Reprinted with the artist's permission.

the codices—that is, "the element of surprise when the missionaries realize the gaze of the *tlacuilo* is looking back at them."[56]

Once more, Chagoya's peculiar superhero imagery choices enrich and deepen his work's themes of confrontational, transborder encounter. Most irreverent and pertinent: The *Codex Espangliensis* liberally quotes from the first-ever intercompany crossover *Superman vs. The Amazing Spider-Man* (1976), a landmark event in comics publishing and the mainstream superhero genre, with story by Gerry Conway and art by Ross Andru. The borrowings include the "swatted" Superman mentioned above, along with his dialogue ("Whoof!" etc.);[57] in plate 10, the Man of Steel's famous flying pose from the cover, though now he is soaring out of a detail of the same 1598 de las Casas print depicting Spanish atrocities against Haitians utilized in *Uprising of the Spirit*; and in plate 3 Spider-Man's body (also from the 1976 cover, though here fused with George Washington's head) leaping into the fray of another sixteenth-century de las Casas print, this one depicting the torments of Arawak Indians committed by Christopher Columbus's men.

---

56. Rabasa, *Tell Me the Story*, 195.
57. Conway and Andru, "Superman vs. the Amazing Spider-Man," 4.

The codex (again, reading right to left) in fact opens with a superhero as privileged signifier of border crossing: A completely red Superman[58] shoots forth from an infernal turn-of-the-century Posada print, "The Shepherdess Flora and Gil Plagued by Their Opposing Demon," as if out of the mouth of hell. His body traverses the fold to confront three Mixtec warriors armed with atlatls (spear-throwers) from the *Codex Zouche-Nuttall* (fourteenth to fifteenth centuries). An emissary between two worlds, an intermediary, crimson Superman is also a conqueror, a death's herald—as marked by the skull replacing the "S" on his chest emblem (see figure 6.3).

But perhaps Chagoya's most subtly productive use of superhero pastiche in *Codex Espangliensis* occurs in plate 9, showing, from left, a pair of levitating soldiers firing shoulder-mounted lasers, from the 1992–1993 "Death of Superman" storyline.[59] Instead of firing at the villain Doomsday, however, here the soldiers attack a crowd of civilians being brutalized by Porfirio Díaz's cavalry in Posada's 1892 print "Anti-Reelection Protest." A hovering helicopter from Jurgens's story covers the event, exclaiming, "Move in closer! We're broadcasting this *live!*"[60] A Kirby/Plastino Superman from *Forever People*[61] flies to the right, once more crossing the accordion fold, hands bloody, toward a version of Alberto Korda's iconic 1960 photograph "Guerrillero Heroico," composed of the repeated word "Che." A red dot over Guevara's chest, with the red word "Bang!" next to it, presumably denotes the revolutionary's 1967 execution in Bolivia.

Just below this portrait, we see a silent rectangular panel showing Robin, Batman, and Wonder Woman, immediately before the latter engages Mongul in combat in the aforementioned *Superman Annual* #11 story.[62] The incorporation of this piece into a conceptualist work obsessed with alternate worlds bears particular significance; Moore and Gibbon's Gothic tale explores, as Brad Ricca puts it, "the abject of superheroism" through a plot in which Superman/Kal-El is haunted by a psychologically repressed alternative version of his life.[63] In sum, the superhero imagery Chagoya inserts in his work, far from perfunctory, tends to derive from thematically apposite narratives

---

58. Chagoya takes this (reversed) portrait from *Superman and Spider-Man* (1981), the sequel to the 1976 crossover. At this point in the story, Clark Kent has just changed into his costumed identity and flies over the city on his way to oppose the Hulk.
59. Jurgens, et al. "Doomsday!"
60. Chagoya and Gómez-Peña, *Codex Espangliensis*.
61. Kirby, "Forever People," 242.
62. Moore and Gibbons, "For the Man Who Has Everything," 284.
63. Ricca, "'I Fashioned a Prison That You Could Not Leave,'" 161.

**FIGURE 6.3.** Superman confronts the Mixtec (*Codex Espangliensis*). Reprinted with the artist's permission.

about displacement, cross-cultural collision, and histories that never "really" happened.

## "Whiteness That Haunts"

For a work that partly self-identifies as "comix," it seems not unfitting to frame Chagoya's allusion-driven *Codex Espangliensis* in terms more familiar to comics fans: He essentially engages in a glorified, narratively informed species of swiping. A colloquial expression for comics industry redrawing practices (especially in the context of deadline-based commercial work), swiping holds a time-honored place in fan culture, whether as respectful homage, craven plagiarism, or, indeed, as invisible, constituting "a medium-specific way of citing that inscribes the graphic novelist's practice into a multi-layered memory of comics," according to Benoît Crucifix. Swiping, "whether practiced in an overt or shameful manner, whether it gets noticed or not," reminds us of comics' reiterative, nostalgic, artifice-driven proclivities.[64] The strategy also recalls Ole Frahm's conceptualization of graphic narrative as "a parody on the referentiality of signs."[65] As he expounds:

> The reading of comics is precisely *not* about reconstructing unity (of whatever) but rather to appreciate the heterogeneous signs of script and image in their peculiar, material quality which cannot be made into a unity....

---

64. Crucifix, "Cut-Up and Redrawn," 312, 313.
65. Frahm, "Weird Signs," 179.

> These constellations of signs peculiar to comics make them parodies of the common notion of how signs and reality, signs and reference, relate.[66]

For Frahm, comics as a medium bears an inescapably conceptualist ("parodic") function above and beyond any narratival impulse. These considerations on the meaning-(un)making capacities of comics have some bearing, I want to suggest, on the matter of superheroes' presumptive whiteness, even in such sardonic *détournement* practices as Chagoya's. In short, by inverting history and "cannibalizing the cannibalizers" (figured as Superman, Spider-Man, etc.) through insistently intertextual swiping, *Codex Espangliensis* correlates the core "parodic" nature of signs in comic art with the fundamental instability of whiteness—even though such a deconstructive approach risks draining the work of much of its anti-colonialist critique.

In their discussion of what they call "oxymoronic whiteness," Tammie Kennedy and colleagues write that the term "invites us to identify multiple contradictions in discursive uses of whiteness, whether the term is directly employed or serves as a haunting."[67] This "whiteness that haunts" reminds us of its protean nature, how it functions

> as a trope with associated discourses and cultural scripts that socialize people into ways of seeing, thinking and performing whiteness and non-whiteness. Both white and nonwhite bodies may perform whiteness, albeit to different ends and often with different success. As such, whiteness has historically been defined in different ways, for example, as a performance of acting white, violence and terror, the drive to consume land and cultures, religious hypocrisy, denial and ignorance.[68]

Whiteness, then, need not attend particular bodies and minds, but—like power for Foucault—shifts along with historical and other contingencies. As Klor de Alva rather saucily phrased the issue in regard to the racialization of Latinx peoples: "The Commerce Department didn't know what to do with Latinos; the census takers didn't know what to do with Latinos; the government didn't know what to do with Latinos, and so they said, 'Latinos can be of any race.'"[69] Similarly, in her call for a Foucauldian intervention in whiteness studies, Ladelle McWhorter contends: "What we need instead of

---

66. Frahm, "Weird Signs," 177. But see Cook's objections to and elaborations upon Frahm's thesis in "Metacomics."
67. Kennedy, Middleton, and Ratcliffe, *Rhetorics of Whiteness*, 7.
68. Kennedy, Middleton, and Ratcliffe, *Rhetorics of Whiteness*, 5.
69. De Alva, Shorris, and West, "Our Next Race Question," 487.

avowals and exposés of whiteness as a racial identity is a genealogy of race and a network of counter-memories to begin to build alternative accounts of raced existence and possibilities of living race differently."[70]

This way of articulating whiteness informs my reading of *Codex Espangliensis*'s fifteenth screen (the final one, if reading right to left). With Europzin Tezpoca's armies presumably having conquered the new continent of Europe, a group of pre-Columbians feast on the body parts of various vanquished enemies (including Mickey Mouse).[71] An accompanying text from the San Diego Historical Museum reads, "Please place the following species in the appropriate category." A list is overlaid on the image of the diners. Like a grotesque menu from a cannibal restaurant, the offerings include "Aztec," "Apache," "Chicano," "Anglo Saxon," and so on. To the left, the final/first page depicts Superman lurching from a punch, signified by the sound effect "KAPOW,"[72] though here Spider-Man's fist is replaced by a Posada print skull, next to a bleeding cartoon heart. Finally, in another panel to the left, Superman appears again, now prostrate amid rubble, a tattered "S" logo flag waving in the wind. Superhero fans will readily recognize the source: It is the climax of the "Death of Superman" storyline, from the previously mentioned *Superman #75*, where the hero lies deceased at the hands of the bludgeoning monster Doomsday. The bold phrase "Threatened endangered or extinct?" is superimposed over the scene.

But something funny happened on the way to the superhero holocaust. Given the oxymoronic instability of whiteness—its incessant "haunting," in Kennedy et al.'s formulation—Chagoya's alternate history turning of the tables (victorious Mesoamericans, conquered European whites) seems to alchemize an unforeseen side effect, an unintended reversal. If, as he says, "Often the white superheroes . . . in my work represent the Western cultural colonialism expanding not only in the Americas but all over the world,"[73] then in *Codex Espangliensis*'s parallel reality it is Europzin Tezpoca and his super-hordes who enact whiteness, the fallen heroes who futilely resist invasion of their "New World." In this "mirror history," enunciated largely through Frahm's destabilizing, "parodic" comics discourses, white-

---

70. McWhorter, "Where Do White People Come From?," 552. See also Singh, who agrees that "whiteness and blackness as well as other modern racial forms emerge as subject positions, habits of perception, and modes of embodiment that develop from the ongoing risk management of settler and slave capitalism, and more generally racial capitalism (i.e., capitalism)." "Whiteness," 1096.

71. Chagoya recycled this image from his codex *Insulae Canibalium (Cannibal Island, 1995)*.

72. Conway and Andru, "Superman vs. the Amazing Spider-Man," 50.

73. Chagoya in discussion with the author, November 25, 2017.

ness itself is parodied—indeed, flipped; never a stable category to begin with, adhering to no particular racial/biological formation, whiteness stands revealed as predicated on particular polarities of power. The codex oddly reifies what it condemns: Someone still gets conquered, someone still does the conquering. Or not, since the rules set out by Chagoya subvert any linear narrative or finalizable meaning. We could certainly read the panel sequence/double portrait of the living/dead Superman at the end/beginning of *Codex Espangliensis* as "the death of whiteness." Or, indeed, as "long live whiteness."

If the question "Threatened endangered or extinct?" pertains to whiteness, Chagoya's rather mealymouthed answer seems to be: "None of the above." In the Mexican artist's peculiar twilight of the gods, whiteness seems inextricable not from superheroes, but from super*villainy*.

## Bibliography

Baca, Damián. *Mestiz@ Scripts, Digital Migrations, and the Territories of Writing*. New York: Palgrave Macmillan, 2008.

Chagoya, Enrique. "Imagery." In *Codex Espangliensis: From Columbus to the Border Patrol*, by Enrique Chagoya, and Guillermo Gómez-Peña. San Francisco: City Lights Books, 2000.

———. Tales from the Conquest Codex. 1992. Collage/codex. SF MOMA.

Chagoya, Enrique, and Guillermo Gómez-Peña. *Codex Espangliensis: From Columbus to the Border Patrol*. San Francisco: City Lights Books, 2000.

Coleman, Jerry (writer), and Wayne Boring (artist). "The Super Key to Fort Superman." In *The Greatest Superman Stories Ever Told*, edited by Mike Gold and Robert Greenberger, 103–14. New York: DC Comics, 1987.

Conway, Gerry (writer), and Ross Andru (artist). "Superman vs. the Amazing Spider-Man." In *Superman vs. The Amazing Spider-Man*, 1–92. New York: Marvel/National, 1976.

Cook, Roy T. "Metacomics." In *The Routledge Companion to Comics*, edited by Frank Bramlett, Roy Cook, and Aaron Meskin, 257–66. New York: Routledge, 2017.

Cortez, Constance. "The New Aztlan: Nepantla (and Other Sites of Transmogrification)." In *The Road to Aztlan: Art from a Mythic Homeland*, edited by Virginia M. Fields, Victor Zamudio-Taylor, and Los Angeles County Museum of Art, 358–73. Los Angeles: Los Angeles County Museum of Art, 2001.

Crucifix, Benoît. "Cut-Up and Redrawn: Reading Charles Burns' Swipe File." *Inks: The Journal of the Comics Studies Society* 1, no. 3 (Fall 2017): 309–33.

"Culture Clash Chicano Superheroes." DailyMotion video, 1:33. Posted by Kellen Aanya, 2015. https://www.dailymotion.com/video/x2txyod.

Cunningham, Scott. "From Pop back to Popular: Art & Comics." *Poliester* 2, no. 6 (Summer 1993): 46–53.

De Alva, Klor, Earl Shorris, and Cornel West. "Our Next Race Question: The Uneasiness Between Blacks and Latinos." In *Critical White Studies: Looking Behind the Mirror*, edited by Richard Delgado and Jean Stefancic, 482–92. Philadelphia: Temple University Press, 1997.

Díaz, Gisele, and Alan Rodgers. *The Codex Borgia: A Full-Color Restoration of the Ancient Mexican Manuscript*. New York: Dover Publications, 1993.

Eisenstein, Sergei. *Film Form; Essays in Film Theory*. Translated by Jay Leyda. New York: Harcourt, Brace, 1949.

Encalada Egusquiza, Yorki J., Catherine D. Gooch, and Joshua D. Martin. (2016) "Transnationalism, Xicanosmosis, and the U.S.–Mexico Border: An Interview with William Nericcio." *disClosure: A Journal of Social Theory*: Vol. 25, Article 20.

Evanier, Mark. "Jack Kirby's Superman." *News from Me*, August 22, 2003, https://www.newsfromme.com/2003/08/22/jack-kirbys-superman/.

Frahm, Ole. "Weird Signs: Comics as a Means of Parody." In *Comics and Culture: Analytical and Theoretical Approaches to Comics*, edited by Anne Magnuson and Hans Christiansen, 177–91. Copenhagen: University of Copenhagen Press, 200.

Friedenthal, Andrew J. *Retcon Game: Retroactive Continuity and the Hyperlinking of America*. Jackson: University Press of Mississippi, 2017.

Gómez-Peña, Guillermo. "Texts." In *Codex Espangliensis: From Columbus to the Border Patrol*, by Enrique Chagoya and Guillermo Gómez-Peña. San Francisco: City Lights Books, 2000.

González, Jennifer. "*Codex Espangliensis* Critical Commentary." Moving Parts Press, 2015, http://movingpartspress.com/publications/critcom.

———. Introduction to *Codex Espangliensis: From Columbus to the Border Patrol*, by Enrique Chagoya, and Guillermo Gómez-Peña. San Francisco: City Lights Books, 2000.

Gutiérrez-Jones, Carl. "Humor, Literacy and Trauma in Chicano Culture." *Comparative Literature Studies* 40, no. 2, 2003: 112–26.

Hanley, Sarah Kirk. "Visual Culture of the Nacirema: Chagoya's Printed Codices." *Art in Print* 1, no. 6 (March–April 2012): 3–15.

Hickson, Patricia. "Borderlandia Unbound: An Abbreviated Guide to the Visual Anthropology of Enrique Chagoya." In *Enrique Chagoya: Borderlandia*, edited by Patricia Hickson, Robert Storr, and Daniela Pérez, 1–7. Des Moines: Des Moines Art Center & University of California, Berkeley, 2007.

Howes, Franny. "Imagining a Multiplicity of Visual Rhetorical Traditions: Comics Lessons from Rhetoric Histories." *ImageTexT: Interdisciplinary Comics Studies* 5, no. 3, 2010.

Jurgens, Dan (writer/penciller), Brett Breeding (penciller), Glenn Whitmore (colorist), and John Costanza (letterer). "Doomsday!" Superman, vol. 2, #75. Jan. 1993.

Karlstrom, Paul. "Oral Interview with Enrique Chagoya." *Smithsonian Archives of American Art*, July–August 2001, https://www.aaa.si.edu/collections/interviews/oral-history-interview-enrique-chagoya-12495.

Kennedy, Tammie M., Joyce Irene Middleton, and Krista Ratcliffe, eds. *Rhetorics of Whiteness: Postracial Hauntings in Popular Culture, Social Media, and Education*. Carbondale: Southern Illinois University Press, 2017.

Kirby, Jack (writer/artist). "The Forever People." In *The Greatest Superman Stories Ever Told*, edited by Mike Gold and Robert Greenberger, 231–54. New York: DC Comics, 1987.

Kukkonen, Karin. "Navigating Infinite Earths: Readers, Mental Models, and the Multiverse of Superhero Comics." *Storyworlds: A Journal of Narrative Studies* 2, no. 1 (2010): 39–58.

Leibsohn, Dana. "Seeing in Situ: The Mapa de Cuauhtinchan No. 2." In *Cave, City, and Eagle's Nest: An Interpretive Journey through the Mapa De Cuauhtinchan No. 2*, edited by David Carrasco and Scott Sessions, 389–426. Albuquerque: University of New Mexico Press, 2007.

Leith, Sam. "One of These Comic Heroes Really Is Dead." *The Telegraph*, March 12, 2007, http://www.telegraph.co.uk/comment/personal-view/3638405/One-of-these-comic-heroes-really-is-dead.html.

Licona, Adela C. "(B)orderlands' Rhetorics and Representations: The Transformative Potential of Feminist Third-Space Scholarship and Zines." *NWSA Journal* 17, no. 2 (2005): 104–29.

Loria, Daniela Miranda. "Painted (Hi)stories: The Subversive Power of Codex and Comics Elements in Codex Espangliensis: From Columbus to the Border Patrol." *International Journal of Comic Art* 15, no. 2 (Fall 2013): 55–76.

Maggin, Elliot S. and Swan, Curt. "Must There Be a Superman?" In *The Greatest Superman Stories Ever Told*, edited by Mike Gold and Robert Greenberger, 255–71. New York: DC Comics, 1987.

McCloud, Scott. *Understanding Comics*. Northampton, MA: Kitchen Sink Press, 1993.

McWhorter, Ladelle. "Where Do White People Come From?: A Foucaultian Critique of Whiteness Studies." *Philosophy & Social Criticism* 31, no. 5–6 (2005): 533–56.

Moore, Alan (writer), and Dave Gibbons (artist). "For The Man Who Has Everything." In *The Greatest Superman Stories Ever Told*, edited by Mike Gold and Robert Greenberger, 272–311. New York: DC Comics, 1987.

Moraga, Cherríe. "Codex Xeri: El Momento Historico." In *The Chicano Codices: Encountering Art of the Americas*, edited by Patricia Draher, 20–21. San Francisco: Mexican Museum, 1992.

Noriega, Chon A. "The City of Dreams . . . and Shoes." *Tate Etc.* no. 23 (Autumn 2011). http://www.tate.org.uk/context-comment/articles/city-dreamsand-shoes.

Rabasa, José. *Tell Me the Story of How I Conquered You: Elsewheres and Ethnosuicide in the Colonial Mesoamerican World*. Austin: University of Texas Press, 2011.

Ricca, Brad. "'I Fashioned a Prison That You Could Not Leave': The Gothic Imperative in 'The Castle of Otranto' and 'For the Man Who Has Everything.'" In *Alan Moore and the Gothic Tradition*, edited by Matthew J. A. Green, 159–78. Manchester, UK: Manchester University Press, 2013.

Sanchez-Tranquilino, Marcos. Foreword in *The Chicano Codices: Encountering Art of the Americas*, edited by Patricia Draher, 3. San Francisco: The Mexican Museum, 1993.

Schmidt, Rob. "Superman vs. The Mexica." *Indian Comics Irregular* #63, August 10, 2001. https://groups.yahoo.com/neo/groups/IndianComicsIrregular/conversations/topics/49.

Singh, Nikhil Pal. "The Whiteness of Police." *American Quarterly* 66, no. 4 (2014): 1091–99.

Storr, Robert. "Stratagies." In *Enrique Chagoya: Borderlandia*, edited by Patricia Hickson, 29–32. Des Moines, IA: Des Moines Art Center, 2007.

Torres, Anthony. "Enrique Chagoya @ Gallery Paule Anglim." *Whitehot Magazine*, February 2011, https://whitehotmagazine.com/articles/enrique-chagoya-gallery-paule-anglim/2210.

Watkin, Mel. "Utopian Cannibal: Adventures in Reverse Anthropology." In *Utopian Cannibal: Adventures in Reverse Anthropology—an Exhibition of Work by Enrique Chagoya*, edited by Mel Watkin and Manuel Ocampo, 7–30. St. Louis, MO: Forum for Contemporary Art, 2001.

PART II

# Reaching toward Whiteness

CHAPTER 7

# SEEING WHITE

## Normalization and Domesticity in Vision's Cyborg Identity

ESTHER DE DAUW

FIRST INTRODUCED in Marvel Comics's *The Avengers* #57 (October 1968), Vision is a cyborg created by the artificial intelligence Ultron. Rebelling against his creator, Vision joins the Avengers and, throughout the ensuing decades, explores the conditions and limitations of humanity. By focusing on Vision's origin story and highlighting key moments in the character's publication history, this chapter demonstrates how white domesticity functions as a gateway to hegemonic privilege. As a character within a multi-authored, transmedial fictional universe, Vision demonstrates how comics, as a media platform, engage with dominant social and cultural narratives defining white masculinity through the lens of white domesticity. Especially in the miniseries *The Vision and the Scarlet Witch* (1985), Vision's relationship with Wanda Maximoff (Scarlet Witch) simultaneously solidifies his status as a man and draws it into doubt through fears of miscegenation. In 2004, Wanda kills Vision, framing nonwhite femininity as corrupting white masculinity, leading to the destruction of heteronormative domesticity. The 2015 *The Vision* series follows a similar narrative where the Other haunts and infects white domesticity. This analysis reveals how, historically, Vision has embodied the link between white masculinity and domesticity, while the Other inevitably fails to adequately perform either.

## White Masculinity as Superhero Norm

Superhero comics are often accused of failing to engage with race in meaningful ways, partly because there are so few superheroes of color. Yet, such claims play into comics' engagement with whiteness as the invisible, nonracial norm. As anthropologist Jane H. Hill argues, whiteness constructs itself as inherently superior to nonwhite cultures and people, whose moral failings, rather than institutionalized forms of discrimination, prevent them from reaching parity with white people.[1] Most superheroes protect this status quo, including black superheroes whose performance of whiteness is informed by adherence to the white status quo. In contrast stands Kenneth Ghee's culture-bound superhero, who "is working to save *his own* people *first*, in the context of saving humanity."[2] Considering the white status quo as fundamentally discriminatory, superheroism itself must be newly conceptualized for it to adequately portray the values attributed to it. Superheroes of color who are not culture bound, despite their explicit or implicit engagement with race, perform whiteness and reaffirm white-as-norm standards. Additionally, the racial Other is literally white in aliens/mutants as race metaphors, for example in the Atlanteans, Kryptonians, and the majority of the X-Men.[3] The superhero cyborg falls into a similar category. Feminist theorist Donna Haraway makes a compelling case for the cyborg's ability to complicate social categories of race, gender, and sexuality, rendering it a threatening figure to rigid identity structures.[4] However, literary critic Malini Johar Schueller suggests that the cyborg's commitment to blurring boundaries is suspect.[5] Because of white-as-norm culture, the cyborg's supposed lack of racial markers does not necessarily indicate a post-race existence, but confers whiteness instead. Caught between Haraway and Schueller, the cyborg is an ominous figure who performs whiteness convincingly, until it does not, at which point the threat of its nonwhite identity must be contained or destroyed.

Marvel's Vision represents such a cyborg Other. As a technological being, Vision is supposedly devoid of race and yet is often constructed as white through his relationship with or search for humanity. From the very beginning, storylines focusing on Vision are concerned with his status as a man, both in terms of humanity and masculinity. This human masculinity

---

1. Hill, *The Everyday Language*, 23
2. Ghee, "Will the "Real" Black Superheroes Please Stand Up?!," 231.
3. Singer, "Black Skins," 110.
4. Haraway, *Simians, Cyborgs and Women*, 154.
5. Schueller, "Analogy and (White) Feminist Theory," 77.

is defined through performances of domesticity, reflecting hegemonic masculinity's inevitable enmeshment with heterosexuality in dominant American narratives.[6] While the dimensions of white masculinity's investment in white domesticity have shifted over the long history of their entanglement, their core idealization of the benevolent white patriarch, the obedient wife, and their children inheriting a white legacy has remained the same. It is this hegemonic position—white, masculine, and paternal—that Vision strives to inhabit by becoming both the rightful heir of the white patriarch and the white patriarch himself.

## Origins of the Heir

When Vision first appears as an enemy of the Avengers in 1968, he is described as "every inch a human being . . . except that all his bodily organs are constructed of synthetic materials!"[7] Vision's status as either man or machine is made complex over the course of his early appearances, especially by the nebulous definition of humanity wielded by *The Avengers*. If Vision is "every inch" the human, even when his body is mechanical or artificial, what about him is human and how does the comic define humanity? Initially, Vision refers to himself as artificial and wonders "if a creature such as I be allowed to have emotions!"[8] But when confronting Ultron, Vision claims that he has risen above the "mere imitation of a human being" Ultron intended him to be.[9] To Vision, his humanity is both questionable and readily apparent. Hank Pym insists that Vision is a man "trapped forever in an android body," but other characters and the narrator often accuse Vision of being cold and robot-like despite his internal(ized) humanity.[10] These early Vision storylines maintain the tension between the insistence that Vision is human but also not-human, or not human enough, and set the tone for the character's development for decades.

After the Avengers and Vision defeat Ultron together, they discover that Ultron stole the brain patterns of Simon Williams, also known as Wonder Man, to create Vision's mind. The link to white Wonder Man as a proto-Vision strengthens the illusion that Vision's "natural," or even biological, identity is white. This allows him to further reject Ultron as his creator

---

6. Kimmel, *Manhood in America*, 105.
7. Thomas, Buscema, and Rosen, "Behold . . . The Vision!"
8. Thomas, Buscema, and Rosen, "Behold . . . The Vision!"
9. Thomas, Buscema, and Rosen, "Behold . . . The Vision!"
10. Thomas, Buscema, and Rosen, "Even an Android Can Cry."

in order to establish a white lineage. Vision's white masculinity is further cemented through the familial bonds he establishes with other characters, especially his romantic interest, Wanda. Initially, Vision struggles to accept his feelings, believing that his "electronic emotions do not include—human—love."[11] Not until Vision is confronted by Wonder Man's brother, the Grim Reaper, in *Avengers* #107 (January 1973) does he consider himself to be his own man. The Grim Reaper reveals that he has recovered Wonder Man's body and offers to place Vision's brain inside of it. This would restore Wonder Man completely and give Vision the chance to literally join humanity. Vision refuses and realizes that he does not consider himself to simply be Wonder Man's copy. He considers himself a (hu)man, regardless of his synthetic body. As a result, Vision accepts his feelings for Wanda and pursues a romantic relationship with her. Vision's self-acceptance as (hu)man leads to the realm of domestic heteronormativity, demonstrating how white masculinity and heterosexuality are consolidated into a definition of humanity that is culturally exalted.

The comics' conflation of whiteness, masculinity, and humanity becomes increasingly apparent as Vision establishes familial ties with other white male characters. In *The Avengers* #116 (October 1973), the team discovers that Ultron did not build Vision's robot body.[12] Instead, he modified the already existing synthezoid or android body of the original Human Torch made during WWII.[13] This revelation further cements Vision's masculinity and claim to whiteness, as both Vision's body (Human Torch) and his mind (Wonder Man) are inherited from white men. Furthermore, the Human Torch was designed by Phineas Horton, establishing a white father figure for Vision to emulate. By becoming the heir to a white father, Vision conceptualizes himself as a white man. Rejecting Ultron was Vision's first step toward becoming a superhero, as it constitutes an initial rejection of the cyborg's potential Otherness and reifies a commitment to white normativity. Choosing to serve with the white superheroes and following in his white father's footsteps seals Vision's commitment to white superheroism and white masculinity.

---

11. Englehart, Starlin, Tuska, and Vladimir, "The Master Plan."
12. Englehart, Esposito, and Costanza, "The Avengers vs the Defenders."
13. Burgos and Schomburg, "Introducing Toro."

## Vision's Domestic Whiteness: The Son Becomes the Father

Vision's whiteness as rooted in domestic normalcy is particularly evident in the twelve-part 1985 miniseries *The Vision and the Scarlet Witch*, which focuses on Vision and Wanda's marriage and their life in white suburbia. Here, Vision and Wonder Man (who came back from the dead in 1984) establish a close, brotherly connection, and together they visit Wonder Man's mother, who Vision declares is also his mother. Through his connection with Wonder Man, Vision gains a white human family, prompting him to tell Wanda he wants them to have children. Taking place in the 1980s, the series's scenes of domesticity reveal a preoccupation with white middle-class suburbia and the state of American domesticity, as all of Vision and Wanda's neighbors, family, and friends are white. The 1980s Vision, building on the masculinity established in the late 1960s and early 1970s, lays the groundwork for a fundamental aspect of white masculinity: white procreation and maintaining a white legacy for his offspring to inherit.

Vision and Wanda's move into the suburbs to start married life and raise a family plays into important racial narratives about desegregation and white flight in postwar America. Urban historian Kevin M. Kruse documents how the political rhetoric of segregation (particularly in terms of housing, schools, and public services) in the 1960s evolved into the 1980s language of middle-class concerns about city life and suburban communities. In the 1950s and 1960s, white segregationists charged that integration would cause the destruction of their community. Since the 1950s concept of "togetherness," suburbia was hailed as a (white) couple/family's retreat from the outside world, and integration was framed as an attack on the white father's right to protect his family and the community they belonged to. Campaigning to prevent their neighborhood from "going black," "whites in borderline neighbourhoods began stressing their common ties, their common rights, and their common goals" in order to "present a united front."[14] The rhetoric of white suburban communities revolved around the preservation of white spaces for future generations. When black families did move into predominantly white neighborhoods, whites fled to white enclaves.[15] By the 1980s, most of the rhetoric around white flight and white suburbia in mainstream American culture lost its explicitly racial tones, even while it remained rooted in a racist history and ideology. Instead, the political rheto-

---

14. Kruse, *White Flight*, 80.
15. Kruse, *White Flight*, 264.

ric characterized suburbia as a neutral and nonpolitical atmosphere for raising children. Implicitly, the suburbs were white, affluent, and middle-class while the city was poor, black, and crime-ridden. In the explicit discourse of 1980s America, however, suburban families were only looking for a community in which to raise families, free from the pollution and political unrest of the city. White flight was characterized by a desire to preserve white spaces as a legacy white offspring could inherit to maintain whiteness as an institutionalized way of life. White masculinity, in turn, is predicated on the ability to sustain whiteness, now and in the future, through white procreation and the preservation of the white community.

Vision and Wanda's decision to move into the New Jersey suburb of Leonia mirrors white flight's explicit rhetoric and its implicit investment in the preservation of white supremacy. Vision and Wanda move to Leonia because they are looking for a quiet place to settle down together as newlyweds and take a break from the Avengers lifestyle. Their entry into suburbia is resisted by the community, further playing into cultural narratives surrounding white flight. For instance, on Halloween, their house is burned down and they are forced to temporarily move back into the Avengers Mansion. Eventually, they decide to leave the Avengers permanently and return to Leonia, which is depicted as an ideal suburb, "small and forested, residential."[16] Their realtor, Norm Webster, explains that "the climate for tolerance in this area's not what it once was."[17] Webster goes on to say that he is "proud to have two Avengers living in Leonia, and so are—most of my friends!"[18] Norman's insistence on being tolerant and having tolerant friends mirrors the dialogue used in the debates of suburban resistance to urban expansion in the 1980s. The white community considered itself progressive and deflected its own racism by externalizing the violence done to nonwhite people as perpetrated by the fringe few, which maintained white-as-norm culture.[19] Vision and Wanda insist that all they have to do is demonstrate their humanity and their neighbors will accept them. In effect, this perpetuates the idea that if nonwhite people could only act "normal," meaning white, they could gain access to white spaces and institutionalized white privilege.

When Vision and Wanda are moving into their second home in *The Vision and the Scarlet Witch* #4 (January 1986), one group of residents attempts to intimidate Webster into sabotaging the purchase of their house. Webster refuses and claims the men are living in the past, playing into the rhetoric

---

16. Englehart, Migrom, and Orzechowski, "Sons!"
17. Englehart, Howell, and Buhalis, "Lovers."
18. Englehart, Howell, and Buhalis, "Lovers."
19. Kruse, *White Flight*, 80.

of racism as a dated, superseded ideology.[20] While these men are framed as an extreme minority, the narrative also insists that these men are good, normal, white people, leaders of their community who are only confused by the changing times—a presentation that echoes the rhetoric of 1980s normalization of white suburbia and segregation. They are worried Vision and Wanda will bring the problems of the city to their peaceful suburbs and endanger their families, reiterating the cultural narrative of the black city as a threat to white suburbs. The problem with this narrative is that Vision and Wanda initially pass as white, which means that their ability to function as an allegory for racial discrimination falls flat. There is no way for whiteness to embody the racism faced by nonwhite peoples. Comics scholar Marc Singer points out that when white superheroes symbolically represent race, they fail to represent real instances of racism, erasing racial experiences and differences instead, further normalizing white hegemony.[21] Vision and Wanda perpetuate this discourse as they represent the Other while performing whiteness in a narrative that furthers white-as-norm culture.

In *The Vision and the Scarlet Witch* #3 (December 1985), Vision and Wanda decide to have children despite Vision's mechanical body, and Wanda channels a powerful magic that impregnates her. In the following issue, Wanda insists that because Vision was holding her and she could feel his love, he's the father. Even as the Avengers and other characters express surprise at Wanda's pregnancy, most seem to accept this process as natural, with Dr. Strange vouching for the magical pregnancy's normalcy. In the following issue, when the men who set fire to their first house attack Vision and Wanda, she reveals she is pregnant and says that since they are all parents, they "want the same thing—a quiet and secure place to raise our families!"[22] Her pregnancy serves as proof of Vision's masculinity, as the ability to father white children is crucial in the construction of white domesticity. It is Vision's fathering of children that lends legitimacy to their claim to domesticity. Reflecting the common rhetoric of families fleeing the city for a more secure place to raise their children, Wanda explicitly unites the ideals of white suburbia with heteronormativity as fundamental to domesticity and hegemonic masculinity. Her appeal succeeds and the previously antagonistic residents leave Vision and Wanda alone. While the narrative of Vision and Wanda's struggle to be accepted into Leonia can be read as an analogy for the discrimination that black and other nonwhite people face, their performance of whiteness reinforces the ideology of white suburbia and its tradi-

---

20. Englehart, Howell, and Rosen, "Mutant Romance Tales."
21. Singer, "Black Skins," 110–11.
22. Englehart, Howell, and Rosen, "Mutant Romance Tales."

tional gender roles. Vision and Wanda's success rests on their phenotypically white appearance, which temporarily allows them to participate in whiteness. In the miniseries, Vision and Wanda function as a superpowered couple who protect their white family from threatening outside forces, like all families in the suburbs do, and bring their extended family closer together. This particular narrative in the midst of the Reaganite 1980s portrays Vision as the benevolent white patriarch who protects all his (white) dependents, like the superhero protecting (white) society from dangerous outside (non-white) forces, thereby reinforcing white-as-norm culture even as Vision and Wanda's underlying subjectivities upset it.

## Miscegenation and White Manhood Destroyed

Vision's search for humanity is intimately connected to his masculinity, which is defined through his heterosexual relationship. His time with Wanda highlights his humanity, but when their relationship falls apart, Vision's Otherness becomes more apparent. In *West Coast Avengers #37* (October 1988), Vision and Wanda decide to return to the Avengers. They leave the supposed safety of the suburbs for the more urban Avengers compound in Los Angeles and the narrative increasingly Others their family, in the process destroying Vision's white masculinity. In *West Coast Avengers #42–45* (March–June 1989), Vision is kidnaped by a government agency and disassembled.[23] When dismantled, his memory is erased and his backup files in the Avengers' computers are destroyed. While he has been given all available information about his life as it was, he has no emotional connection to the events, the Avengers, or Wanda. With his memory and humanity lost, Vision also loses his familial and domestic connections to Wanda, his children, and his adoptive family. Wonder Man rejects Vision as a brother because he considers Vision to be a copy of his own soul. This also erases Vision's connection to Wonder Man's mother. Phineas Horton returns and reveals that Vision's body is not the Human Torch's after all, nor was he built by Horton. Wanda struggles to accept this new Vision as her husband and their children do not interact with this new Vision. In the span of several issues, Vision loses all his ties to his white inheritance and the white masculinity it bequeathed him. In the eyes of the Avengers, Vision's loss of manhood delegitimizes his humanity, his masculinity, his marriage, and his fatherhood.

---

23. Byrne, Sienkiewicz, and Buscema, *Avengers West Coast: VisionQuest*.

Vision's white manhood, partly established through his white family with Wanda, is further eroded through Wanda's Otherness. During "Vision-Quest," the narrative occasionally turns to Wanda's children, William and Thomas, demonstrating how the children mysteriously disappear and reappear. In *West Coast Avengers* #52 (December 1989), Agatha Harkness, Wanda's former teacher, reveals that the children disappear because Wanda no longer actively thinks about them. She explains that they "are not real, child. They are manifestations of Wanda's will."[24] When Wanda is not channeling her power, the children vanish. In the late 1980s, Wanda's desire to leave her children with a nanny while she works renders her femininity suspect and endangers the children's existence. The mass media of the 1980s focused intensely on the working woman who turned away from her career because she preferred to stay at home. As feminist journalist Susan Faludi points out, while there was no statistical evidence to support this narrative, the media focused on anecdotal evidence to prove its point that with the gains of feminism, women now realized they preferred to stay home.[25] The phenomenon was referred to as "cocooning" and, similar to the 1950s concept of "togetherness," projected the idea that families preferred to stay at home and spend all their time together. The crucial difference between the two is that while the 1950s concept referred to the home as a man's refuge from the outside world, the 1980s version was a trend "defined not as *people* coming home but as *women* abandoning the office."[26] Cocooning was informed by the national myth that sending children to day care was damaging to the mother-child bond and could cause irreparable damage to children's psyche.[27] While Vision and Wanda's time in suburbia is exemplary of both togetherness and cocooning, her return to work and leaving the children with a nanny is framed as destructive to their family, ultimately causing her and Vision's white progeny to literally cease existing.

John Byrne's *West Coast Avengers* run insists that Wanda's creation of her children is an unavoidable and natural consequence of her upbringing and heritage. Wanda's Otherness and monstrous identity, as a mutant, Romani, or a witch, are framed as biological. This narrative plays into the exoticization of Romani women as having a supernatural sexual allure that is irresistible to white men and seduces them away from deserving white women to the detriment of future white generations. Vision's failure to bodily and technologically father children is a failure to contain not only Wanda's "nat-

---

24. Byrne and Oakley, "Fragments."
25. Faludi, *Backlash*, 109–10.
26. Faludi, *Backlash*, 109–10.
27. Faludi, *Backlash*, 64–65.

ural" feminine desire for children but also her Romani heritage and sexual power. Her nonwhite identity perverts the normative masculine role within traditional white heterosexual domestic life. In effect, she sabotages Vision's attempts to create white offspring, which is fundamental to establishing a white masculinity. When Vision cannot control his wife and children, he no longer passes as white and his role as a superhero within the Avengers diminishes. At the end of *Avengers West Coast* #52, the children are destroyed and Agatha Harkness erases Wanda's memory of them. Vision and Wanda separate and, for the next two decades, have an on-again-off-again relationship. However, in the "Avengers Disassembled" storyline, appearing in *Avengers* #500–503 (September–December 2004) and *Avengers: Finale* #1 (January 2005), Wanda regains her memories. She takes revenge on the Avengers for stealing her children, destroys Avengers Mansion, and kills several team members, including Vision. Dr. Strange reveals that Wanda's actions are the result of a mental breakdown caused by her powers.[28] He places the source of Wanda's instability in her mutant identity, which the comics have historically conflated with her stereotyped Romani heritage. This frames Wanda as a threatening Other whose monstrosity is rooted in a racialized and gendered identity, the intersection of which threatens and ultimately destabilizes the superiority claims of white masculinity. With Vision dead and the Avengers disbanded, the Other's destruction of white domesticity leads to the destruction of white superheroism and white masculinity.

## The Return of the Destructive Other

In 2015, Marvel began publishing *The Vision*, which details Vision's attempts to construct a new life and family by building a cyborg wife (Virginia) and cyborg twins (Vin and Viv). Most of the art by Gabriel Hernandez Walta in *The Vision* features a comforting middle-class domestic aesthetic with open floor plans and nicely trimmed yards. However, there is something uncanny in the art's stereotypical 1950s nostalgia, revealing the dark truths hidden underneath the respectable veneer of white domesticity. The family's performance of domestic normalcy and, by extension, of whiteness, continuously fails as the outside world intrudes and the racialized cyborg Other haunts the narrative.

According to historian Stephanie Coontz, 1950s American media was invested in creating the nuclear family as a completely self-sufficient unit

---

28. Bendis and Finch, *Avengers Disassembled*.

while "sociologists argued that modern industrial society required the family to jettison traditional productive functions and wider kin ties."[29] In order to construct a family that would properly benefit the child and the parents, the family's energy had to be focused solely inward. The concept of "togetherness" promoted the idea that couples should do everything together and rely only on each other. White suburbs supposedly facilitated this, as a lack of political unrest and the presence of a suitably traditional (read: white) community would allow a white patriarch to construct a safe space for his family. This rhetoric reappeared in different forms in the 1960s segregation debate focusing on the preservation of the white community. White homeowners in the 1960s insisted that the relationship between the community and the nuclear family was symbiotic. The nuclear family functioned as a retreat from the outside world and the community was an extension of that retreat. In effect, white families maintained their domestic isolation by creating a community that served as a buffer between them and the (black) city. Without the community, the nuclear family would fall apart and vice versa. This narrative resurfaced in the 1980s discourse of cocooning, and in contemporary nostalgia for and idealization of the 1950s.

In *The Vision*, Vision's family is completely isolated. Since they were built by Vision, Virginia and her children have no extended family, and while Vision often speaks to his work colleagues and other Avengers, the family itself rarely interacts with nonfamily members. The children attend school, but they do not really establish close ties to other children "their age," even when Vision purposefully splits them up to attend different classes. Virginia is still trying to settle on a career, and she is often depicted as being alone in the house or observing her family from afar. While this domestic isolation is often framed as a source of comfort in wider American media, both in the 1950s and in contemporary 1950s nostalgia productions, the comic seemingly depicts it as sinister. The family's performance of the 1950s nuclear family is desperate, almost farcical. Supposedly, the white family can be fully nurtured and protected by the white father, but Vision fails to properly embed his family within the community. Their domestic isolation stands apart from the white community, instead of reinforcing it.

On the surface, the Visions are a perfect family and Vision's creation of this family secures his white masculinity. The father works, their mother reviews the children's homework after they have all sat down together for dinner, and they go to bed at reasonable hours. Except, of course, that the children's homework does not need to be checked because their brains do

---

29. Coontz, *The Way We Never Were*, 26.

not make errors, and they sit down together at the dinner table, but they do not eat. They lie down in the dark but do not require sleep. Virginia, Viv, and Vin are constructed fully in Vision's image, sharing his abilities: flying, phasing, and the use of a solar laser. However, Vision insists that they always present themselves as human. Suppressing their special abilities, which Vision purposefully gave them when he built them, is fundamental to passing as human. White-as-norm culture requires the active suppression of the Other by white-passing individuals in order to construct whiteness. Despite (or because of) this consciously created suppression of the Other, the Visions' white performance fails. The dangers of the city and the past, namely Vision's origins and his relationship with Wanda, continuously intrude on the isolation of the family.

In many ways, *The Vision* is a retelling of the 1985 *The Vision and the Scarlet Witch* miniseries. Both are premised on Vision and his female partner moving into the suburbs to start a new life and raise children. As in the 1985 miniseries, in *The Vision*, the family is confronted with prejudice in the neighborhood and, in one instance, has their garage door vandalized. In 2015, *The Vision* creative team directly engaged with Vision and Wanda's past as the series draws parallels between Vision's past relationship with Wanda and his current relationship with Virginia. Wanda's violent actions, attributed to her biological nature, haunt the narrative from within Virginia. In the first issue, Vision wakes from an artificial sleep cycle and finds "himself in a state of dread, his thoughts caught on a repeating image of the day he first saw his wife open her eyes. Over and over he saw her eyelids rise, her pupils grow and recede, like a camera lens adjusting to the light. And for a reason he could not understand, this scared him."[30] Virginia's very existence haunts Vision as once again, nonwhite femininity threatens white hegemonic masculinity. In issue #7, the narrative reveals Virginia is based on a copy of Wanda's brain patterns.[31] Vision is consistently unsettled by the cyborg woman he built and her neurological similarity to Wanda, the violent ex-wife who killed him as a result of her mental breakdown. He attempts to simultaneously rewrite the past by using Wanda's brain patterns, incorporating her into the new story, and purge its violence by building Virginia, whose body is meant to function as a white filter to purify Wanda's nonwhite heritage, allowing her to embody whiteness the same way Vision does. Throughout the series, he lingers on his relationship with

---

30. King, Walta, Bellaire, and Cowles, "Visions."
31. King, Walsh, Bellaire, and Cowles, "I Too."

Wanda and attempts to recreate special moments between them in his relationship with Virginia.

Vision's past marriage with Wanda continually resurfaces. The Grim Reaper, obsessed with the idea that Vision is a copy of his brother, Wonder Man, attacks the family, almost kills Viv, and injures Vin. Virginia, in an attempt to protect her children, kills the Grim Reaper. The villain's death sets off a cycle of events that causes the neighborhood to grow increasingly hostile toward the cyborg family, prompting Virginia's further attempts to protect them, all of which end in death and destruction. Virginia consistently responds to threatening situations in an emotional and violent manner, mimicking Wanda's hysterical emotionalism in 2004 when she destroyed the Avengers. Virginia kills not only the Grim Reaper but also Chris Kinzky, a young white boy who goes to school with Viv, and puts his father, Leo Kinzky, in a coma. When Vision becomes aware of the situation, he is compelled to lie to protect Virginia and increasingly compromises his own moral position. This leads the Avengers to become increasingly suspicious of where Vision's loyalty lies. They send another cyborg, Victor Mancha, to spy on the family and report back. The Avengers, as the guardians of institutionalized white superheroism, begin to suspect Vision is no longer one of them, of having become Other. In effect, they suspect his (lack of) white masculinity. Events spiral out of control even further when Victor accidentally kills Vin and Vision decides to kill Victor in return. In the end, Virginia kills Victor before Vision can and she commits suicide after confessing all of her crimes. Accidentally, but inevitably, Virginia destroys the family, and this violence spills out into the community Vision strove to be a part of.

Vision's choice to protect Virginia instead of the white status quo corrupts his enactment of white masculinity and superheroism, turning him into a threatening Other. Vision fails to control his wife, which both is the cause of and is caused by his lack of white masculinity. His inability to control Virginia causes her Otherness to infect his performance of white masculinity, mirroring his relationship with Wanda. Yet, the narrative insists that the attempt must be made, again and again. The search for white domesticity by those outside of whiteness is framed as normal and even morally correct while its (inevitable) failure is depicted as sad and tragic. Even as Viv explains to her father that she is not normal, they remain in the family house in the suburbs and Viv continues to attend school. While the narrative demonstrates that the performance of white identity cannot be sustained and will not grant nonwhite individuals access to privileged spaces, it maintains the idea of whiteness as fundamental to existence. In the series' last few panels, Vision is seen attempting to rebuild Virginia in secret, implying that whiteness must be sought out even in death. The panels are disturbingly sinister and Vision, who seems poised to become a new villain rather than a superhero, fully inhabits the destructive and threatening Other.

## Conclusion

As a white-performing character, Vision falls into two categories. As a cyborg, he fits into well-established patterns of using white-passing identities as an allegory for the racial Other. He also performs white manhood through his search for a white heritage and family. However, his partners' presentation of nonwhite femininity corrupts their relationship and, by extension, his own manhood. It is Vision's failure to control and contain nonwhite femininity that destroys his white masculinity. The cyborg identity becomes Othered and is the source for his failing as a man and as a superhero. The four-decade character history of Vision offers a case study into how superhero comics and American culture construct whiteness and masculinity as inextricably linked, and how failure to successfully perform the identity of the white man leads to social, and often real, death. Vision simultaneously promotes the performance of whiteness as the only way to gain access to privileged spaces, while also highlighting how the venture is inevitably doomed for nonwhite individuals. While cultural narratives present the inability to construct white domesticity as a personal, individual weakness, they simultaneously present that weakness as being grounded in the Other's nature instead of the structural inequalities kept in place by hegemony. These narratives inscribe performance of whiteness as the only possible moral lifestyle the superhero may embody, protect, and promote. For Vision, and the Other, there is no way in or out of whiteness.

## Bibliography

Bendis, Michael Brian (writer), and David Finch (artist). *Avengers Disassembled.* New York: Marvel Comics, 2005.

Burgos, Carl (writer, letterer), and Alex Schomburg (artist). "Introducing Toro, the Flaming Torch Kid." *Human Torch Comics*, vol. 1, #2. New York: Marvel Comics, October 1940.

Byrne, John (writer, artist), and Bill Oakley (letterer). "Fragments of a Greater Darkness." *Avengers: West Coast*, vol. 1, #52. New York: Marvel Comics, December 1989.

Byrne, John (writer), Bill Sienkiewicz (artist), and John Buscema (penciller). *Avengers West Coast: VisionQuest.* New York: Marvel Comics, 2005.

Coontz, Stephanie. *The Way We Never Were: American Families and the Nostalgia Trap*. London: Hachette UK, 2016.

Englehart, Steve (writer), Mike Esposito (artist), and John Costanza (letterer). "The Avengers vs the Defenders Chapter 2: Betrayal!" *The Avengers*, vol. 1, #116. New York: Marvel Comics, October 1973.

Englehart, Steve (writer), Richard Howell (artist), and Lois L. Buhalis (letterer). "Lovers." *The Vision and the Scarlet Witch*, vol. 2, #1. New York: Marvel Comics, October 1985.

Englehart, Steve (writer), Richard Howell (artist), and Joe Rosen (letterer). "Mutant Romance Tales." *The Vision and the Scarlet Witch*, vol. 2, #4. New York: Marvel Comics, January 1986.

Englehart, Steve (writer), Al Migrom (artist), and Tom Orzechowski (letterer). "Sons!" *West Coast Avengers*, vol. 2, #2. New York: Marvel Comics, November 1985.

Englehart, Steve (writer), Jim Starlin (artist), George Tuska (artist), and Denise Vladimir (letterer). "The Master Plan of the Space Phantom!" *The Avengers*, vol. 1, #107. New York: Marvel Comics, January 1973.

Faludi, Susan. *Backlash: The Undeclared War against Women*. New York: Random House, 2010.

Ghee, Kenneth. "'Will the "Real" Black Superheroes Please Stand Up?!' A Critical Analysis of the Mythological and Cultural Significance of Black Superheroes." In *Black Comics: Politics of Race and Representations*, edited by Sheena C. Howard, 223–38. New York: Bloomsbury Academic, 2014.

Haraway, Donna. *Simians, Cyborgs and Women: The Reinvention of Nature*. New York: Routledge, 1991.

Hill, Jane H. *The Everyday Language of White Racism*. Chichester, UK: Wiley-Blackwell, 2008.

Kimmel, Michael. *Manhood in America: A Cultural History*. New York: Princeton University Press, 2008.

King, Tom (writer), Gabriel Hernandez Walta (penciller, inker), Jordie Bellaire (colorist), and Clayton Cowles (letterer). "Visions of the Future." *The Vision*, vol. 2, #1. New York: Marvel Comics, January 2016.

King, Tom (writer), Michael Walsh (penciller, inker), Jordie Bellaire (colorist), and Clayton Cowles (letterer). "I Too Shall Be Saved by Love." *The Vision*, vol. 2, #7. New York: Marvel Comics, July 2016.

Kruse, Kevin M. *White Flight: Atlanta and the Making of Modern Conservatism*. Princeton, NJ: Princeton University Press, 2013.

Schueller, Malini Johar. "Analogy and (White) Feminist Theory: Thinking Race and the Color of the Cyborg Body." *Signs* 31, no. 1 (2005): 63–92.

Singer, Marc. "'Black Skins' and White Masks: Comic Books and the Secret of Race." *African American Review* 36, no. 1 (2002): 107–19.

Thomas, Roy (writer), John Buscema (artist), and Sam Rosen (letterer). "Behold . . . The Vision!" *The Avengers*, vol. 1, #57. New York: Marvel Comics, October 1968.

———. "Even an Android Can Cry." *The Avengers*, vol. 1, #58. New York: Marvel Comics, November 1968.

CHAPTER 8

# "BEWARE THE FANATIC!"

Jewishness, Whiteness, and Civil Rights in *X-Men* (1963–1970)

MARTIN LUND

THE PROTAGONISTS of *X-Men*, created by Jewish American comics creators Stan Lee and Jack Kirby and premiering in September 1963, were different from contemporary superheroes. Their powers came not from alien physiology, cosmic rays, or radioactive spider bites; they were mutants. The cliché today is that the X-Men are outsiders, feared and hated by a world they have sworn to protect. Within the comics' universe, mutants' difference has inspired fears among nonmutants and has fostered many of the prejudices that have historically plagued marginalized minority groups. These have included, among other things, forced or voluntary segregation, conspiracy theories about mutants' aims as a group, racial slurs, violent persecution, and genocidal campaigns. But this was not a central theme in the series' initial run, which was cancelled in March 1970. Initially, they were committed Cold Warriors. In their first adventure, for example, the X-Men helped the US military avert sabotage of a nuclear test, while their second ended with a showdown on the White House lawn over stolen American military plans.

Indeed, as products of the Cold War, the early X-Men mostly sought to win other mutants over to their side, while supervillain Magneto's communist-coded Brotherhood of Evil Mutants tried the same, as if the groups were NATO and the Warsaw Pacters, struggling over influence and allies among the unaligned.[1] Moreover, the five WASPish teens that composed the X-Men team and their mentor, Dr. Charles Xavier, lived a lavish, upper-middle-class life in a posh Westchester suburb. While many of their villains were menacing, ugly, or grotesque, the X-Men were attractive and passed as human, even Angel, with his wings hidden by a special harness. Although identity was always a concern, systemic mutant persecution did not become a prevailing theme until after the series' 1975 relaunch, under writer Chris Claremont and various artists.

Nevertheless, because Lee and Kirby were Jewish, and because common wisdom claims that the X-Men have always been outsiders, mutantcy[2] is often read as a coded Jewishness, but mutants have also been called stand-ins for LGBTQ or disabled people or for people of color.[3] The last reading presents the comics as a civil rights allegory and often includes the claim that Xavier and Magneto were modeled on Martin Luther King Jr. and Malcolm X. Setting aside concerns raised by even a quick contextual look—Where is Malcolm X's Islamic theology in Magneto's politics? Where is King's radicalism? What of their mutual respect for one another or the fact they were both growing closer to each other's philosophy by the time of Malcolm X's assassination in 1964?[4]—such readings of Xavier and Magneto are informed by a long-running mythologization of the two black civil rights leaders: King is often sanitized as an inoffensive (to whites' sensibilities) accommodationist while Malcolm X is perennially viewed as only and always an angry separatist. This chapter will argue that perspectives like these oversimplifications are indeed a keynote of early *X-Men* comics, but if King and Malcolm X were in any way inspirations, they were filtered through and subsumed under a white view of the civil rights movement and its discontents. Indeed, to the extent that *X-Men* did eventually engage with civil rights issues, it did so in a way that largely failed to empathize with the oppressed and downtrodden, and that was deeply informed by white fears of the nonwhite Other.

---

1. For another example of Cold War coding, see Lund, "'Introducing the Sensational Black Panther!'"

2. This chapter uses "mutantcy," rather than the more established "mutancy." This distinction is made to mark off the former's fictional nature: "Mutancy" denotes the natural, actual, and real state of being subject to a genetic mutation, whereas "mutantcy" is the state of being a superpowered "mutant" in the Marvel Universe.

3. For a discussion of different readings of this type, see Lund, "The Mutant Problem."

4. See Malcolm X and Haley, *Autobiography of Malcolm X*; King, *The Radical King*; Blake, "Malcolm and Martin."

Ultimately, however, early *X-Men* reads as a negotiation between different understandings and shades of whiteness.

## Ambiguous Mutantcy and Rights Consciousness

The X-Men franchise has a long history of addressing identities, prejudices, and oppressions, if often allegorically and in ways that privilege whiteness. This focus on identity did not appear fully formed, but emerged over time. Lee has claimed that using mutants was a shortcut, simply giving them a "scientific" origin (his scare quotes); mutants existed in nature.[5] Here, Lee trod familiar ground: The mutant "homo superior" trope had been common in science fiction in the 1940s and 1950s.[6] While Lee has said that he eventually came to see mutants as a good metaphor for bigotry, he denies ever having viewed them in terms of Jewishness.[7] That "homo superiors" would be feared if their existence became known was a common idea, so, to the extent that Lee marked mutants as Other, he was again repeating the familiar.[8]

Still, *X-Men*'s eventually becoming a site to address rights consciousness is unsurprising. Labeled a race from the outset, Marvel's "homo superior" mutants were well positioned to broach such topics. Civil rights were highly visible in 1960s US public culture and, by 1965, rights consciousness had begun to seem "all-conquering."[9] Talk of inclusion regardless of sex, race, or creed had become central to the nation's self-definition against communism; the Soviet Union, activists said, denied its citizens equality.[10] More than any other white group, Jewish Americans took part in the struggle. Alongside prominent figures like Martin Luther King Jr. could be seen several influential Jewish American leaders.[11] But mutantcy in *X-Men* was never categorically defined, and when the issue of rights was addressed, it was most often from a cautious or critical perspective.

Indeed, Marvel comics from the 1960s are largely quiet about the decade's social and cultural unrest. Conflict is often handled conservatively, as when the X-Men serve US Cold War interests. Still, Marvel did not com-

---

5. Lee and Mair, *Excelsior!*, 165.
6. Attebery, *Decoding Gender*, 63–64; Trushell, "American Dreams of Mutants," 153–54.
7. Brevoort and Lee, "The Jewish Thing."
8. See Attebery, *Decoding Gender*, chap. 4.
9. Patterson, *Grand Expectations*, 474–78, 480–83, 524–25, 542–47, 579–87.
10. Greenberg, *Troubling the Waters*, chap. 5.
11. Takaki, *Different Mirror*, 389–94; Sarna, *American Judaism*, 306–15.

pletely ignore the civil rights movement. But it is important to not let later developments in the franchise's continuity and politics affect the reading of earlier stories: When *X-Men* began touching on the issue, the X-Men policed mutants who were vocally demanding rights and security, and they fought not to give mutants a place of their own *as mutants,* but to show that "good" mutants were just as good citizens as anyone else. In short, translated into the terms of the day's racial politics, they followed a liberal assimilationist line rather than a radical one, and they actively opposed those who championed the latter. In the mutant world, as in the real US, radical rights activism was a threat to white hegemony and assimilationism a potential way of securing it.

## Identity Emergent

Racialized rhetoric appeared already in *X-Men* #1, when Xavier tells his new student, Jean Grey, about the X-Men's mission, saying that humanity is not yet ready to accept those with powers: "Here we stay, unsuspected by normal humans, as we learn to use our powers for the benefit of mankind . . . to help those who would distrust us if they knew of our existence!"[12] Beyond motivating *X-Men*'s use of the secret identity trope, this line reads as an integrationist appeal: Acceptance will come if mutants demonstrate their worth. While fear and mistrust of mutants is occasionally asserted as an aside in the early *X-Men*, the integrationist impression is deepened by the fact that the team initially works with the US military, the government, and the FBI and are sometimes hailed as heroes by the public.[13] Conversely, many villains, Magneto in particular, express the view that mutants are born to rule, which only serves to deepen their un-American and undemocratic characterization.[14]

The X-Men's integrationism is unsurprising. While US anti-Semitism had reached its historical peak during WWII, phenotypically white Jewish Americans were increasingly accepted in the postwar years. Historian Peter Novick writes: "An integrationist rather than a particularist consciousness was the norm in the postwar decades: difference and specificity were

---

12. Lee et al., *Essential Uncanny X-Men Vol. 1 (hereafter EUX1),* #1, 10. See also #7, 3. See also *EUX1,* #6, 2 and #14, 1, for similar exchanges.
13. Lee et al., *EUX1,* #1, 23; #2, 2, 4, 13, 19; #4: 6; #5, 4; #10, 4; #9, 11; #11, 6, 10, 19; #16, 13; #17, 2.
14. Examples include Lee et al., *EUX1,* #2, 10–11; #3, 23; #4, 5, 9; #5, 8; #7: 5, 8–9; #18, 3; #20, 1.

at a discount; a 'brothers under the skin' and 'family of man' ethos was dominant."[15] Xavier's comments display such a sentiment, reminiscent of ideas that informed much Jewish American civil rights activism. In surveys around the time, many Jewish Americans responded that they "fervently believed" that "Jews are like everyone else," even in the face of the suburban "five o'clock shadow" that kept Jewish and non-Jewish after-work socializing to a minimum. Still, white Jewish Americans were conscious of being marked as different despite their sameness, real or imagined. For his part, Lee confronted Jewish difference when he (wrongly) feared that his mother would not accept his Episcopalian wife, and later when the couple had trouble adopting, because theirs was a "mixed marriage."[16]

There are hints in some Lee/Kirby X-Men stories of double consciousness, a sense of being fully American but not quite full participants in American life,[17] which can easily breed ambivalence or defeatism. In #7 (September 1964), the mutant villain Blob rejects both the Brotherhood and the X-Men: "I'm thru with mutants—thru fighting *other* people's fights!" As the Blob walks away, the X-Man Cyclops replies that "there are good mutants, and bad mutants! And there are also some who *hate* being mutants—some who turn away from the great responsibility their power imposes upon them!"[18] The same message returns in the next issue, when the Beast briefly quits the X-Men after encountering human mob mentality: "I'm *through* risking my life for humans . . . For the *same* humans who fear us, hate us, want to *destroy* us! I think Magneto and his evil mutants are *right* . . . Homo Sapiens just aren't *worth* it!"[19] Before long, however, the Beast realizes that he has the power to fight and, therefore, the responsibility.

Coupled with early *X-Men*'s Cold War coding of inter-mutant struggle, these debates can be read in light of the perceived Cold War threat posed by those "too willing to shirk their public duties to stand up to the communists."[20] Blob betrays the national struggle while Beast comes to his patriotic senses. This reading does not preclude a connection to civil rights, however: Since equality defined the day's juxtaposition of American freedom with communist evil, the events can be read as critiquing those on the

---

15. Peter Novick, *Holocaust in American Life*, 114.
16. Prell, *Fighting to Become Americans*, 157–61, 164–69; Goldstein, *The Price of Whiteness*, 212; Lee and Mair, *Excelsior!*, 69, 74–75.
17. See Prell, *Fighting to Become Americans*, esp. 163–65; Brodkin, *How Jews Became White Folks*.
18. Lee et al., *EUX1*, #7, 22.
19. Lee et al., *EUX1*, #8, 6.
20. Costello, *Secret Identity Crisis*, 27.

civil rights sidelines. Speaking just before King's "I Have a Dream" speech in 1963, for example, Rabbi Joachim Prinz had stressed the importance of the struggle, enlisting the Holocaust as both a universalist motivator for antiracist activism and as a rationale for Jewish participation. Prinz said that as a response to racial injustice, silence was complicity.[21]

## Different Perspectives

In June 1964, President Johnson signed the Civil Rights Act and urged "every American" to join in the effort to "bring justice and hope to all our people—and to bring peace to our land."[22] Not only was it the right thing to do, it was the law. The above-cited comics, then, if they were connected with civil rights, said that equality was everybody's fight. Indeed, Jewish Americans had been by far the most represented white group in the nonviolent and integrationist wing of the civil rights movement, cooperating with activists of color for religious, ideological, and pragmatic reasons. By mid-decade, however, when the movement's gaze increasingly turned to the northern US, cooperation started waning because the movement's aims began to clash with other issues dear to some Jewish American activists, because of increased black nationalism and a concurrent rise in affirmations of Jewishness, purges of white members from civil rights organizations, and an apparent increase in black anti-Semitism.[23]

Highlighting how immigrants had struggled in America and supposedly pulled themselves up by their bootstraps, many white ethnics felt that people of color had the same opportunities, and that seeking group-based considerations and rights or redress for oppression through radical means was unwarranted: Blacks were not especially disadvantaged, the historically unmoored argument went, they were simply latecomers to America.[24] In this context, *X-Men*'s integrationist configuration of the "homo superior" trope appears as an extension of a common failure among liberal Jewish Americans (and among white Americans generally) to identify the structural white privilege that had assisted Jewish and white ethnic social mobility. This failure, which anthropologist Karen Brodkin labels "a Jewish version of Horatio Alger," has led some Jewish American organizations to adopt

---

21. Sarna, *American Judaism*, 310.
22. Johnson, "Remarks upon Signing the Civil Rights Bill."
23. See Dollinger, *Quest for Inclusion*, chaps. 6–7, and *Black Power, Jewish Politics*; Novick, *Holocaust in American Life*, 172–74.
24. See Frye Jacobson, *Roots Too*.

racist attitudes toward African Americans and to oppose affirmative action for people of color, inspiring many Jewish and white liberals to be more willing both to accept compromise and the status quo and to eschew or condemn black radicalism.[25] If one reads early *X-Men* as a civil rights allegory, the struggle between the X-Men and the Evil Mutants then emerges as an argument over tactics along the lines that would ultimately break up the so-called black–Jewish civil rights alliance, such as it was; the X-Men stand for peaceful racial liberalism of a type common among Jewish American rights activists, while the Evil Mutants stand for emergent Black Power and other radical activism.

But a failure of empathy does not necessarily lead to wholesale abandonment. One of Lee and Kirby's most influential stories appeared in *X-Men* #14–16 (November 1965–January 1966). In it, anthropologist Bolivar Trask denounces the "mutant menace": "We've been so busy worrying about cold wars, hot wars, atom bombs, and the like, that we've overlooked the greatest menace of *all!* Mutants walk among us! Hidden! Unknown! Waiting—!—Waiting for their moment to *strike!*"[26] Channeling Trask's anti-mutantism, the press publishes fearmongering stories that enlist shades of McCarthyism, fears of communist influences over civil rights, and racist and nativist-sounding rhetoric about threats to American culture, as expressed, for instance, by the right-wing John Birch Society and the 1964 Republican presidential candidate Barry Goldwater.[27]

In response, Xavier calls for a debate, hoping to "stop the wheels of persecution that have been set in motion" by showing that Trask's theories "are both erroneous and potentially *dangerous!*"[28] During the debate, Trask unveils his mutant-hunting robot Sentinels, which almost immediately go out of control.[29] In the Sentinels' own words, they "were created to be the *guardians* of mankind! And to guard them properly, we must *rule* them completely!"[30] They even threaten to destroy a city if Trask refuses to build

---

25. See Brodkin, *How Jews Became White Folks* (quote from p. 26); Greenberg, *Troubling the Waters*, chap. 6; Frye Jacobson, *Roots Too*, chaps. 4–5; Goldstein, *Price of Whiteness*, 215. This stance also ignores Jewish Americans of color, who face both anti-Semitism and racism.

26. Lee et al., *EUX1*, #14, 3.

27. Patterson, *Grand Expectations*, 156–57, 417, 476, 477; Greenberg, *Troubling the Waters*.

28. Lee et al., *EUX1*, #14, 6.

29. Lee et al., EUX1, #14, 8–9.

30. Lee et al., *EUX1*, #14, 11, 19; also #15, 7.

more Sentinels. Hatred thus takes on a life of its own, and the intolerance of the few becomes a threat to all.[31]

Ultimately, convinced by Beast's articulation of the X-Men's mission to protect humanity, Trask sees the error of his ways.[32] He sacrifices himself to end the threat he created: "In my ignorance, my fear, I created an evil far greater than the menace it was built to destroy!"[33] Trask's lesson, heavy-handedly offered to readers, is to *"beware the fanatic! Too often his cure is deadlier by far than the evil he denounces!"*[34] The Sentinels, who want to rule, are dangerous primarily because they impinge on civil liberties, threatening the freedoms of citizens and using totalitarian means, the way 1950s red-baiters like Joseph McCarthy and J. Edgar Hoover had come close to doing. But Trask's conversion also further argues for the rightness of civil rights, while Beast's mission statement echoes repeated assertions by white Jewish American and black civil rights leaders that they were fighting for democracy, against both communism and the totalitarian impulses of anticommunists.[35]

## New Ink, New Fears

As the series progressed, it became more conservative on civil rights. The shift is clearest after 1966, when Roy Thomas, a lapsed Lutheran from the Midwest, took over writing. Initially, Thomas also addressed Cold War geopolitics, but largely put them to rest by the turn of 1968. When, after a lengthy absence, Magneto reentered the X-Men's orbit in *X-Men* #43 (March 1968), he brought a new focus on rights-related radicalism. Antiradicalism had been present throughout the series but came to the fore when Magneto's follower Quicksilver repeatedly speaks about mutant suffering at human hands and rejects humanity for the mutant cause, signaling in turn a realignment of the primary meaning of the Brotherhood's "evil" from communism to rights radicalism.

At this time, white hegemony had been publicly questioned by the rise and increasing visibility of often radical Black Power and particularist Black Nationalism, and challenged by nearly a half-decade of struggle and

---

31. Lee et al., *EUX1*, #15, 10, 12, 14.
32. Lee et al., *EUX1*, #15, 11; also #16, 6, 7.
33. Lee et al., *EUX1*, #16, 16.
34. Lee et al., *EUX1*, #16, 20, 2.
35. See Greenberg, *Troubling the Waters*, chap. 5.

riots.³⁶ This met with significant reaction, exemplified in white politicians like Barry Goldwater, George Wallace, and Richard Nixon, who won the White House in 1968 on the basis of his "Southern Strategy," characterized by race-baiting, xenophobic dog-whistle rhetoric, and antiblack backlash. In the above comic, Quicksilver embraces Magneto's plan to establish a mutant homeland. Mutants can "lead peaceful, normal lives" in such a place, he says.³⁷ Although conceding that it sounds like "the answer to our *prayers*," Cyclops cannot believe that Magneto is willing to do anything for anyone but himself. Quicksilver, says Cyclops, speaking in terms that echo then-contemporary white fears of Black Nationalism, is a "hate-blinded fool" for believing the evil mutant leader.³⁸ For his parochial pro-mutant activism, Cyclops brands Quicksilver a *"traitor to the human race,"* indicating an inability to empathize with or to understand many black activists' move away from seeking integration to particularist radicalism.³⁹

Magneto next appeared in a storyline by Jewish American writer Arnold Drake (#49–52, October 1968–January 1969). Again, he leads an army of mutant fanatics in a story that, while totalitarian in rhetoric and iconography, seems to tie into increasingly radical black identity politics rather than anticommunism.⁴⁰ The hypnotic mutant Mesmero leads Magneto's servants in awakening "latent mutants."⁴¹ The threat Magneto and his followers pose, narration proclaims, *"staggers* the imagination—and threatens sanity itself!"⁴² When the X-Men storm the headquarters of beings "that feast on the human *soul* itself," they have no intention of "displaying tear-filled tolerance."⁴³ They are there to quash dissent, to uphold the status quo. Eliminating any doubt that their concern with this threat is rooted in real-world developments, Cyclops tells an enemy he disarms that "I *just* enrolled you in the president's campaign against *civil violence!*"⁴⁴

---

36. Patterson, *Grand Expectations*, 448–49, 550–52, 578–84, 652–68; Takaki, *Different Mirror*, 394–95; Greenberg, *Troubling the Waters*, 217–23. Dollinger, *Quest for Inclusion*, 199 claims that 329 riots took place in 257 different cities between 1964 and 1968.

37. Thomas et al., *Essential Classic X-Men Vol. 2* (hereafter ECX2), #43, 8; #44, 4, 9.

38. Thomas et al., ECX2, #45, 10.

39. Thomas et al., ECX2, #45, 7.

40. Examples include Thomas et al., ECX2, #49, 5; #50, 2–4, 13. I simplify here: A later retcon (in #58) this Magneto is revealed to have been a robot.

41. Thomas et al., ECX2, #49, 6, 13.

42. Thomas et al., ECX2, #50, 1; see #52: 8.

43. Thomas et al., ECX2, #50, 5.

44. Thomas et al., ECX2, #50, 6. Johnson spoke often about "civil violence"; see, for example, "Remarks in Indianapolis" and "Speech to the Nation on Civil Disorders."

Mesmero's plan involves brainwashing Lorna Dane, Magneto's alleged daughter and a friend and ally of the X-Men. Mesmero plays on "the *two* most powerful human elements . . . [f]ilial duty and the inner need for *power!*"⁴⁵ This reads like a direct indictment of black identity politics: Increasingly, many Jewish American liberals were starting to view (sometimes anti-Semitic) Black Power as antithetical to pluralism and a danger to democracy.⁴⁶ By repeatedly remarking on her blood ties to Magneto, Lorna symbolically stresses the ostensibly politically destructive and paralyzing potential of parochialism and suggests the growing difficulty among liberal Jewish American civil rights proponents to reconcile competing liberal positions, such as the relationship between activism and respect for law and the democratic process, or between advocating immediate equality and working within the system. Despite having just met Magneto and in spite of her doubts about his agenda, Lorna switches sides, leaving the X-Men for her supposed father and saying in unselfconsciously blunt terms that "the genes we share command me more than *laws* and ethics."⁴⁷ Iceman, on the other hand, underlines how she has been corrupted by such essentialist talk: "They've twisted you—turned you against all that's good!"⁴⁸ *X-Men*, then, was willing to admit that injustices existed, but could not acknowledge any means of opposing them other than individualist integrationism.⁴⁹

## The Dream of Sameness

After a yearlong hiatus, Thomas returned to scripting in *X-Men* #55 (April 1969), and immediately turned what had been a run-of-the-mill action storyline into an anti-prejudicial story with anti-McCarthyist elements. One Judge Chalmers has founded a Federal Council on Mutant Activities and, working with Bolivar Trask's son Larry, is trying to prove that "mutants are a *menace* to human dominance on Earth . . . !" Falsely claiming that the X-Men killed his father, Trask has started a new Sentinel program and captured the X-Men

---

45. Thomas et al., ECX2, #51, 2.
46. Greenberg, *Troubling the Waters*, 222.
47. Thomas et al., ECX2, #50, 11; #51, 2#52, 413; see Greenberg, *Troubling the Waters*, 215, 220–21.
48. Thomas et al., ECX2, #50, 13; #51, 3.
49. Johnson, "Remarks upon Signing the Civil Rights Bill," "Speech before Congress on Voting Rights," and "Remarks on Signing the Civil Rights Act." This argument was made in Marvel comics into the 1970s; see Costello, *Secret Identity Crisis*, 124.

and other mutants.[50] His goal is to demonstrate the "true depths of *mutant depravity*" by fabricating evidence and showing it to the media.[51]

When Trask finds out that he too is a mutant, he attempts, to no avail, to countermand his order to the Sentinels to exterminate the prisoners. Again, hatred takes on a life of its own; Trask is not human, and thus has no authority over the Sentinels. In the end, it is the internal logic of the robots' programming that proves to be their undoing. Cyclops tells them that the human race, like all life forms, is the result of mutation. Thus, if they are truly to protect humanity, they have to neutralize the source of that mutation, the sun. Seemingly recalling the Holocaust, which was at the time slowly transitioning into American public discourse but still not with today's cataclysmic or specifically Jewish connotations,[52] the Sentinels resolve to effect "the *ultimate* resolution to the *mutant question*" and leave for *"the very heart of the raging sun itself!"* Their actions become an argument that the logic of prejudice can turn self-destructive, that inflexibility can lead to dangerous extremes.[53] But, narration suggests, these logics are petty in a dual sense: "On the surface of this world of solar winds . . . of moment-to-moment thermonuclear cataclysm . . . a handful of humanoid forms will make but the most imperceptible of ripples . . . !"[54]

In the final two issues of the initial series (#65–66, February–March 1970), Thomas struck particularly high-sounding notes. In the former, an alien invasion threatens the world and Xavier telepathically summons the compassion of half the planet to beat the enemy. This mental siphoning awakens, among other things, "an *urgency* . . . a fierce desire to right the wrongs of *centuries*" in the multiracial cross-section of humanity from which power is drawn.[55] And in the latter, the series ends on a moralizing and hopeful note: "There are *wrongs* to be righted . . . a *world* to be saved from evil mutants . . . and from *itself*," Xavier tells his students that "it's a *good* world, basically . . . one well *worth* the saving . . . as long as there are people in it like . . . the X Men!"[56]

---

50. Thomas et al., *Essential Classic X-Men Vol. 3* (hereafter *ECX3*), #57, 13–15, 18.
51. Thomas et al., *ECX3*, #58, 2–4; #59, 8–9.
52. See Novick, *Holocaust in American Life*.
53. According to Sanderson, "Interview," 89–90, this resolution was Chris Claremont's idea. Claremont would later state much the same view as the one advanced here in relation to the Nazis and the Moral Majority.
54. Thomas et al., *ECX3*, #59, 18–19.
55. Thomas et al., *ECX3*, #65, 15–19.
56. Thomas et al., *ECX2*, #66, 20.

Despite such pluralist language and hopefulness, however, difference remained uncelebrated and conformity continued to be rewarded. During the X-Men's last pre-cancellation battle with Magneto (#62–63, November–December 1969), the villain creates new mutants for his cause, a plan described as a "twisted, tortured vision of a world ruled by *evil mutants!*"[57] When Magneto is defeated, his victims revert to human form, as if his corrupting separatist ideology was what marked them as Other: "As mutants, they'd have been mere *outcasts* of a society that *hated* them! They'll be *happier* when they're back to *normal!*" The team's ally is not as sure: "*Who* would be happier to . . . to lose vast powers which set them *apart* from other men?" The X-Men's reply is surprising: "Did you say . . . who? *Offhand* [. . .] I can think of at least *five* people, without even *trying!* / And their initials, jungle man, are . . . the *X-Men!*"[58] Even as identity was becoming more and more of a concern for minorities in the US, these X-Men resisted diversity and deemphasized difference in favor of a perceived fundamental unity and human sameness that was expressed in near-monocultural terms, and defended the established social order against those who demanded a change in circumstances.

The difference between this perspective and the one Lee expounded in his "Soapbox" column that appeared regularly in Marvel's comics is small, but telling. Giving voice to a type of thinking that was similarly becoming increasingly criticized in these days, especially by black leaders, Lee wrote in September 1968 that even though the Marvel bullpen shared the same diversity of opinion as Americans everywhere, there was one thing they all agreed on:

> We believe that Man has a divine destiny, and an awesome responsibility—the responsibility of treating all who share this wondrous world of ours with tolerance and respect—judging each fellow human on his own merit, regardless of race, creed, or color. . . . [W]e'll never rest until it becomes a fact, rather than just a cherished dream![59]

---

57. Thomas et al., *ECX3*, #63, 20.
58. Thomas et al., *ECX3*, #63, 20.
59. Reprinted in Lee, *Stan's Soapbox*, 14. A year earlier, African American studies scholar Harold Cruse had chided black integrationists who "have accepted the full essence of the Great American Ideal of individualism" and "want to be full-fledged Americans, without regard to race, creed, or color." Quoted in Schulman, *The Seventies*, 60.

Lee's was still the same Otherhood-informed, liberal universalist, integrationist, and individualist philosophy that stressed tolerance, not sameness, that he had begun the series with. It was that perspective that had made Lee and Kirby's X-Men see their difference as a responsibility and not, as Thomas's did, a burden.

## Concluding Remarks

Stan Lee has denied ever thinking about mutantcy in terms of Jewishness, but from the above it can be argued that under him and Kirby, the X-Men's struggles were at least formulated in a way that converged with contemporary Jewish American majority positions on the major issues that were addressed in the comics. The heroic mutants' anticommunism was staunch, as it was among liberal Jewish Americans in general, and the comics' reconfiguration of the civil rights struggle was not out of place when compared to many other areas of Jewish American life at the time. These X-Men were, if anything, racially liberal, but not radical; they fought for equality of opportunity and integration on the individual level, not social equality for their group as a whole, as was the case for much liberal Jewish American rights activism.[60]

During the Lee/Kirby years, *X-Men* engaged with civil rights from a position of relative privilege over people of color and then, in Roy Thomas's run and Arnold Drake's issues, with definitive privilege. This is only to be expected: Following the rapid postwar acceptance and integration of phenotypically white American Jews, all four comics creators were positioned as white Americans. Lee and Kirby's X-Men, to the extent they are to be regarded as ethno-racially marked by their powers, were a model minority. They used their difference in "constructive" ways, contributed to US security and society, and deferred to authority. This "constructive" use of difference resonates with how sociologist Nathan Glazer and other Jewish Americans intellectuals were at the time representing American Jews as entering the majority through what they perceived as the compatibility between their culture and the country as well as Jews' superiority to African Americans.[61]

---

60. See Greenberg, *Troubling the Waters*.
61. Brodkin, *How Jews Became White Folks*, 144–53. "Glazer's treatment of Jews is a paean to their success at becoming solidly middle-class educationally and occupationally. This he attributes to a strong diaspora culture, strong families, little family breakup, and a 'good' kind of voluntary self-segregation and a low rate of intermarriage.... The

It would appear, from the ways the different perspectives of the X-Men and the Brotherhood were represented, that neither Lee and Kirby nor Thomas or Drake could empathize with those who demanded restitution for systemic inequalities. That the Evil Mutants were always instigators, engaged in "destructive" behaviors, and were never framed as being legitimate in their radicalism signifies an affinity with the continued—and continuing—white inability to identify or empathize with people of color.[62]

Still, there are whitenesses of different stripes. Lee and Kirby's *X-Men* was marked, if implicitly, by a white Jewishness that emerges when one looks at the difference in intensity of opposition to radical activist stances between their run and the scripts of Thomas and Drake. Lee and Kirby expressed a perspective that appears to have been informed by a Jewish double consciousness, which afforded a modicum of sympathy for the Other. Conversely, the Thomas run and Drake's issues proffer a more vehement resistance that appears to have been informed by a more secure whiteness and, perhaps, a reaction to intense and prolonged criticism of "whitey," the Establishment, and the majority culture, to which Thomas, as a white Midwestern Protestant, belonged by default. Similarly, Drake's story was written when the black–Jewish civil rights alliance had split beyond reconciliation. Thus, the X-Men as represented by Lee and Kirby can be said to interact with American culture on terms that were common to Jewish Americans at the time, and to reflect their Jewish American experience, but mutantcy as a semantic marker was not metaphorized Jewishness. It was, at first, the uneasy whiteness of the racially in between that only later turned into the combative whiteness of the old guard or the recently whitened. This is the foundation upon which the always problematic outsiderhood of Marvel's mutants was built.[63]

---

virtues and rewards that they claimed for themselves as good Jewish sons depended upon showing how similar Jewish culture was to bourgeois cultural ideals and upon differentiating Jewish culture from a depraved and unworthy African American culture." 145.

62. See Patterson, *Grand Expectations*, 380–84, 478–85, 637–38, 649; Frye Jacobson, *Roots Too*.

63. For examples of how mutantcy has been employed in problematic ways, see Shyminsky, "Mutant Readers"; Lund, "'X Marks the Spot.'" See also Shyminsky's chapter in this volume.

# Bibliography

Attebery, Brian. *Decoding Gender in Science Fiction.* New York: Routledge, 2002.

Blake, John. "Malcolm and Martin, Closer Than We Ever Thought." *CNN*, May 19, 2010, http://www.cnn.com/2010/LIVING/05/19/Malcolmx.king/index.html.

Brevoort, Tom, and Stan Lee. *The Jewish Thing: Transcript.* Interview by Brooke Gladstone and Bob Garfield. http://www.onthemedia.org/2002/aug/02/the-jewish-thing/transcript/?utm_source=sharedUrl&utm_media=metatag&utm_campaign=sharedUrl.

Brodkin, Karen. *How Jews Became White Folks and What That Says About Race in America.* New Brunswick, NJ: Rutgers University Press, 1998.

Costello, Matthew J. *Secret Identity Crisis: Comic Books and the Unmasking of Cold War America.* New York: Continuum, 2009.

Dollinger, Marc. *Black Power, Jewish Politics: Reinventing the Alliance in the 1960s.* Lebanon, NH: University Press of New England, 2018.

———. *Quest for Inclusion: Jews and Liberalism in Modern America.* Princeton, NJ: Princeton University Press, 2000.

Frye Jacobson, Matthew. *Roots Too: White Ethnic Revival in Post–Civil Rights America.* Cambridge, MA: Harvard University Press, 2008.

Goldstein, Eric L. *The Price of Whiteness.* Princeton, NJ: Princeton University Press, 2006.

Greenberg, Cheryl Lynn. *Troubling the Waters: Black-Jewish Relations in the American Century.* Princeton, NJ: Princeton University Press, 2006.

Johnson, Lyndon Baines. "Remarks in Indianapolis at a Luncheon with Indiana Business, Labor, and Professional Leaders." *The American Presidency Project*, July 23, 1966, http://www.presidency.ucsb.edu/ws/index.php?pid=27734.

———. "Remarks on Signing the Civil Rights Act." *Miller Center of Public Affairs*, April 11, 1968, http://millercenter.org/president/speeches/detail/4036.

———. "Remarks upon Signing the Civil Rights Bill." *Miller Center of Public Affairs*, July 2, 1964, http://millercenter.org/president/speeches/detail/3525.

———. "Speech before Congress on Voting Rights." *Miller Center of Public Affairs*, March 15, 1965, http://millercenter.org/president/speeches/detail/3386.

———. "Speech to the Nation on Civil Disorders." *Miller Center of Public Affairs*, July 27, 1967, http://millercenter.org/president/speeches/detail/4040.

King, Martin Luther Jr. *The Radical King.* Edited by Cornel West. Boston: Beacon Press, 2015.

Lee, Stan. *Stan's Soapbox: The Collection.* New York: Marvel, 2008.

Lee, Stan (writer), Jack Kirby (artist), Roy Thomas (writer), Alex Toth (penciller), Werner Roth (penciller), Paul Reinman (inker), Chic Stone (inker), Vince Colletta (inker), Joe Sinnott (inker), and Dick Ayers (inker). *Essential Uncanny X-Men Vol. 1.* New York: Marvel Comics, 1999.

Lee, Stan, and George Mair. *Excelsior! The Amazing Life of Stan Lee.* New York: Simon & Schuster, 2002.

Lund, Martin. "'Introducing the Sensational Black Panther!' *Fantastic Four* #52–53, the Cold War, and Marvel's Imagined Africa." *The Comics Grid: Journal of Comics Scholarship* 6 (2016): 1–21.

———. "The Mutant Problem: *X-Men*, Confirmation Bias, and the Methodology of Comics and Identity." *European Journal of American Studies* 10, no. 2 (2015). http://ejas.revues.org/10890.

———. "'X Marks the Spot': Urban Dystopia, Slum Voyeurism and Failures of Identity in *District X*." *Journal of Urban Cultural Studies* 2, no. 1–2 (2015): 34–56.

Malcolm X and Alex Haley. *The Autobiography of Malcolm X*. New York: Ballantine Books, 1999.

Novick, Peter. *The Holocaust in American Life*. Boston: Houghton Mifflin Harcourt, 2000.

Patterson, James T. *Grand Expectations: The United States, 1945–1974*. New York: Oxford University Press, 1997.

Prell, Riv-Ellen. *Fighting to Become Americans: Jews, Gender, and the Anxiety of Assimilation*. Boston: Beacon Press, 1999.

Sanderson, Peter. "Interview with Chris Claremont." In *X-Men Companion I*, edited by Peter Sanderson, 89–122. Stamford, CT: Fantagraphics Books, 1982.

Sarna, Jonathan D. *American Judaism: A New History*. New Haven, CT: Yale University Press, 2004.

Schulman, Bruce J. *The Seventies: The Great Shift in American Culture, Society, and Politics*. Cambridge, MA: Da Capo, 2002.

Shyminsky, Neil. "Mutant Readers, Reading Mutants: Appropriation, Assimilation, and the X-Men." *International Journal of Comic Art* 8, no. 2 (Fall 2006): 387–405.

Takaki, Ronald T. *A Different Mirror: A History of Multicultural America*. New York: Back Bay Books/Little, Brown, 2008.

Thomas, Roy (writer), Arnold Drake (writer), Dennis O'Neil (writer), Don Heck (penciller), Werner Roth (penciller), Neal Adams (penciller), Sal Buscema (penciller), Vince Colletta (inker), Sam Grainger (inker), and Tom Palmer (inker). *Essential Classic X-Men Vol. 3*. New York: Marvel, 2009.

Thomas, Roy (writer), Gary Friedrich (writer), Arnold Drake (writer), Werner Roth (penciller), Jack Sparling (penciller), Dan Adkins (artist), Ross Andru (penciller), et al. *Essential Classic X-Men Vol. 2*. New York: Marvel Publishing, 2006.

Trushell, John M. "American Dreams of Mutants: The X-Men—'Pulp' Fiction, Science Fiction, and Superheroes." *Journal of Popular Culture* 38, no. 1 (August 2004): 149–68.

CHAPTER 9

# MUTATION, RACIALIZATION, DECIMATION

The X-Men as White Men

NEIL SHYMINSKY

IN THE FIRST of his three years writing *New X-Men* (2001–2004), Grant Morrison introduced Mutant Town and the idea that mutants possessed a sexy and influential, if marginalized, subculture. "Mutant music, mutant styles, mutant ideas are becoming more and more fashionable," a TV news anchor tells us.[1] It was a long time coming. To the extent that mutants had a distinct culture during the first forty years of the X-Men franchise, it was an impoverished one: Aside from the ubiquitous X-logo itself, readers would be hard-pressed to name or describe the symbols or cultural practices of Marvel's mutant communities. The mutant renaissance of Morrison's X-Men had limits, though. In an early issue of his run, Morrison's narration tells us that mutant fashion designers can only "dream of seeing mutant models on the Paris fashion catwalks."[2] Mutant styles are popular, but mutants themselves? Not so much.

The ambivalence of nonmutant mainstream culture toward emergent mutant culture within the comic's storyworld should sound familiar. To pull examples from May 2017 alone, a range of nonblack artists as eclectic as Katy Perry, Lilly Singh, and Damien Hirst came under fire for appro-

---

1. Morrison, *New X-Men Vol. 2*.
2. Morrison, *New X-Men Vol. 4*.

priating the aesthetics of black cultural practices piecemeal and discarding their politics. Cultural critic bell hooks explains how appropriation is like "eating the Other," turning blackness into a fetish object to be consumed. "The over-riding fear," she writes, "is that cultural, ethnic, and racial differences will be continually commodified and offered up as new dishes to enhance the white palate—that the Other will be eaten, consumed, and forgotten."[3] Indeed, when Morrison introduces us to the eccentric mutant fashion designer Jumbo Carnation, it is only to show Carnation's murder at the hands of nonmutant autograph seekers.[4]

While I do not want to exaggerate the importance of a character who is murdered in his single, two-page appearance, it is meaningful that Morrison explores this idea of a mutant culture industry and that he finds it a contradictory and problematic space. Just as people outside the Western mainstream have long found themselves dehumanized and commodified for the enjoyment of white consumers and audiences, so too are mutants. "Being a mutant became cool in the same way that being black is cool," writes comics blogger David Brothers about Morrison's run.[5] "You can buy clothes and music made by mutants and be down. You can even hang out in Mutant Town after dark to show how open-minded and cool you are. At the same time, that only goes so far—no one wants to be black, or a mutant, when the things go down or the cops show up."[6] Sure, nonmutants can party with mutants, wearing all sorts of nonhuman costumes in a display of solidarity and community. But when the party ends, the blue makeup and wings come off. Likewise, white and other nonblack peoples can step in and out of blackness with relative ease, affecting a blackcent in one moment and dropping it—and any association with blackness—when it is no longer useful or amusing. "Within commodity culture," adds hooks, "ethnicity becomes spice, seasoning that can liven up the dull dish that is mainstream white culture."[7]

While we typically associate whiteness's use of that "seasoning" with cultural appropriation rather than with overt, physical violence, Morrison connects the two with his addition of John Sublime and the U-Men. In the U-Men—a nonmutant terrorist group, organized and led by John Sublime, that dismembers mutants and surgically grafts the superpowered body parts to themselves—those acts of representational theft and violence become lit-

---

3. hooks, "Eating the Other," 359.
4. Morrison, *New X-Men Vol. 4*.
5. Brothers, "Grant Morrison."
6. Brothers, "Grant Morrison."
7. hooks, "Eating the Other," 359.

eral. "We like to model your behavior, you see," Sublime tells the X-Man Cyclops, shortly before attempting to cut off his head. "To learn from your every move, so we can be more like you."[8] With the U-Men and his framing of mutant culture, Morrison offered a critique of the X-Men's creators and audience, groups of mostly white men who both fear and desire the Otherness that mutants represent.[9]

Through the metaphorical uses of mutantcy, white creators and audiences have historically had a space in which to enact racial fantasies of oppression: not just of imitating or becoming the Other, as Morrison elucidates in the examples above, but of reaffirming the racial fetishes and stereotypes that underpin white supremacy and American hegemony. It has often been argued that mutantcy in the Marvel Universe is analogous to Otherness, and racial Otherness in particular.[10] For instance, the "dream" of X-Men founder Professor Xavier, that mutants and humans might live peacefully as equals, evokes comparisons with Martin Luther King Jr. in both its name and content; the franchise's main antagonist, Magneto, is a mutant separatist who often spars verbally with Xavier, predictably evoking comparisons with Malcolm X; the island of Genosha, where a human minority had built a utopian society on the backs of mutant slave-labor, was described by its creator as an explicit analogy for the South African apartheid state; fans have often pointed out the similarities between HIV/AIDS and the Legacy Virus that targeted and killed several mutants in the 1990s; and, more simply, mutants are a hated and feared minority whose very existence has been deemed a social problem and, at times, even criminalized. However, it does not necessarily follow that the X-Men stories are opposed to white supremacy or make a coherent argument in favor of progressivism or racial equality. As comics critic Julian Darius first contended, if mutants are black, then "blacks are indeed a serious threat to the white social order. And let us make no mistake: it is the white social order."[11]

Given the speed and frequency with which superhero comics cycle through creative teams and directions, many of Morrison's developments were bound to be abandoned or erased. But are the X-Men still, as Darius argued in 2002, defenders of the white supremacy rather than its opponents? How have Marvel editorial and subsequent X-Men creators responded to criticism, and have their responses ameliorated or exacerbated the comics' problematic relationship to race? With a particular focus on status-quo-alter-

---

8. Morrison, *New X-Men Vol. 4*.
9. Shyminsky, "Mutant Readers," 390.
10. Shyminsky, "Mutant Readers," 388.
11. Darius, "X-Men Is Not an Allegory."

ing storylines like 2006's "Decimation" and 2012's "Avengers vs. X-Men," this chapter argues that while Marvel has become more conscious of race politics and responsive to critiques, the X-Men remain beholden to a white social order.

## White Skin and Racial Erasure

The X-Men franchise's problematic relationship to race starts with the most obvious aspect of representation: the visual. Among Marvel's mutants, white characters abound. Of the roughly two dozen characters who called themselves X-Men during the comic's first twenty-five years, Storm was the only person of color who remained a member for more than three issues. Absurdly, until 1990, people of color were outnumbered by white men covered in blue fur. "White people are not racially seen and named," argues film theorist Richard Dyer, and so "they/we function as a human norm."[12] Unlike, for instance, blackness, which is associated with a particular set of racialized, stereotypical signs and behaviors such as aggression and hypersexuality, whiteness manifests only as the *absence* of race. To call a character white, then, is to point out that he or she has no markers of racial or ethnic specificity at all, instead occupying the role of a universal subject. For instance, while Summers is a Scottish family name also common in England, there is nothing about Scott Summers's—Cyclops's—backstory that associates him with either country or its national culture. His presumptive British origin doesn't suggest a particular type of character, nor does his reputation for being serious play into any stereotype of white, ostensibly Christian, men. Cyclops's whiteness does not register as a particular race so much as a lack of race. We are far more aware of what he is not—not black like Storm, not Jewish like Kitty Pryde—rather than what he *is*, and so he can be perceived as simply a human. "Other people are raced," writes Dyer, "we are just people."[13]

That white mutants are popularly understood to represent nonwhite, Otherized subject positions is a significant problem. The white mutant creates a contradictory condition. On the one hand, mutantcy is more often than not a metaphor for racialized Otherness; on the other, the predominantly white mutants of the X-Men lack race and typically pass as "just people." But in spite of their exceptional powers and abilities that mark

---

12. Dyer, *White*, 1.
13. Dyer, *White*, 1.

them as the Other, most of the X-Men would not be out of place within mainstream, white America. This is owed to the fact that, at least within Western culture, vision is the dominant way of knowing. "The visual field is not neutral to the question of race," explains philosopher Judith Butler. "It is itself a racial formation, an episteme, hegemonic and forceful."[14] The fact that the X-Men are mostly white, mostly men, and able-bodied makes the experience of reading about them entirely different than it would be were they people of color, women, or disabled.

Consider, for instance, Orion Martin's art project "X-Men of Color," where he recolors images from the X-Men comics "so that every mutant had a skin color that was some shade of brown."[15] Martin argues that the recolored panels reveal that something is lost in the metaphorical "translations from reality to fantasy and fantasy back to reality."[16] As an example, Martin argues that the recoloring of characters dramatically alters the way these characters are read. "Wolverine is a symbol of wild, untamed, white male power," writes Martin, "but when I recolor his skin to imagine him as a person of color, his snarling, predatory aggression reads as a stereotype of wild black men."[17] Of course, comics historians and critics never place Wolverine within a tradition of the black savage, mandingo, or blaxploitation—even though the latter emerged as a film genre around the same time that Wolverine appeared—opting instead for comparisons with white figures like Clint Eastwood and John Wayne. Skin color makes all the difference.

But what do the comics themselves have to say about how the X-Men look? "You look like movie stars," complains Kaga, a murderous Japanese super-genius who appeared in *Astonishing X-Men* (vol. 3) #34 (August 2010), three years after Morrison's run. Kaga's in-utero exposure to radiation from the atom bomb in Hiroshima has disfigured, paralyzed, and nearly killed him.[18] "Your clothing reeks of boastful sexuality, the fashion wear of action heroes. Do you think *you* have been badly served by the world?"[19] Kaga makes a point that the X-Men are loathe to concede, namely that these mansion-dwelling and physically attractive heroes have more privilege than other and Otherized mutants. When Kaga heard of the X-Men, he imagined people who could empathize with his experience of mutation. What he found, instead, was a cruel irony: "I dreamed I might have a family some-

---

14. Butler, "Endangered/Endangering," 17.
15. Martin, "What if the X-Men Were Black?"
16. Martin, "What if the X-Men Were Black?"
17. Martin, "What if the X-Men Were Black?"
18. Ellis and Jimenez, *Astonishing X-Men Vol. 6*.
19. Ellis and Jimenez, *Astonishing X-Men Vol. 6*.

where, and that together we might make some kind of a life, where we didn't have to hide in basements. And then I saw you. Perfect men and women who pose and strut and punch people uglier than yourselves."[20] However, it does not appear that Warren Ellis, the story's writer, shares Kaga's opinion. When the X-Men defeat Kaga, Cyclops is genuinely confused that "there are people who hate us because we're not outcast enough," and Wolverine's response is basically a shrug.[21] In the end, Kaga's criticisms of the X-Men's unearned privileges, exclusivity, and lack of self-awareness is successfully dismissed as nothing more than the ravings of another evil, hateful madman.

In demanding that Kaga justify himself and then subsequently disregarding his reasons, the X-Men align themselves with hegemonically white ways of seeing and understanding racial privilege and oppression. "Black and Third-World people are expected to educate white people as to our humanity," writes Audre Lorde.[22] "Women are expected to educate men. Lesbians and gay men are expected to educate the heterosexual world. The oppressors maintain their position and evade their responsibility for their own actions."[23] Philosopher Nora Berenstain calls this rhetorical strategy "epistemic exploitation," where the privileged endlessly demand evidence of oppression and, further, that oppressed people educate their oppressors. As Berenstain explains, "marginalized persons often do not have the option to simply disengage from an epistemically exploitative situation without being subjected to harm as a result of their perceived affront."[24] Berenstain calls this a "double bind" because the marginalized person here is in a no-win scenario. When experiencing epistemic exploitation, a person of color may be asked to explain why something is racist. The scenario is a double bind because such a person has only two options: to accept the expectation that it is their responsibility to educate and to expend that time and energy, or to refuse and confirm beliefs of their irrational, emotional, and antisocial character. Having already demonstrated the latter when he removed himself from society, Kaga is asked to educate the X-Men. He refuses, but the reader has already concluded, by this point, that he is an irredeemable villain.

In another example where the X-Men are shown to perceive the world and mutants' relation to it from a characteristically white perspective, consider the now-infamous scene from *Uncanny Avengers* #5 (May 2013) where

---

20. Ellis and Jimenez, *Astonishing X-Men Vol. 6*.
21. Ellis and Jimenez, *Astonishing X-Men Vol. 6*.
22. Lorde, "Age, Race, Class, and Sex," 281.
23. Lorde, "Age, Race, Class, and Sex," 281.
24. Berenstain, "Epistemic Exploitation."

the newly announced leader of the Avengers Unity Squad, the mutant Havok, resoundingly rejects the very idea of mutant identity politics:

> I don't see myself as born into a mutant cult or religion. Having an X-gene doesn't bond me to anyone. It doesn't define me. In fact, I see the very word "mutant" as divisive. Old thinking that serves to further separate us from our fellow man. We are all humans. Of one tribe. We are defined by our choices, not the makeup of our genes. So please, don't call us mutants. The "m" word represents everything I hate.[25]

Comics critic Steve Morris writes that "the idea that 'mutant' is an 'm-word' is comprehensively wrong. The idea that equality is reached via erasing differences is wrong."[26] What Havok describes is a sort of gene-blind or post-mutant society, implying that a distinct and separate mutant community is undesirable, if not simply wrong, and that identifying with what makes you different only makes things worse. When a reporter asks Havok what language he proposes to replace "the m word," he responds, "How about Alex?," discarding his mutant identity altogether.[27] "That's not a message of inclusion," opines Andrew Wheeler for *Comics Alliance*, "that's a message of assimilation. That's a message of erasure."[28]

## The Racial Fetishism of Mutant Dystopia

"Mutants are almost always facing apocalyptic scenarios," writes James Whitbrook in the introduction to his *Gizmodo* article "8 Times the X-Men Were Nearly Wiped Out Forever."[29] 1980's "Days of Future Past" was the first story to portend a near-future where mutants are hunted to near-extinction, but hardly the last. The conclusion of 1993's "X-Cutioner's Song" saw the release of the Legacy Virus, an airborne plague that infects only mutants and would kill several characters over the next decade. The 1995 "Age of Apocalypse" crossover depicted an alternate reality where war between humans and mutants has killed millions of people and renders a sizeable section of the world uninhabitable. It also inaugurated the trope whereby a mutant becomes a global dictator—repeated with Magneto in 2005's "House of M"

---

25. Remender and Cassaday, *Uncanny Avengers Vol. 1*.
26. Morris, "Uncanny Avengers Introduces 'The M-Word.'"
27. Remender and Cassaday, *Uncanny Avengers Vol. 1*.
28. Wheeler, "Avengers Assimilate."
29. Whitbrook, "8 Times the X-Men Were Nearly Wiped out Forever."

and Cyclops in 2012's "Avengers vs. X-Men," both of whom create a world that is, ironically, far more inequitable. Morrison's four-year run on *New X-Men* opened with the destruction of the mutant "homeland" of Genosha and the deaths of the roughly sixteen million mutants who live there. Beginning with M-Day at the conclusion of "House of M," when the number of mutants was magically reduced to roughly 200, until the end of "Avengers vs. X-Men," the mutant X-Gene is all but removed from reality. And even after the X-Gene was restored, mutants faced a new threat when the Terrigen Mists, a gas cloud that activates Inhuman superpowers, appeared in 2015. It either killed or sterilized every mutant it encountered, forcing most mutants to temporarily leave the Earth.[30]

But what makes dystopia such a compelling and recurring genre among the various X-Men comics? "In Western fiction," writes popular culture critic Noah Berlatsky, "dystopic stories often ask, 'What if this atrocity had happened to white people instead?'"[31] Though Berlatsky was writing generally about dystopia, he might as well have been describing the X-Men specifically. Marvel's mutants have often been used by white creators to muse about the nature of oppression in ways that betray a lack of familiarity with the topic.[32] "There are just way too many friggin' mutants in the Marvel Universe!" complained Joe Quesada, Marvel's editor-in-chief, when asked to explain why he felt it necessary to reduce the number of mutants in the Marvel Universe from millions to only a few hundred on M-Day during the "Decimation" event.[33] Explains Quesada, "X-Men at its core is about a group of people who are a minority, they are the downtrodden, they are looked strangely upon because they're special, weird, strange, different, freaks—take your pick. The bottom line is at the very core of the X-Men metaphor is the fact that they are a small minority who have this special ability."[34] It is worth adding, here, that this was already the second time that Que-

---

30. Dystopian race wars appear in two of the films as well: 2006's *X-Men: The Last Stand* and 2014's *X-Men: Days of Future Past*.
31. Berlatsky, "Both Versions of *The Handmaid's Tale*."
32. Joe Quesada, one of the creators responsible for setting the X-Men's agenda over the past fifteen years, complicates this "white creator" claim somewhat. Quesada, a second-generation Cuban American, has described himself as Hispanic and is white-passing. However, his racialization does not necessarily exempt him from the effects of white supremacy, which often demands that racialized people internalize racism and reproduce the conditions of their own marginalization. "White supremacy's controlled transgression continues to be embedded in its popular imagination," writes Tokawa, "and even strengthened by marginalized reproduction." "Racialized Self-Misrepresentation," 163.
33. "Joe Fridays—Week 21."
34. "Joe Fridays—Week 21."

sada greenlit the removal of millions of mutants from the Marvel Universe, having earlier approved Cassandra Nova's genocidal attack on the mutant nation of Genosha—"we got rid of that, thank god"—and its sixteen million inhabitants.[35] For Quesada, oppression necessarily means an unsustainably small population: "staggeringly low," he adds, so that we "feel for these characters again."[36] Quesada necessarily ties his ability to empathize with mutants to the ever-present threat of extinction, such that "when one gets injured or dies, it really matters, it's going to really affect the populace and hopefully our loyal readers."[37] If readers do not fear that the X-Men and mutantkind might end tomorrow, then Marvel does not expect them to care.

Needless to say, oppression does not function in the way Quesada imagines. Half of the world is female, and yet sexism and misogyny persist. There are indeed nations that are composed of mostly people of color that are not immune to racism, the legacy of colonialism, or the effects of white supremacy, and states where the ethnic or faith group that composes the majority of the population is nonetheless disempowered and dispossessed. In prescribing his specific definition of a highly specific, visible, and demographically minor population as constituting oppression, Quesada engages in a form of racial fetishism, a discourse that uses particular narratives and stereotypes that purport to speak the truth of entire communities of racial Others so as to marginalize them.[38] Consider, for instance, how the rate at which black American men were accused of raping white women skyrocketed following the Civil War or how cultural narratives fixated on black men's supposedly unquenchable, animalistic sexuality. Following their liberation at the end of the war, large numbers of freed black men posed a threat to white power. Lacking a clear and available legal recourse, their racial fetishization provided a lasting justification for the existing social and moral order, one in which the Other remained—and still remains—separated and contained.[39] That same logic of racial fetish is at work in Quesada's justification of the wholesale elimination of mutants. As their number has expanded, Marvel's ability to define what it means to be mutant and, by extension, what it means to be Other had slipped away.

However, this is not to say that M-Day was motivated by overt racism. "Well-intentioned Whites often dismiss, negate, and minimize the experiential reality of POC [people of color]," write psychologist Derald Wing Sue

---

35. "Joe Fridays—Week 21."
36. "Joe Fridays—Week 21."
37. "Joe Fridays—Week 21."
38. Mercer, *Welcome to the Jungle*, 175.
39. See Dray, *At the Hands of Persons Unknown*.

and his colleagues in their description of aversive racism, a practice white people use to "question the racial realities of POC" because such realities implicate them.[40] While ostensibly trying to represent the racial realities experienced by people of color, Quesada questions whether racist oppression is possible when danger is not genocidal in scale, offering a definition of oppression that elides and excludes any nuance: Everyday hate crimes, much less the systemic nature of white supremacy, do not register. Simply put, M-Day functions to redefine what it means to be oppressed.

What, then, does this post-M-Day reality look like? Predictably, it is a Kafkaesque vision of what it means to be a mutant and X-Man. "Half my school has been killed, the other half spent time in hell . . . literally, hell," explains Northstar to the reader, summarizing the events that followed the appearance of the first mutant baby after M-Day.[41] To be a mutant, under these new conditions, is to either be dead or to experience something similar to it. In 2007's "Endangered Species," a mega-crossover story with a name that is perhaps too on the nose, Mercury, a student at the X-Mansion, seems to paraphrase Quesada's stated goals when she describes what it means to be a mutant after M-Day thusly: "This is all we are now . . . a few dazed refugees staggering around after an earthquake or something."[42] Having been reduced to fewer than 200, the X-Men now finally resemble the sufficiently and undeniably oppressed group that Quesada imagined.

## Cyclops's Narrative of Terror

So far I have discussed only those points in Quesada's interview that, while betraying a lack of understanding or awareness of how racism functions, are not themselves obviously racist. Unfortunately, Quesada unmistakably crosses this line when describing why it became necessary to create M-Day and eliminate the X-Gene from the Marvel Universe, even after killing sixteen million Genoshan mutants, because "mutants now were breeding so quickly that eventually they were going to be the majority on the planet."[43] Though Quesada does not expand on or extend this train of thought, his word choice—"breeding"—and argument echo the logics of the white genocide conspiracy theory. While theories of "white genocide," which posit that declining birth rates among white people will lead to their displacement and

---

40. Sue et al., "Racial Microaggressions."
41. Young, "Blend In."
42. Carey, Gage, and Yost, *X-Men: Endangered Species*.
43. "Joe Fridays—Week 21."

oppression, have existed since at least the Third Reich, they have become increasingly and worryingly mainstream in recent years.[44] As well, implicit in such arguments is the suggestion that nonwhite peoples will not simply become a dominant national or global force once they are the majority, but that, by virtue of being able to enact this plan now, they are already dominant.

It is in the context of racial fetishism and white genocide conspiracy theorizing that I now want to consider Cyclops, the longtime leader of the X-Men and follower of Xavier's dream. In recent years, Cyclops has been rebranded as a mutant terrorist and villain, fulfilling Magneto's earlier role. While foreshadowed in his creation of Haven, an artificial island built from the remains of Magneto's former asteroid home, after M-Day, Cyclops's turn to villainy began in earnest when he broke from Wolverine during "Schism" in 2011 and created the Extinction Team, a group powerful enough that they "could stare gods in the eye until they blink."[45] "Iraq didn't have weapons of mass destruction," explains Cyclops, drawing an analogy that discomforts at least one of his teammates, but "every time this team goes into the field, we remind the world that we do."[46] Cyclops's allusions to tyrannical governments—he also compares his team to North Korea—prove prescient, as he is shortly thereafter leading the Phoenix Five, a team of cosmically empowered superheroes-turned-dictators. "The Phoenix Five, from the start, fit neatly into the pro-active/fascist super-hero mold," writes comics scholar Tony D'Agostino: "The X-Men's Phoenix Five have gone from protecting a world that fears and hates them to creating-slash-ruling."[47]

As leader of the Phoenix Five, Cyclops immediately orders the "remaking" and "transforming" of the Horn of Africa, the Gobi Desert, and Russia's far north. "We have given you . . . the very key to modernity," announces Cyclops to the United Nations, but the Phoenix Five are figured as the villains in 2012's "Avengers vs. X-Men."[48] "We have a history of forward progress," explains President Obama to the Avengers immediately after Cyclops's announcement, implying that the Phoenix Five represent a disruption of that narrative, rather than its continuation. Obama continues, "But when the world works it's because there has always been some outlying culture of accountability. Right now. These X-Men do not have that . . . And

---

44. See Lane, "White Genocide Manifesto."
45. Gillen, *Uncanny X-Men.*
46. Gillen, *Uncanny X-Men.*
47. D'Agostino, "AvX #6."
48. Aaron et al., *Avengers vs. X-Men.*

something has to be done."⁴⁹ We might well ask, "Accountable to whom?" and the answer can only be American or nonmutant human hegemony, if not also white supremacy. According to historian Kaja Silverman, "hegemony depends upon the maintenance of what is at least to some degree a shared universe," and so "it necessarily implies not only a common identification, but a shared reality."⁵⁰ To ignore the authority of the president of the United States and his representatives in the Avengers, as the X-Men do, is thus regarded as a rejection of the moral and legal order within which the president and Avengers function and that their existence guarantees. If the X-Men no longer consider themselves answerable or accountable to American hegemony, then they are necessarily figured as its villains.

It is worth noting that the story briefly offers a critique of this Americentric view of Cyclops's villainy. The Black Panther, an Avenger and king of the Central African nation of Wakanda, observes that "instead of running from conflict and hunger, refugees are leaving Wakanda and returning north to Ethiopia and Sudan," adding that "certainly these things merit consideration."⁵¹ Indeed, they should, which is why it becomes necessary for the creators of these comics to pile on additional evidence of villainy, just in case readers find themselves sympathizing with the wrong side. These villainous acts are often personal: The newly telepathic Cyclops reads the mind of his mentor, Professor Xavier, without consent; Cyclops's romantic partner, Emma Frost, has a psychic affair with Namor; siblings Colossus and Magik grow to distrust each other so deeply that they beat one another into unconsciousness. But if that were not enough, the Phoenix Five also strip their enemies of their humanity and freedom: They take telepathic control of most of the X-Men's minds and imprison those heroes they cannot brainwash.

Importantly, these tropes of villainy serve a dual symbolic purpose, working to both delegitimize the Phoenix Five and to reassert the legitimacy of the hegemony they oppose. Cyclops is figured not simply as unfit to lead, but as someone who must be beaten down and controlled. "The narratives of terror," writes postcolonial scholar Sherene Razack about the ways in which tales of native savagery have been used throughout history to justify European rule, "could reflect back to the colonizers their reality as civilized and business-like only if they were controlled through acts of savagery. Savages, mythically endowed with great strength, had to be put down."⁵² In light of the acts cited above, the Phoenix Five's feeding of the

---

49. Aaron et al., *Avengers vs. X-Men*.
50. Silverman, *Male Subjectivity at the Margins*, 24.
51. Aaron et al., *Avengers vs. X-Men*.
52. Razack, *Casting Out*, 79.

hungry and poor is viewed with suspicion, a small part of the X-Men's long game, rather than a beneficial act that might "merit consideration" regardless. The Phoenix Five could never really be revolutionaries or liberators.

The idea that nonmutant humans are threatened by mutant unity and the creation of an alternative to the Americentric, nonmutant—and, metaphorically, white—world order is a recurring feature of Cyclops's speeches. "My fellow mutants," Cyclops announces to a TV camera in a deliberate evocation of a presidential address, "I know you're out there and I know you can hear me. No one else is going to do it for us. We have to fight for ourselves."[53] Though not explicitly violent, Cyclops's words are nonetheless suggestive of violence. And as much as Cyclops's message is for mutants, it is as much, if not more, a performance for the benefit of the X-Men's enemies. In another speech to TV cameras, this time with most of the mutant community standing before him, Cyclops declares that "the humans' worst nightmare is that we would unite and attack. Unite and conquer. Unite and come after them. Well, here we are. United. And . . . isn't it beautiful?"[54] Again, Cyclops hints at violence, teasing the possibility that mutants might live up to the fears of nonmutant humans while playfully refusing to confirm it.

What makes Cyclops dangerous, however, is less his threat of physical violence than his threat to political hegemony. For nation-states that rely on and derive their power from the passive acceptance of white supremacy and a monopoly on violence, Cyclops's overtures to a nascent mutant nation presents a philosophical, as well as practical, problem to nonmutant states. For Max Weber, the "legitimate authority" of the modern state is predicated on a monopoly over physical violence and domination of its people, and so the loss of that monopoly endangers the state's very legitimacy.[55] When he launches the Extinction Team, one of Cyclops's stated goals is to replace the Avengers as the world's premier super-team.[56] Given that the Avengers are beholden to governmental bodies and the X-Men are not, this is not merely a symbolic goal. Indeed, when, following *Avengers vs. X-Men*, Cyclops is freed from prison and immediately rescues two American mutants from police custody, he demonstrates precisely how threatening a mutant order might be. The prerogative power of the US to use violence, and the very basis of their claim to legitimacy, no longer belongs to government. It is unfortu-

---

53. Bendis and Bachalo, Uncanny X-Men Vol. 1.
54. Bendis and Bachalo, *Uncanny X-Men*, vol. 1, #600.
55. Bendix, *Max Weber*, 295.
56. Gillen, *Uncanny X-Men*.

nate, then, that Cyclops's mutant world order is never presented as a viable alternative.

## Closing Thoughts

Ultimately, while the X-Men have been able to critique white hegemony, they have hardly been able to challenge it, much less propose how it might be effectively subverted. So long as Marvel imagines a world in which Havok is heroic for disidentifying with the word "mutant" and Cyclops's team is figured as the world's most feared terrorist organization, the status quo is unlikely to be threatened.

Where might Marvel take the X-Men and their mutant metaphor from here? The words of the X-Men's own writers might be telling. When readers and critics responded negatively to Havok's "m-word" speech, Marvel's staff decided to double down on their message of racial erasure. When *Ladies Making Comics*, a feminist comics wiki, took to Twitter to suggest that "telling people whose rights have been trampled for decades 'But we're all people! Let's get along!' [is] guaranteed to piss them off," *Uncanny Avengers* writer Rick Remender took offense.[57] Per Remender, Havok was "trying to make people stop seeing a 'mutant' and start seeing a 'person,'" and "mutants come from all races and sexual orientation. It's not an apt analogy you're making."[58] Fellow X-Men writer Jason Aaron went a step further, responding that X-Men comics are "not the story of what it means to be black or gay in today's society."[59] Recalling Dyer's argument that the Other can never be "just people," this interpretation of the X-Men seems not only at odds with the goals of identity-based politics but antithetical to them. If the X-Men are "just people," then the *X-Men* is just another comic about white people.

---

57. Shyminsky, "The X-Men."
58. Shyminsky, "The X-Men."
59. Shyminsky, "The X-Men."

# Bibliography

Aaron, Jason, Brian Michael Bendis, Ed Brubaker, Matt Fraction, and Jonathan Hickman (writers). *Avengers vs. X-Men.* New York: Marvel Comics, 2012.

Bendis, Brian Michael (writer). *Uncanny X-Men,* vol. 1, #600. New York: Marvel Comics, 2015.

Bendis, Brian Michael (writer), and Chris Bachalo (penciller). *Uncanny X-Men Vol. 1: Revolution.* New York: Marvel Comics, 2013.

Bendix, Reinhard. *Max Weber: An Intellectual Portrait.* Berkeley: University of California Press, 1977.

Berenstain, Nora. "Epistemic Exploitation." *Ergo: An Open Access Journal of Philosophy* 3, no. 22 (2016), http://dx.doi.org/10.3998/ergo.12405314.0003.022.

Berlatsky, Noah. "Both Versions of *The Handmaid's Tale* Have a Problem with Racial Erasure." *The Verge,* June 15, 2017, https://www.theverge.com/2017/6/15/15808530/handmaids-tale-hulu-margaret-atwood-black-history-racial-erasure.

Brothers, David. "Grant Morrison Ruined the X-Men." *4thletter!,* November 6, 2009, http://4thletter.net/2009/11/grant-morrison-ruined-the-x-men/.

Butler, Judith. "Endangered/Endangering: Schematic Racism and White Paranoia." In *Reading Rodney King/Reading Urban Uprising,* edited by Robert Gooding-Williams, 15–22. New York: Routledge, 1993.

Carey, Mike, Christos Gage, and Christopher Yost (writers). *X-Men: Endangered Species.* New York: Marvel Comics, 2008.

D'Agostino, Tony. "AvX #6: The X-Men Get Their 'Pro-Active/Fascist Super-Hero Moment' and It Doesn't Suck at All . . . Especially if You Are White, at Least Middle Class, and Living in the U. S." *Cosmic Utility Infinity Ring,* July 17, 2012, http://cosmicutilityinfinityring.blogspot.ca/2012/07/avx-6-x-men-get-their-pro-activefascist.html.

Darius, Julian. "X-Men Is Not an Allegory of Racial Tolerance." *Sequart Organization,* September 25, 2002, http://sequart.org/magazine/3201/x-men-is-not-an-allegory-of-racial-tolerance/.

Dray, Philip. *At the Hands of Persons Unknown: The Lynching of Black America.* New York: Modern Library, 2003.

Dyer, Richard. *White: Essays on Race and Culture.* New York: Routledge, 1997.

Ellis, Warren (writer), and Phil Jimenez (penciller). *Astonishing X-Men Vol. 6: Exogenetic.* New York: Marvel Comics, 2011.

Gillen, Kieron (writer). *Uncanny X-Men by Kieron Gillen Vol. 1.* New York: Marvel Comics, 2012.

hooks, bell. "Eating the Other: Desire and Resistance." In *The Consumer Society Reader,* edited by Juliet B. Schor and Douglas B. Holt, 343–59. New York: The New Press, 2000.

"Joe Fridays—Week 21." *Newsarama.com,* http://archive.li/49qfa.

Lane, David. "White Genocide Manifesto." *White Resister,* http://whiteresister.com/index.php/17-opinion/163-david-lane-the-white-genocide-manifesto.

Lorde, Audre. "Age, Race, Class, and Sex." In *Out There: Marginalization and Contemporary Cultures,* edited by Russell Ferguson, Martha Gever, Trinh T. Minh-ha, and Cornel West, 281–88. New York: The New Museum of Contemporary Art, 1990.

Martin, Orion. "What if the X-Men Were Black?" *The Hooded Utilitarian,* December 16, 2013, http://www.hoodedutilitarian.com/2013/12/what-if-the-x-men-were-black/.

Mercer, Kobena. *Welcome to the Jungle: New Positions in Black Cultural Studies.* New York: Routledge, 1994.

Morris, Steve. "Uncanny Avengers Introduces 'The M-Word.'" *The Beat,* March 28, 2013, http://www.comicsbeat.com/uncanny-avengers-introduces-the-m-word/.

Morrison, Grant (writer). *New X-Men Vol. 2: Imperial.* New York: Marvel Comics, 2002.

———. *New X-Men Vol. 4: Riot at Xavier's.* New York: Marvel Comics, 2005.

Razack, Sherene. *Casting Out: The Eviction of Muslims from Western Law and Politics.* Toronto: University of Toronto Press, 2008.

Remender, Rick (writer), and John Cassaday (penciller). *Uncanny Avengers Vol. 1: The Red Shadow.* New York: Marvel Comics, 2013.

Shyminsky, Neil. "Mutant Readers, Reading Mutants: Appropriation, Assimilation, and the X-Men." *International Journal of Comic Art* 8, no. 2 (2006): 387–405.

———. "The X-Men Don't Represent What You Think They Represent." *Guilty Displeasures,* May 16, 2013, http://neilshyminsky.blogspot.ca/2013/05/the-x-men-dont-represent-what-you-think.html.

Silverman, Kaja. *Male Subjectivity at the Margins.* New York: Routledge, 1992.

Sue, Derald Wing, Christina M. Capodilupo, Kevin L. Nadal, and Gina C. Torino. "Racial Microaggressions and the Power to Define Reality." *American Psychologist* 63, no. 4 (2008). doi:10.1037/0003-066X.63.4.277.

Tokawa, Kenji Haakon. "Taking Seriously the Power of Racialized Self-Misrepresentation." In *Ruptures: Anti-colonial & Anti-racist Feminist Theorizing,* edited by Njoki Wane, Jennifer Jagire, and Zahra Murad, 157–65. Rotterdam: Sense Publishers, 2013.

Wheeler, Andrew. "Avengers Assimilate: Identity Politics in 'Uncanny Avengers." *Comics Alliance,* March 29, 2013, http://comicsalliance.com/uncanny-avengers-5-rick-remender-identity-politics-mutants/.

Whitbrook, James. "8 Times the X-Men Were Nearly Wiped out Forever." *Gizmodo,* November 16, 2015, http://io9.gizmodo.com/8-times-the-x-men-were-nearly-wiped-out-forever-1742816773.

Young, Skottie (writer and artist). "Blend In." *X-Men: Divided We Stand* #1. New York: Marvel Comics, 2008.

CHAPTER 10

# WHITE PLASTICITY AND BLACK POSSIBILITY IN DARWYN COOKE'S *DC: THE NEW FRONTIER*

SEAN GUYNES

DARWYN COOKE'S *DC: The New Frontier*, a six-issue miniseries published by DC Comics in 2004, is an unabashed, nostalgic paean to the vast history of DC's intellectual properties and narrative and artistic legacies. It is not, however, uncritical or unaware of the problems of representative inequality, bound up with real-world systemic oppression, that plague that history and those legacies. Cooke's *New Frontier* retells the origin story of DC's superhero team the Justice League of America (JLA), strategically bridging the historical gap between the WWII-era Golden Age heroes Superman, Batman, the Justice Society of America, and Wonder Woman and the Cold War's Silver Age versions of Green Lantern, the Flash, and others, while weaving a new story of how the JLA was founded and how it fits with lesser-known contemporaneous DC properties, such as Adam Strange, the Challengers of the Unknown, and the Losers. Cooke sets the bulk of his narrative of the JLA's founding between 1955 and 1960, ending with the historical JLA's first appearance in a battle against an alien starfish in *The Brave and the Bold* #28 (March 1960). Though populated by dozens of recognizable characters, *New Frontier* focuses on Hal Jordan, a white test pilot who becomes the Green Lantern, and Martian Manhunter, an alien accidentally brought to earth by a deep-space communications experiment and forced to keep himself secret lest humans' "fear of the unknown" and "hatred of things they can't control or understand" prove his demise.¹

Cooke tells this story in the energetic, cartoony style he pioneered as a storyboard artist for DC's animated television shows in the 1990s and that brought him acclaim for freelance work at DC and Marvel in the early 2000s. *New Frontier* melds Cooke's signature style with the aesthetics of 1950s Populuxe design to render a nostalgic glimpse of early Cold War America and its superheroes. Cooke offers a reconsideration of our nostalgia-mediated collective memory of the early postwar era, unsettling sanitized memories of America's history and of the racial politics of DC's publication record, which excluded superheroes of color until the 1970s, when a series of black superheroes appeared in various titles, including John Stewart as the first black Green Lantern in 1971, and culminating with *Black Lightning* in 1977, the first solo title about a nonwhite superhero. Key to *New Frontier*'s racial politics, Cooke retroactively inserts, or "retcons," the 1990s black superhero Steel into the JLA origin story, transforming him into the black folk hero John Henry, who originally inspired Steel's creation, and making the character a KKK-fighting vigilante in 1950s Tennessee.

In this chapter, I argue that Cooke's *New Frontier* responds to DC's racially unjust history and to the overwhelming whiteness of its superheroes through two narratives, one of Martian Manhunter, who represents a liberal-progressive fantasy of integration and the erasure of racial difference, and the other of John Henry. In the context of the mid-century American racial formation as understood in the pioneering work of Michael Omi and Howard Winant, John Henry signifies what was understood then to be the historical impossibility of the black superhero, unable to be written into the comics of the 1950s, let alone to be thought of as possible by the white-dominated comics industry. But his presence in Cooke's revisionist comic also gestures to the possibility of the black superhero's emergence—its ability to be imagined, then created, sold, and consumed—within the racial formation of the "post-"civil rights decades.² In telling his history of the JLA, Cooke does not retroactively include black superheroes; he does not sanitize

---

1. Cooke, *DC*, 191.

2. Omi and Winant eponymous conceptualization in *Racial Formation* outlines race as a both a fundamentally ideological formation—that is, a symbolic and historically situated discourse—as well as the set of real-world social, economic, and other effects of that discourse on black life. I refer to the period after the "'classical' phase" of civil rights struggle (1954–1965) as untenably "post-" in order to recognize—after Hall, "The Long Civil Rights Movement," 1234—that the struggle for racial justice and inequality is not over and done.

DC's legacy, but reinscribes the company's decision (and, indeed, the genre's tendency) to exclude black superheroes until the chorus of civil rights had grown so loud as to demand greater social realism in comic book representation. Martian Manhunter and John Henry's narratives point to the plasticity of whiteness when it is posited as the sole racial category to which superheroes may belong, making the critique of superhero comics' racial history integral to Cooke's otherwise nostalgic vision of the JLA story.

While Leo Spitzer refers to nostalgia as "the selective emphasis on what was positive in the past," the 1950s were only "positive" in any real sense for the white middle-class heterosexuals most often designated "average Americans."[3] Despite its seeming embrace of the past, Cooke's comic is hardly wedded to notions that the 1950s were a better time. Instead, Cooke places his nostalgic renderings of the past in tension with narratives about race, difference, and belonging. Nostalgia, he knows, acts as a powerful form for thinking about the history and present of racial and gender formations, deployable in ways both reifying and probing. Thus, *New Frontier* exemplifies what Sinead McDermott calls "critical nostalgia" and "uses the past to unsettle the present," thus rejecting notions that the text seeks to restore a better history.[4] As a work of critical nostalgia, Cooke's comic plays form, narrative, and history off one another to reenvision the past and think through questions of racial justice in the history of superhero comics.

Through Manhunter and John Henry alike, the metaphors of alienness and superheroism Cooke deploys, and the real histories of blackness that he builds from, he reimagines DC Comics's racial legacy in *New Frontier*. In doing so, he points to the possibility of a more just racial history for the superhero, one that acknowledges the key role of whiteness while also foregrounding the possibilities for the emergence of the black superhero in later decades. At the same time, Cooke underscores the fundamental whiteness of the superhero and its continual erasure of racial difference from the superhero figure.

## Martian Manhunter and the Plasticity of Whiteness on the New Frontier

The historical New Frontier from which Cooke's comic takes its name was an administrative policy as well as a cultural attitude. Articulated in John F.

---

3. Spitzer, *Hotel Bolivia*, 153.
4. McDermott, "Memory, Nostalgia, and Gender," 401–5.

Kennedy's speech accepting the 1960 democratic presidential nomination, it was the New Deal for a "new generation of [American] leadership." The New Frontier was defined by significant advances in technology, especially the development of the atomic bomb, but Kennedy assured that despite the threat of nuclear annihilation, "the changing face of the future is equally revolutionary." His political vision, furthermore, linked the techno-scientific with the social, stressing that "beyond [the New Frontier] are the uncharted areas of science and space, unsolved problems of peace and war, unconquered pockets of ignorance and prejudice, unanswered questions of poverty and surplus."[5] Cooke's *New Frontier* lives in Kennedy's rhetoric. His reimagining of DC's superheroes corroborates liberalism's hope for a more equal, more just America driven by techno-scientific advancement and outraged at racist violence, while also demonstrating the fundamental failure of liberalism to achieve lasting justice through structural changes to systems like race. The shapeshifting alien superhero Martian Manhunter operates as the crux of this historical critique of who does and does not belong, who is and is not white, in mid-century America and in the superhero comic more generally.

Martian Manhunter was created by science fiction and comics writer Joseph Samachson, son of Russian Jewish émigrés to the US, and comics artist Joe Certa. The green-skinned alien first appeared in a backup story published in *Detective Comics* #225 in 1955. He was conceived as something of a cross between Batman and Superman, mixing the former's detective skills with the latter's alien origins, nigh invulnerability, and outlandish list of superpowers. Manhunter's original story saw him using his shapeshifting powers to spend life on Earth as the white police detective John Jones. Outside of this disguise, he looks strikingly like Superman in form, the only real difference being his sharp, heavy brows and green skin. A relatively popular backup character throughout the late 1950s, Manhunter became a founding member of the JLA when Gardner Fox dreamed the team up in 1960. After that, Manhunter appeared regularly in JLA comics and less often as his alter ego John Jones. *New Frontier* changes little of Samachson's story, but instead imagines how Manhunter is discovered by other superheroes, joins their cause, and becomes a central member of the JLA. In doing so, the comic stresses the tension between the human (white male) life he leads and the alien he is, turning the latter into a metaphor for race that is typical of

---

5. Kennedy, "1960 Democratic National Convention."

science fiction and that undermines the real damage wrought by race and a lack of representation in people of color's lives.[6]

In the narrative world of *New Frontier*, superheroes have been outlawed as un-American vigilantes by the House Un-American Activities Committee (HUAC). The only legally sanctioned superheroes are Wonder Woman and Superman, the two superheroes with the greatest powers and thus the most to offer in helping assert US policy abroad in the fight against communism; Cooke presents the former as an adamant feminist disenchanted with US foreign policy, and the latter as a naive, consensus-bound patriot. Other superheroes, all white, keep their former identities hidden or are hunted down by law enforcement. A mock-up newspaper article inserted into the comic details one superhero's death during a police chase as "the latest and most tragic chapter in the Eisenhower Administration's efforts to register and reveal the identities of the nation's" superheroes.[7] But as the story unfolds, a massive, chthonic enemy predating all life on Earth, known as the Centre, enters US territory and attacks. With the military unable to defend against the threat, superheroes become a national defense necessity after the Centre seemingly kills Superman (he is later discovered alive); once they band together to defeat the enemy, they are deemed integral to the nation-state and incorporated via the JLA into the military-industrial complex. This narrative metaphorizes the superhero as a minority political group, like the alien-as-race metaphor, and plays out a key liberal fantasy that imagines this group, formerly the target of discriminatory legislation, integrated into American political culture and now working for rather than (supposedly) against the state.

In this context, Martian Manhunter serves as the only image of color in a landscape of white superbodies: His is a hypervisible green body on display, barely covered by the blue underwear and boots, yellow belt, and thin, chest-crossing red straps that constitute his costume. Manhunter's story follows the same trajectory from exclusion to integration into the white, liberal body of American democracy that the comic's plot traces for the superhero figure, but at the same time his narrative generates anxieties about what it means to belong in America when one is (as a metaphor) racially marked. Cooke signals these anxieties about belonging and, ultimately, about the adaptability of whiteness as a racial category both visually and through Manhunter's dialogue. When Manhunter first appears on Earth, the victim of a telecommunications experiment conducted by the scientist Dr. Erdel, he

---

6. On this generic trope, see Lavender, *Race in American Science Fiction*; James, "Yellow, Black, Metal, and Tentacled"; and Kilgore, "Difference Engine."

7. Cooke, *DC*, 52.

is a monstrous figure, a tall, lanky, vegetal green humanoid with a conical head and demonic red eyes. His visage gives Dr. Erdel a heart attack, though the scientist does not blame Manhunter. He warns Manhunter before dying: "You *must* be *very careful*. This world isn't ready for . . . you. Mankind is a suspicious, violent creature. You *must not* reveal yourself."[8] Heeding this warning, and discovering that he cannot return to Mars, Manhunter hides himself away to study humanity so that he can assimilate and live among them—so that he can "pass" as human.

Manhunter spends weeks "studying life on earth with the help of this charming device they call the television. It is giving me all the information I need to act like a typical citizen of this nation called America."[9] Cooke demonstrates the plasticity of the Martian's identity and physical form alike, as Manhunter utilizes his shapeshifting ability to emulate realistic and animated images from television—first Groucho Marx, then Bugs Bunny and the Indian-head test pattern that followed television station sign-offs at the end of the broadcasting day, and finally the identity he settles on—the key image of the "typical citizen of this nation called America": "police detective John Jones. . . . [O]ne of the good guys."[10] Manhunter effortlessly assumes the visual identity of a white man and proves a formidable detective as John Jones, but not until after demonstrating the limitless extent of his body's plasticity to mimic form, shape, and aesthetic. And yet, though his ability to perform identity is seemingly boundless, whiteness—like the plastic so evocative of the period—cannot exceed certain tolerances. Although passing easily for white as Jones, Manhunter is nonetheless estranged from his human colleagues, who think that Jones talks strangely, as though a character in a film noir, and that he violates the behavioral norms of mid-century white folks on account of his dual obsession with civil rights and aliens.

In a pivotal scene, Jones stands in his office staring at his wall covered in newspaper articles. On the one side are articles about the recent lynching of John Henry (a *Time* cover article titled "Black America Today"), about Rosa Parks, KKK attacks and black retaliations, and even an anachronistic article about Malcolm X; on the other wall are clippings about life on Mars, alien abductions, UFO sightings, and Area 51. As Manhunter narrates it: "My interest in subjects like racism and UFO sightings has made me something of an eccentric to my fellow officers."[11] But as a result of his expertise, he is asked to take a statement from Harry, a "nutty" "fruitcake," as Jones's

---

8. Cooke, *DC*, 78.
9. Cooke, *DC*, 89.
10. Cooke, *DC*, 90.
11. Cooke, *DC*, 221.

colleagues mockingly describe him, who sees "little green men." Harry turns out to be a technician on the space flight project led by federal agent King Faraday, with Hal Jordan (Green Lantern) as test pilot.[12] He tells Jones of a government conspiracy to hide knowledge of alien life from the public and that "the last five years have been spent developing a rocket to reach Mars" in order to eradicate Martian life before it attacks Earth.[13]

When Faraday steps in to remove Harry, Manhunter reads Faraday's mind and discovers that the seeming ravings are true and, moreover, that Dr. Erdel's experiment that brought Manhunter to earth tipped off the US military to the existence of alien life on Mars and to Manhunter's terrestrial presence. To Faraday, who leads the space flight project and seeks to drop nuclear bombs on Mars, and by extension to the military-industrial complex that Faraday stands in for, the alien Other represents the antithesis of the human and a grave threat to national security. But framed against Manhunter's insistence that racial and alien difference are alike in kind, the white G-man Faraday's insistence on American dominance over and destruction of an entire alien species takes on overtones of a war for racial supremacy—a war in which Manhunter sees both himself and the black folk hero vigilante John Henry fighting on the same side.

Manhunter's realization that he is being hunted by Faraday leads him to try to escape Earth, which he does by sneaking into the interstellar test flight base, but he misses his chance to escape in order to save Faraday's life after the G-man attempted to kill Manhunter. But this wins him no favors; Faraday instead imprisons Manhunter at the rocket test site on Nellis Air Force Base, a privately owned enterprise contracted to the US Air Force. Through a series of interrogations, however, Manhunter and Faraday become friends, they play chess, and Manhunter gives Faraday insight into the growing threat posed by the Centre, to which Manhunter is unwillingly connected via telepathy. With Faraday, Manhunter sits revealed in his true Martian form, not as Jones or as the sleek Superman-esque visage he later adopts, suggesting a level of trust and camaraderie that bridges (metaphorically) racial and specific differences.

In the end, the alien whose species Faraday had intended to eradicate as a measure of interplanetary Cold War containment works for the G-man, at first as a G-man himself and then as a superhero fighting the Centre with other future JLA heroes. Manhunter's ability to shapeshift once again signals his plasticity of identity and his ability to pass, racially and otherwise. As

---

12. Cooke, *DC*, 222.
13. Cooke, *DC*, 224.

he and Faraday leave for the battle against the Centre, Manhunter presents himself to Faraday as the bright-green, bald-headed superhero familiar to DC readers in the late 1950s. Manhunter calls this a *"friendlier* appearance," "more like the hero Superman."[14] But Faraday disagrees, suggesting a more normative, all-American appearance: "Real men wear pants."[15] Manhunter immediately morphs his attire into a blue suit with a tie and dons black glasses, the clichéd image of the G-man, now the assimilated alien standing side by side with his former enemy.

Manhunter's story of anxiously passing, of keeping tabs on the race (and the alien) question, of being hunted and persecuted by the government, and of eventually becoming the G-man himself is not a novel narrative trajectory for stories about race in the US. Indeed, as countless works of American ethnic literature have demonstrated and as scholarship about the Irish or Jews or Italians becoming white has strived to chart,[16] whiteness, like Manhunter's fantastical Martian body, is plastic. Although a formidable structure in American social, cultural, political, and economic life, race and its attendant meanings are contingent. Whiteness in particular can be fashioned anew in order to consolidate greater amounts of power over those excluded from the category, a process of racial alchemy that has been called the "racial bribe."[17]

As cultural historian Colin Salter argues of the Australian and Canadian contexts of whiteness, though equally germane to the US,

> the malleability of whiteness, its variability and changing contours, is located in its ability to adapt. The normativity of whiteness, the apparent universality, is rooted in an ability to absorb (co-opt) difference, in adapting to changes and societal variations [over time and space]. These abilities expose the hegemonic nature of whiteness, what we might describe as a dynamic equilibrium. An ability to absorb any potentially destabilising challenges.[18]

---

14. Cooke, *DC*, 327.
15. Cooke, *DC*, 327.
16. See, for example, Brodkin, *How the Jews Became White Folks*; Guglielmo, *White on Arrival*; Ignatiev, *How the Irish Became White*; Jacobson, *Whiteness of a Different Color*.
17. Alexander, *The New Jim Crow*, 234, uses the term "racial bribe" to describe attempts to expand the social-control powers of whiteness over blackness (and other nonwhite racial formations) by granting whiteness to formerly non- or not-entirely-white groups, promising ultimately that the former status quo of what she terms the "racial caste system" will "reemerge in a new form."
18. Salter, *Whiteness and Social Change*, 47–48.

Manhunter's physical form shifts in step with the social form of whiteness, and in so doing he becomes an assimilated American, a G-man, a superman. By the end of *New Frontier*, gone is the Manhunter who, in a moment of fear after having his life threatened in his Jones persona by Batman, anxiously reverts to his original Martian form while still in his work clothes. This scene occurs roughly in the middle of the miniseries, after Manhunter has just seen a sensational science fiction film, *Invasion from Mars*. Watching the film, he laughs at what he deems its ridiculous imagination of a human–alien encounter while the all-white audience screams. Manhunter takes this experience as evidence that Americans fear the unknown and hate "things they can't control or understand," proof that he will never be accepted.[19] He repeats this line to himself in his half-alien, half–white man state after Batman's threat, revealing his ultimate fear that the differences between alien Others and humans, like those between the KKK and John Henry, are irreconcilable. But with time, Kennedy's vision of an America able to put difference aside for the cause of global good proves the fulfillment of Manhunter's wish for acceptance.

Martian Manhunter gets to become, like the Superman he sees perform in animated shorts before the science fiction film, a superhero admired by and serving the nation. Yet, even so, in the end he takes a form designed to be friendly to that "typical citizen of this nation called America" that he worked so long to pass with. Manhunter's is a story of liberalism's efforts to integrate in the Kennedy era and its mild successes, but at the same time, to borrow historian David Roediger's phrasing, race survives integration, and its meanings migrate and its signs proliferate in new ways.[20] This is the result of liberalism's failure in the New Frontier era to fundamentally alter the systemic bases that make race so oppressive for people of color in the US, in the process maintaining what Toni Morrison calls the "habit of ignoring race" throughout American history, which she notes as "a graceful, even generous, liberal gesture" premised on the idea that race is, especially in the postwar and "post–"civil rights era, "an already discredited difference."[21] While Manhunter demonstrates the possibilities for passing and the hope for integration and inclusion, Cooke is not as shortsighted as Manhunter, and offers his character John Henry as a reminder that the superhero figure is enmeshed with a racial politics that champions whiteness and that marks out and excises blackness.

---

19. Cooke, *DC*, 194.
20. Roediger, *How Race Survived*.
21. Morrison, *Playing in the Dark*, 9–10.

# John Henry and the Possibility of the Black Superhero

Martian Manhunter's narrative arc destabilizes whiteness, if only briefly before seeing him incorporated into the power structure of whiteness as one of its central beneficiaries via the JLA. At the same time, his demonstration of the plasticity of whiteness, insofar as it is the primary racial identity of the superhero, opens up space for the nonhegemonic superhero to emerge. And while, as Cooke knows, DC's history does not see a nonwhite superhero appear for nearly two decades after the JLA's initial publication, his reimagining of the company's history brings to life Cold War America's domestic struggles with race, carving out room for thinking the possibility of the black superhero while at the same time making clear the black superhero's latent presence in the narratives of so many comic book superheroes like Manhunter, Superman, and others written as alien outsiders passing in a normative world of whiteness in the comics of the 1950s and 1960s.

*New Frontier* trades in two metaphors that have been central to narratives of race in American popular culture. The more recent of these sees the superhero as a surrogate for racial differences, a clichéd tokenism that, as comics scholar Marc Singer has pointed out, can be used to powerful, socially critical effect, but often instead offers "deceptively soothing stereotypes" that "obscure minority groups even as the writers pay lip service to diversity."[22] Such are the superheroes in *New Frontier,* who are shunned by US society and hunted by the government, though they lead otherwise successful lives as white Americans. Much older, and occasionally overlapping with the superhero-as-race metaphor—as evidenced by Superman and Manhunter; in Singer's reading, by the Legion of Superheroes; and in numerous, often muddled analyses of the X-Men[23]—is the use of the alien as an allegorical figuration of racial (and, at the turn of the century, colonial) Otherness. These metaphorical renderings of race, both of which are present in Cooke's comic, efface more nuanced considerations of the very formation of power they purport to represent, and thus do damage to the painful histories of race while obscuring or downplaying the dangers of whiteness.

Cooke is aware of the implications of these metaphors, as Manhunter's fascination with the relationship between alienness and blackness, and his ultimate rejection of that relationship in order to become white and a member of the superhero elite, underscores. Cooke's assertion of John Henry's story of real racial struggles in the midst of these metaphors also challenges

---

22. Singer, "'Black Skins' and White Masks," 107, 118.
23. On the problematic, multiple, shifting interpretations of the X-Men's Otherness, see Shyminsky, "Mutant Readers, Reading Mutants"; Lund, "The Mutant Problem."

any reading that would dismiss Cooke's understanding of their ability to erase history in superheroic and science fiction narratives. Rarely do superhero comics both assert the alien- or superhero-as-race metaphor and also undermine it through the actual presentation of race. Even rarer are uses of that presentation to critique the failures of the metaphors. Cooke allows histories of political uses of the superhero to collide and chafe at the generic figure's constitutive whiteness. Indeed, Cooke's critique comes through clearly in the comparison of Manhunter's and John Henry's narratives: Where Manhunter insists on the links between blackness and alienness as two comparable things Americans fear, as a shapeshifting alien superhero he is able to assimilate, but as a black man in 1950s Tennessee, John Henry meets with fatal violence.

As a result of editorial and creator prejudices or fears that black superheroes would hurt comics sales in the early decades of superhero comics, black superheroes didn't exist, so they certainly were not eligible for membership when the JLA debuted in 1960 with all its metaphorical diversity, featuring a white Amazon princess, a white scientist-athlete, a white space ranger, a white Atlantean king, and a green Martian. As Cooke put it in his annotations of *New Frontier*: "The problem [with retroactively writing about a black superhero in the 1950s] was DC catered to white culture."[24] Given the racial legacy of the genre at mid-century, then, Cooke's John Henry appears briefly, albeit in key moments, throughout the comic—and when he does appear, it is not as a superhero, but rather as a manifestation of the black folk hero of the same name.

John Henry is perhaps the most famous black folk hero, and certainly the one about whom the most has been said; he was also, as historian Scott Reynolds Nelson discovered, a real railroad worker in Reconstructionist West Virginia.[25] The legend is easily told but signifies powerfully onto the history of blackness: John Henry, a masterful steeldriver, challenged his foreman that he could drive more steel in one day than the foreman's new steam-powered engine; he did, but the effort cost him his life. These exploits were immortalized in dozens of songs about John Henry, reflecting a complex relationship in America between blackness and labor; the songs were "fantasies of escape" from a labor situation haunted by "the almost constant specter of death."[26] The subject of "the most researched folk song in the United States, and perhaps the world," John Henry was "appropriated to tell the story about the position of black men during Jim Crow, . . . about

---

24. Cooke, *DC*, n.p.
25. Nelson, *Steel Drivin' Man*, chap. 2.
26. Nelson, *Steel Drivin' Man*, 32, 36.

the coming of the machine age, about nostalgia for the past, ... about capitalism, and about the Black Power movement."[27] Foremost, the song was a warning against overwork and the dangers of racial capitalism to the black body. The folk hero became the inspiration for DC superhero Steel (John Henry Irons), a black construction worker-become-superhero, co-created by white writer Louise Simonson and white artist Jon Bogdanove in 1993 as one of four replacements for Superman after his "death"; the character proved mildly popular, landing his own series (1994–1998) and a film starring Shaquille O'Neal (1997).

Cooke's John Henry recasts Steel for an era when he could not have existed. In 1950s America, he is a vigilante driven by a classically generic origin story magnified by the horrors of Jim Crow: John Wilson and his family are hung by the KKK, but Wilson's rope breaks and he survives; Wilson dons an executioner's hood, cinched with the broken noose from his hanging, forges two massive hammers, and attacks KKK members to protect Southern blacks. Media brand him the "Modern Day John Henry."[28] His story numbers a mere eleven of the comic's four hundred pages, making him one of *New Frontier*'s minor characters; he appears in three short vignettes in issue #3 and dies in issue #4. As Cooke put it in his annotations, "I wanted the reader to know that there was no hope for him, and America was still years away from a time when there would be that hope."[29]

Bringing a more sincere connection to the source material, Cooke uses lyrics from several John Henry songs, plus his own lyrics, to tell Wilson's story. The lyrics overlay and lend a mythic significance to Wilson's few scenes, and Cooke wields the lyrics' meaning to fine effect, as for example during Wilson's first confrontation with the KKK as John Henry, which Cooke narrates using portions of the John Henry songs about his pledge to defeat the machine. In the final image of the scene, a single-page splash, Wilson/John Henry is shown from low-angle perspective, his massive size spread out before a blazing black church set alight by the KKK, his hammers at rest after the confrontation: "*John Henry told the captain that a man is just a man, and I swear by all that's right and wrong I'll kill you where you stand.*"[30] This threat is likely Cooke's own lyric, since it promises a violent confrontation with the foreman rather than just the contest with the steam-engine steeldriver. Cooke juxtaposes the machine and its ties with racial capitalism, acknowledging their survival of Reconstruction, *de jure* through Jim Crow

---

27. Nelson, *Steel Drivin' Man*, 2, 40.
28. Cooke, *DC*, 221.
29. Cooke, *DC*, n.p.
30. Cooke, *DC*, 184.

and *de facto* through racist violence perpetrated by the KKK and unchecked by local, state, or federal officials.

While *New Frontier* is a love letter to DC superheroes on the cusp of the Silver Age, John Henry's narrative is the crux of Cooke's critical nostalgia. John Henry exists in a period when the superhero has been outlawed, and though isolated from other characters except through news reports read and overheard by Manhunter, he has all the trappings of the superhero: a (tragic) original story, a secret identity, an iconic costume, and a pro-social mission.[31] But whereas the superheroes of *New Frontier* prevail through their HUAC-led persecution to become integral members of the US nation-state and the Cold War military-industrial complex, the black superhero goes unrecognized as a superheroic figure, remaining instead a "Modern Day" folk hero.[32] The denial of *New Frontier*'s black superhero is triple: It occurs within the storyworld, in the history that Cooke draws on, and in part in Cooke's own rhetoric for including a proto-version of Steel. For Cooke, "any effort to insinuate the DCU[niverse] into the real world of the 1950s wouldn't have been complete without looking at the civil rights issues of the day."[33] While John Henry is a serious vector for telling the story of blackness and race in America, his presence is mandated by a more just telling of history, one inclusive of race, rather than any inclination toward giving a black superhero his own story alongside the JLA greats. This is not to say that Cooke's motivation is wrongheaded, but rather to point out that the black superhero emerges only in the context of race issues, is always a means to talk about race or to satisfy a need for diversity. After all, the superhero, unmarked, is white, even when metaphorizing Otherness. The black superhero is only possible, John Henry suggests, through a narrative process of marking that makes him something other than the superhero.

John Henry's death is therefore necessary, since he will remain forever marked, first as black in a world where race matters, then—and only then—like the others, as a superhero in a world where superheroism is briefly outlawed. While John Henry's role is thematically and politically significant to *New Frontier*, Cooke uses John Henry, his story, and his death to emphasize Manhunter's identity quest. When, for example, John Henry is killed—betrayed by a white girl[34] whom he asks for help, then burned to death by KKK—and news of his death is broadcast nationwide, it deals a devastating

---

31. Coogan, *Superhero*, 30.
32. Cooke, *DC*, 221.
33. Cooke, *DC*, n.p. (annotations).
34. Cooke, writing on the blond white girl in his annotations: "the most innocent creature I could imagine." *DC*, n.p.

blow to Manhunter's faith in humanity (and by proxy, Americans) to deal with difference. Learning the news while in John Jones disguise at a bar with his detective partner, Manhunter remarks, "That man was a hero . . . A *freedom fighter!* A symbol of hope and resistance," or all that is definitive of a patriotic American. His partner explains, "This is America, not some sugar-coated utopia," prompting Manhunter to ask: "What do you think they'd do if they ever found one of those aliens they always talk about?"[35] Manhunter conflates alienness and race, and draws the conclusion that he, too, could be lynched. But not unsurprisingly, the metaphorical connections between alienness and blackness break down. It is not John Henry's death, in the end, that prompts Manhunter's attempt to leave Earth; no, he makes this decision later when the Flash takes over a news broadcast to announce he is giving up being a superhero because of government persecution.[36] Manhunter chooses the meaning of his alienness, between race and the superhero, between blackness and whiteness, and aligns himself ultimately with the group more easily integrated into DC's postwar America. As one able to be and become white, he does what John Henry cannot; he chooses his identity, he lives, and he becomes a superhero.

## Coda

One of the final images Cooke gives us of Manhunter appears in the epilogue, after Manhunter and the future JLA have defeated the Centre. The epilogue includes scenes from the lives of the various characters featured throughout *New Frontier*, each paired with a consecutive portion of Kennedy's "New Frontier" speech, the pairing often highlighting the relationship between the comic's narrative and the historical circumstances of the dawning Kennedy era. Cooke gives us, for example, an image of a young black boy with the name "Irons" on his jersey (and thus, ostensibly, the future 1990s Steel) reading next to the mossy gravestone of "John Wilson AKA John Henry," paired with the text of Kennedy's speech that stresses "a peaceful revolution for human rights—demanding an end to racial discrimination in all parts of our community life."[37] And a panel showing a black boy passing

---

35. Cooke, *DC*, 239. In an expert formal juxtaposition, following the partner's comment that America is not a utopia, Cooke's next page offers a sensuous glimpse at utopian life on Wonder Woman's Paradise Island, beginning a scene in which Wonder Woman rejects American political self-righteousness.
36. Cooke, *DC*, 247.
37. Cooke, *DC*, 399.

a "WHITE ONLY" water fountain tops a later page, paired with Kennedy claiming, "Today some would say that those struggles are all over—that all the horizons have been explored—that all the battles have been won—that there is no longer an American frontier."[38] The suggestion from Cooke's inventive juxtaposition is that, just as W. E. B. Du Bois called "the problem of the Twentieth Century . . . the color-line," that problem remained as Kennedy's very own American frontier, even as Kennedy meant something wholly different: the frontier of America's techno-scientific, social, economic, and geopolitical global dominance.[39]

Sandwiched between the pages bearing these two images of the new American frontier that Cooke articulates as race is a full-page splash that features Superman and Manhunter, side by side as friends, turning away from the reader, looking out across a rich field of wheat, both heroes bathed in the golden light of a storm breaking and casting sunlight onto the field. Paired to this image is a lengthy selection from Kennedy's speech about the pioneering spirit of those who first set out across the old American frontier, "determined to make that new world strong and free, to overcome its hazards and its hardships, to conquer the enemies that threatened from without and within."[40] Martian Manhunter, now a JLA superhero alongside his equal and idol Superman, an icon of assimilated difference, has become not just a G-man but a triumphal pioneer of the new American frontier. Yet the images of the black boys circling Manhunter's triumph of belonging throw their shade, casting doubt on the possibility of integration, signaling the limits of whiteness's plasticity in an age of heightened racial tensions. Though a wide-ranging and nostalgic love letter to DC Comics's history, *New Frontier* is at the same time a racial critique of the superhero comic. Cooke utilizes the destabilized, plastic, and racially ambiguous body of Martian Manhunter—who by all rights, as an alien, should sit beyond the discourses of race in America—to complicate and point to the power of racial structures, and in particular whiteness, to incorporate differences, while at the same time demonstrating the ultimate contingency of whiteness in the field of racial formation.

---

38. Cooke, *DC*, 401.
39. Du Bois, *Souls*, 20.
40. Cooke, *DC*, 400.

# Bibliography

Alexander, Michelle. *The New Jim Crow: Mass Incarceration in the Age of Colorblindness.* New York: The New Press, 2010.

Brodkin, Karen. *How Jews Became White Folks and What That Says about Race in America.* New Brunswick, NJ: Rutgers University Press, 1998.

Coogan, Peter. *Superhero: The Secret Origin of a Genre.* Austin, TX: MonkeyBrain Books, 2006.

Cooke, Darwyn. *DC: The New Frontier.* New York: DC Comics, 2016.

Du Bois, W. E. B. *The Souls of Black Folk.* Mineola, NY: Dover Publications, 1994.

Guglielmo, Thomas A. *White on Arrival: Italians, Race, Color, and Power in Chicago, 1890–1945.* Oxford: Oxford University Press, 2004.

Hall, Jacquelyn Dowd. "The Long Civil Rights Movement and the Political Uses of the Past." *The Journal of American History* 91, no. 4 (2005): 1233–1263.

Ignatiev, Noel. *How the Irish Became White.* New York: Routledge, 2009.

Jacobson, Matthew Frye. *Whiteness of a Different Color: European Immigrants and the Alchemy of Race.* Cambridge, MA: Harvard University Press, 1999.

James, Edward. "Yellow, Black, Metal, and Tentacled: The Race Question in American Science Fiction." In *Black and Brown Planets: The Politics of Race in Science Fiction,* edited by Isiah Lavender III, 199–222. Jackson, MS: University Press of Mississippi, 2014.

Kennedy, John F. "1960 Democratic National Convention, 15 July 1960." John F. Kennedy Presidential Library and Museum, www.jfklibrary.org/Asset-Viewer/AS08q50Yz0SFUZg9uOi4iw.aspx.

Kilgore, De Witt Douglas. "Difference Engine: Aliens, Robots, and Other Racial Matters in the History of Science Fiction." *Science Fiction Studies* 37, no. 1 (March 2010): 16–22.

Lavender, Isiah III. *Race in American Science Fiction.* Bloomington: University of Indiana Press, 2011.

Lund, Martin. "The Mutant Problem: X-Men, Confirmation Bias, and the Methodology of Comics and Identity." *European Journal of American Studies* 10, no. 2 (Summer 2015): http://journals.openedition.org/ejas/10890.

McDermott, Sinead. "Memory, Nostalgia, and Gender in *A Thousand Acres.*" *Signs: Journal of Women in Culture and Society* 28, no. 1 (2002): 389–407.

Morrison, Toni. *Playing in the Dark: Whiteness and the Literary Imagination.* Cambridge, MA: Harvard University Press, 1992.

Nelson, Scott Reynolds. *Steel Drivin' Man: John Henry, the Untold Story of an American Legend.* Oxford: Oxford University Press, 2008.

Omi, Michael, and Howard Winant. *Racial Formation in the United States: From the 1960s to the 1990s.* 2nd ed. New York: Routledge, 1994.

Roediger, David R. *How Race Survived U. S. History: From Settlement and Slavery to the Obama Phenomenon.* New York: Verso, 2010.

Salter, Colin. *Whiteness and Social Change: Remnant Colonialisms and White Civility in Australia and Canada.* Newcastle upon Tyne: Cambridge Scholars Publishing, 2013.

Shyminsky, Neil. "Mutant Readers, Reading Mutants: Appropriation, Assimilation, and the X-Men." *International Journal of Comic Art* 8, no. 2 (Fall 2006): 387–405.

Singer, Marc. "'Black Skins' and White Masks: Comic Books and the Secret of Race," *African American Review* 36, no. 1 (Spring 2002): 107–19.

Spitzer, Leo. *Hotel Bolivia: The Culture of Memory in a Refuge from Nazism*. New York: Hill & Wang, 1999.

PART III

# Whiteness by a Different Color

CHAPTER 11

# WHITE OR INDIAN?

Whiteness and Becoming the White Indian Comics Superhero

YVONNE CHIREAU

## Introduction

Whether viewed as hilarious or horrifying, few comics characters are as racially anomalous as the white Indian superhero. We see him with pink-tinged skin and azure eyes, as Manzar the Bright Arrow, thundering into battle on horseback in a feathered war bonnet. As Firehair, a freckled redhead wearing a youthful warrior's buckskin. Statuesque, arms folded, blond hair wrapped in leather, he is Rojhaz, a time-traveling, Indian version of Steve Rogers/Captain America in the year 1602. As the romantic leading man Injun Jones, he dons warpaint to become a chieftain in the Piegan Nation. Elsewhere, he exudes rugged strength as a wilderness survivor in the heroic epic *White Indian*. Finally, he blasts onto the scene, a relentlessly violent action figure without tribe or sanctuary, as Scalphunter, Ke-No-Woh-Tay, He Who Is Less Than Human.

"Indian or White Man?" demands the tagline on the cover of *The Apache Kid* (1950), a comic about a white cowboy with a secret Native American crime-fighter alias.[1] But how is race visualized when a white protagonist

---

1. Maneely, "The Comanches Strike!." *Apache Kid* ran for nineteen issues, from 1950 to 1956.

assumes the body and persona of a Native American? Is the Apache Kid's "whiteness" represented as distinct from his "Indianness"? In this chapter, I examine graphic figurations of white comics characters who become Indian superheroes. In highlighting whiteness as a mutable concept in these graphic narratives of racial self-definition, we can see the ways that the white Indian is "raced" with illustrations of his biography, including his remarkable origins and his acquisition of fantastic powers—the stuff that makes superheroes.[2]

This discussion draws from an array of Golden, Silver, and Bronze Age comics (c. 1938–1986) and considers the continuity of some white Indian characters into the twenty-first century. Most white Indian comics were created in the post–World War II period of the mid-1940s and 1950s. For the most part, American Indians played secondary and background roles to the white cowboys, gunslingers, and outlaws who occupied the exciting landscape of Wild West comics. Although rare and occasional, indigenous characters such as in the eponymous *Mantoka* (1940), *Bird Man* (1940), and *Nelvana* (1941) appeared alongside other players in this formative era of superhero comics. Popular in radio and film, cowboys soon eclipsed the masked avengers, detectives, and crime-fighting superheroes of the Golden Age, and white Indians flourished.[3] By the 1960s, an increasing number of Native Americans had entered into the comics and the predominance of the white Indian diminished, but his mythology would be revitalized in Hollywood films such as *A Man Called Horse* (1976), *Dances with Wolves* (1990), and, more recently, *Avatar* (2009) and *The Lone Ranger* (2013). While the archetype of the solitary white male whose heroic journey leads him to "become Indian" has all but disappeared from present-day comics, its legacy has endured, underscoring the contradictions and allure of cultural appropriation and its attendant narratives of white supremacy in popular media.[4]

## Playing Indian

Ironically, from the start an impressively diverse cast of characters populated white Indian comics, including a woman (*Firehair*, 1948), a Comanche (*Straight Arrow*, 1950), a child (*Johnny Injun*, 1954), and even a revenant (*Phantom Rider*, 1967). The first white Indian comics superhero was the Black Marvel, a masked and caped crime fighter who debuted in the omnibus

---

2. Rosenberg and Coogan, *What Is a Superhero?*, 7.
3. Savage, *Comic Books and America*, 69.
4. Barbour, From Daniel Boone to Captain America; Pavlik et al., *Native Apparitions*.

*Mystic Comics* (1940). Black Marvel's origin account tells the story of the white protagonist Dan Lyons, who defeats "a hundred of the finest braves in the country" in a series of tests of skill, strength, and endurance to "carry on the great traditions" of the "Blackfeet Chiefs." Gifting Lyons with a magical artifact and a new name, the elderly patriarch of the tribe, Man-to, gasps with amazement: "The white man has proved himself . . . bestow the Mantle of Black to the *new* Marvel!"[5] At the other end of the spectrum of white Indianness are two long-running Western comics brands, *Tomahawk* (1947)[6] and *Jonah Hex* (1972)[7]—the former about a rugged, deerskin-wearing frontiersman (see figure 11.1), and the latter, a Bronze Age, ex-Confederate, scarfaced bounty hunter whose white Indian legend recounted his exile from the Apache nation. Both drew copiously from the tropes of racial assimilation and appropriation that would become familiar in white Indian comics narratives.

Although Anglo-Indian encounters in Western genre comics tended to function as extraneous plot coupons, white Indian comics resituated narratives of historical interactions between Native Americans and non-indigenous peoples within the abiding fictions of white cross-racial passing. By foregrounding whiteness, the comics also underlined a vital subtext: the ensuing dependency of the white superhero upon indigenous Others as benefactors. Accordingly, these indigenous saviors would patronize whiteness as a superior racial formation. In what follows, we will see that in graphic accounts of superhero becoming, whiteness functions as both sign and signifier, bringing Indians to life in white bodies, and displacing real indigenous presence by way of a complicated racial mimesis.

In a detailed study of white Indian themes, Chad A. Barbour discusses the rhetorical meanings of indigenous appropriation in art, graphics, and literature and shows how ideologies of nationalism, race, and gender advanced the cultural production of white Indians as appealing vessels for promoting popular fantasies of a strong, masculine, and virtuous American male identity. Barbour concludes that the signifying racial performance of the white Indian organized its own "metonymic logic" with icons, items, and behaviors nominally affiliated with Indian traditions, even though the

---

5. Gabriele, "The Black Marvel."

6. Tomahawk is one of the longest-running characters in the Western comics genre. Originating in *Star-Spangled Comics* (1947), he would star in his own series from 1950 to 1972. The white Indian frontiersman character was also promoted as a tie-in with Hollywood cowboy comics stars. See Fox and Frazetta, "The White Indian Chief."

7. Jonah Hex made his first appearance in DC's *All-Star Western* (1972), before branching off with his own series (Fleisher and García-López, "Vengeance for a Fallen Gladiator"), which ran from 1977 until 1985.

FIGURE 11.1. Tomahawk as comics superhero (*Tomahawk* #68). © DC Comics. Image presented under fair use legislation.

cultural pluralism and material survivance of real Native American peoples was rendered invisible in the comics text. The temporal and spatial distance of historical Indian cultures was used to justify the creation of these contrived forms of indigeneity. Furthermore, with the "amplification of visual signs of Indianness" by white Indians, actual Native American presence was obscured. "Playing Indian," Barbour explains, "is a superficial masquerade, a performance of Indianness, usually originating from non-Native sources, with little connection to or regard for genuine history, ongoing traditions, and particular peoples."[8] In reviewing white Indian images, we can see how this superhero embodies both a negation and an affirmation of Indianness. I would also suggest that as a pervasive device of the comics imaginary, the

---

8. Barbour, *From Daniel Boone to Captain America*, 9.

white Indian superhero speaks to the power of whiteness to assert claims on racial Others so as to create its own virtual racial identity and to dominate, possess, and extract what is useful to itself.

In this chapter, I focus on representations of the white Indian as a comics superhero. The conventions associated with superheroes, including their use of spectacular, recognizable costumes, their secret identities, and their acquisition of incredible powers, correlate with graphic depictions of white Indians. We might interpret narratives of the white Indian as a kind of redface minstrelsy, the vestiges of similar, widely accepted traditions of staged racial fantasy and performance in the US during the nineteenth and early twentieth centuries. It may be that these comics characters reflect cultural anxieties associated with the reification of whiteness in America during the postwar period.

Of course, white Indians are not unique to comics. Historically, iterations of racial appropriation have simultaneously co-opted and marginalized Native American bodies in many areas of popular culture, as was the case with Hollywood movies throughout much of the twentieth century, when it was common practice for non-Native actors to claim Native American identities and re-present them in stereotyped and outlandish forms. Entirely produced by non-indigenous creators, the white Indian of the comics does much of the same work in film media while externalizing fears of, and fascination with, corporeal absorption by the racial Other, in graphic formats. For it is not only by displaying "key signature items" of the Indian's costume, as Chad Barbour notes—the buckskins, headbands, moccasins, feathers, and warpaint accoutrements by which the white Indian comics character creates the visual effect of his heroic persona—but by his physical embodiment of Indian "ways" that this superhero constitutes whiteness as Indianness.[9] A review of white Indian comics indicates that (1) far from being neutral and non-situated, whiteness establishes its own visible material essence in white Indian comics superhero images, and (2) although disguised by the Indian costume, whiteness becomes Indianness, paradoxically, through the medium of the white racialized body. Accordingly, the white Indian superhero cannot become an Indian without transmuting his own whiteness. One might say that the transmutation of whiteness—made possible by the metaphorical appropriation of an Indian body through rites of passage—is the requisite "superpower" widely deployed by these comics protagonists.

So what is "white" about the white Indian comics superhero? And what does whiteness look like in an Indian body? Let us consider the white Indian as visual subject. Whether he is blond or pale, bearded or redheaded, freck-

---

9. Barbour, *From Daniel Boone to Captain America*, 5.

led or swarthy, the white Indian comics character enacts Indianness in a composite form. If, as sartorial design scholars Barbara Brownie and Danny Graydon argue, the superhero costume (in this case, iconographic "traditional" Native American regalia) functions as a mask that enables "two identities" that are "seemingly incompatible," what can one say about the coinciding embodiment of dual racial identities in the persona of the white Indian?[10] The white Indian registers race by marking difference in and on the graphic body. But which body, which race? "Can a man be white—with the free, fighting heart of a redskin?" asks the header in the comics series *Blazing West* (1948) (see figure 11.2).[11] On the inset of the first panel, we see the portrait of a stern man of deep hue and fierce visage, clasping a war hatchet, gazing out across the page. With dark-brown skin painted with stripes the color of blood, a beaded headband, and piercing blue eyes, his anomalous physiognomy presses the question: "Indian or White Man?" With this striking facsimile, the reader confronts the instability of race, even as the superhero drama propels the biography forward.

The white Indian is indelibly linked to a discursive practice known as "playing Indian."[12] Playing Indian, similar to "going Native," encompasses cultural appropriation, racial disguise, impersonation, and other acts of imitation of indigenous people by non-Natives. Comics critic and Caddo scholar Michael Sheyahshe discusses playing Indian and Native American comic book stereotypes in relation to the "Mohican Syndrome," referring to the frontier stories of nineteenth-century novelist James Fenimore Cooper, whose portrayals of civilization, noble red men, and savages shaped modern notions of indigeneity in the US.[13] Sheyahshe characterizes the Mohican Syndrome as a comics device that involves a protagonist who becomes a superlative representative of indigenous traditions by virtue of his participation in Native ways of life. The white Indian acquires knowledge and proficiency, says Sheyahshe, by his "absorption" of Native American heritage and attains Indian identity through "some sort of osmotic metamorphosis."[14] A reformulation of the Mohican Syndrome is seen in most comics that deploy white Indian tropes. And although Sheyahshe asserts that there are no superpowers associated with the white Indian character, I would argue that the ability to simultaneously deracinate and racialize the self might be considered one of the great superpowers—and one of the more advantageous and devious

---

10. Brownie and Graydon, *The Superhero Costume*, 28–29.
11. Hughes et al., "Injun Jones."
12. On the history of this phenomenon, see Deloria, *Playing Indian*.
13. Sheyahshe, *Native Americans in Comic Books*, 13–14.
14. Sheyahshe, *Native Americans in Comic Books*, 14.

FIGURE 11.2. Injun Jones, blue-eyed Indian (*Blazing West* #1). © American Comics Group. Image presented under fair use legislation.

privileges of whiteness—that is enacted by the white Indian comics hero. As we will see, these characters become superheroes not only by appropriating the identity of the racial other but by transmuting whiteness so as to become the Other.

## Whiteness in a Red Body

The Fiction House series *Indians* (1950) sets forth a conspicuous pattern in postwar-era white Indian comics: a protagonist's dramatic transformation from ordinary everyman to powerful Native American hero. On the cover of the first issue (see figure 11.3), Manzar the Bright Arrow charges forward on horseback, bow raised and drawn, leading a group of indistinguishable braves. The "wildest son of the savage Sioux," with blue eyes and white skin he evokes a commanding presence, as befits his assumed identity as a Lakota chieftain. "When the smoke-sign spelled danger in the Black Hills, Dan Carter the trader, vanished," announces the title montage, "and blazing along the peril-trails rode *Bright Arrow*, blue-eyed son of the Sioux, shouting the battle-cry . . . *Hoka-Hai!*"[15] Manzar's secret alter ego, an effete businessman named Dan Carter, stands in stark contrast to this mighty Indian warrior. In his covert identity as Dan Carter, he appears as a weak and sometimes cowardly city-bred rancher, but as Manzar he is a fearless defender of righteousness and truth on the frontier.

The duality of these extremes between hidden whiteness and public Indianness is symbolized by the contrast between strength and vulnerability, and savagery and civilization, a consistent pattern in white Indian comics. For the white Indian superhero, illustrations of this dualism emphasize his transformed, reinvigorated appearance, his semi-clad, muscular physique, his fierce martial prowess, and his mastery of traditional Indian skills such as hunting, bow and arrow, horseback riding, and tracking. Similarly, in the Timely Comics series *The Apache Kid* (1950), we see the apotheosis of a mild-mannered white cowboy into a magnificent Native American protector of justice.[16] In *The Apache Kid*, a shiftless saddle tramp named Aloysius Kare becomes the avenging Apache Kid, a "valiant champion of right," raucously touted in the comic's promotional blurb as "the West's most mysterious warrior!"[17] With the Apache Kid, the classic superhero secret identity device is used with great purpose in sequences that show Kare's quick costume change from white man's dress to the feathers and warpaint of an Indian super-chief. Like Manzar, the Apache Kid requires a superficial disguise, for with his fair skin, painted facial stripes, and noble bearing, he is seen, compellingly, to enact an inner "Indianness" that overlays his exteriorized racial identity.[18]

In their moments of visual transubstantiation, White Indian protagonists are fully white, yet fully Indian, inhabiting racialized qualities that signal heroic virtue. "White man trained to think and act like an Indian, but live like a white man!"[19] roars the banner for *The Golden Warrior* (1951), one of the few masked white Indian superheroes in this era. The Golden Warrior elaborates several familiar superhero conventions. As a fair-haired youth named David Brown, he is cared for by the Cheyenne after his parents die at the hands of outlaws, receiving his calling as he comes of age. "Now you must leave us . . . you must give your life to stamp out all evil, whether it be Indian or white man!" pleads his elderly father Chief Mountain Thunder,

---

15. Starr, "Hoka-Hai!"
16. Buscema, "Massacre at Fort Madison!" The Apache Kid debuted in 1950 in *Two-Gun Western*, later receiving his own title, thereafter *Apache Kid*, from 1950 to 1956.
17. Maneely, "The Comanches Strike!"
18. Barbour, *From Daniel Boone to Captain America*, 134–36.
19. Cameron, "Golden Warrior."

FIGURE 11.3. Manzar, the white Indian chief (*Indians* #1). © Fiction House Publishing. Image presented under fair use legislation.

before sending him away on his mission.[20] With a skirted loincloth, a quiver of magical arrows strapped against his chest, and a circle of gold on his brow, his profile suggests a classical Grecian figurine (see figure 11.4). When among his Cheyenne compatriots, he uses the crudely scripted gibberish of comics dialogue that passes for a Native American vernacular—"*Hamaw Yestar!*" "*Tankaz Harf!*"—while in his form as David Brown, his timid and

---

20. Cameron, "Golden Warrior," 6.

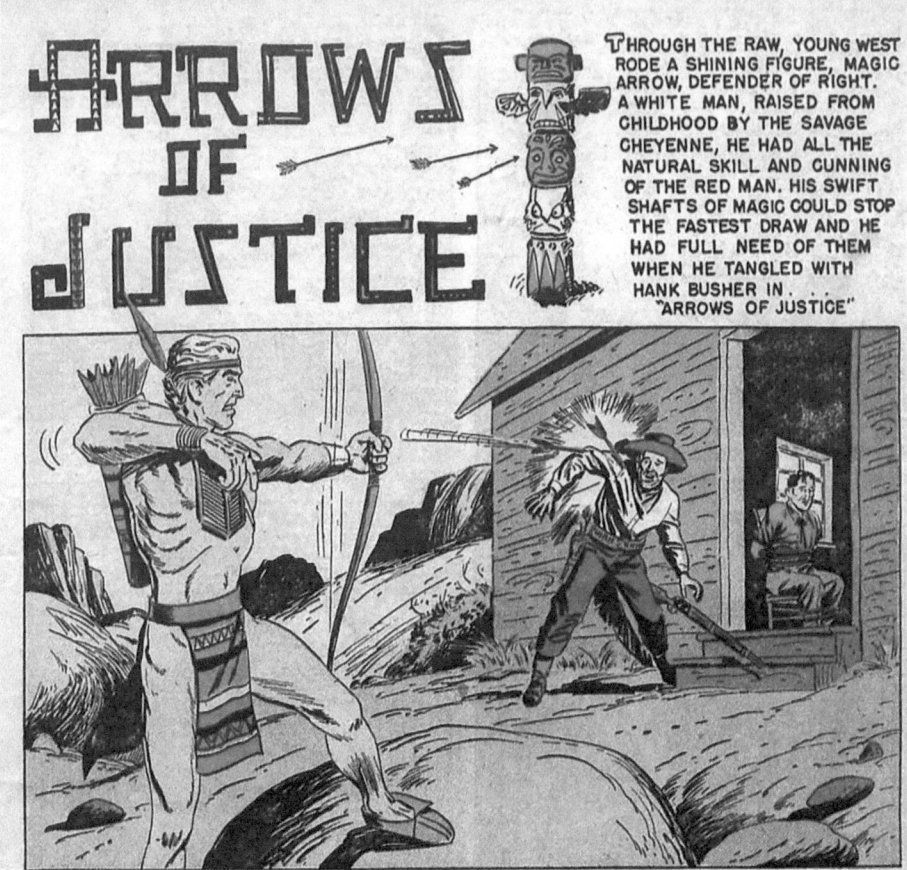

FIGURE 11.4. David Brown, the Cheyenne-adopted Golden Warrior (*Indian Fighter* #2). © Youthful Magazines. Image presented under fair use legislation.

blond alter ego, he is known to "talk queer for a cowboy," his broken English adding intrigue to his dissimulation.[21]

We can contrast visuals of the Golden Warrior with those of his comics contemporary in *Pawnee Bill* (1951), "white chief of the Pawnee Indian scouts," touted as *"cleverer than his fellow white men and craftier than the Indians among whom he lived!"*[22] Pawnee Bill sports a yellow mustache and shoulder-length hair in a style reminiscent of Buffalo Bill Cody, the real-life Wild West showman upon whom this character is loosely based. Pawnee Bill has

---

21. Cameron, "Golden Warrior," 6.
22. Cameron, "Trail of the Ambush Killers," 1; Cohen, Kiemle, and Larson, "Pawnee Bill."

no secret identity and moves easily between the white and Indian worlds. Among his Native peers, he goes shirtless and wears a feathered headband, bellowing in the clichéd drawl of the Western cowboy, *"No yuh don't, yuh dry gulchin' hoot owl!"*[23] The linguistic incongruity between Indian and white man's talk is acknowledged within the text itself, as it is an instance in which white Indian racial self-definition exists in tension with its Indianness. Nonetheless, the anomalies of graphic representation allow for this, since it is by his embodiment of whiteness that the character qualifies as a superhero. No matter how incongruous or maladroit his appearance, he is seen to balance his public performance as an Indian against his private, "white" self.

Herein lies the paradox of the white Indian. In accordance with superhero comics conventions, in which the transformation of a civilian into a superhero is normally accomplished with technological or magical means, the white Indian relies upon a process of racialization to achieve the same results. His whiteness must be made visible to register the transmutation. The act of racial appearance and disappearance is a sleight of hand that is "conjured," says Barbour, "through material or visual symbols, specific objects, designs, or props" so as to impart an "idealized projection of Indianness."[24] The white Indian maintains his whiteness "while adopting Indianness in his dress and abilities" as the visual distinctions between his public and secret identity are "raced" with extravagant bodily metamorphoses.[25] It is the negation of the Indian phenotype that I wish to call attention to, the visual displays of his subjectivity. It is by maintaining physical characteristics associated with embodied whiteness that a white Indian superhero is imagined as absorbing "Indianness" but not assimilating into it.

The white Indian superhero constitutes his racial disguise with distinct signifiers. For example, the transference of embodied whiteness to embodied Indianness in "quick change" panels manifests evidence of an outer and inner modification, with whiteness disguised by Indianness, so to speak. Although suited for this kind of presentation, the graphic production of phenotypes to designate racial difference are unstable and often inconsistent. Take, for example, the composition of Ke-Woh-No-Tay/Brian Savage in *The Scalphunter* (1972), one of the few white Indian characters introduced in the Bronze Age.[26] An orphan rescued by Kiowa Indians during a massacre at

---

23. Cameron, "Trail of the Ambush Killers," 8.
24. Barbour, *From Daniel Boone to Captain America*, 5. See also Deloria, *Playing Indian*, 120.
25. Barbour, *From Daniel Boone to Captain America*, 6.
26. Fleisher, Ayers, and Evans, "Scalphunter."

his family's homestead, Ke-Woh-No-Tay enacts a life story that aligns with those of other white Indians, albeit with a caveat that turns the offense of race prejudice back onto the comic's indigenous characters: Due to his Anglo ancestry, the tribe will not accept Brian Savage/Ke-Woh-No-Tay as a full member of the Kiowa nation. Because his adopted Kiowa will not honor him as one of their own, Ke-Woh-No-Tay strives to "gain strong magic" so that one day he will be recognized as a warrior. Lost and deranged, like a Dark Knight of the frontier, he exacts vigilante justice against Wild West reprobates with the murderous practice associated with his nickname, Scalphunter. "When the Great Spirit looks down from his Sky Valley and sees these scalps," he shouts, bloody locks in hand, "he will know that I am brave and I have slain my enemies!"[27] Notwithstanding this editorial gesture toward a false equivalency between inter-ethnic tribalism and anti-Indian racial prejudice, the story of *Scalphunter* is that of a hero's struggle to inhabit a dual identity in a world that will not allow him to do so, for Brian Savage, a white man, believes "in his heart, in his soul, he is a Kiowa."[28]

The themes of racial erasure and appropriation envisaged in *Scalphunter* are enhanced with sketches of Brian Savage/Ke-Woh-No-Tay that illustrate his anomalous whiteness, concurrent with his suitably "ethnic" Native American physiognomy. His form alternates between that of an objectified Indian male, with brown skin, glossy black hair, and high cheekbones, and in other cases, images that use the representational iconography of white comics savages like Conan the Barbarian and Kull the Conqueror.[29] The ambiguous images exteriorize the character's turbulent inner conflict by projecting his inability to resolve the meaning of his racial origins, as seen in this exchange between Ke-Woh-No-Tay and his elderly, bedridden birth father, Matt Savage:

MATT SAVAGE: I-is that really you, Brian? Are yuh my long-lost boy?
KE-WOH-NO-TAY: . . . I can speak! I am not your son! I am Ke-Woh-No-Tay, warrior of the Kiowa!
MATT SAVAGE: Why, you ain't no Kiowa, boy! Yuh got eyes as blue as lake water, just like your mother had! . . . An yuh ain't no warrior, either! Look at yuh!
KE-WOH-NO-TAY: No! You lie! . . . I am *not* a white man! I am *not* your son! I am a *Kiowa!*[30]

---

27. Conway, Ayers, Evans, Serpe, and Simek, "City of Shame!"
28. Fleisher, Ayers, Evans, and Berube, "The Mark of a Warrior."
29. Fleisher, Ayers, Evans, and Berube, "The Mark of a Warrior."
30. Fleisher, Ayers, and Evans, "Scalphunter."

Although represented to display an idealized superhero masculinity, the white Indian is often cast as the Other who becomes the object of denigration, ridicule, and scorn by antagonists, or by his own compatriots, who elicit suspicion toward his racially marked body, perceiving it as strange, even monstrous. Consider the 2009 science fiction/fantasy film *Avatar*, in which the protagonist integrates his human consciousness into the blue body of an alien being called a Na'vi. In this transhuman tale of tribal adoption and assimilation, Jake Sully is the white human-alien who goes Native with a bioengineered form of the Indian-styled Na'vi. And although he has ostensibly become a Na'vi, he is viewed by the indigenous beings as ugly, freakish, a poor counterfeit: "These aliens *try* to look like people," sneers a Na'vi warrior with contempt, "but they *can't*."[31]

They *try*, but they *can't*: The white outcast who embodies Indianness remains white. His affective claim to Indianness turns on a compelling execution of Native American subjectivity. The graphic representation demands that by highlighting phenotypic characteristics such as blond hair and blue eyes, these physiognomic markers might affirm the white Indian's racialized whiteness. Visually, the incongruity of the white Indian character—in particular his hybrid nature—serves the aesthetic function of defining racial hierarchy within the ideological lens of whiteness. The juxtaposition between the hero's racial features and his racial ambiguity as conveyed in the text positions whiteness as explicitly superior. The arrogance of whiteness asserts that the white Indian body should be valorized for its appearance, since it is an impressive—though still anomalous—object of cultural production.

From the postwar era onward, the concept of playing Indian in the comics would go mainstream, with episodic masquerades by superheroes such as Captain Marvel (1948), Superman (1950), Batman (1954), and even a canine Indian chief, Rex the Wonder Dog (1955).[32] And although it would be decades before Native Americans achieved fair representation, by the final quarter of the century some white Indian comics advanced more nuanced treatments of racial themes. The presentation of heroic self-discovery and heroic becoming through racial identity formation would be established in these late iterations of the white Indian.

---

31. Cameron, *Avatar*.
32. Barbour, "When Captain America Was an Indian," 269.

## Transmutation of Whiteness in the White Indian Body

With their divergent graphic biographies, the figurative dilemma of white Indian characters is how to present whiteness as an embodied identity. Of course, the idea fits well with the idea of the superhero's secret alias. After all, these texts of transformation and empowerment establish whiteness as superheroic *becoming*. With every costume change from ordinary civilian to Native warrior, or every cosmetic shift from mild-mannered protagonist to super-Indian, a racialist conceit supports the premise that white can become red through the metamorphosis of an inner essence, sometimes described idiomatically as "soul" or "spirit" (although "blood" remains the authorized metaphor within contemporary regimes of tribal classification by the United States government).[33] The white Indian superhero demonstrates the instability of race as a biological and physical construct, even as whiteness is made and remade in anomalous presentations in the comics narratives. Transfigurations of embodied whiteness by costume change and physical disguise may be understood as the product of allegorical rites of passage that validate the racialized persona of the hero, grounding and authenticating his role as an adept, a superior Indian—in a white body. I argue that through rites of passage, the white Indian protagonist transmutes his whiteness by a profound reformation of the self. His Indianness is conferred by transitions of status that are marked by trauma, for with few exceptions chronicles of the white Indian include a crisis at the origin point, precipitating a rupture in the social moorings of the hero's world.

Dan Brand, for example, star of the *White Indian* series (1953), commences the journey into Indianness when he, a wealthy eighteenth-century Philadelphian, plunges into the dangerous wilderness after the tragic death of his fiancée.[34] Similar concerns of estrangement and revenge animate the plot of the series *Tomahawk* (1950), about a Daniel Boone–styled character whose travails are illustrated with perilous scenes of his captivity, ferocious animal attacks, and desperate wilderness survival sequences. Like Dan Brand's White Indian, the buckskin-clad, coonskin hat–wearing frontiersman Thomas Hawkins's adventures begin when he is an adult. For white Indian stories following this pattern, the protagonist assumes the role of an exile, a castaway, or an abject figure who is torn away from family, freedom, and the trappings of civilization. Plot structures thus incorporate the emotional and material challenges faced by the hero and exemplify the American frontier mythos of individual self-determination through raw courage, brute

---

33. Barbour, *From Daniel Boone to Captain America*, 183.
34. *White Indian* started as a short-story series in *The Durango Kid* (1949), before branching off with *White Indian Comics* from 1953 to 1955.

strength, and physical will. Graphic scripts that display the robust and virile masculinity of the white Indian are so normative that their elaboration is routine.³⁵

It is noteworthy that transitions from whiteness to Indianness are modeled after fabricated and reconfigured renderings of indigenous traditions that are presented as genuine Indianized rites of passage. Indeed, within indigenous cultures such initiations and status transformations are forged within a crucible of sacred practices and beliefs that confer meaning during significant life changes such as birth, puberty, marriage, and death. Universally, the white Indian stories reprise initiation narratives to depict the process of becoming by which a protagonist enters the Native American world with the help of a tribal father figure, who later becomes his most significant patron. Adoption-initiation provides thematic framing in support of a character's Indianization, allowing a reimagining of whiteness as an abstracted state of being. Here again the white protagonist invariably shows himself as a prodigy amongst his tribal family, displaying his natural superiority with Native heritage abilities such as tracking, hunting, fighting, and athletics. In white Indian storylines, fictitious initiations provide elaborate staging for the protagonist's transmutation of his whiteness. Consider, for example, the 1975 comic series about a freckle-faced, redheaded, green-eyed Blackfoot boy named Firehair, whose coming of age featured a sweat lodge ceremony and a psychic vision quest.³⁶ In *Firehair*,³⁷ issues of racial discrimination and ethnic prejudice preceded the hero's entry to adulthood, with the white body envisioned as a proving ground of identity formation. In his constructed role as a troubled outcast with angsty teenage sensibilities, Firehair attends to themes of alienation and alterity that were familiar to readers of Bronze Age comics, with its outsider characters, mutant misfits, and ethno-racial minorities whose stories reflected the cultural sensibilities of the insurgent youth and social protest movements in the US of the 1960s and 1970s.³⁸ "Repelled by the whites because of his Indian-like appearance, and rejected by the Indians because of his white heritage," Firehair undergoes trials that also bring to mind pop culture forays into indigenous mysticism, with extravagant displays of out-of-body journeys, nightmarish apparitions, and psychedelic visionary experiences.³⁹

---

35. Wright, *Comic Book Nation*, 68; Barbour, *From Daniel Boone to Captain America*, 104–12.

36. Kubert and Costanza, "The Shaman!"

37. The original Firehair, the "white queen of the Indians," played recurring roles in Western-themed comics, including *Ranger Comics* (1947) and *Pioneer West Romances* (1950), as well as her own *Firehair* series (1951).

38. Wright, *Comic Book Nation*.

39. Kubert and Costanza, "The Shaman!"

The specious commodification of indigenous religions culminated with the rise of "instant shaman" Native American superhero tropes in the 1980s and 1990s.[40] Similar portrayals of white racial transmutation by rites of passage were depicted in *Avatar*, with scenes of the white Indian superhero and his indigenous counterparts navigating dreamtime rituals of initiation and using hallucinogenic sacred medicines. While memes of shamanism inspired fanciful takes on Native American initiation practices in Bronze Age comics, white Indian characters began to engage issues of racial conflict and miscegenation, allegorizing their racial rites of passage in rituals of transmutation. *Son of Tomahawk* (1970), a short-lived spinoff of the older *Tomahawk* series, featured the half-Apache, half-white progeny of the original white Indian frontiersman.[41] As with other white Indian characters, "Hawk" Hawkins presents as a starkly anomalous figure. A young rebel with the "dark slit eyes of a hawk," his embodied whiteness is literalized with a blond streak dividing his jet-black hairline. In an episode recounting his persecution as a "half-breed" at the hands of a sadistic bounty hunter, Hawk is determined to make sense of his racial identity. Confronted by his criminal nemesis, he is forced to run a deadly race for his own survival, a ritualized contest similar to that depicted on-screen in the sensationally violent film *Run of the Arrow* (1957). In both accounts, the hero enacts the running ordeal as a white Indian's rite of passage. "I've got to be *all-Indian* to outlive the bounty hunter," Hawk shouts, barefoot and bare-chested, as he hurtles into what is literally a run for his life. "Here's where we both find out . . . how much Indian I really am!"[42]

Similar racialized and transformative rites of passage can be seen in *A Man Called Horse* (1970), a film about a blond, blue-eyed British aristocrat who assimilates the "savage ways" of the Sioux Indians in the Dakota territory during the nineteenth century. The dramatic center of this cinematic epic is a mortification ceremony called the "vow to the sun," in which the white Indian protagonist is shown suspended high above the earth, bone hooks embedded in his flesh, in a tortuous sacrament of endurance, agony, and ecstasy. An identical scene is re-created in *Shaman's Tears* (1993), a comic about a modern Sioux Irish detective who becomes a superpowered Indian crime fighter after undergoing initiation rites, a graphic vow to the sun that is ostensibly modeled after the Lakota "Sun Dance."[43] Here we see that the consolidation of racialized whiteness, corporeality, and superhero identity exerts a powerful impetus as white Indian characters become "Indianized"

---

40. Sheyahshe, *Native Americans in Comic Books*.
41. Kanigher et al., "Hang Him High!"
42. Kanigher, Costanza, and Thorne, "Hawk Faces the Scalp Hunter!"
43. Grell et al., *Shaman's Tears*.

through initiation practices that are presented as authentic forms of Native American ceremonialism. These fabricated traditions provide effective scripting for spectacular scenes for the violent purging of the superhero's whiteness through the ritual process. The price of attaining Indianness for the white Indian, it would seem, is to survive the dangerous crossing into liminality and back again to reintegrate the self—actions that necessitate the symbolic annihilation of embodied racial identity, with the concomitant hazards and risks of surrendering one's very being.

## Conclusion

White or Indian? I would suggest that the racialized portrayal of the white Indian superhero requires identification with, and subversion of, both. For although this superhero is able to contain and absorb indigenous identity, his claim to Indian subjectivity is complicated, since he relies on its erasure. The long path that carries the white Indian from identification to identity collapses in the absence of colonized Native American bodies to support it. Literary critic Armando Prats asserts that "representation presupposes appropriation: the figure itself of the Other already substantiates the dominance of the Same."[44] The imaginary, idealized white Indian was the quintessential vehicle for asserting superhero whiteness in a racialized form. Says Prats: "The Western present[ed] its most complete Indian through the white hero," a character who, paradoxically, embodied the indigenous Other.[45]

Although whiteness has persisted as a seemingly unassailable figural authority for the creation of comic book subjects, Native American characters like Red Wolf (1970), Moonstar (1982), and Rainmaker (1994), superhero teams like Alpha Flight (1979), and the independent squad Tribal Force (2002) would deliver more authentic comics visions of indigenous superhero identity, not based in whiteness. It is ironic—if not egregiously cynical—that for a time the white Indian superhero was promoted as the "protector of the innocent," his biography revising America's chronicles of conquest so as to identify *him* as Other, as those who had been targeted in genocidal campaigns of war, removed from ancestral lands, and ravaged by the destruction of their religions in the wake of America's colonizing aspirations. "In the end," Prats concludes, "the Indians of the revisionist Western ... vanished ..., the white hero remained to tell their story—and to claim, if implicitly, sole exception from complicity in their disappearance."[46] With his

---

44. Prats, *Invisible Natives*, 175.
45. Prats, *Invisible Natives*, xiv–xv, 174.
46. Prats, *Invisible Natives*, 173.

iconic costumes, his extraordinary powers, and his righteous, all-consuming mission of justice, the white Indian superhero recapitulated white supremacy in graphic media by appropriating the Native American. Utilized in service of an overdetermined whiteness or an anomalous whiteness, white Indian characters pushed beyond the limits of their own racial subjectivity to normalize whiteness using the formulaic codes of superheroism, irrespective of the form and the conditions of their *becoming* the embodiment of the very peoples they had displaced.

## Bibliography

Barbour, Chad A. *From Daniel Boone to Captain America: Playing Indian in American Popular Culture.* Jackson: University Press of Mississippi, 2016.

Barbour, Chad. "When Captain America Was an Indian: Heroic Masculinity, National Identity, and Appropriation." *Journal of Popular Culture* 48.2 (2015): 269–84.

Brownie, Barbara, and Danny Graydon. *The Superhero Costume: Identity and Disguise in Fact and Fiction.* New York: Bloomsbury, 2016.

Buscema, John (artist). "Massacre at Fort Madison!" *Two-Gun Western* #5, Timely Comics, November 1950.

Cameron, James. *Avatar.* Beverly Hills, CA: 20th Century Fox Home Entertainment, 2010.

Cameron, Lou (artist). "Golden Warrior and the Raiders of Terror Canyon." *Pawnee Bill* #3. Story Comics, July 1951.

———. "Trail of the Ambush Killers." *Pawnee Bill* #3. Story Comics, July 1951.

Cohen, Sol (writer), H. W. Kiemle (artist), and Howard Larson (artist). "Pawnee Bill." *White Chief of the Pawnee Indians.* Avon Periodicals, 1951.

Conway, Gerry (writer), Dick Ayers (artist), George Evans (artist), Jerry Serpe (artist), and Jean Simek (letterer). "City of Shame!" *Weird Western Tales* #47. DC Comics, July–August 1978.

Deloria, Philip. *Playing Indian.* New Haven, CT: Yale University Press, 1998.

Fleisher, Michael (writer), Dick Ayers (artist), and George Evans (artist). "Scalphunter." *Weird Western Tales* #39. DC Comics, March–April 1977.

Fleisher, Michael (writer), Dick Ayers (artist) George Evans (artist), and Liz Berube. "The Mark of a Warrior." *Weird Western Tales Starring Scalphunter* #40. DC Comics, May–June 1977.

Fleisher, Michael (writer), and José Luis García-López (artist), "Vengeance for a Fallen Gladiator!" *Jonah Hex* #1. DC Comics, March–April 1977.

Fox, Gardner (writer), and Frank Frazetta (artist). "The White Indian Chief." *Jimmy Wakely* #3. DC National Comics, October 1949.

Gabriele, Al (artist). "The Black Marvel." *Mystic Comics* #5. Timely Comics, March 1941.

Grell, Mike (writer), Brian Snoddy (artist), Joe Chiodo (artist), and Steve Haynie (letterer). *Shaman's Tears* #1. Image Comics, May 1993.

Hughes, Richard E. (writer), Ed Moritz, (artist), Paul Cooper (artist), and Max Elkan (artist). "Injun Jones." *Blazing West* #1. American Comics Group, Fall 1948.

Kanigher, Robert (writer), John Costanza (artist), and Frank Thorne (artist). "Hang Him High!" *Tomahawk* #131. DC Comics, November–December 1970.

———. "Hawk Faces the Scalp Hunter!" *Tomahawk* #133. DC Comics, March 1971.

Kubert, Joe (writer), and Costanza, John (art). "The Shaman!" *Showcase* #87. DC Comics, December 1969.

Maneely, Joe (artist). "The Comanches Strike!" *Apache Kid* #53. Marvel Comics, December 1950.

Pavlik, Steve, M. Elise Marubbio, and Tom Holm. *Native Apparitions : Critical Perspectives on Hollywood's Indians.* Tucson: The University of Arizona Press, 2017.

Prats, Armando Jose. *Invisible Natives: Myth and Identity in the American Western*, Ithaca, NY: Cornell University Press, 2002.

Rosenberg, Robin S., and Peter Coogan. *What Is a Superhero?* New York: Oxford University Press, 2013.

Savage, William W. *Comic Books and America, 1945–1954.* Middletown, CT: Wesleyan University Press, 1990.

Sheyahshe, Michael A. *Native Americans in Comic Books: A Critical Study.* Jefferson, NC: McFarland & Company, 2016.

Starr, John (writer, artist). "Hoka-Hai!" *Indians: Picture Stories of the First Americans* #2. Fiction House, June 1950.

Wright, Bradford W. *Comic Book Nation : the Transformation of Youth Culture in America.* Baltimore: Johns Hopkins University Press, 2001.

CHAPTER 12

# "A TRUE SON OF K'UN-LUN"

The Awkward Racial Politics of White Martial Arts Superheroes in the 1970s

MATTHEW PUSTZ

THANKS TO the television program *Kung Fu* (1972–1975), films like *Five Fingers of Death* (1972), and especially the charisma of Bruce Lee, interest in both the genre and the actual practice of martial arts exploded in the early 1970s. Comic books of the era were filled with advertisements for karate, kung fu, and other martial arts programs that promised to give young men fighting skills beyond those of their peers. It is not surprising, then, that publishers began to tell the stories of various martial arts warriors. Marvel's *Master of Kung Fu* (1973), starring Shang-Chi, was the longest-running martial arts comic of the decade. Two other characters—Marvel's Iron Fist (1974) and DC's Richard Dragon, Kung Fu Fighter (1975)—were not as successful as Shang-Chi but provide cultural historians with insights into not only the martial arts genre but also the racial politics of the era. Unlike most of the characters appearing in the Hong Kong–made martial arts films of the 1970s, both Iron Fist and Richard Dragon are white. As these characters easily master their martial arts disciplines, their stories quickly fall into the "white savior" trope, where white characters are able to use elements of non-Western cultures in heroic ways.

In effect, their stories demonstrate that both Iron Fist and Richard Dragon have become masters of a universal form of martial arts that is both

Asian and not Asian at the same time. For mainstream comic book readers in the 1970s, the martial arts as portrayed in these comics would be both exotic and familiar. Iron Fist and Richard Dragon clearly practiced kung fu and disciplines that followed the martial traditions of China and other East Asian cultures. Their stories featured diverse supporting casts that were consistent with the multicultural character of martial arts movies and their audiences. At the same time, though, the inclusion of magic and even science fiction elements meant that these martial arts comics fit the expectations of superhero fans. These comics also undermined the connections between the martial arts and their cultural origins, never challenging the superhero audience's racial sensibilities, which ultimately created "whitened" versions of the disciplines practiced by Iron Fist and Richard Dragon.

This new way of framing the martial arts helped promote the image of the hyper-competent white man for whom any challenge—any cultural barrier—can be overcome. This adaptability raises the issue of cultural appropriation. This is, perhaps, inevitable. After all, both Iron Fist and Richard Dragon are unquestionably white men practicing traditionally Asian martial arts (which, in the 1970s, meant kung fu and karate). Although readers are not given any information or clues about their ethnicities, they are unambiguous in their generic whiteness. Dragon is a redhead and Danny Rand, Iron Fist's not-so-secret identity, is blond. Significantly, though, both of them receive their martial arts training from Asian teachers who instill in them Eastern philosophies. Danny learns martial arts while living in K'un-Lun, a mystical city in the Himalayas. Monks from the city discover him at nine years old in the frozen wastes after the death of his parents. They raise him like one of their own, with the wise and skillful Lei-Kung training him in the martial arts. After ten years, and having gained the power of the Iron Fist by defeating a dragon in combat, Danny is ready to go out into the world.[1]

Richard Dragon's story begins in Kyoto, Japan, where he is a petty thief. One day, he encounters a martial arts teacher named O-Sensei who explains to him that the martial arts can help "a man discover himself!" Shortly thereafter, Dragon is defeated in a fight by Ben Turner, O-Sensei's African American student. Ben tells him that O-Sensei "teaches a few of us to become ourselves—better'n ourselves," while O-Sensei adds that "the goal is wisdom! The path is the discipline of the martial arts!" They offer Dragon a place in their school because O-Sensei believes he has vast potential for

---

1. Wein, Hama, and Giordano, "Heart of the Dragon!," 27.

greatness. After three years of study, Dragon graduates, ready to fight for the honor of the school alongside Ben, whom he now considers his best friend.[2]

This relationship is emblematic of the multicultural flavor of both *Richard Dragon, Kung Fu Fighter* and *Iron Fist*, and hence helps to establish the exotic nature of the 1970s comic book version of the martial arts. Ben is a nearly constant presence in *Richard Dragon*; early issues feature his face on the masthead alongside the title character. Later in the series, the pair is joined by a Chinese woman named Sandra Woosan—also a martial artist and nearly an equal to Dragon—going by the name Lady Shiva.

Iron Fist has a similar diverse supporting cast. Danny's first friend in the US is Colleen Wing, the Japanese American daughter of a professor of "Oriental" studies. Not surprisingly, she is also a martial artist, having been taught the ways of the samurai in Japan by her grandfather. Although half-white, Colleen is so devoted to the concept of bushido and other traditions she learned as a girl that her grandfather describes her soul as being "all Japanese."[3] (Danny, on the other hand, as an example of white competence, hard work, and adaptability, is never described as having this natural, essentialist connection to the martial arts.) Colleen is also a private investigator, working side by side with Misty Knight, an African American former police officer with a bionic arm. By the end of his solo series, Iron Fist and Misty are romantically involved. After his own series is cancelled, Iron Fist is partnered with Marvel's most prominent African American superhero in the long-running *Power Man and Iron Fist* (1978–1986), creating a comic book version of the blaxploitation/martial arts double bills that were popular during the mid-1970s.

It is not surprising that these white martial artists would be surrounded by multiracial supporting casts. Martial arts comics of the 1970s were in general much more diverse than typical superhero comics of the same era. Asian characters like Lady Shiva rubbed elbows with African Americans like Ben Turner in *Richard Dragon* at the same time nonwhite characters were rare in superhero comics. Racially mixed characters in martial arts comics include Shang-Chi, the son of Fu Manchu and a white American mother, Japanese Americans Colleen Wing and Karate Kid of the Legion of Super-Heroes, and the German Vietnamese Mantis of the Avengers. The best example of the racial and ethnic diversity in martial arts comics is the Sons of the Tiger, a team that starred in Marvel's magazine-sized *Deadly Hands of Kung Fu*. The group consists of Lin Sun (Chinese American), Bob Diamond (white),

---

2. Dennis and Durañona, "Coming of a Dragon!," 3, 5.
3. Claremont and Rogers, "Daughters of the Dragon," 8.

Abe Brown (African American), and Lotus Shinchuko (whose nationality is never defined but who is coded as a generic, generalizable Asian). What unites the team (or at least the men, as Lotus is a later addition) is that they are given parts of a tiger medallion by Lin's late teacher, Master Kee; the sections of the medallion grant them additional strength and swiftness.[4] Eventually, though, romantic tension over Lotus causes the group to break up, and the men toss their parts of the medallion in a nearby alley. They are soon found by Hector Ayala, a Puerto Rican college student. He puts on the medallion and promptly transforms into the White Tiger, becoming Marvel's first Latino superhero.[5]

It is possible that the writers and editors behind these series saw this diversity as a way to attract the nonwhite audiences who were attending martial arts movies in droves (at least until American producers began filling them with white leading men like Chuck Norris). Film theorist and historian David Bordwell explains that many African American and Latinx youth of the 1970s were "inspired by [Bruce] Lee's fearless confrontation with white power."[6] The presence of Jim Kelly, for example, helped the movie *Enter the Dragon* (1973) appeal to African American audiences, which, in turn, resulted in martial arts becoming a common element in many blaxploitation films. In an essay about the audiences for 1970s kung fu films, historian Sundiata Cha-Jua argues that part of the appeal of martial arts movies came from the fact that they had similar plots to those found in blaxploitation films. In both, "the winning formula called for an explosion of rage and retribution by a long-suffering protagonist who finally embarks on a journey of revenge against a vicious amoral antagonist."[7] Cha-Jua adds that the politics and skill of Bruce Lee also contributed to the appeal of martial arts movies for African Americans in the 1970s. Lee's movies, he argues, "introduced themes of racial oppression and class exploitation," and his fighting style demonstrated his "preference for eclectic polycultural mixtures." Ultimately, Cha-Jua writes, both martial arts movies and blaxploitation films "were nationalist visions of self-defense or retaliatory violence against racial oppression, albeit fueled by individual grievances."[8]

The diverse supporting casts of *Iron Fist* and *Richard Dragon, Kung Fu Fighter* were not just window dressing, though. They played significant roles in the comics and were frequently integral to the heroes' success. While Ben

---

4. Conway and Giordano, "The Sons of the Tiger!"
5. Mantlo, Perez, and Abel, "An Ending!"
6. Bordwell, *Planet Hong Kong*, 50.
7. Cha-Jua, "Black Audiences," 200.
8. Cha-Jua, "Black Audiences," 216, 217.

Turner seemed to spend many of the early issues recovering from gunshots, he is clearly Dragon's closest and most dedicated friend. In the final issue of the series, Dragon falls into a deep depression because he thinks Ben is dead. Lady Shiva tells him that he has been lax with his training and complains that he has "become a travesty of [his] former self." To motivate him, she urges him to get involved in stopping a martial arts tournament run by organized crime. The police show up after Dragon defeats his opponent, and Dragon is caught in a cross-fire between them and the mob, but a mysterious character called the Bronze Tiger saves him. In the final panels of the story, Dragon discovers that the Bronze Tiger is, in fact, Ben, and this gives the title character a renewed sense of confidence and purpose.[9]

Misty Knight and Colleen Wing are both integral parts of Iron Fist's life. The relationship shared by Iron Fist and Misty Knight is based on mutual love, respect, and concern. At one point, Iron Fist blindly decides to engage the entire X-Men team in battle when he thinks that they are the reason Misty is missing from her apartment.[10] Later, Misty abandons an important undercover assignment when she finds out that Iron Fist is in mortal danger.[11] They frequently go into battle together, supporting each other in the process. Further, while there are no romantic connections between Colleen Wing and Danny, she is most likely his closest friend. This is especially true after he is forced to use the power of the Iron Fist to heal her after her mind is shattered by the supervillain Angar the Screamer. This "mind-meld" effect results in a permanent psychic bond between the two friends.[12] And then, when the weakened Iron Fist is on the verge of being murdered by Master Khan's minions, it is Colleen who snaps out of the mental fog induced by Angar to save her friend in a dramatic, full-page panel, killing Iron Fist's potential executioners.[13]

The fact that diverse supporting casts are featured in both *Iron Fist* and *Richard Dragon* is significant in terms of both establishing the uniqueness of these series (in comparison to the generally whiter comics published at the same time by Marvel and DC) and demonstrating the racial positionality of the lead characters. Significantly, Ben, Lady Shiva, Misty, and Colleen exist in these stories to help Richard Dragon and Iron Fist. While the supporting characters do, on occasion, rescue the leads, it is clear that the titular white characters are the stars. They are the ones who have the special abilities, and

---

9. O'Neil and Estrada, "The Secret of the Bronze Tiger," 7, 17.
10. Claremont, Byrne, and Green, "Enter, the X-Men."
11. Claremont, Byrne, and Hunt, "Night of the Dragon."
12. Claremont, Byrne, and Chiaramonte, "Death Match!," 27.
13. Claremont, Byrne, and Chiaramonte, "Iron Fist Must Die!," 3.

they are the ones who are able to master the intricacies of the martial arts on the highest level. Ben Turner, for example, studied kung fu under O-Sensei for years before Dragon showed up, but once he "graduates," Dragon is clearly the superior fighter. It seems almost as if the supporting cast exists in both these comics to remind readers that, ultimately, it is white people—and perhaps especially white men—who have special access to the martial arts. Their comics might establish that the martial arts are universal, but they also suggest that white men have a special connection to their truths.

Still, both *Iron Fist* and *Richard Dragon* try to depict the cultural roots of the martial arts. One way the series do this is by showing the characters developing their skills through training. The earliest appearances of Iron Fist are filled with panels of him practicing with his sensei Lei-Kung in scenes that would not be out of place in a Hong Kong martial arts film. On at least three occasions, readers are reminded that being good at the martial arts is a skill, not a superpower, and that it must be practiced. In *Marvel Premiere* #24 (1975), Iron Fist is training with Colleen Wing, a proficient martial artist in her own right. Later, the story in *Marvel Team-Up* #63 (1977) opens with two pages of Iron Fist training by himself. A caption explains, "It's been two years since you [Iron Fist] chose to leave K'un-Lun for Earth, and in that time the fine edge of your skills has been blunted. You've neglected your training—the honing of mind and spirit that complements that of the body—and you've paid the price. And so you've played the hermit these past weeks, pushing yourself hard, seeking to regain what's been lost."[14] Finally, in *Power Man and Iron Fist* #59 (1979), Danny is training with Bob Diamond, from the Sons of the Tiger, because he thinks that he is "out of shape" since all he and Luke Cage seem to do is fight "hired thugs and street punks."[15] In *Richard Dragon, Kung Fu Fighter*, spirituality is emphasized as we frequently see the main character in his personal quarters, sitting, with his legs crossed, in front of a Buddha statue. For example, in the fourth issue, Dragon is in his room meditating, "motionless, emptying his mind, his heart, preparing" for the battle to come.[16]

At the same time, though, the creators behind these series wanted to make their worlds and plots familiar to the readers of superhero comics. To do that, a number of stories take the martial arts out of their Asian cultural traditions. In fact, some stories seem to argue that kung fu and karate did not actually originate in Asia. The origin of Mantis, a martial artist introduced in 1973, was finally told in *Avengers* #134 (1975), showing readers

14. Claremont, Byrne, and Hunt, "Night of the Dragon," 1.
15. Duffy, Von Eeden, and Gordon, "Big Apple Bomber," 7.
16. O'Neil, Estrada, and Wood, "A Time to Be a Whirlwind!," 7.

that the people who taught her the martial arts, "the Priests of Pama," were actually refugees who escaped the galaxy-spanning Kree empire thousands of years ago, not Vietnamese monks, as was previously revealed. In response to this new information, Hawkeye asks, "If those kung fu pacifist types were in Asia that long ago, could they have been the guys who kicked that weird [martial arts] scene off on Earth?"[17] No one gives him an answer, but the implications seem clear: In the Marvel Universe, the Kree created the martial arts, not human beings living in Eastern Asia.

The same thing is implied in the mythos surrounding Iron Fist and K'un-Lun. The city is located in the Himalayas, but it only appears in the physical world once every ten years. For the rest of the time, it exists in its own plane of existence, far away from the influence of the modern world. On the surface, K'un-Lun appears to be Chinese—or, rather, a kind of faux Chinese that the writers and artists might have picked up from movies or visits to Chinese restaurants. The scenes set there feature architecture invoking ancient Chinese styles, and the dragon iconography throughout K'un-Lun draws on popular culture images of "Oriental" culture. Many of its citizens have names that replicate the common two-syllable, hyphenated pattern of Chinese names rendered in English. For example, Danny Rand has to battle a martial artist named Shu-Hu, and to gain the power of the Iron Fist he has to defeat a dragon called Shou-Lao the Undying. His teacher Lei-Kung even wears a hexagram from the *I-Ching* on his chest. Their dialogue often reflects a stereotyped, orientalist vision of "Asian" mysticism, with its inevitable "ancient Chinese secrets" and inscrutable aphorisms. For example, after the death of the man who killed his father, Iron Fist reflects on advice given him by Yü-Ti, the ruler of K'un-Lun: "Vengeance, my son, is a double-edged sword, for it cuts not only its victim, but also its perpetrator!"[18]

Many of these characters are masked, so we do not get a visual sense of their race or ethnicity, but we find out that the people in K'un-Lun might not actually be Chinese or even Asian. Just before Iron Fist leaves the city, he learns that his blond-haired and clearly white father was, in fact, Yü-Ti's biological brother.[19] In a flashback, he remembers friends and rivals from before he came to New York City. Those include a blond woman named Miranda (who might be Danny's sister) and a brown-haired man named Conal. There is even the suggestion that, like the Priests of Pama, the people of K'un-Lun might not even be from Earth: Iron Fist's rivals call him "dog of an outworlder" and "Earther," emphasizing that the city—and its martial

---

17. Englehart, Buscema, and Staton, "The Times That Bind!," 31.
18. Moench, Hama, and Giordano, "Death-Cult!," 2.
19. Wein, Hama, and Giordano, "Heart of the Dragon!," 27.

arts teachings—belong to a whole other world.[20] If this is true, then in the universe of Iron Fist, the martial arts are equally alien to all human beings, and are certainly not the special right of people from Asia.

In addition to this science fiction element, magic is also a presence in *Iron Fist* and *Richard Dragon*. This tends to undermine the cultural authenticity of the martial arts depicted there by contradicting the idea that kung fu and other disciplines require training, practice, and an understanding of their philosophical and spiritual foundations. Magic essentially transforms the martial arts into another comic book superpower, putting them on the same level as having a mutation or gaining access to alien technology. Looking at it from the point of view of 1970s superhero comics, connecting the martial arts to magic is another attempt at making them less Asian. Creators seemed to be making the effort to keep kung fu and karate in the realm of what was familiar to a typical mainstream comic book reader who, most likely, would have been more knowledgeable about imaginary sci-fi technology and the speculative (at best) impact of cosmic rays on human genetics than Chinese or Japanese culture as they actually existed in the real world. In contrast to *Iron Fist* and *Richard Dragon*, Marvel's *Master of Kung Fu* does not attribute its hero's ability to magic in the least. Significantly, *Master of Kung Fu* is not really a superhero comic, focusing more on the espionage genre.

Magic is important in the superhero milieu, though, and Iron Fist and Richard Dragon are clearly superheroes. Danny Rand gains the power of the Iron Fist, for example, because he defeated an immortal dragon in battle.[21] Early in *Richard Dragon*, the main character gains power through his knowledge and expertise. Later, though, the hero uses a jade dragon's claw medallion to focus his power. After touching the claw, there is "a shimmering in the air ... and, for an instant, a wraith seems to appear ... the spectre of the beast," as we see the image of a dragon surround him.[22] In issue #5, he uses the dragon claw while meditating; as a result, he is "transformed into the fierce being that is his soul ... the dragon!"[23]

While the inclusion of magic tends to flatten out the cultural distinctiveness of the martial arts, it also reinforces certain stereotypes of Asian peoples and cultures. Many Americans in the 1970s still lumped people from China, Japan, and elsewhere into a single group—Asians, Orientals, or sometimes worse—that was seen as inscrutable, mysterious, and sometimes even mystical. For example, countercultural discussions of Eastern religions like Bud-

---

20. Claremont, Byrne, and Chiaramonte, "Valley of the Damned!," 2.
21. Wein, Hama, and Giordano, "Heart of the Dragon!," 14.
22. O'Neil, Kirby, and Berry, "Claws of the Dragon!," 12.
23. O'Neil, Estrada, and Wood, "The Arena of No Exit!," 9.

dhism and Taoism often focused on their metaphysical elements as a way to differentiate them from Christianity. Integrating magic into the comic book version of the martial arts suggested that the people among whom these disciplines developed were different from people of other races, but it made them different in a way that was familiar to Marvel and DC fans. They became like other mysterious beings who are able to grant powers to (mainly white) heroes.

At the same time, Asian characters in *Iron Fist* and *Richard Dragon* are often robbed of their racial and cultural identity. Other times, that identity is relegated to stereotypes. The challenge of showing Asian people as being racially distinctive without slipping into stereotypes became a significant concern when Marvel began publishing the adventures of Shang-Chi in 1973. His first appearance establishes that he is the son of the archvillain Fu Manchu. From the beginning, Shang-Chi is colored with a golden-bronze hue, perhaps to accentuate his resemblance to Bruce Lee, but Fu Manchu is a sickly, pale yellow. This coloring harkens back to fears of the "Yellow Peril" and racist depictions of Japanese and Chinese immigrants in the nineteenth century that led to the Chinese Exclusion Act of 1882 and other actions that would limit and control the lives of Asian newcomers to the US. Later, in World War II, Japanese characters in comic books were colored in a similar yellow shade, often accompanied by other dehumanizing visual tropes. In the 1950s and 1960s, this iconography was transferred to Marvel villains like the Yellow Claw and the Mandarin. Fu Manchu's long history in popular culture, beginning with Sax Rohmer's original 1913 novel, helped to shape these images. There, he is described as "tall, lean and feline, high-shouldered, with a brow like Shakespeare and a face like Satan, a close-shaven skull, and long, magnetic eyes of true cat-green." For Rohmer, Fu Manchu was meant to represent "all the cruel cunning of an entire Eastern race."[24]

This racist imagery would not be as easily accepted in the 1970s as it was earlier in the twentieth century. Artist Jim Starlin, co-creator of Shang-Chi, was shocked by the racism when he read the original Rohmer novels. Criticism from friends of Asian descent prompted him to leave the series.[25] Comics fan and frequent correspondent William Wu often complained in the *Master of Kung Fu* letters page about racist imagery in the visual depiction of characters in the series. In issue #33, after two previous attempts to raise the subject, he finally got a public response. The editors revealed that writer Doug Moench was also concerned about the appearance of Asian charac-

---

24. Quoted in Wu, *Yellow Peril*, 165.
25. Howe, *Marvel Comics*, 146.

ters, asking why they were colored with any shade of yellow. The response concluded, "It was decided that with the exception of firmly established characters (Shang-chi and Fu Manchu being obvious answers), all future Asian characters would be colored in the same flesh tones as are Caucasian characters."[26] So, when that issue introduced the Chinese secret agent Leiko Wu, she was shown as white.[27] This policy didn't last, however; by issue #51, Leiko is colored bronze, just like Shang-Chi. When Fu Manchu returns from the dead in issue #83, he too is bronze.

Although this coloring convention had become the standard style for depicting people of Asian descent in mainstream comics, there was still a lot of inconsistency across martial arts comics throughout the 1970s. The Cat, a Chinese martial artist who appears in various issues of *Master of Kung Fu*, is sometimes colored as white, sometimes bronze. Many of the enemies that Iron Fist and Richard Dragon battle are similarly white, despite having Asian backgrounds. And while the half-Chinese, half-white Shang-Chi is colored with the conventional bronze to designate him as Asian, other mixed-race characters (like Colleen Wing) are typically depicted as white. Karate Kid, for example, had been depicted as white since his introduction in July 1966. In 1975, though, his origin is finally revealed, establishing him as the son of a Japanese supervillain and a white American government agent.[28] Artist Mike Grell wanted to go further depicting him as Asian by "slightly altering Karate Kid's look." The goal of this, according to the editors of the comic, was not to achieve some notion of racial justice, but rather to "model" the character on Bruce Lee.[29]

This racial ambiguity subsumed Asian culture and people into a universe of whiteness, limiting their roles, especially in white-centric comics like *Iron Fist* and *Richard Dragon*. This narrowed the possibilities for characters coded as Japanese or Chinese. In white-centric martial arts comics, they can only be martial arts heroes if they are part of a group (like Lin Sun of the Sons of the Tiger) or support white characters (like Lady Shiva). They can, however, be teachers, like Master Kee or O-Sensei, so long as they are providing their wisdom to white people. Mixed-race heroes can only function if they disparage the authentic origin of their talent by associating it with evil (Shang-Chi and Karate Kid) or by suggesting that it is not really Asian (Mantis). Or, the mixed-race hero can basically be depicted as white (Colleen

---

26. "Missives to the Master!," 32.
27. Moench, Gulacy, and Adkins, "Wicked Messenger of Madness," 11.
28. Shooter and Grell, "The Lair of the Black Dragon," 25.
29. Sacks, *American Comic Book Chronicles*, 193.

Wing), ignoring his or her cultural background except when it is needed to explain a character's stereotypical actions and abilities.

Characters like Richard Dragon and Iron Fist, on the other hand, symbolically demonstrate in this context that white people are understood as having unlimited potential, that with some training (and the addition of magic), they can easily develop a mastery of ancient Asian techniques for self-defense. Whiteness, as it is portrayed in these comics, bestows flexibility and adaptability. Whites, in this view, are not culturally limited or stuck in the traditions of their own heritage. Rather, they are able to colonize the practices of other cultures through mastery of their skills and a true understanding of their spiritual dimensions. This, of course, is a perfect definition for cultural appropriation, something that happens, according to film scholar Sean M. Tierney, when "a white person seeks to emulate or imitate the actions and/or beliefs of someone ethnoculturally different from themselves."[30]

Cultural appropriation—here, seen as the mastery of a universalized form of the martial arts by white superheroes—is demonstrated in *Marvel Team-Up* #63–64 (1977) costarring Iron Fist and Spider-Man. In the early issues of *Iron Fist*, readers had been introduced to an angry man named Davos who left K'un-Lun vowing revenge against Danny Rand. As the son of Lei-Kung, he believes that he is the rightful heir to the power of the Iron Fist and that Danny stole it from him. After stalking Danny and gradually robbing him of his "Chi," Davos—now calling himself the Steel Serpent—nearly kills him in single combat, taking the last of the Iron Fist power in the process. Proclaiming his victory, he announces that he is "a *true* son of K'un-Lun, where this boy was no more than a half-breed." Inevitably, though, Danny regains the power of the Iron Fist as he defeats his out-of-control rival.[31]

Essentially, this is a story about the triumph of a whitened version of the martial arts. Iron Fist reclaims his power from the representative of its original source with the help of his multicultural friends. This is how whites can gain—or maybe steal, if Davos's claim on the Iron Fist has any legitimacy—the power of the martial arts. Danny defeats Steel Serpent one-on-one, but it is the assistance from his friends that puts him in the position to do so. Misty Knight saves Danny from Davos at the end of the first half of the story. Later, Spider-Man helps Misty and Colleen Wing lead the Steel Serpent back to the park for the final confrontation. Finally, it is Colleen who convinces Misty

---

30. Tierney, "Themes of Whiteness," 608.
31. Claremont, Byrne, and Hunt, "Night of the Dragon," 15.

and Spider-Man that they need to let Danny face Davos alone. "Being Iron Fist is more than wearing a fancy costume and having a fist that glows in the dark," she explains. "It's an ideal, a dream—it's believing in a code of honor and tradition that's lasted a million years. Don't you see?! Iron Fist has to prove—here and now, to himself more than anyone—that he is worthy of his name and all that goes with it."[32] Her appeal to honor establishes that Danny connects with the cultural origins of the martial arts; in fact, the story suggests that it is the white Danny who is more in touch with the spiritual basis of the martial arts than the nominally Asian Davos. The comic ends with a scene showing Lei-Kung remotely watching the outcome of the battle and approving of Danny's victory, which reinforces the notion that Iron Fist, not the Steel Serpent, is the rightful custodian of K'un-Lun's power.[33]

In effect, Iron Fist is racially passing. He is a wealthy white man, but when it suits him, he is able to pass into the exotic tradition of the martial arts. This is an essential part of the stories of both Iron Fist and Richard Dragon as they prove themselves supremely deserving of martial arts knowledge and wisdom. Ultimately, the comics starring these characters establish a unique version of white racial identity. Through flexibility and adaptability, and with help from teachers coded as Asian and a multicultural supporting cast, it is their whiteness that allows them to become masters of the martial arts.

## Bibliography

Bordwell, David. *Planet Hong Kong: Popular Cinema and the Art of Entertainment*. Cambridge, MA: Harvard University Press, 2000.

Cha-Jua, Sundiata K. "Black Audiences, Blaxploitation and Kung Fu Films, and Challenges to White Celluloid Masculinity." In *China Forever: The Shaw Brothers and Diasporic Cinema*, edited by Poshek Fu, 199–223. Urbana: University of Illinois Press, 2008.

Claremont, Chris (writer), John Byrne (artist), and Dan Adkins (inker). "Kung Fu Killer!" *Iron Fist*, vol. 1, #10. New York: Marvel Comics, December 1976.

Claremont, Chris (writer), John Byrne (artist), and Frank Chiaramonte (inker). "Death Match!" *Iron Fist*, vol. 1, #6. New York: Marvel Comics, August 1976.

———. "Iron Fist Must Die!" *Iron Fist*, vol. 1, #7. New York: Marvel Comics, September 1976.

———. "Valley of the Damned!" *Iron Fist*, vol. 1, #2. New York: Marvel Comics, December 1975.

---

32. Claremont, Byrne, and Hunt, "If Death Be My Destiny," 14.
33. Claremont, Byrne, and Hunt, "Night of the Dragon," 17.

Claremont, Chris (writer), John Byrne (artist), and Dan Green (inker). "Enter, the X-Men." *Iron Fist*, vol. 1, #15. New York: Marvel Comics, September 1977.

Claremont, Chris (writer), John Byrne (artist), and Dave Hunt (inker). "If Death Be My Destiny." *Marvel Team-Up* vol. 1, #64. New York: Marvel Comics, December 1977.

———. "Night of the Dragon." *Marvel Team-Up*, vol. 1, #63. New York: Marvel Comics, November 1977.

Claremont, Chris (writer), and Marshall Rogers (artist). "Daughters of the Dragon." *Deadly Hands of Kung Fu*, vol. 1, #32, 4–24. New York: Marvel Comics, January 1977.

———. "Sword of Vengeance." *Deadly Hands of Kung Fu*, vol. 1, #33, 39–58. New York: Marvel Comics, February 1977.

Conway, Gerry (writer), and Dick Giordano (artist). "The Sons of the Tiger!" *Special Collector's Edition*, vol. 1, #1, 53–67. New York: Marvel Comics, 1975.

Dennis, Jim (writer), and Leopoldo Durañona (artist). "Coming of a Dragon!" *Richard Dragon, Kung-Fu Fighter*, vol. 1, #1. New York: DC Comics/National Periodical Publications, May 1975.

Dennis, Jim (writer), Jim Starlin (artist), Alan Weiss (artist), and Al Milgrom (inker). "A Dragon Fights Alone!" *Richard Dragon, Kung-Fu Fighter*, vol. 1, #2. New York: DC Comics/National Periodical Publications, July 1975.

Duffy, Mary Jo (writer), Trevor Von Eeden (artist), and Al Gordon (inker). "Big Apple Bomber." *Power Man and Iron Fist*, vol. 1, #59. New York: Marvel Comics, October 1979.

Englehart, Steve (writer), Sal Buscema (artist), and Joe Staton (inker). "The Times That Bind!" *Avengers*, vol. 1, #134. New York: Marvel Comics, April 1975.

Howe, Sean. *Marvel Comics: The Untold Story*. New York: Harper Collins, 2012.

"Iron Fistfulls" (letters page). *Iron Fist*, vol. 1, #12, 18. New York: Marvel Comics, April 1977.

Mantlo, Bill (writer), Sal Buscema (artist), Mike Esposito (inker), and Frank Giacoia (inker). "Tiger in a Web!" *Peter Parker, the Spectacular Spider-Man*, vol. 1, #10. New York: Marvel Comics, September 1977.

Mantlo, Bill (writer), George Perez (artist), and Jack Abel (inker). "An Ending!" *Deadly Hands of Kung Fu*, vol. 1, #19, 44–61. New York: Marvel Comics, December 1975.

"Missives to the Master!" (letters page). *Master of Kung Fu*, vol. 1, #33, 19, 32. New York: Marvel Comics, October 1975.

Moench, Doug (writer), Paul Gulacy (artist), and Dan Adkins (inker). "Wicked Messenger of Madness." *Master of Kung Fu*, vol. 1, #33. New York: Marvel Comics, October 1975.

Moench, Doug (writer), Larry Hama (artist), and Dick Giordano (inker). "Citadel on the Edge of Vengeance." *Marvel Premiere*, vol. 1, #17. New York: Marvel Comics, September 1974.

———. "Death-Cult!" *Marvel Premiere*, vol. 1, #19. New York: Marvel Comics, November 1974.

O'Neil, Denny (writer), and Ric Estrada (artist). "The Secret of the Bronze Tiger." *Richard Dragon, Kung-Fu Fighter*, vol. 1, #18. New York: DC Comics/National Periodical Publications, December 1977.

O'Neil, Denny (writer), Ric Estrada (artist), and Wally Wood (inker). "The Arena of No Exit!" *Richard Dragon, Kung-Fu Fighter*, vol. 1, #5. New York: DC Comics/National Periodical Publications, January 1976.

———. "A Time to Be a Whirlwind!" *Richard Dragon, Kung-Fu Fighter*, vol. 1, #4. New York: DC Comics/National Periodical Publications, November 1975.

O'Neil, Denny (writer), Jack Kirby (artist), and D. Bruce Berry (inker). "Claws of the Dragon!" *Richard Dragon, Kung-Fu Fighter*, vol. 1, #3. New York: DC Comics/National Periodical Publications, September 1975.

Sacks, Jason. *American Comic Book Chronicles: The 1970s*. Raleigh, NC: TwoMorrows Publishing, 2014.

Shooter, Jim (writer), and Mike Grell (artist). "The Lair of the Black Dragon." *Superboy*, vol. 1, #210, 20–30. New York: DC Comics, August 1975.

Thomas, Roy (writer), Gil Kane (artist), and Dick Giordano (inker). "The Fury of the Iron Fist!" *Marvel Premiere*, vol. 1, #15. New York: Marvel Comics, May 1974.

Tierney, Sean M. "Themes of Whiteness in *Bulletproof Monk*, *Kill Bill*, and *The Last Samurai*." *Journal of Communication* 56 (2006): 607–24.

Wein, Len (writer), Larry Hama (artist), and Dick Giordano (inker). "Heart of the Dragon!" *Marvel Premiere*, vol. 1, #16. New York: Marvel Comics, July 1974.

Wu, William F. *The Yellow Peril: Chinese Americans in American Fiction, 1850–1940*. Hamden, CT: Archon Books, 1982.

CHAPTER 13

# THE WHITEST THERE IS AT WHAT I DO

Japanese Identity and the Unmarked Hero in *Wolverine* (1982)

ERIC SOBEL

**AMONG THE FIRST** superhero comics to extensively represent Japanese culture from an American perspective, *Wolverine* (1982), written by Chris Claremont and illustrated by Frank Miller, throws the title character and star of *Uncanny X-Men* into a fictional Japanese landscape. In a story permeated with stereotypes of East Asia, its cultures, and its peoples, Claremont and Miller's characters negotiate clichéd Japanese and at times more generalized "Asian" identities alike. Of course, Asian stereotypes are nothing unusual in American comic books, whether it's Captain America fighting fang-toothed Japanese soldiers during World War II or Iron Man combating the prideful, power-hungry Mandarin in the 1960s. Miller himself is no stranger to unusual, often problematic Japanese representations, having introduced the evil, mysterious organization of ninjas known as The Hand in the pages of *Daredevil* the year before *Wolverine*, following it up with his limited series *Ronin* (1983), which pushed his fascination with East Asian culture to even greater extremes.

In *Wolverine*, Claremont and Miller revel in "Japanese" stereotypes, both in terms of imagery but more importantly in their representation of the values that supposedly contribute to Japanese identity. Wolverine's love interest in the miniseries, Mariko, and her father, Shingen, are exemplary of the stifling strictures that Orientalizing brings to Japanese characters in the large white mediascape of American superhero comics. Mariko and Shingen, though exceedingly different in temperament and morality, are united in how the flattening effects of Orientalism paint them as one-dimensional and leave them with little capacity for the expression of identity. As "geisha" and "gook" types, as described by Asian American activist and historian Helen Zia,[1] both characters remain trapped in rigid roles, one as a timid, submissive woman who is bound by honor and the other as an untrustworthy gangster.

While significant in highlighting ways that comic creators employ a racist logic in their handling of those who are nonwhite, the limited ability of the Japanese characters to develop and move beyond fairly fixed, flat identities creates a point of comparison for Wolverine. It is against this backdrop of one-dimensional renderings of Asianness in *Wolverine* that we are able to more starkly see what the creators have to say about being white. A hero armed with the privilege and invisibility whiteness affords, Wolverine, unlike the foreign characters he encounters, is able to easily move between different identities without placing his whiteness and the agency it bestows in any real jeopardy. His journey of redemption and self-discovery climaxes with his triumphant defeat of the gangster Shingen, which dramatically denotes his personal growth and elevates the character to the level of a "true" samurai, a title that his scheming Japanese foe could never truly earn within the logic of *Wolverine*. The harmful effects of Wolverine's appropriation of Japanese culture in the narrative and the historical contexts that have produced and informed said culture are all but ignored in the comic, while the character's inherent, "natural" moral righteousness is continually reinforced. The prominent depiction of Wolverine's muscled white body, in conjunction with his extraordinary ability to heal wounds, further assist in solidifying his innate goodness in contrast to the Other and justify his exploitation and appropriation of nonwhite culture.

## Introducing Wolverine

While synonymous with the X-Men today, Wolverine, whose secret identity was at first simply "Logan," was established as an adversary to the Hulk in the final page of 1974's *Incredible Hulk* #180. He was portrayed as a bull-headed, rough-around-the-edges antihero, typical of the morally gray macho men that emerged in the last quarter of the twentieth century, includ-

---

1. Zia, *Asian American Dreams*, 119.

ing the gun-toting Punisher, hero-for-hire Luke Cage, and the supernatural motorcyclist Ghost Rider. John M. Trushell characterizes Wolverine as essentially a Libertarian, a "rugged antihero" whose commitment to individualism reflected a cynicism toward the social revolutions of the previous decade and a government marred by war and scandal.[2] Wolverine's special abilities were soon revealed to be a healing factor that allowed him to recover from even the most horrific injuries and that slowed his aging; an indestructible skeleton made from the fictional metal adamantium; and razor-sharp adamantium claws that emerged from each hand. Wolverine's ascent to prominence among the readership began the following year, in 1975's *Giant Size X-Men* #1, in which the character was added as the Canadian element of a consciously—albeit majority white—international team. Among future X-Men mainstays such as Nightcrawler from Germany, Colossus from Russia, and Storm from sub-Saharan Africa, Wolverine stood out as the brash American type, despite being nominally Canadian. This "All New, All Different" group of X-Men, as they would be characterized on the covers that followed this issue, appeared to expand the diversity of the cast, though this gesture toward multiculturalism did not necessarily correspond with more progressive characters rooted in real-life oppression.

Although possessed of extraordinary superhuman abilities, mutants in Marvel comics are feared and hated for being different, and the X-Men's challenges are therefore often read as a metaphor for the real-world challenges of the oppressed.[3] Indeed, an appeal of the X-Men is that their struggle can supposedly represent anyone's struggles, which "implies an equivalence between all of the various readers' oppressions,"[4] according to Neil Shyminsky, allowing those with a privileged status, such as countless white male comic readers, to appropriate a position of marginality. By sheer nature of being a member of the X-Men, Wolverine is granted a sympathetic victim status that no doubt facilitates his exploitative use of whiteness at the expense of Japanese characters in Claremont and Miller's *Wolverine*.

Published in 1982 as a spin-off of the hugely successful Claremont-scripted Marvel comic, *Uncanny X-Men*, *Wolverine* looked to capitalize on and develop a character that was quickly gaining popularity in the industry. While there are countless comics that could be used to spark fruitful discussion of whiteness as presented in the publishing history of Wolverine's character, I find the 1982 miniseries to be a useful starting point. As the

---

2. Trushell, "American Dreams," 157.

3. See the chapters on the X-Men by Neil Shyminsky and Martin Lund in this volume.

4. Shyminsky, "Mutant Readers," 388.

star and sole X-Men character in the book, the specificities of Wolverine are afforded greater attention and thus a closer focus that would otherwise be diluted if he were sharing space with other superheroes. By taking place in Japan and featuring Japanese supporting characters, the comic puts Wolverine's whiteness into stark contrast with those around him. Lastly, while this comic contains character types and narrative tropes that are indicative of the superhero genre Wolverine belongs to, it stands relatively well on its own as a comprehensible, self-contained text in a way that an ongoing monthly comic, in many cases, does not.

Claremont and Miller's *Wolverine* depicts adventures in Japan set in motion after all of Wolverine's letters to his Japanese girlfriend, Mariko, return unopened. He soon learns that her father, Shingen, is head of the criminal Clan Yashida and has recently reappeared, after being presumed dead. After his return, Shingen seeks to reclaim his position and to arrange for Mariko to marry another man due to a debt he had incurred. Having come to Japan to investigate and subsequently perceived as a threat to Clan Yashida, Wolverine is seemingly defeated by Shingen in a *bokken* (wooden practice swords) duel in the presence of Mariko, who is unaware that her true love was poisoned before the fight. Although demoralized after his unfair loss, Wolverine redeems himself by the narrative's conclusion, having perfectly adopted the ethnoracially marked Japanese qualities of honor and nobility that Mariko deeply values, to the point that she compares him to a samurai and claims that he embodies characteristics definitive of her lineage and culture.[5] In effect, the mysterious white character becomes a more successful expression of the qualities upheld by the Japanese characters in Claremont and Miller's imagined Japan than any of the Japanese characters themselves.[6]

## Mariko and Wolverine: The Geisha and the White Man

Of the miniseries' various interpretations of Japanese identity, Wolverine's love interest, Mariko, proves to be the most rigidly confined by historical stereotypes. From her initial appearance in the first issue, we are presented with a character that exemplifies the Orientalized image of the "geisha," a passive, submissive Asian female type.[7] Lisa Lowe describes the stereotypi-

---

5. Claremont, Miller, and Rubenstein, "Wolverine #1–4 (1982)," 115.
6. For more on white superheroes' Orientalist appropriations of nonwhite cultures, see the chapters in this volume by Matthew Pustz and Jeffrey A. Brown.
7. Zia, *Asian American Dreams*, 119.

cally "Oriental" woman as simultaneously sexually enticing and "impassive, undemanding and insensate herself; her Oriental mystery never fails to charm."[8] The impassiveness of the geisha type, bound up in a Western imagination of Asian women's submission to men, is exemplified by Mariko, for example, when she is questioned by Wolverine about the reason behind her marriage to the abusive Noburu, as arranged by her father. Mariko responds: "If my father, in honor, gave his solemn word, then I, his daughter, am honor-bound not to foreswear him. If you cannot comprehend and accept that, Logan, you do not truly know me at all."[9] Unlike her father, a criminal who carefully presents a façade of honor and tradition in order to project a respectable, trustworthy persona for personal gain, Mariko has deeply internalized such values, claiming them as a foundation of her personal and familial identity. Within a few short sentences, she not only defines herself in relation to a patriarch but uses language entrenched in the lexicon of the honorable Asian stereotype. Whereas Wolverine describes himself as a superhero and warrior, and Shingen boasts of his status as head of Clan Yashida, Mariko is unable to create an identity unattached to either cultural tradition or a dominant male figure.

The sense of family and honor that so heavily define Mariko are reinforced by the way her character describes swords that have belonged to the Yashida clan for 800 years. Discussions of these highly revered weapons, "crafted by the supreme swordsmith, Masamune," bookend the miniseries. During the first such scene, Mariko states that "they are the soul of my family. All that we were and are and are yet to be is represented by these two swords."[10] After Wolverine defeats Shingen during the comic's climactic final battle, Mariko willingly gives a sword to a reluctant Wolverine, stating that it belongs to "the samurai who best exemplifies" the "reality and spirit" of her clan.[11] Mariko's fascination with the swords highlights the underlying theme of honor and portrays an essentialized family identity tied to the past, an identity made as static as the ancient blades themselves. Honor and family, while ostensibly favorable and perhaps true to the historical reality of Japanese women's lives, do little to elevate the character's status in the narrative and more than anything cause Mariko to appear as little more than a flat replication of an Orientalist figure.

It is in this conclusion that Claremont and Miller most clearly highlight Wolverine's privileged status and differentiate him from the inferior Japa-

---

8. Lowe, *Critical Terrains*, 76.
9. Claremont, Miller, and Rubenstein, "Wolverine #1–4 (1982)," 39.
10. Claremont, Miller, and Rubenstein, "Wolverine #1–4 (1982)," 38.
11. Claremont, Miller, and Rubenstein, "Wolverine #1–4 (1982)," 115.

nese characters. Mariko's language mirrors her previous discussion of the weapons, stating that each blade Masamune has "crafted is said to possess a portion of his essential character. His soul. This represents all we were and are and wish to be."[12] Claiming that Shingen did not possess the nobility and grace necessary to wield such a weapon, Mariko grants one to Wolverine, whom she deems worthy. Despite this gesture of defiance against her father—the effect of which is, of course, diminished greatly by the fact that he is now dead—Mariko continues to be defined in stereotypical, antiquated terms. Instead of transcending the limits imposed by her lineage and abstract, ambiguously defined codes of honor and duty, she simply positions her father as someone who was a disgrace to this system, while continuing to see it as valid and an invaluable aspect of her life. Unquestioning of the stereotypes and rigid limitations that shape her life, Mariko now gives herself to another man, this time to Wolverine.

As Wolverine's love interest, cynically offered up for an arranged marriage for business reasons by a father counting on her loyalty, and someone who is clearly suffering as the result of her father's corrupt behavior, Mariko is certainly presented as sympathetic. Indeed, she is the "good Asian" in a world that also includes "bad Asians" such as Shingen, suggesting a balanced look at another culture on the part of white comic creators. This view, however, fails to acknowledge the implications of Asian representation by whites, specifically in the way that white superiority is maintained. In Georganne Nordstrom's discussion of *The Last Samurai* (2003), she builds off of the work of Michel de Certeau to argue that in representing the Other, even if the representation appears "authentic" and is intended to portray the non-white culture in a favorable light, white storytellers disguise their assertion of authority: "The simulacrum masks the appropriation."[13] Even favorable representations of Japanese-ness by whites become problematic because these representations imply that the characters and culture are being treated fairly. To be coded as "good" by a white writer or artist is no substitute for real authorship, as true agency is never in the hands of those people being represented.

---

12. Claremont, Miller, and Rubenstein, "Wolverine #1–4 (1982)," 114.
13. Nordstrom, "Embracing the Other," 181.

## Shingen: The Gangster

While Claremont and Miller present Mariko as a character who has deeply internalized a sense of honor toward her family, her father Shingen, while perhaps represented as having greater awareness of the weight that signifiers of Japanese identity carry (at least for the context of a largely white readership), similarly embodies his own set of clichés. The head of a criminal empire, Shingen is conscientious of traditional gendered expectations of Japanese identity and uses this knowledge to his advantage, putting up a façade of honor while secretly engaging in murder, theft, and other illegal operations. Shingen occupies an ancestral stronghold near Tokyo, possesses ancient swords with which he is exceptionally skilled, and heads his own criminal organization. During Shingen's initial encounter with Wolverine, the crime lord comments that "our family is as old as the Emperor's with as legitimate a claim to the throne," while in his next breath he acknowledges that concepts such as lineage "have become as ephemeral as the morning dew."[14] He claims status by surrounding himself with ancient relics and inhabiting an ancient building, but hints at their artificiality, suggesting to the reader that he is acutely aware of the power of symbolism and how to manipulate it for personal gain. Utilizing the guise of a confrontation between two evenly matched opponents, Shingen invokes samurai integrity only to undermine it with devious, self-serving motives and means. Shingen not only crafts a scenario in which he presents himself as a noble warrior, but humiliates Wolverine in the process. Not tied to the same codes that govern Mariko, Shingen nevertheless exercises some degree of control in his ability to manipulate these stereotypes. However, this further reinforces his character as a ruthless crime lord, locking him in another stereotype regularly applied to Asian characters in the American scheme of racial representations.

An event toward the conclusion of the second issue excellently demonstrates Claremont and Miller's portrayal of Shingen as an Asian man willing to hide his nefarious motives behind the pretense of acceptable Japanese social conventions. We are introduced to the cowardly Noburu, Shingen's son-in-law and husband of Mariko, who is meeting with rival gang leader Katsuyori in a kabuki theatre. This encounter is merely a façade so that Shingen's main rival can be brought out into the open and assassinated. The two men witness the performance of the play *Chūshingura*, described by Wolverine in narration as "a tale of honor, of loyalty, of samurai determination"

---

14. Claremont, Miller, and Rubenstein, "Wolverine #1–4 (1982)," 41.

that "embodies all the qualities the Japanese revere most in their national character and heritage."[15] Shingen's awareness of expectations does little to distance him from racist, essentializing ideology in that he never moves beyond his role as a manipulative, morally questionable criminal.

Despite Claremont and Miller's depiction of Shingen as someone with the ability to manipulate imagery and find spaces for constructing identity, the character ultimately remains an incredibly unsympathetic character example of what Zia labels the "gook" type,[16] an evil, conniving, and untrustworthy Japanese or Asian man. Although he is given some room to sidestep the shackles of honor and nobility embodied by his daughter, perhaps attributable to male privilege afforded by a male writer and artist, he remains one-dimensional and is overtly coded as a criminal foil to Wolverine's increasingly heroic persona. The kabuki play provides an apt metaphor for Shingen's deception, as a play about the indisputably commendable qualities of loyalty and determination that acts as a front for an assassination. In the case of both the play and Shingen, there is a presentable surface concealing something menacing. In *Wolverine*, male Japanese identity, as represented most centrally by Shingen, centers around untrustworthiness and selfishness. Such people partake in criminal activities and show little concern for who is harmed as a result. Shingen, while never truly signifying honor and lineage, is nonetheless tied to them in that his failures are measured in his inability to uphold such seemingly noble concepts.

The persistent reminders of Shingen's rather blatant failure to uphold Japanese honor correspond to a concurrent attempt by Claremont and Miller to elevate Wolverine and portray him as someone who is perfectly suited to embody honor. As trapped as the Japanese characters are by tradition in Claremont and Miller's Oriental imaginary, the qualities of honor and nobility they purport to uphold are indeed portable, as exemplified when Mariko informs Wolverine that he is "what Shingen could never hope to be."[17] As the story concludes, we are presented with failed, inadequate "Japanese" identity as represented by a "Japanese" character, serving as a clear contrast with Wolverine, the only true, successful samurai as sanctioned by the series. Ultimately, we are shown that Japanese traditions and qualities neither belong to the Japanese nor are they necessarily best exemplified by the Japanese. The gruff white man from Canada, who is granted much greater freedom from the strictures of identity, emerges as the best "Japanese" character in a less than subtle way.

---

15. Claremont, Miller, and Rubenstein, "Wolverine #1–4 (1982)," 64.
16. Zia, *Asian American Dreams*, 119.
17. Claremont, Miller, and Rubenstein, "Wolverine #1–4 (1982)," 115.

Not simply a triumph of good over evil, Wolverine's surpassing of Shingen demonstrates whiteness's facility for casting the Other as inferior. Sean M. Tierney notes, "the White imitator's display of the appropriated mastery both *to* and *through* the Asian practitioner nullifies the Asian's relationship to (and possession of) the mastery."[18] Claremont and Miller not only transplant mastery to Wolverine, who has earned it in a seemingly just way, but the qualities of a samurai are now presented as belonging to a white man, all while the evil Asian lies in defeat to support the hegemonic notion that the Other is inferior. Deborah Root notes how appropriating cultural artifacts is a means of "marking and remarking the defeat of the enemy and is always closely linked to the repetition of the moment of conquest, a repetition that can occur in how the world comes to be represented aesthetically."[19] While easily dismissible as entertainment that simply upholds the importance of one's internal quality, comics, especially those as iconic as *Wolverine*, play active roles in shaping how we characterize, judge, and exploit race.

## Wolverine's Invulnerable Whiteness

Wolverine's adoption of Japanese identity, while an evident display of the notion that it takes a white man to embody the forces of good and emerge as the hero, stems from a greater issue of the freedom of expression and identity that is granted by whiteness. Much like Richard Dyer's discussion of Tarzan film adaptations, in which the white hero becomes king of the jungle while effortlessly befriending the good and defeating the bad African natives, Claremont and Miller similarly portray Wolverine as able to prove his moral and physical superiority regardless of his role in relation to nonwhite characters.[20] The opening pages of *Wolverine* portray a plainspoken protagonist exploring the wilderness and reflecting on his various social (and generic) roles as a mutant and superhero. Initially failing as a "worthy" samurai type against Shingen, by the series' conclusion he has progressed to noble warrior, surpassing every other character to become an exemplary Japanese figure. Although whiteness is not explicitly used to characterize Wolverine, it nonetheless finds a strong presence in the narrative.

In contrast to the limited number of ways in which Mariko is defined by Claremont's script and Miller's art, almost exclusively as an obedient daughter, Wolverine is constantly identified in different ways. He classifies

---

18. Tierney, "Themes of Whiteness," 613.
19. Root, *Cannibal Culture*, 188.
20. Dyer, *White*, 157.

himself as "a mutant . . . a secret agent . . . [and] a super hero"[21] at the story's beginning, only to work through a multitude of identifiers, noting variously how he is a drunk, a warrior, a loner, a tiger, a scrapper, and, finally, just a man—a plain, unmarked identity available only to white men. As unmarked both in terms of his unknown past and, perhaps more significantly, his whiteness, Wolverine gains and discards labels with relative ease. The diversity of such labels, despite some of their negative or even dehumanizing connotations, suggests that Wolverine is not trapped by any one identity, and thus is granted more freedom than the characters around him.

While "Japanese" is a rigid category for certain characters, particularly Mariko, Wolverine fairly easily negotiates the boundaries of whiteness and nonwhite identities alike. From the hero's debut in 1974, a major defining characteristic has been his mysterious past, a point that would be further reinforced during Barry Windsor-Smith's *Weapon X* (1991) comic that introduced the idea that Wolverine was given artificial memories while part of a government experiment. In contrast to Mariko, Wolverine is not tethered to an ancient lineage, nor does he know his true last name—a distinction that often carries with it connotations of ethnicity and nationality. As Wolverine reflects on Mariko, whom he considers the love of his life, he notes, "She can trace her lineage back almost 2,000 years. Me, I know my father—that's as far as it goes."[22] Already in the opening pages, then, Wolverine's status as unmarked is explicitly anchored and contrasted to Mariko's ancient and ethnically tethered ancestry. Indeed, Wolverine in many ways is unmarked, not only in his whiteness but also in his freedom from his own history and the associations that accompany the label of names. Without an ancestral heritage to inform his present, Wolverine clearly represents the reshaping of identity on a constant basis.

Wolverine's ability to shift between identities and ultimately take on what is framed as the most revered Japanese qualities is facilitated by the framing of whiteness as transparent. Because of his whiteness, Wolverine can claim different cultural practices without any change in identity formation. In addition to undermining the cultural appropriation that takes place in white hero stories like *Wolverine*, the framing of whites' adoption of "Japanese" characteristics is framed as an extension of universal humanity that "writes out the history, politics, struggles, and the conditions that produced these specific cultural practices."[23] In the narrative, Wolverine's ascendance to the role of samurai is quite simple: He has a good spirit and "fought for

---

21. Claremont, Miller, and Rubenstein, "Wolverine #1–4 (1982)," 29.
22. Claremont, Miller, and Rubenstein, "Wolverine #1–4 (1982)," 32.
23. Drzewiecka and Wong, "Dynamic Construction," 206.

the good of others."[24] Sean M. Tierney similarly remarks how the inherent entitlement of whiteness "shows how the unquestioned invisibility of whiteness rationalizes the adoption and appropriate of Others' cultural activities as an expression of a universal, human impulse or right."[25] Wolverine is not portrayed as a white man who is granted so much authority that he is allowed to freely take from another culture, but rather as a virtuous man who takes on non–culturally specific qualities that can be achieved regardless of one's position, as long as one is worthy. As such, the hero is granted, without question, what Edward Said would refer to as "flexible positional superiority,"[26] in that he is able to move among various positions in relation to the Orientalized characters while always remaining superior.

The sense of freedom and agency provided by Wolverine's whiteness is amplified even further when *Wolverine* is placed in the broader context of the comic book world. In the pages of *Uncanny X-Men* and its various offshoots, mutants such as Wolverine are Othered by society and seen as a menace by a bigoted, paranoid majority, to the point where the series is commonly read as an allegorical comment on real-world struggles of minority groups. As popular X-Men historian Peter Sanderson has stated, many "regarded mutants as dangerous freaks, threatening the existence of the 'normal' human race."[27] The blue-skinned Nightcrawler, for example, is believed to be a demon in his native Germany and hunted by the God-fearing people of his village, while the Morlocks, a group of mutants who live in the sewers of New York, are deemed too hideous and bizarre by traditional standards, and so remain hidden from society. Not all mutants carry signifiers of privilege.

However, in *Wolverine*, the hero's unusual abilities are only referenced in passing and the human/mutant dichotomy so prevalent in *Uncanny X-Men* is replaced by a clear white/nonwhite binary. No longer labeled in terms of his mutant identity, Wolverine is identified by his Western status. In the new context of Japan, he is able to shed his previous signifier of Otherness, allowing his whiteness to help him emerge victorious in the midst of Japanese Others. The tenuous, albeit long-held, notions of mutants as representations of the righteous struggle of the oppressed is blatantly abandoned as Wolverine is effectively switched from mutant to white man. Nowhere is this clearer than during the final showdown with Shingen, in which the hero is without his iconic mask. The whiteness of Wolverine's face clearly contrasts with the sinister, slant-eyed gaze and devious smirk of his Japanese oppo-

---

24. Claremont, Miller, and Rubenstein, "Wolverine #1–4 (1982)," 115.
25. Tierney, "Themes of Whiteness," 609.
26. Said, *Orientalism*, 2.
27. Sanderson, *Ultimate X-Men*, 9.

nent. By the story's end, it is Logan the white man who kills Shingen and symbolically triumphs over the Other, not his elusive alter ego of Wolverine that is obscured by a mask.

Of course, while the narrative elevates Wolverine above the lowly status typically attributed to mutants, we are nonetheless left with a character who, as explicitly described in the story and supported by thousands of portrayals across countless media, is in fact not human, is not normal, and possesses a set of exceptional abilities. The character notes on several occasions throughout the miniseries how he differs from the average person. He states that "what makes me a mutant is my body's ability to heal virtually any wound, counter-act any disease."[28] Less overt, perhaps, is the way whiteness is privileged and upheld as a feature of such powers. I would like to suggest that his nature as an exceptional being, who is able to avoid physical suffering and quickly return to a perfect state of health, prevents him from fully immersing himself in the human experience, which ultimately upholds the importance of whiteness and makes his connection, as a mutant and member of the X-Men, to real-life marginalized groups even more tenuous. Paul Gilroy, in full acknowledgment that race is not based in genetics, argues that by focusing on the human body and what it means to live in the world as a human being, we can begin to move beyond the harmful restrictions brought on by race. Gilroy welcomes the "constraints of bodily existence"[29] and offers that "awareness of the indissoluble unity of all life at the level of genetic materials leads to a stronger sense of the particularity of our species as a whole."[30] Wolverine possesses an indestructible skeleton, artificially implanted against his will in order to make him the ultimate soldier, as well as a natural mutant ability to heal from nearly any wound, and as such, he does not truly live as a human being who may suffer from prolonged or indefinite physical pain. Indeed, as each scar, injury, or physical imperfection simply goes away, his whiteness is stubbornly upheld and perpetually preserved. Wolverine, as a character in general, is unhelpful in critiquing race because he is unable to experience the same pain and suffering that Gilroy suggests are able to create a bond among humans of all races. He cannot immerse himself in the lived, human, bodily existence that characterizes human experience, gives humans a sense of commonality with all other humans, and hopefully begins to expose the socially constructed nature of identifiers such as race.

---

28. Claremont, Miller, and Rubenstein, "Wolverine #1–4 (1982)," 40.
29. Gilroy, "The Crisis of 'Race' and Raciology," 269.
30. Gilroy, "The Crisis of 'Race' and Raciology," 271.

It is, however, difficult to ignore the way Wolverine's healing factor correlates to the more immediate, practical benefits of white privilege, specifically the opportunity to be physically healthy. George Lipsitz, in his extensive examination of how whiteness dramatically impacts many of the most significant (and quotidian) aspects of our lives, argues that "white Americans are encouraged to invest in whiteness, to remain true to an identity that provides them with resources, power, and opportunity."[31] In America, this includes greater access to medical treatment and higher life expectancies than the ethnic minorities who are hurt the most by the neoconservative assault on government spending for services that assist with transportation, housing, and, of course, health care.[32] As opposed to addressing institutionalized privilege that disproportionately benefits the physical and mental well-being of whites, the writers and artists behind Wolverine have, in much more dramatic fashion, heightened the results of such privilege and built them into the character's abilities. The advantageous effects that being white can have on one's body are literalized by Wolverine's superhuman anatomy.

If the white body is to represent "purity, cleanliness, and goodness"[33] Wolverine's mutant power, in the way it heals wounds, slows his aging, and returns him to a state of physical perfection, continually prevents the character from presenting anything less than the ideal for very long. He not only physically heals in preparation for tussling with the next supervillain but restores a site in which whiteness' symbolic power of superiority is dangerously normalized. Wolverine, of course, as a superhero, possesses a traditional, muscled physique as well. Although the white body could undermine white authority, in that it reminds us that white men are merely human like everyone else, Richard Dyer reminds us that the built, contoured white body can combat the fluid categories of race and gender. Dyer states that "only the hard, visibly bounded body can resist being submerged into the horror of femininity and non-whiteness."[34] The built, white, male body, as a symbol of whiteness as a rigid category, is always restored and always upheld by Wolverine and any fears of the feminine are, as Shyminsky has argued, "alleviated through identification with Wolverine's naturalized mutant maleness."[35] He becomes a rather blatant expression of whiteness as something both fixed and inherent to those who possess it, his body a literalization of the notion that whiteness is normalized on the human body.

---

31. Lipsitz, *Possessive Investment*, vii.
32. Lipsitz, *Possessive Investment*, 19.
33. Warren, "Bodily Excess," 93.
34. Dyer, *White*, 153.
35. Shyminsky, "Mutant Readers," 398.

Susan Bordo warns us of the dangers of being conditioned to believe that we simply choose our own bodies, as if this choice is somehow reflective of our character. She states that "the firm, developed body has become a symbol of correct *attitude*; it means that one 'cares' about oneself and how one appears to others, suggesting willpower, energy, control over infantile impulse, the ability to 'shape your life.'"[36] Wolverine, then, embodies perpetual agency and represents those highly valued internal qualities that are worn on the muscled, white body. As Shyminsky has said, "his very powers reinscribe the singular, biological, and essential notion of traditional white maleness—a muscled, animalistic body that, in addition to his moral code, serves to appeal directly to the desires of adolescent male readers."[37] The concept of white privilege becomes a little less abstract with Wolverine, who wears the signifiers of self-reliance, determination, and upstanding moral character on his body while putting in minimal effort to maintain that state of perfection. Indeed, most comic book heroes' physiques are not subject to the effects of time and the realistic dangers of partaking in the extreme activities required of such adventurers. After all, keeping these commercial characters in their physical prime would appear to be economically advantageous. However, in case that is not enough, Wolverine has his mutant powers. If "the bodies of a culture's practitioners can be called upon to supply proof of where that culture fits in the inevitable hierarchy of value,"[38] then Wolverine is a constant reminder that whites belong at the top.

## Conclusion

Though much has improved since the slant-eyed, fang-toothed Japanese soldiers portrayed in World War II–era *Captain America*, *Wolverine* demonstrates that by the early 1980s, mainstream superhero comics were far from overturning the hegemonic privileging of the white male that has been, and continues to be, so pervasive in the genre. As one considers the ways in which Japanese identity is negotiated throughout the narrative, a hierarchy emerges in which the Westerner is allotted the most freedom in defining himself. Although Japanese characters are no longer compared to Nazis or equated with vampires, comics such as *Wolverine* still manage to Other them, defining them in incredibly narrow terms. Wolverine's role as the white character and Shingen's careful use of clichés are indicative of a

---

36. Bordo, *Unbearable Weight*, 195.
37. Shyminsky, "Mutant Readers," 398.
38. Gilroy, "The Crisis of 'Race' and Raciology," 274.

comic that, while keenly aware of the performed, superficial quality of racial identity, presents characters that are nonetheless unable to transcend these limitations.

As part of the first in a wave of American superhero comics to take up Japanese characters and culture, which would soon also lead to Frank Miller's own series, *Ronin* (1983), and the commercial juggernaut of the *Teenage Mutant Ninja Turtles* (1984–), *Wolverine*, like many of its contemporary comics, remains steeped in a racist logic, privileging the perspective of the white protagonist, who is able to negotiate the aspects of his identity with ease in contrast to the "ethnic" characters who surround him. While X-Men such as Nightcrawler, Beast, and the Morlocks are Othered by physical difference and suggest fairly easy connections to real-world racial struggles, the books' standout star, Wolverine, while certainly not devoid of personal issues, is unmarked by signifiers of race. Enhanced senses, accelerated healing, and an indestructible skeleton seem useful for a hero such as Wolverine, but as the 1982 miniseries *Wolverine* demonstrates, few superpowers can compare to being white.

## Bibliography

Bordo, Susan. *Unbearable Weight: Feminism, Western Culture, and the Body*. Berkeley: University of California Press, 2003.

Claremont, Chris (writer), Frank Miller (penciller), and Josef Rubenstein (inker). "Wolverine #1–4 (1982)." In *The Best of Wolverine*, edited by Jeff Youngquist, 25–117. New York: Marvel Comics, 2004.

Drzewiecka, Jolant, and Kathleen Wong. "The Dynamic Construction of White Ethnicity in the Context of Transnational Cultural Formations." In *Whiteness: The Communication of Social Identity*, edited by Thomas K. Nakayama and Judith N. Martin, 198–216. Thousand Oaks, CA: Sage, 1999.

Dyer, Richard. *White: Essays on Race and Culture*. London: Routledge, 1997.

Gilroy, Paul. "The Crisis of 'Race' and Raciology." In *The Critical Studies Reader, Third Edition*, edited by Simon During, 264–80. London: Routledge, 2007.

Lipsitz, George. *The Possessive Investment in Whiteness: How White People Profit from Identity Politics*. Philadelphia: Temple University Press, 1998.

Lowe, Lisa. *Critical Terrains: French and British Orientalisms*. Ithaca, NY: Cornell University Press, 1991.

Nordstrom, Georganne. "Embracing the Other: Illusions of Agency." *The International Journal of Diversity in Organizations, Communities, and Nations: Annual Review* 5, no. 2 (2006): 179–86.

Root, Deborah. *Cannibal Culture: Art, Appropriation, and the Commodification of Difference*. Boulder, CO: Westview Press, 1996.

Said, Edward W. *Orientalism*. New York: Pantheon Books, 1978.

Sanderson, Peter. *Ultimate X-Men*. New York: Marvel/DK, 2000.

Shyminsky, Neil. "Mutant Readers, Reading Mutants: Appropriation, Assimilation, and the X-Men." *International Journal of Comic Art* 8, no. 2 (2006): 387–405.

Tierney, Sean M. "Themes of Whiteness in *Bulletproof Monk*, *Kill Bill*, and *The Last Samurai*." *Journal of Communication* 56, no. 3 (2006): 607–24.

Trushell, John M. "American Dreams of Mutants: The X-Men—'Pulp' Fiction, Science Fiction, and Superheroes." *Journal of Popular Culture* 38, no. 1 (2004): 149–68.

Warren, John T. "Bodily Excess and the Desire for Absence: Whiteness and the Making of (Raced) Educational Subjectivities." In *Performance Theories in Education: Power, Pedagogy, and the Politics of Identity*, edited by Bryant K. Alexander, Gary L. Anderson, and Bernardo P. Gallegos, 83–104. London: Routledge, 2005.

Zia, Helen. *Asian American Dreams: The Emergence of an American People*. New York: Farrar, Straus, and Giroux, 2001.

CHAPTER 14

# THE DARK KNIGHT

Whiteness, Appropriation, Colonization, and Batman in the *New 52* Era

JEFFREY A. BROWN

BATMAN, LIKE MOST comic book superheroes, is a white American man and thus perpetuates an association of heroism, power, and moral superiority with whiteness. Of course, the relative invisibility of Batman's whiteness as a definitive character trait is not unique to the Caped Crusader. Western culture, and American popular culture in particular, has long presented whiteness as the default normative identity. As indigenous rights scholar Aileen Moreton-Robinson argues, whiteness is a baseline position "constitutive of the epistemology of the West; it is an invisible regime of power that secures hegemony through discourse and has material effects in everyday life."[1] Batman's status as both a billionaire industrialist and as one of the most dominant superheroes in the fictional DC Comics Universe has long naturalized a persistent Western belief in white exceptionalism. In 2011 DC Comics initiated a reboot of their entire fictional universe under the banner of the "New 52" in order to remove decades of narrative clutter, to update characters for the modern world, and to provide an easier entry point for new readers. This reboot was an opportunity for the superheroes to reflect cultural changes in the real world, including shifting perceptions about ethnicity, international politics, and colonialism. Unfortunately, despite the

---

1. Moreton-Robinson "Whiteness," 75.

best intentions of many of the creators, Batman's comic book adventures in the New 52 era continue to perpetuate and normalize an ideology of white privilege in two key ways: first, through Bruce Wayne's appropriation of exotic skills during his training with ethnic and foreign Others, and second, through Batman's neocolonial approach to enlisting foreign heroes to serve as helpers in his war against crime.

While Batman stories have interacted with Otherness in various ways since the character was first introduced in 1939, it was the repositioning of Batman as a grim and gritty persona in the 1980s that intensified the idea of the Dark Knight acquiring his skills in mysterious foreign lands. In particular, Frank Miller's *Batman: Year One* (1986) established as canon that the adolescent Bruce Wayne traveled the globe seeking out foreign experts who could teach him the skills he would need to become Batman. Since *Year One*, an increasing number of stories have fleshed out Bruce's early travels, documenting his mastery of foreign secrets. In this chapter I focus on Batman comics from DC's New 52 era (2011–2016) to illustrate how whiteness continues to be naturalized even in a time when awareness of diversity issues has become commonplace. That facets of these stories demonstrate an implied white exceptionalism does not mean that the comic books intentionally promote a biased racial perspective. On the contrary, many of Batman's adventures in Gotham City demonstrate an inclusive approach to ethnic diversity. Moreover, Batman himself is often depicted as a relatively liberal champion of tolerance and acceptance (even if his adventures never really bring about cultural changes). But contemporary comics are also bound up with dominant American cultural values, ideologies, and narratives, and have as such portrayed Batman's dealings with predominantly nonwhite cultures through the lenses of appropriation and colonization.

## White Knight

Batman's commercial success seems to know no bounds. In recent years Batman as intellectual property has generated billions of dollars for Time-Warner through live-action feature films and television series, cartoons, video games, toys, T-shirts, and countless other forms of merchandising.[2] Moreover, Batman continues to headline DC's best-selling comics while featuring in no less than eight monthly series.[3] Unsurprisingly, the character

---

2. Santiago, "10 Highest Grossing Superhero Franchises in the US."
3. Mayo, "Why Is Batman the Benchmark?"

has undergone dramatic changes over his roughly eighty years of existence, from a gun-wielding vigilante, to a campy do-gooder, to an obsessive devotee of justice. But, as media theorists Roberta E. Pearson and William Uricchio point out in their landmark work on Batman, through all the changes and variations there remain important "minimal components"[4] of the character's identity. Specifically, Batman is identifiable via his secret identity as orphaned billionaire Bruce Wayne, his iconic costume and accessories, his Gotham City setting, his detective skills, and his equally iconic rogues gallery. Furthermore, the dominant perception of Batman is solidified around several identifiable characteristics: He is also tacitly acknowledged as a white, heterosexual, American man in his early thirties. It is these implicit characteristics of Batman (and most superheroes) that naturalize a persistent valorization of racial, gendered, and economic privileges. The basic conception of Batman/Bruce Wayne has always been one of exceptional privilege. Yes, he is a tragic and sympathetic character, but as both Batman and Bruce Wayne he personifies a decidedly hegemonic position.

At the same time, the Gotham City of contemporary comics is depicted as home to many different cultural groups—not unlike the major coastal metropolises in the US—but racial politics are rarely part of Batman's adventures. Characters on both sides of the law represent far more diversity than in decades past, with numerous black, Asian, and Latinx figures assuming pivotal roles, especially and increasingly as superheroes. The once all-WASP Batman family now includes African American Duke Thomas and Asian American Cassandra Cain. Former Latina Gotham City police officer Renee Montoya has taken on the role of The Question, a mysterious superhero long adjacent to Batman. African American tech genius Luke Fox now fights alongside Batman in sophisticated armor as Batwing. And the current Robin, Bruce's biological son Damien Wayne, is a biracial product of a union between Batman and the Middle Eastern villainess Talia Al Ghul. Still, most of Batman's adventures in the New 52 era ignore race as a pivotal issue, suggesting instead that anyone, regardless of structural inequalities, can be a hero if they work hard and seek justice.

These stories present what Eduardo Bonilla-Silva refers to as an image of America as "colorblind."[5] In eliding racial politics, Batman's whiteness remains invisible—it is neither questioned nor challenged. Batman's preeminence as a costumed hero is presented as a logical result of his determination, training, and intelligence. The unmarked status of Batman's whiteness

---

4. Pearson and Uricchio, "I'm Not Fooled by That Cheap Disguise," 186.
5. Bonilla-Silva, *Racism without Racists*.

naturalizes the relationship between his seemingly innate superiority in all areas and his racially hegemonic status. Batman's masculine privileges may occasionally be questioned by the likes of Batgirl and Catwoman, his normative heterosexual position may be ridiculed by his lesbian cousin Batwoman, and even Bruce Wayne's wealth is openly discussed as one of the unfair advantages the character has by some of his young allies like Spoiler and Duke Thomas. But Batman's whiteness is never foregrounded, which allows the stories to reinforce assumptions of racially specific privileges as natural.

In his pioneering work, *Orientalism*, postcolonial theorist Edward Said detailed the long-standing racial logic adopted by Western cultures that naturalized and assumed white superiority over other cultures and peoples. The term "Orientalism" refers to an "imaginative geography" of the Orient narratively constructed in Western representations and, consequently, imagined by Westerners. Travel literature, academic and missionary accounts, art, and literature have historically presented non-Western cultures and people as mysterious, beguiling, dangerous, and uncivilized. As Said argued: "The Orient was almost a European invention, and had been since antiquity a place of romance, exotic beings, haunting memories and landscapes, remarkable experiences."[6] The imaginative language of Orientalism survives today, reinforced through the discursive terrain of mass culture, including comic books. Orientalism, and the concomitant concept of an "Other" diametrically opposed to the Western "self," structures a colonialist logic of Western superiority and a right to exploit or dominate foreign lands and peoples.

The basic binary structure of Orientalism has adapted to account for numerous other socially constructed dichotomies. As film scholar Matthew Bernstein argues, "the regime of knowledge that Orientalism encompasses—structured around a basic dichotomy between East and West, and Other and Self—share an ontological norm (white Western culture) with constructions of race, ethnicity, and sexual orientation in Western culture."[7] Batman's implicit characteristics and all the associated qualities that accompany his multiple markers of privilege (white, male, heterosexual, wealthy, American) construct him as a figure against which all Otherness is measured—and usually found wanting. The valorizing of white heroism becomes explicit when Batman's adventures bring him into contact with representatives of other nations and ethnicities. In this way, Batman perpetuates a colonialist belief in white dominance that has become a trope among characters in the Western heroic tradition. "For centuries," neocolonial critic Casey Kelly

---

6. Said, *Orientalism*, 1.
7. Bernstein, introduction, 3.

notes, "tales of white heroism and conquest in foreign lands have sustained misguided beliefs in the superiority of Western culture, the backwardness of non-Western societies, and the imperative to 'civilize' the world."[8] Batman's adventures reinforce this idea of whiteness as a dominant position through his mastery of the "Orient" and his (neo)colonial relationships with non-American heroes.

## Batman and Appropriation

Batman origin stories in the 2010s often recount how he acquired his skills during decade-long travels by interweaving flashbacks or in backup features. For example, the backup story in *Batman* #21 (June 2013) depicts a nineteen-year-old Bruce Wayne in Rio de Janeiro completing six weeks of training with Don Miguel, a famed getaway driver.[9] Bruce has become an expert at high-speed chases, but in his final lesson he uses the car they are driving to trap Miguel for the police. Similarly, in *Batman* #23 (August 2013), a twenty-four-year-old Bruce learns to surpass the limits of human endurance in a remote part of Norway.[10] Fighting a death match for twenty-eight hours straight, Bruce defeats dozens of challengers but refuses to kill the men to gain his own freedom. Eventually the men refuse to fight any more because they are afraid of this fierce warrior. And in *Batman* #52 (May 2016), flashbacks depict young Bruce learning martial arts in the Hida Mountains of Japan, how to withstand extreme cold in Canada, and how to survive jumping from a plane without a parachute in Yugoslavia.[11] One of the more detailed stories about Bruce's time abroad occurs in *Detective Comics* #0 (September 2012).[12] The tale takes place "somewhere in the Himalayas," with a twenty-something Bruce learning from "the legendary Shihan Matsuda. Zen-Buddhist monk warrior, master of mind control." Bruce explains that previously he had also learned from experts in dozens of exotic locations. Under Matsuda's tutelage, Bruce learns swordsmanship, a new martial art, and meditation techniques that allow him total control over his body. And, in a three-issue story arc published in *Legends of the Dark Knight* #38–40 (February–April 2013), Alfred recounts the exploits of an adolescent Bruce Wayne learning the art of vanishing in Thailand from the exotic Mekhala,

---

8. Kelly, "Neocolonialism and the Global Prison," 332.
9. Snyder and Capullo, "Where the Hell Did He Learn to Drive?!"
10. Snyder, and Capullo, "The Pit."
11. Snyder, Tynion, and Rossmo, "The List."
12. Hurwitz and Daniel, "The Final Lesson."

the daughter of a rebel leader.[13] Mekhala agrees to teach Bruce the skills she has learned from her father in gratitude for his saving her from the corrupt police.

These contemporary stories about Bruce Wayne's early world travels are depicted in other twenty-first-century Batman media as well. Christopher Nolan's *Batman Begins* (2005) devotes a significant amount of screen time to Bruce's training in the "Orient." The *Justice League Unlimited* episode "Dead Reckoning" (2006) addresses Batman's early martial arts lessons among the monks of the mythical Asian temple Nanda Parbat. Likewise, the lighthearted LEGO movie *Justice League: Gotham City Breakout* (2016) sees Batman return to the mysterious dojo of Madame Mantis, where he was the only student to learn Mantis's infamous "Forbidden Move." The consistent theme in all of these New 52–era stories, and many more, across disparate media is that in order to become Batman, Bruce must first travel the world, gaining incredible abilities and discovering ancient secrets from a range of non-American and typically nonwhite masters. As the stories repeatedly demonstrate, Bruce not only studies these skills but also becomes the best at whatever he learns. Batman is shown time and again surpassing rival students, even those who have trained for significantly longer. What all of these stories about Bruce's preparations in foreign lands reveal is not just a mastery of exotic skills, but an Orientalist appropriation of signifiers.

Bruce's quest to become Batman demonstrates the logic whereby if a white Westerner is determined enough, he can become the best at anything he wants. For the Westerner, there is no barrier that impedes becoming a master of Others' traditions. Batman's fascination with foreign cultures and the skills he easily appropriates from them is not unique to the Dark Knight, but he is the most famous of superheroes to appropriate Otherness. White Western comic book superheroes like DC's Black Canary, Richard Dragon, and Karate Kid, as well as Marvel's Wolverine, Daredevil, and Iron Fist, all learned their martial arts skills while studying in the Orient.[14] Likewise, Hollywood films often retell the fantasy of a white Westerner who becomes part of a supposedly more primitive culture and in doing so becomes its savior, as for example in *Lawrence of Arabia* (1962), *Dances with Wolves* (1990), *The Last Samurai* (2003), and *Avatar* (2009). More specifically, Western fictions repeatedly portray a white character mastering exotic abilities, exhibiting what Said describes as a belief that whites "can imitate the Orient without

---

13. Williamson and Craig, "I Hate It When He Does That."
14. See Matthew Pustz's chapter in this volume on the racial politics of 1970s white martial arts superheroes.

the opposite being true."[15] In his discussion of American martial arts films like *Kill Bill* (2003) and *Bulletproof Monk* (2003), film scholar Sean M. Tierney argues these movies utilize a "repetitive framework of superiority in which the White person achieves and/or comes to *possess* skill, mastery, and recognition (as well as mastery over and acquiescence of Others)," which, Tierney continues, "displays a colonialist attitude that reinforces Western hegemony."[16] Batman's training implies the same colonialist attitude about a white character's abilities to master skills associated with ethnic Others, and even surpass native experts. Batman's appropriation of countless Eastern skill sets demonstrates his preeminence as a superhero, but also, and more politically significant, his advantages as a white and Western figure of privilege.

Tierney reasons that the easy, seemingly magical way that white protagonists become proficient at martial arts is evidence of how media tropes perpetuate and reinforce an assumption of white superiority. That heroes like Batman, who may only train for a few weeks or months, can best natives who have been training their entire lives implies that Westerners have an inherent capacity and right to usurp the cultural traditions of Others. "The ability of the White practitioner to defeat Asians, using an Asian skill, in Asia," observes Tierney, "propagates the theme of a ubiquitous, even inevitable White supremacy of global proportions."[17] White Western characters are repeatedly shown in popular culture to be physically, mentally, and morally superior to Easterners. The colonialist presumption is that Westerners are naturally better at everything and thus able to master the simplistic traditions of Other cultures if they only put their mind to it. This colonialist fantasy routinely offered by Hollywood is taken to an extreme with Batman. Where white film protagonists may master the skills from a single foreign culture, Batman does so with dozens of exotic cultural groups. There is seemingly no fighting style, detective ability, or crime-fighting talent that Bruce Wayne cannot perfect. Bruce's ten-year sojourn around the globe described in New 52–era comics allowed him to collect and appropriate every expertise desired—like a wealthy tourist purchasing souvenirs, a demonstrable commodification and possession of Otherness.

Contemporary Batman stories extend the Orientalist presumptions beyond the traditional dichotomy of West versus East. The tales of Batman's training in various locations demonstrate that from an American perspective, Orientalism indicates *anywhere* else in the world. Thus, European nations,

---

15. Said, *Orientalism*, 160.
16. Tierney, "Themes of Whiteness," 614.
17. Tierney, "Themes of Whiteness," 614.

and even Canada, are now as likely to be cited as exotic places where Bruce acquires skills. This perception that anywhere outside the US is mysterious and potentially dangerous reflects a post-9/11 xenophobia. One comic to position Europe as an Orientalist Other is the "Born to Kill" storyline from *Batman and Robin* #1–8 (September 2011–April 2012).[18] The new costumed villain in Gotham, dubbed Nobody, is actually Morgan Ducard, the vengeful son of one of Bruce's old teachers, Henri Ducard. Batman recalls how years earlier he found and trained under Henri in his native Paris. Bruce spent months learning how to track even the most elusive criminals from the Ducards. Eventually Bruce tries to leave, so Henri sends Morgan to kill him. But Bruce emerges victorious and deposits a bloody Morgan on his father's desk. In Tomasi's story, France is as dangerous as any war-torn Middle Eastern country and the Ducards are as untrustworthy as any stereotypically depicted Other. Yet again, young Bruce proves himself the better fighter, the better person. Batman's appropriation of foreign skills, drawing on the Orientalist presumption of Western superiority, implies that white American masculinity is the pinnacle of physical, mental, and moral achievement. Even if Batman faces some initial defeats, he is always able to overcome his adversaries in the end.

Likewise, Batman is portrayed as preternaturally intelligent—able to solve any mystery or outthink any opponent. In fact, as media theorist Richard Dyer notes in his analysis of 1950s peplum films starring white bodybuilders in exotic lands, colonial logic suggests that the physical and mental superiority of heroic white men is often intertwined. Dyer argues that the muscular white body is assumed to be the result of thought and planning, and that the white hero is "better able to handle his body, to improvise with what is at hand, to size up situations. . . . The built white physique may be fabulous, but what made it, and makes it effective, is the mind in the body."[19] Moreover, Batman's unwavering morality consistently characterizes him as incredibly ethical. He is incorruptible, he refuses to kill or allow others to kill, and he always serves a larger sense of justice, if not the letter of the law. In a sense, where Batman's brawn and brains mark him as physically ideal, his morality confirms not just his heroic status but also an almost saintly position. This stance conforms to colonialist ideas about whiteness as a symbol of being inherently more civilized and inherently closer to divine perfection than the "savage heathens" of other lands. As Bruce describes his pre-Batman acquisition of the skills of ethnic and national Others in *Batman*

---

18. Tomasi and Gleason, "Born to Kill."
19. Dyer, "The White Man's Muscles," 311.

*and Robin* #5 (January 2012), each skill added "an integral piece to the arsenal I'd be carrying back to Gotham."[20] Clear parallels exist between Bruce taking what he wants from other cultures for his own purposes and the long history of the West exploiting the East.

## Batman and Colonization

Several New 52–era Batman stories explore the flip side of Western Orientalist thinking, not just taking *from* but taking *over*. Rather than merely appropriating from Others as young Bruce did, the more mature Batman imposes his world view and crime-fighting methods on other nations and cultures. Most obviously, the Grant Morrison–scripted series *Batman Incorporated* (2010–2013) depicts the character's efforts to combat crime on a global scale. To do so, Batman enlists vigilantes around the world, sanctioning them in his own image. Bruce informs the board of his multinational company Wayne Enterprises that it is

> time to use our resources not only to improve Gotham, but to change the world . . . I plan to build and support a network of international crime-fighting agents. From London to Hong Kong, from Buenos Aires to Moscow . . . We're creating a ubiquitous international crime-fighting franchise.[21]

In interviews Morrison described the idea behind extending Batman's brand internationally as a form of the character's benevolence: "*Batman Inc.* is an attempt to reimagine what a good corporation can be. . . . [T]his will be Bruce Wayne's attempt, and I think it's going to be quite progressive."[22] The merger of Bruce Wayne's corporate approach with Batman's global crime-fighting goals reveals the neocolonial ideology that undergirds the project of establishing Batman franchises around the world.

Morrison's *Batman Incorporated* was inspired by the hokey "Batmen of All Nations" that appeared originally in *Detective Comics* #215 (1955). Where the original Batmen of All Nations were six cheery do-gooders who independently adapted the idea of Batman to their own native countries, Morrison's series has Batman recruiting, testing, and employing fledgling or second-tier foreign heroes. Among the Batman-like costumed adventurers conscripted for Batman, Inc. are Batwing (Democratic Republic of the Congo), El Gau-

---

20. Tomasi and Gleason, "Born to Kill."
21. Morrison et al., "Brand Building."
22. Thill, "Grant Morrison's *Batman, Inc.*"

cho (Argentina), Nightrunner (France), Dark Ranger (Australia), Chief Man-of-Bats (Native American), Knight and Squire (England), Jiro the Batman of Japan, and Ravil the Batman of Moscow. As terms like "incorporated," "investors," and "international franchises" (all used in the comic to describe Batman's crime-fighting structure) suggest, Batman's personal quest for justice mirrors the neoliberal approach to global commerce. Specifically, it is an approach rooted in Western ideas about colonizing other nations and the modern neocolonial version of international corporate expansion. The hegemonic whiteness of Bruce in his role as CEO of Wayne Enterprises and of Batman as the head of Batman Incorporated reproduces a long-standing inequity between wealthy, white Westerners and the exploitable labor of ethnic Others.

Though the era of European colonialism came to a close shortly after World War II, the general ideology of Western supremacy carries on and has become more covert through neocolonial practices. Colonialism, in a classic sense, designates the tradition of nations using force to appropriate land and conquer indigenous populations of foreign territories. Since the 1950s, military attempts at empire building have been outlawed, but the practice of neocolonialism extends the ideology of colonialism through systems of persuasion rather than force. "Neocolonial rhetoric is representational though inferential," notes media scholar Casey Kelly, "not an overt endorsement but a discourse symptomatic of repressed and unexamined colonial ideologies."[23] Neocolonialism is an imperial project—colonizing the minds, hearts, beliefs, and bank accounts of indigenous people around the world. Not directed by governments and militaries, neocolonialism is often deployed by corporate interests. Neocolonialism is globalization as Americanization: not planting a flag on foreign soil but erecting instead McDonalds, Starbucks, and Walmarts.

*Batman Incorporated* follows this business model as a way to expand and control vigilantism. Rather than flying an American flag to claim territories, a Bat-Signal shines in the sky above foreign cities. As comics journalist Emmet O'Cuana argues: "Wayne's strategy is to execute socially progressive crime-fighting measures across the world through the franchising of the Bat-brand, applying the model of a corporation to the work of a superhero."[24] Similarly, legal theorist Chris Comerford notes that the structure of Batman, Inc. is analogous to the American government's approach to foreign policy after 9/11. Batman, Inc. is "headed by and answerable to a Western—specifi-

---

23. Kelly, "Neocolonialism," 334.
24. O'Cuana, "'Morrison Inc.,'" 212.

cally American—figure of authority," as Comerford argues, "overseen from the United States and executing worldwide activities . . . necessary and for the sake of justice."[25] Despite Grant Morrison's stated desire to explore what a "good corporation can be," *Batman Incorporated* is ultimately revealed as a neocolonial narrative branding justice with the well-known American symbol of Batman and interpellating foreign heroes into Batman's world view. "Good corporation," in this context, is equated with neocolonial protectorate.

Batman's recruitment of foreign operatives takes place across the first issues of the series, with some stories far more detailed than others. Throughout *Batman Incorporated* there are consistent themes of Batman's superiority as a costumed hero, the neophyte's admiration for Batman, and their willingness to join his noble crusade against crime. There is an emphasis in the recruitment stories on the Otherness of the Batman, Inc. associates. In typical comic book fashion, all of the heroes from other nations are Orientalized in broad strokes. The heroes from the US, Australia, and France are drawn from disenfranchised ethnic populations: Chief Man-of-Bats and his sidekick Raven Red, both of the Sioux nation; the Australian Dark Ranger, pseudonym of the Aborigine Johnny Riley; and Bilal Asselah, an Algerian Sunni Muslim immigrant, going by the codename Nightrunner. As the series unfolds, Batman's vision of an incorporated global crime-fighting force is wrapped up in a neocolonial logic wherein a powerful white American man leads a diverse group of ethnic Others, steering them toward his view of justice. Perhaps more important, Batman is presented as the pinnacle of heroic achievement that these lesser ethnic heroes should aspire to, thus implying that Batman's whiteness is also an aspirational category.

The introduction of Bilal Asselah as France's Nightrunner in 2011's *Detective Comics Annual* #12 and *Batman Annual* #28, in particular, demonstrates the neocolonial approach taken with foreign heroes. Bruce is in Paris lobbying for permission to establish a branch of Batman, Inc., while Batman tries to quell racially charged riots spurred by the assassinations of public figures involved in both sides of an immigration debate. Bruce and Dick Grayson (formerly Robin) team up with Nightrunner, a masked, parkour-running vigilante who is the son of Arab immigrants who began crime fighting to defend fellow Muslims. Fighting alongside Batman, Nightrunner thinks to himself: "Under my mask, I'm grinning like a lunatic. This is it! I'm a hero! . . . I'm working *with* them. They accept me without question. I've proved myself. It feels good."[26] After the heroes defeat the criminal organi-

---

25. Comerford, "The Hero We Need," 195–96.
26. Hine and Padilla, "All the Rage."

zation instigating the civil unrest for their own financial gain rather than for any political agenda, Wayne Enterprises is permitted to set up a Batman, Inc. franchise and Bruce endorses Bilal as the Batman of France. Bruce provides Bilal with a lavish base of operations, cutting-edge equipment, and several weeks of personal training with Dick Grayson.

While presenting Bilal with a new gray-and-black suit adorned with a Batman symbol, Bruce explains: "To unite a city we have to give the people something to unite *about*, Bilal. We have to give them someone who doesn't fight for one side, but who fights for one goal. We have to give them a *symbol*. What I want, Bilal, is for The Nightrunner to help me save Paris."[27] Batman's endorsement, sponsorship, and training of Nightrunner may establish Bilal as a costumed hero for Paris, but only as a reflection of Batman himself. As a hero, Nightrunner is colonized to willfully and enthusiastically accept Batman's ideas, methods, and purpose. Batman insists on his conservative view of justice that maintains the status quo and resists truly transformative social change. Bilal may have started out as a champion for Arab and Muslim immigrants, but Batman's ideology repositions Nightrunner as a mitigating presence defending innocents on both sides of the political debate. In effect, Batman contains and redirects Bilal's anti-colonialism, guiding him to a more "civilized" (white and Western) perspective.

The establishment of a Batman franchise in Japan follows a similar neocolonial pattern. As told in *Batman Incorporated* #1 and #2 (November and December 2010), Batman and Catwoman travel to Tokyo looking to recruit the vigilante Mr. Unknown, aka Jiro Osamu. When Jiro meets Batman, he immediately declares: "Bruce Wayne's Batman Incorporated, right? . . . *I'll take the offer.*"[28] But since Jiro used a gun to avenge his mentor's assassination, Batman rescinds his offer. Eventually Jiro earns Batman's respect and trust and is enlisted as the Batman of Japan. In the story's final panel, readers see Jiro swearing an oath to Batman by candlelight, blatantly suggesting the almost religious level of loyalty that Batman expects from his underlings and the presumption that validity to act for justice within one's own nation and culture is granted by a white figure of authority from the US. Batman establishes franchises around the world and persuades foreign agents to adopt his methods and morality as the superior paths to justice. As feminist scholars David Oh and Doreen Kutufam have argued, "where White masculinity differentiates itself from non-White masculinities is the belief that White masculinity tempers savage primitivism with self-discipline and

---

27. Hine and Padilla, "All the Rage."
28. Morrison and Burnham, "In the Eye of the Leviathan."

control, constructing non-White men as not having tamed their primitive selves."[29] Batman's rules and methods reconstruct these ethnically diverse characters as acceptable heroes. In essence, Batman's insistence on the use of *his* techniques and *his* morality functions to whiten the diverse cast of indigenous heroes. These Other Batmen can only be validated for readers when they conform to Batman's iconic white, Western version of heroism. Batman's admonishment of Jiro's use of a gun, for example, is a very literal tempering of his savagery (and an ironic one considering Batman used a gun himself in his first adventures in 1939). In Orientalist terms, Batman evidences and valorizes white masculinity and Western culture as the pinnacle of human achievement that can benefit lesser foreign characters that he personally endorses as worthy if they accede to his world view. Batman colonizes the Other heroes from different nations to work for him, to be like him, and to extend his personal vision, tied up as it is with an Americanized notion of global policing.

The narrative premise of *Batman Incorporated* is presented as an extension of Batman's altruistic impulse to protect people, here pushed well beyond the confines of Gotham City. Indeed, in his analysis of Morrison's major works, Emmet O'Cuana refers to the ideology of *Batman Incorporated* as "benevolent capitalism."[30] The global expansion of Batman's war on crime is a novel idea for the comic book superhero genre. But the stories of Batman recruiting international allies also suggest a pastiche of older American and European imperialist concepts like noblesse oblige, Manifest Destiny, and the white man's burden, especially given Batman's alter ego as businessman Bruce Wayne. Despite Morrison's best intentions, Batman's intervention in spaces outside of the US implies that only a powerful white man can achieve justice for the globally disenfranchised. As Richard Dyer argues, there is a very thin line between international assistance and colonial ideology:

> The ideas of intervention and restoration, of acting on behalf of those who cannot act on behalf of themselves, are the centerpieces of neocolonialist rhetoric. Colonialism had long claimed that imperial possession brought, and was even done in order to bring benefits to the natives, and this informed the policy of the Western nations toward their former colonies in the postwar era, headed by the idea of the United States as world policeman.[31]

---

29. Oh and Kutufam, "The Orientalized 'Other,'" 153.
30. O'Cuana, "Morrison Inc.," 211.
31. Dyer, "The White Man's Muscles," 304.

As *Batman Incorporated* moved toward its conclusion after a three-year run, it became apparent that rather than "benevolent capitalism," this conglomerate of Bat-heroes were recruited to help Batman himself more than they were gathered so that Batman could help fight crime in their countries.

Throughout *Batman Incorporated,* Batman instructs his agent-employees to battle the emissaries of a mysterious evil organization known only as "Leviathan." Despite the apparent complexity and global reach of Leviathan, it is eventually revealed that Talia al Ghul is the mastermind behind everything. Talia is mother to Damian Wayne (Robin) and former lover of Batman. Leviathan's sole purpose is to take away everything Batman values in revenge for his rejection of Talia. In other words, the global threat masks an entirely personal one focused on Batman and Gotham City. Most of the members of Batman, Inc. come to Gotham to help defeat Talia. Despite the claims made in *Batman Incorporated* about bringing Batman-like justice to every corner of the globe, the exact opposite happens. Gotham in effect becomes the colonial metropole, the geographic center that all of the colonized agents serve and defend. Some of the foreign heroes even give their lives to help Batman. Moreover, in the end, Batman completely dissolves Batman, Inc., leaving the foreign heroes to their own devices, no longer backed by the American hero's guidance or financial resources. Likewise, DC Comics completely abandoned the international characters after they served their narrative purpose as supporting characters in Batman's global foray. In other words, the demise of Batman, Inc. mirrored the devastating effects on foreign economies and cultures when multinational conglomerates unilaterally withdraw from various markets. The only *Batman Incorporated* hero to remain in circulation was David Zavimbe, the African Batwing, who was featured in his own eponymous series. But, by *Batwing* #19 (April 2013), Zavimbe was replaced by the African American character Luke Fox and his adventures were moved to Gotham City. For the most part, the nonwhite heroes bolstered Batman's mythical white superheroism and then were quickly discarded.

Batman's implicit identification as a white American, as the ultimate fantasy of unassailable hegemonic masculinity, helps normalize whiteness as a racial and cultural ideal. The assumption of white privilege is camouflaged as heroic adventure through stories of young Bruce Wayne's world travels to acquire exotic skills, and the more mature Batman's recruitment of foreign costumed agents to expand his war on crime. The character of Batman is complicit in perpetuating an Orientalist world view in which white Westerners easily master even the most difficult of foreign skills in a remarkably short period of time, and naturally assume command of more feeble nonwhite figures and guide them to be better allies and to adopt a more sensible (and Western) perspective. Cultural appropriation and neocolonial colonization are two of the central tenets of Orientalist thinking that privilege the civilized West over the mysterious East, whiteness over the nonwhite Other. The premise that Batman acquired or appropriated his physical skills while traveling the Orient has been part of the general Batman mythology since the late 1980s. But the constant retelling of specific events whereby young Bruce Wayne trained with foreign masters continues to reinforce assumptions about white privilege. Batman's effort to recruit foreign operatives to work for him is a new trope that has not been explored in the past, but rather than authentically diversifying the Bat-universe, this accumulation of Other Batmen only served to further validate the superiority of the white American character. The cumulative result of Batman's appropriation and colonization of Otherness in the 2010s is a strained attempt to incorporate diversity within the character's fictional world, and an unintended perpetuation of America's assumption of normative whiteness as the pinnacle of achievement.

## Bibliography

Bernstein, Matthew. Introduction to *Visions of the East: Orientalism in Film*, edited by Matthew Bernstein and Gaylyn Studlar, 1–18. New Brunswick, NJ: Rutgers University Press, 1997.

Bonilla-Silva, Eduardo. *Racism without Racists: Color-Blind Racism and the Persistence of Racial Inequality in America*. Lanham, MD: Rowman & Littlefield, 2003.

Comerford, Chris. "The Hero We Need, Not the One We Deserve: Vigilantism and the State of Exception in *Batman Incorporated*." In *Graphic Justice: Intersections of Comics and Law*, edited by Thomas Giddens, 183–200. New York: Routledge, 2015.

Dyer, Richard. "The White Man's Muscles." In *Race and the Subject of Masculinities*, edited by Harry Stecopoulos and Michael Uebel, 286–314. Durham, NC: Duke University Press, 1997.

Hine, David (writer), and Agustin Padilla (artist). "All the Rage, Part One." *Detective Comics Annual* #12. New York: DC Comics, June 2011.

———. "All the Rage, Part Two." *Batman Annual* #28. New York: DC Comics, July 2011.

Hurwitz, Gregg (writer), and Tony Daniel (artist). "The Final Lesson." *Detective Comics*, vol. 2, #0. New York: DC Comics, September 2012.

Kelly, Casey. "Neocolonialism and the Global Prison in National Geographic's *Locked Up Abroad*." *Critical Studies in Media Communication* 29, no. 4 (2012): 331–47.

Mayo, J. "Why Is Batman the Benchmark? Comic Book Sales Data, Explained." *Comic Book Resources*, April 13, 2017, https://www.cbr.com/comic-book-sales-data-explained/.

Moreton-Robinson, A. "Whiteness, Epistemology, and Indigenous Representation." In *Whitening Race: Essays in Social and Cultural Criticism*, edited by A. Moreton-Robison, 75–88. Canberra: Aboriginal Studies Press, 2005.

Morrison, Grant (writer), and Chris Burnham (artist). "In the Eye of Leviathan." *Batman Incorporated* #1–2. New York: DC Comics, November–December 2010.

Morrison, Grant (writer), Chris Burnham (writer), and Frazer Irving (artist). "Brand Building." *Batman Incorporated* #0. New York: DC Comics, November 2012.

O'Cuana, Emmet. "'Morrison Inc.' and Themes of Benevolent Capitalism." In *Grant Morrison and the Superhero Renaissance: Critical Essays*, edited by Darragh Greene and Kate Roddy, 205–22. New York: McFarland Press, 2015.

Oh, David C., and Kutufam, Doreen V. "The Orientalized 'Other' and Corrosive Femininity: Threats to White Masculinity in 300." *Journal of Communication Inquiry* 38, no. 2 (2014): 149–65.

Pearson, Roberta E., and William Uricchio. "'I'm Not Fooled by That Cheap Disguise.'" In *The Many Lives of the Batman: Critical Approaches to a Superhero and His Media*, edited by Roberta E. Pearson and William Uricchio, 182–213. New York: Routledge, 1991.

Said, Edward. *Orientalism*. New York, NY: Random House, 1979. Reprinted in 1994.

Santiago, Amanda Luz Henning. "The 10 Highest Grossing Superhero Franchises in the US." *Business Insider*, July 7, 2017, http://www.businessinsider.com/highest-grossing-superhero-franchises-in-the-us-2017-7.

Snyder, Scott (writer), and Greg Capullo (artist). "The Pit." In *Batman* Vol. 3, No. 23 New York: DC Comics, August, 2013.

———. "Where the Hell Did He Learn How to Drive?!" *Batman*, vol. 3, #21. New York: DC Comics, June 2013.

Snyder, Scott (writer), James Tynion (writer), and Riley Rossmo (artist). "The List." *Batman*, vol. 3, #52. New York: DC Comics, May 2016.

Thill, Scott. "Grant Morrison's *Batman, Inc.* Births Comics' First Zen Billionaire." *Wired Magazine*, November 2, 2010, https://www.wired.com/2010/11/grant-morrison-batman-inc/.

Tierney, Sean M. "Themes of Whiteness in *Bulletproof Monk*, *Kill Bill*, and *The Last Samurai*." *Journal of Communication* 56 (2006): 607–24.

Tomasi, Peter J. (writer), and Patrick Gleason (artist). "Born to Kill." *Batman and Robin*, vol. 3, #1–8. New York: DC Comics, September 2011–April 2012.

Williamson, Joshua (writer), and Wes Craig (artist). "I Hate It When He Does That." *Legends of the Dark Knight*, vol. 2, #38–40. New York: DC Comics, February–April 2013.

AFTERWORD

# EMPOWERMENT FOR SOME, OR TENTACLE SEX FOR ALL

NOAH BERLATSKY

YOU CAN MAKE a strong case that the first superhero fight scene on film isn't in a pulp serial. Instead, it's in D. W. Griffith's notoriously racist 1915 film *Birth of a Nation*. A straight, tall, upstanding white man with a rakish broad-brimmed hat enters a gin mill in search of a black rapist. The crowd in the gin mill sets upon him. Though he is outnumbered more than ten to one, he easily holds his own, tossing his assailants about like sacks of flower, smashing chairs across their heads, and forcing them to flee from the ramshackle dwelling like clowns leaping from a burning clown car. Our hero is only defeated when one of the black villains shoots him in the back. Even then it takes multiple bullets to do him in, foreshadowing the entirely bulletproof heroes to come.[1]

Comics scholar Chris Gavaler has pointed out that the superhero has important roots in racist KKK adventure fiction. Thomas W. Dixon's 1905 novel *The Clansman*, the main source for *Birth of a Nation*, popularized many familiar elements of superhero stories, such as dual identities and vigilante violence to protect the weak. As Gavaler writes,

---

1. "Watch Scene from D. W. Griffith's 'Birth of a Nation.'"

when innocent people are brutalized, villains go unpunished, and corrupt police fail to act, a hero must rise to save the country he loves. His secret identity hidden behind a mask, the Grand Dragon leads his team of loyal companions in a battle to restore law and order.[2]

The fight scene in *Birth of a Nation* shows that the connection between KKK fiction and superhero stories is even deeper than these narrative parallels suggest, though. The battling white man in Griffith's film is superpowered because he is white—or more precisely, he has superpowers because he is white and the people he is fighting are black. Superness is a mark of physical and moral virtue that sets the hero apart from the run-of-the-mill riff-raff. The (white) hero's empowerment is inextricable from the (less white) rabble's disempowerment. Superness, like whiteness, is dependent on a world in which some people are more equal than others.

Many contributors to this volume have shown that superness and whiteness aren't just parallel, but—as in *Birth of a Nation*—intertwined. In their introduction, Martin Lund and Sean Guynes point out that early Superman stories "were larded with denigration and marginalization of women and people of color," and "laid the groundwork" for a genre in which the default vision of a superhero is "the white heterosexual man." Olivia Hicks argues that the superhero Dagger's superpower is her whiteness: "She is a vision of white innocence exaggerated to superpower status." Osvaldo Oyola notes that "race has always defined Captain America." Since American heroism is innately white, Sam Wilson, a black man, was marked for failure as soon as he donned the Captain America mask.

Critic James Lamb in an essay on *The Hooded Utilitarian* points out that in the films as well, Sam Wilson serves to bolster and dramatize Steve Rogers's power and superness:

> Take *Captain America: The Winter Soldier*: early in the film we watch an athletic Black man sprint effortlessly around the National Mall in Washington, D. C. Wearing exercise shorts and a shapeless grey sweatshirt on a crisp spring day, viewers indulge athleticism, defined. Landscape shots capture republican majesty at the Washington Memorial and the U. S. Capitol. Suddenly a blurry blonde humanoid whizzes past, and frenetic limbs pump faster than the naked eye can detect. Comical frustration darkens Grey Sweatshirt's expression: once, twice, thrice, the splendid blond beast laps

---

2. Gavaler, "How the KKK Shaped Modern Comic Book Superheroes."

the public track while Grey Sweatshirt bellows disbelief at his strained cardiovascular system's futile effort.[3]

*Winter Soldier* premiered in 2014, almost a full century after *Birth of a Nation*. Yet both films use the trope of black inferiority to define and glorify white heroism. A superhero, to be super, requires nonsuper people to serve as a foil, just as white people require nonwhite people to assure them of their eugenic superiority and status.

Thus, in Alan Moore and Alan Davis's *Marvelman*, the competent, deadly black operative Mr. Cream is overawed and then regressed by the blinding whiteness of Marvelman. "Why not shiver and roll your eyes in the dark, Mr. Cream?" the character asks himself. "Why not shiver and say, 'Lawsy! I'se spooked!'" The vision of a white superhero does not empower Cream; instead it boxes him into racist stereotype as a bumbling, subhuman minstrel sidekick. Soon enough, and inevitably, he sacrifices his life for Marvelman, fertilizing the power of whiteness with his corpse.[4]

Superheroes are built on a foundation not just of whiteness, but of white supremacy; these heroes are super specifically because they are better than nonwhite people. As a result, simply creating more superheroes of color can't really address or fix the underlying whiteness of the genre. When a black man becomes Captain America, as Oyola shows, he simply ends up demonstrating that a black man makes an unsuitable Captain America. Similarly, Eric Berlatsky and Sika Dagbovie-Mullins illustrate how black heroes like Black Lightning and Moon Girl are either positioned as inferior to white heroes like Superman, or else are defined as provisionally white in comparison to some more stereotypically debased blackness.

The celebrated film *Black Panther* (2018) shows the limitations of using black superheroes to undermine or rethink the whiteness of the genre. The film provides an exhilarating range of exciting, nuanced roles for black actors. It also engages directly and thoughtfully with issues of global black liberation that are rarely discussed in the superhero genre. The villain, Killmonger (Michael B. Jordan), explicitly blames white Western racism and imperialism for the suffering of black people around the world, and his analysis (though not his solution) is validated by both the film and the hero.

But while Black Panther (Chadwick Boseman) acknowledges the injustice of inequity, oppression, and whiteness, the superhero genre nonetheless requires him to reproduce what he denounces. Black Panther is a heredi-

---

3. Lamb, "Figures of Empire."
4. Moore and Davis, "The Approaching Light."

tary monarch, chosen by bloodline and combat. His superspeed and superstrength are emphasized by his super-authority—he makes the decisions in Wakanda, and everyone else must obey him. Despite its casting, *Black Panther* still can't imagine a country in which black people are free.

Moreover, Wakanda's power is not so much a refutation of white imperialism as a mirror image of it. The film asks, "What if the world's superpower were a black nation rather than a white one?" Wakanda takes the place of the US as the world's most technologically advanced nation—that technological superiority consisting, specifically, of weapons development.

Killmonger wants Wakanda to use its power to conquer the world, mirroring a nineteenth-century vision of imperialist invasion and dominance. Black Panther chooses instead to exercise a more up-to-date strategy, deploying Wakandan soft power to advance global humanitarian goals—which is, of course, what the US claims to be doing in the Middle East and elsewhere. Thus, Wakanda borrows its idea of power and righteousness from an imperial American vision built on inequity. White saviors must travel abroad to uplift the benighted people of the globe. Changing the skin tone of the saviors is an important critique, but the film is still essentially calling on Wakanda to take up the white man's burden. Superheroism remains dependent on the contrast with the less super—a contrast that, in one way or another, is dependent on the example and mystique of whiteness.

If the superhero genre is structured by whiteness, then a superhero story that abandoned whiteness would, in important ways, no longer be about superheroes at all. This is exactly what happens in the work of science fiction author Octavia Butler. Butler was a long-time fan of the superhero genre; according to Gerry Canavan, she loved Superman and followed Marvel comics such as Fantastic Four, Spider-Man, Captain America, and the Hulk. Her own novels show the imprint of her fandom. Her Patternist series (1977–84) is about a family of superpsychics, while her Xenogenesis series (1987–89) imagines (semi-)benevolent aliens manipulating genes to give humans abilities that look a lot like superpowers.[5]

But while Butler's heroes are often superpowered, they aren't really superheroes. The central figure in the Patternist series, for example, is a character named Doro, whose special ability allows him to psychically possess other people. Doro is effectively immortal, as he leaps from mind to mind, killing whoever's body he expropriates. His power is a fairly obvious metaphor for whiteness; he gets his strength from simultaneously enslaving and consuming other, lesser beings. But that power makes him not a protagonist

---

5. Canavan, *Octavia E. Butler*, 40–46, et passim.

in a superhero story, but something more like an unstoppable monster in a horror novel. If some people are super, others are their chattel—and indeed, the Patternist series ends in a dystopian future in which psychics exert absolute control over a human population robbed entirely of free will.

The treatment of superpowers in Butler's Xenogenesis series is more hopeful, and perhaps even more telling. The three books—*Dawn*, *Adulthood Rites*, and *Imago*—are set in a future some time after a nuclear apocalypse. Aliens known as the Oankali saved the few humans remaining following the atomic war, and terraformed and restored the planet. The Oankali did not do this out of altruism, however. They travel from world to world seeking to incorporate genetic material from other races. They literally want to have tentacle sex with earthlings to create new (superpowered) hybrids, to continue the Oankali's journey across the stars.

The Oankali's talent for genetic manipulation allows them to give chosen humans greater strength, improved senses, and great healing abilities. But their goal isn't the creation of superheroes; it's the creation of children. The Oankali don't intend to give certain gifted humans great powers, setting them apart from other, lesser humans. Rather, they want to change humanity entirely by merging with it. It's important, in this context, that the human protagonists of Xenogenesis are mostly black. Lilith, a black woman, is one of the first people the Oankali wake, and one of the first who acquiesces to their breeding program. Her children with the Oankali eventually gain great abilities to manipulate genes and to heal genetic illness and deformities.

That healing ability comes in part from the Oankali. But it also comes from Lilith and from human beings. The Oankali are attracted to humans in large part because humans have untapped genetic potential—genetic potential that manifests as cancer. The rapid growth rate of cancerous cells can be manipulated by the Oankali to allow their progeny to regenerate limbs, or even shapeshift. Superheroes aren't rocketed from Krypton, or bitten by a radioactive spider; they aren't set off from their fellow humans by some act of the gods. Instead, the thing that makes humans special or powerful is shared by everyone, and was seen as a flaw and a disease until the Oankali showed up.

Xenogenesis doesn't just invert whiteness; it creates an entirely new structure for superness that exists at angles to, or completely discreet from, the old one. In superhero stories, whiteness is a superpower doled out to the few. In Xenogenesis, cancer is a superpower doled out to black people, and to everybody else.

Xenogenesis ends with the world being filled up with black superheroes. Essentially, everyone becomes a black superhero. Once whiteness is leached out of superheroes, superheroes disappear, because without whiteness empowerment goes to everyone, not just to a few people in tights.

This isn't to say that Butler's future is a utopia without violence. The Oankali can be read in some ways as colonial exploiters. The series reveals that they eventually plan to devour all of Earth's resources for their ships, leaving behind a shell. Lilith and her children struggle with the question of whether they are joining in a new egalitarian future or merely collaborating with their exploiters. The Oankali have three genders and lots of tentacles, but if you squint in a certain light, you can still see them as white people.

But outside the superhero genre, that whiteness doesn't have to be linked to virtue, and empowerment doesn't necessarily have to mean "more powerful than nonwhite people." Xenogenesis acknowledges a history of colonialism but also reaches tentatively, with those tentacles, for a different distribution of power.

This is not possible within the confines of the superhero genre. Superheroes, by definition, present their audience with individuals who are stronger and more virtuous than the ordinary. Supermen are supermen because they are better than other men. That logic of "better than" is the logic of whiteness. Superheroes can't exist without it.

## Bibliography

Canavan, Gerry. *Octavia E. Butler*. Urbana: University of Illinois Press, 2016.

Gavaler, Chris. "How the KKK Shaped Modern Comic Book Superheroes." *Literary Hub*, November 3, 2017, https://lithub.com/how-the-kkk-shaped-modern-comic-book-superheroes/.

Lamb, James. "Figures of Empire: On the Impossibility of Superhero Diversity." *The Hooded Utilitarian*, May 12, 2015, http://www.hoodedutilitarian.com/2015/05/figures-of-empire-on-the-impossibility-of-superhero-diversity/.

Moore, Alan (writer), and Alan Davis (artist). "The Approaching Light." *Miracleman*, vol. 1, #5. Eclipse Comics, 1986.

"Watch Scene from D. W. Griffith's 'Birth of a Nation.'" *The Washington Post*, July 7, 2017, https://www.washingtonpost.com/video/national/watch-scene-from-dw-griffiths-birth-of-a-nation/2017/07/08/c6c124f8-6345-11e7-80a2-8c226031ac3f_video.html.

CONTRIBUTORS

JOSÉ ALANIZ, professor in the Department of Slavic Languages and Literatures and the Department of Comparative Literature (adjunct) at the University of Washington–Seattle, authored *Komiks: Comic Art in Russia* in 2010 and *Death, Disability and the Superhero: The Silver Age and Beyond* in 2014 (both published by the University Press of Mississippi). His current book projects include *Beautiful Monsters: Disability in Alternative Comics* and a history of Czech graphic narrative.

FREDERICK LUIS ALDAMA is Arts and Humanities Distinguished Professor of English, University Distinguished Scholar, and University Distinguished Teacher at The Ohio State University (OSU). He is the author, coauthor, and editor of thirty-three books; editor and coeditor of eight academic press book series; designer and curator of The Planetary Republic of Comics; and founder/director of LASER/Latinx Space for Enrichment & Research at OSU.

ERIC BERLATSKY is professor and chair of English at Florida Atlantic University. He is the author of *The Real, the True, and the Told: Postmodern Historical Narrative and the Ethics of Representation* and editor of *Alan Moore: Conversations*. He has published articles on the fiction or comics of Dickens, Siegel/Shuster, Woolf, Kundera, Auster, Swift, Spiegelman, Moore/Gibbons, Kureishi, and Simmonds. Additional coauthored work with Sika Dagbovie-Mullins on race and superheroes is forthcoming.

NOAH BERLATSKY is the author of *Wonder Woman: Bondage and Feminism in the Marston/Peter Comics, 1941–1948* (Rutgers University Press, 2015). He was the editor of the comics and culture blog *The Hooded Utilitarian*.

JEFFREY A. BROWN is a professor in the Department of Popular Culture and the School of Critical and Cultural Studies at Bowling Green State University. Brown is the author of numerous articles about gender, ethnicity, and sexuality in media and of the books *Black Superheroes: Milestone Comics and Their Fans* (2000), *The Modern Superhero in Film and Television* (2016), and *Batman and the Multiplicity of Identity: The Contemporary Comic Book Superhero as Cultural Nexus* (2019).

JEREMY M. CARNES is a PhD candidate at the University of Wisconsin–Milwaukee. His research explores the various ways comics depict temporality. Using both queer theory and critical indigenous theory, he argues that the comics form carries radical possibilities for the queering and decolonization of both time and history.

YVONNE CHIREAU is professor in the Department of Religion at Swarthmore College in Swarthmore, Pennsylvania. She has a PhD from Princeton University and is the author of *Black Magic: Religion and the African American Conjuring Tradition* (2003) and the coeditor of *Black Zion: African American Religions and Judaism* (1999). Her writings on Voodoo, comics, and Africana spiritualities can be found at AcademicHoodoo.com.

SIKA A. DAGBOVIE-MULLINS is an associate professor in the Department of English at Florida Atlantic University. She is author of *Crossing B(l)ack: Mixed Race Identity in Modern American Fiction and Culture* (University of Tennessee Press, 2013) and is currently coediting an anthology with Eric Berlatsky that examines representations of racial mixedness and the idea of the superhero. Her other research focuses on representations of slavery in contemporary African American fiction and popular culture.

ESTHER DE DAUW is a comics scholar who completed her PhD in 2017. Her current research focuses on whiteness and race in American superhero comic books and how comics can be used to open up conversations around race and cultural awareness. She has recently published a comics zine, *Missing Panels,* and curated the accompanying exhibit at the David Wilson University Library in Leicester, UK.

SEAN GUYNES is a PhD candidate in English at Michigan State University and journals coordinator at Michigan Publishing at the University of Michigan. He is coeditor of several books and journal special issues, including *Star Wars and the History of Transmedia Storytelling* (Amsterdam University Press, 2017), and editor of *SFRA Review*. Find him online at www.seanguynes.com.

OLIVIA HICKS is a doctorate student at the University of Dundee. Her PhD focuses on the super-girl in British and American girls' comics. She has undertaken a research placement at the British Library, where she researched twenty-first-century British small press comics anthologies, and coedited, with Julia Round, an interview with Trina Robbins that was published in *Studies in Comics*.

MARTIN LUND is senior lecturer in religious studies at the Department of Society, Culture and Identity at Malmö University. He has published widely on comics, including *Re-Constructing the Man of Steel* (Palgrave, 2016) and (as coeditor) *Muslim Superheroes: Comics, Islam, and Representation* (ILEX Foundation/Harvard University Press, 2017).

DR. SHAMIKA ANN MITCHELL is English faculty at Rockland Community College, State University of New York. Her interests are hip-hop, American literature, comics, popular culture, ethnicity, identity, and subjectivity. Her writing has been published in various texts, including *Gloria Naylor's Fiction, Encyclopedia of Black Comics, Icons of Hip Hop*, and *Women on Women: Indian Women Writers' Perspectives on Women*. She is a member of Women in Comics NYC Collective International.

DR. OSVALDO OYOLA's scholarly work focuses on serial comic books, popular music, identity, and collecting practicing. He maintains and edits *The Middle Spaces*, a blog focusing on comics, music, and culture, and serves on the executive committee for the International Comics Art Forum. He recently moved from his beloved hometown of Brooklyn, New York, to Pittsburgh, Pennsylvania.

MATTHEW PUSTZ is the author of *Comic Book Culture: Fanboys and True Believers* (University Press of Mississippi, 2000) and the editor of *Comic Books and American Cultural History* (Bloomsbury, 2012). He teaches American studies and popular culture courses at the University of Massachusetts Boston and Endicott College, in Beverly, Massachusetts. Currently, he is working on a book about comic books in the 1970s.

NEIL SHYMINSKY is an English professor at Cambrian College in Sudbury, Canada. He has previously written about comics in *Men and Masculinities* and *The International Journal of Comic Art* and is currently preparing a book about the X-Men and mutant politics. He recently coedited *The Spaces and Places of Canadian Culture*, a textbook from Canadian Scholars Press, where he also wrote about the cartoonist Seth.

ERIC SOBEL recently completed his master's degree in popular culture from Bowling Green State University. His thesis explored the ways adult action figure collectors and customizers express creativity, negotiate gender codes, and process dominant narratives in response to Internet culture. He is currently interested in the custom action figure fandom fostered through social media, specifically in how fans and creators manipulate popular iconography and construct aesthetic standards.

# INDEX

#BlackLivesMatter (movement), 6, 6n11, 27, 30

Abe Brown (character), 215
Africa, 4, 40–41, 40n8, 52n45, 228; natives of, 234; US relations with, 11
African Americans, xv, 5, 19, 21, 23, 30, 42, 48, 81, 93, 97, 148, 153n59, 154, 154–55n61, 213–15, 244, 255. *See also* black Americans; people of color
Africanist presence, 27, 38–39, 41, 46–47, 49–50, 54, 78
Alex Summers (character). *See* Havok (character)
Alexander, Michelle, 4, 181n17
Aloysius Kare (character). *See* Apache Kid (character)
Amara Aquilla (character), 62–64, 67
America. *See* United States of America
Americanization, 8, 251. *See also* assimilation
Angar the Screamer (character), 216
Angel (character), 58, 143
anticommunism, 148–49
Apache (indigenous people), 58, 195, 208
Apache Kid (character), 193–94, 200, 200n16
*Apache Kid, The* (series, 1950), 193–94, 200
assimilation, 4–5, 8, 20, 59, 85–86, 98, 111, 145, 164, 179, 181–82, 184, 188, 195, 203, 205, 208; into whiteness ("whitening"), 4, 8, 59, 154–55, 154n61, 195, 181, 187; limits of, 184
Australia, 181, 252
*Avatar* (2009), 194, 205, 208, 247
Avengers (fictional group), 58, 127, 129–30, 132–40, 161, 163–64, 214; and state violence, 168–71. *See also* Justice League of America, and military-industrial complex; superheroes, and national defense
*Avengers, The* (series, 1963), 127, 130, 217–18
"Avengers vs X-Men" (2012 event), 165–71
aversive racism, 166–67
Axis, the (WWII), 24–25

Bacon's Rebellions (1676), 4
Badlands, the (fictional place), 66–68
Baldwin, James, xvi, 5
Bannon, Steve, 6. *See also* racism
barbarism, xii, xiv, 4
Barbour, Chad A., 195, 197, 203
Batman (character), 174, 177, 182, 242–56; and cultural appropriation, 246–50; "going Indian," 205; and neocolonialism, 250–56; whiteness of, 242, 245, 252–56. *See also* white privilege
*Batman* (series, 2011), 246, 252
*Batman and Robin* (series, 2011), 249–50
Batman Incorporated (fictional group), 250–56

269

*Batman Incorporated* (series, 2011), 250, 253
"Batmen of All Nations" (fictional group), 250
Batwing (character), 255; Luke Fox as, 244, 255; of 1955, 250
Beast (character), 58, 146–47, 149, 240
Ben Turner (character), 213, 215–17
Berenstain, Nora, 163
Berenstein, Matthew, 245
Berlatsky, Noah, 165
Bilal Asselah (character). *See* Nightrunner
black Americans, xii, xv, 1, 4, 6n10, 6n11, 10, 19–20, 21, 23, 27–32, 38, 42, 48–52, 54–55, 75, 95, 98, 131–33, 143, 147–48, 153, 159, 163, 166, 179, 185–86, 261–62; as American soldiers, 20; anti-Semitism and, 147; black boys, 75, 79, 187–88; bodies of, 21, 24, 42, 53, 78, 185; and civil rights alliances with Jews, 148, 155; culture of, 30, 76, 159, 175n2; and diaspora, 260–61; enslavement of, 38, 77 (*see also* enslaved persons); fear of, 131; and hair, 48; inferiority of, 260; and integration, 153n59; labor of, xv, 77, 184–85; and poverty, xv, 4; and solidarity with colonized peoples, 163; speech of, 50, 159; urban associations with, 90–91, 131–33, 137. *See also* African Americans; people of color and nonwhite people
black liberation, 6, 28, 31, 260. *See also* black nationalism; black power; black radicalism; blackness
Black Lightning (character), 40, 41n12, 42–47, 54, 260; creation of, 41n14
*Black Lightning* (series), 1977–1978, 9, 39, 41–47, 54–55, 175; 1995–1996, 9
Black Marvel (character), 194–95
black men, 1, 21, 39, 45, 55, 72, 74, 81, 84, 93, 166, 184, 259–60; as a threat to white masculinity, 166; as a threat to white women, 81, 83, 162, 258
black nationalism, 147, 149–50, 215; white fears of, 150. *See also* black liberation; black power; black radicalism; blackness
Black Panther (character), 40, 41n12, 44, 54, 169, 260–61

*Black Panther* (film, 2018), 260
*Black Panther* (series), 9; 1977–1979, 9; 1988, 9; 2005, 9; 2009, 9; 2016, 9
black power, 28, 148–51, 185. *See also* black liberation; black nationalism; black radicalism; blackness
black radicalism, 148, 150–51. *See also* black liberation; black nationalism; black power; black radicalism; blackness
black superhero, 8–9, 21–22, 29–31, 38–42, 40n7, 41n12, 46–47, 51, 54, 87, 98, 128, 175–76, 182–84, 186, 244, 262; black folk hero as, 180, 184; exclusion of, 176; (im)possibility of, 175, 182–84, 186. *See also* black (super)villain; superhero, blackness and
black (super)villain, 41n12, 258
black women, 1, 41n14, 47–48, 55, 262; bodies of, 53; sexualization of, 53; as superheroes, 52, 52n45, 161
blackface, 63, 93. *See also* redface
Blackfeet (indigenous people), 195, 207
blackness, 9, 11–12, 25, 28, 31–34, 39–40, 42–43, 46–49, 50–54, 72, 74, 76–78, 81, 98, 119n70, 159, 161, 176, 181n16, 182–84, 187, 260; and alien metaphor, 182–84, 187; and animality, 43, 52; appropriation of, 159; and coolness, 159; and criminality, 41, 45, 45n25; fetishization of, 159; politics of, 98 (*see also* black liberation; black nationalism; black power; black radicalism); and savagery, 162; stereotyping of, 42, 45, 50, 260; super-, 76; and white authorship, 41n14. *See also* whiteness
blaxploitation (genre), 42, 162, 214–15
Blood Syndicate (superhero team), 90, 96, 98, 101
Bonilla-Silva, Eduardo, 244
border consciousness, 105, 110
Bordo, Susan, 239
Bordwell, David, 215
Breitbart News, 6
*Bright Arrow* (series), 199–200
Brothers, David, 159
Brown, Jeffrey A., 9, 51, 93, 98, 100
Brown, Michael, 6. *See also* whiteness, victims of
Brownie, Barbara, 198

INDEX • 271

Bruce Wayne (character). *See* Batman (character)
Burns, Ursula, 48
Butler, Judith, 162
Byrd, Jodi, 59, 59n8

Canada, 233, 246, 249
capitalism, xii, 6n11, 11, 119n70, 185; benevolent, 254–55; racial, 119n70, 185
Captain America (character), 3, 9, 19, 193, 226, 239; as a black man, 21–22, 25, 28, 32–34, 259–60; Bucky Barnes as, 19; as Hydra-Cap, 22, 24–25, 27, 31–34; John Walker as, 19; and redface, 193; Sam Wilson as, 19, 22, 26–34, 259. *See also* Hydra-Cap (character); Sam Wilson (character); Steve Rogers (character)
*Captain America: Sam Wilson* (series, 2015), 24, 26–34, 27n45
*Captain America: Steve Rogers* (series, 2016), 19, 24, 25n18, 26, 29, 34
*Captain America: The Winter Soldier* (2014), 259
Cassandra Cain (character), 244
Caucasian, xii, xiii, 2, 221; as a racialist term, 2
Chagoya, Enrique, 105–20; *Codex Borgia*, 111–12; *Codex Espangliensis*, 112–20; and creation of Mesoamerican codices, 108–12; use of pre-Colombian art, 106–7, 110–11, 113–16, 118–20; use of superheroes, 107–8, 110–11, 113–16, 119–20
Cha-Jua, Sundiata, 215
Charles Xavier (character), 60, 148, 169; compared to Martin Luther King, Jr., 57, 143, 160
Cheyenne (indigenous people), 60–61, 200–201
Chicanx, 103–5; art movement, 103–6, 105n6, 109; era of Chicanismo, 104–5
Chief Man-of-Bats (character), 251–52
Chinese Exclusion Act of 1882, 220. *See also* racism
civil rights, 6, 20, 32, 176; and rights consciousness, 144–46
Civil Rights (movement), 43, 85, 143–49, 151, 154–55, 175–76, 175n2, 179,

182, 186; Jews and the, 146–49, 151, 154–55
Civil Rights Act (1964), 99, 147
civilization, 4, 38–41, 43, 49, 63–65, 68, 84, 169, 198, 200, 206, 245–46, 249, 253, 256
Claremont, Chris, 59–60, 64–65, 73, 143, 152n53, 226, 228, 229, 230, 232–35
class, xv, 2, 4, 7, 50, 97–98, 101, 104, 131–32, 136–37, 143, 154n61, 176, 215. *See also* ethnicity, and class; whiteness, and class
*Cloak and Dagger* (series); 1983, 72, 76, 82–83; 1985, 72, 76
Cloak and Dagger (superhero team), 72–87; as antiheroes, 73; Bill Mantlo's immigrant-story vision for, 73; Cloak's appetite for whiteness, 76–77, 81–84; Dagger and Christian symbolism, 79–90; Dagger as ideal of white femininity, 72–73, 80–81, 83–84, 86–87; and the horror of the black body, 78, 85; racialized superpowers of, 75; sexual connotations of relationship, 83; and supporting cast of ethnic whites, 86; symbolic castration of Cloak, 81 (*see also* Cyborg, castration of)
Cockrum, Dave, 58–60
Cold War, 11, 142, 175, 180, 183, 186; and race, 146–47; and superheroes, 142–47, 175
Colleen Wing (character), 214, 216, 217, 221–23
colonialism, xii, xv, 4, 6n11, 49, 58–59, 61, 63–70, 96, 105, 108, 110–12, 118–19, 166, 183, 209–10, 222, 242–43, 245–46, 248–51, 253–56, 263; anti-colonialism, 106, 253; decolonialism, 69–70; and genocide, 96–97; and indigeneity, 58–59, 59n8, 63–70; and legacy of Christopher Columbus, 96; neocolonialism, 243, 245–46, 248, 250–54, 256; and white supremacy, 245
color line, 2, 5, 188
color-blind(ness), xiv, 7, 20, 221, 244. *See also* post-race
Colossus (character), 169, 228
Comerford, Chris, 251–52
comics; black creators of, 101; black-owned, 9, 90; and diversity, 3, 8, 47, 100, 243; fandom, 3; indigeneity in,

60–61; mainstream, xv; as medium, 127; and Mesoamerican codices, 108–9; nonwhite audiences of, 215; and race, 3, 11; superhero, 3, 7–13, 21, 24, 27, 31–32, 38–39, 43, 46, 48, 54, 114, 140, 160, 176–77, 183–84, 188, 194, 203, 214, 219, 226–27, 239–40, 254; white audience of, 57, 119, 159, 184, 213, 217, 221, 228, 232; white creators of, 41n14, 61, 160, 165, 165n32, 175, 185, 216, 227, 231; whiteness and flesh tone coloring in, 220–21

Cooke, Darwyn, 174–88; on DC's whiteness, 184

Coontz, Stephanie, 136

Cooper, James Fenimore, 198

Corsi and Friedlander (characters), 61, 66–69. *See* "Demon Bear Saga, The" (story arc)

cowboy, 193–94, 200, 202–3; whiteness and the, 200

criminality, xviii, 8, 31, 33, 38–39, 41, 43–47, 54–55, 74, 76, 97, 116, 132, 160, 167, 208, 229–30, 233, 243, 249–50, 252, 254–55; blackness and, 41, 43–47, 45n25, 51, 132; organized, 215, 229, 232–33; and poverty, 97, 132

critical nostalgia, 176, 186

cultural appropriation, 158–60, 195, 213, 222, 227, 231, 234, 243, 246–50, 255–56

Cyborg (character), 9; castration of, 81

Cyclops (character) 58, 146, 150, 152, 160, 161, 165, 167–71; clueless whiteness of, 163

Dakota (fictional place), 90–97, 100–101

Damian Wayne (character), 244, 255

*Dances with Wolves* (film, 1990), 194, 247

Danielle "Dani" Moonstar (character), 9, 60–61, 65–68, 70, 209; and indigeneity, 60; and representation of Native identity, 61, 61n13, 70. *See also* New Mutants, the (superhero team); X-Men (superhero team)

Daredevil (character), 73, 226, 247

Darius, Julian, 160

Dark Ranger (character), 251–52

Davos (character), 222–23

DC Comics, 8, 9, 40, 41, 41n14, 45, 81, 90, 91, 100, 101, 104, 108, 110, 114, 174–77, 181, 183–88, 195n7, 212, 216, 220, 242–43, 247, 255

*DC: The New Frontier* (series, 2004), 174–88

DC Universe, 46, 91, 186, 242

de Certeau, Michel, 231

*Deadly Hands of Kung Fu, The* (series, 1974), 214

"Demon Bear Saga, The" (story arc), 65–69

*Detective Comics* (series), 1937, 177, 250; 2011, 246, 252

Devil Dinosaur (character), 39, 47, 49, 51–52, 54. *See also* Lunella Lafayette (character); *Moon Girl and Devil Dinosaur* (series, 2016)

Dick Grayson (character), 252–53

disability, 8, 25–26, 39, 143, 162; and mutantcy, 143, 162; and superheroes, 8

discrimination, 49, 100; racial, 21, 23, 99, 128, 133, 178, 187, 207

domesticity; and femininity, 127, 135; and masculinity, 127; and whiteness, 127, 129, 131, 133–40

double consciousness, 146; black, 95; Jewish, 155

Drake, Arnold, 150, 154–55

Drug Enforcement Administration, 87

drugs, 72–76, 80, 86–87; whiteness and, 73, 86

Du Bois, W. E. B., 2, 5, 98, 188

Duke Thomas (character), 244, 245

Dyer, Richard, xii, 5, 78, 84, 161, 171, 234, 238, 249, 254–55

Eisenhower Administration, 178

El Gaucho (character), 250–51

empathy; failures of, 143, 166

enslaved persons, 4, 38, 42, 68; labor of, 77, 160

*Enter the Dragon* (film, 1973), 215

"epistemic exploitation," 163

ethnicity, xii, xiv, 9, 13, 48, 57–58, 69, 72–73, 75, 85–86, 159, 161, 166, 181, 213–14, 218, 235, 240, 242–43, 245, 248–49, 251–52, 254; and class, 104; ethnic minority, xv, 39, 42, 104, 238; and indigeneity, 204; prejudice against, 207; and the superhero, 12;

INDEX • 273

white ethnics, 2, 4, 8, 12, 73, 85–86, 147. *See also* blackness; indigeneity; Latinx; race; whiteness

Falcon (character), 9, 19, 40, 42; as black superhero, 40, 42; Sam Wilson as, 19; as sidekick, 9
Faludi, Susan, 83–84, 135
Fanon, Frantz, 12
Fantastic Four (superhero team), 10, 40–41, 44, 261; as symbol of Cold War US, 40
Fawaz, Ramzi, 38–40, 58, 60, 66–67
feminism, 83, 135; backlashes against, 83–84
*Firehair* (series, 1948), 193–94, 207
Frankenberg, Ruth, 5, 19–20
frontier romanticism, 188, 206–7
Fu Manchu (character), 214, 220

gang(ster), 43, 50–51, 86, 227, 232
gay men, xv, 163, 171. *See also* LGBTQ; men; sexuality
"geisha" (stereotype), 227, 229–31
gender, xiv–xv, 2, 7, 39, 54, 57–59, 61, 78, 85, 128, 134, 136, 176, 195, 238, 244–63; gender stereotypes, 229–32. *See also* men; women
Ghee, Kenneth, 128
Gilroy, Paul, 237
Glazer, Nathan, 154
Golden Warrior (character), 200–203
Goldwater, Barry, 148, 150. *See also* racism
"gook" (stereotype), 227, 233–34
Graydon, Danny, 198
Green Lantern (character), 9, 40, 174, 175, 180; as black, 175; Hal Jordan as, 174, 180; Jessica Cruz as, 9; John Stewart as, 9, 40, 175; Simon Baz as, 9
Grim Reaper (character), 130

Haraway, Donna, 128
Hardware (character), 90–91, 94, 97, 100–101
Havok (character), 163–64, 171
Hawkeye (character), 58, 218
heteronormativity, 130
heteropatriarchy, xv. *See also* gender; sexuality

Hill, Jane H., 128
Hitler, Adolf, 6. *See also* racism
HIV/AIDS, 10
hooks, bell, 159
Hoover, J. Edgar, 149. *See also* racism
"House of M" (2005 event), 164–65. *See also* white genocide
House Un-American Activities Committee (HUAC), 178, 186. *See also* anticommunism; Cold War
Hulk, the (character), 51, 53, 116, 227, 261
Hydra (organization), 22, 24–26, 31–32
Hydra-Cap (character), 22, 24–25, 27, 31–34. *See also* Captain American (character)

Iceman (character), 58, 151
Icon (character), 90, 92–98, 100–101; as "black Superman," 93
Ignatiev, Noel, xviii, 5
immigrants, xv, 73–74, 85–86
imperialism. *See* colonialism
Inca (indigenous people), 62–65, 67
*Incredible Hulk, The* (series, 1962), 227
Indianness, 3, 194, 200; absorption of, 203; embodied, 203; and savagery, 200; objectification of, 204; obscuration of by whiteness, 196; white performances of (*see* redface). *See also* indigenous
indigenous/indigeneity, xii, 4, 9, 59–70, 193–94; appropriation of, 197, 198, 204, 205; and DNA, 67n31; "going Native," 68, 205 (*see also* redface); racialization of, 63–64; and rites of passage, 197, 206–8; sovereignty, 65; terminology for, 58n6; white contrivances of, 196, 207, 208–9; and whiteness, 60–70, 254. *See also* Native American; white Indian
Inhumans (fictional characters), 48, 52–53, 165
integrationism, 142–55, 182
interracial relationships, 3
intersectionality, xii–xiii, 3, 6, 136
Irish, 4, 85, 181, 208
Iron Fist (character), 212–23, 247
*Iron Fist* (series, 1974), 214, 215, 216, 217, 219, 220, 221, 222

Isabella, Tony, 41, 41n14
Italians, 8, 85–86, 181

Jean Grey (character), 58, 145
Jewish-comics connection, 10
Jews, 4, 8, 10, 25, 142, 144–48, 150–51, 154–55, 161, 177, 181; civil rights alliances with blacks, 148, 155
Jim Crow, 6, 98, 184–86
Jiro Osamu (character), 251, 253–54
John Henry (black folk hero), 175, 184–85; songs about, 184–85
John Henry (comics character), 176, 179–80, 182, 183–88
*Johnny Injun* (series, 1954), 194
Johnson, Lyndon B., 147; and "civil violence," 150
justice, 3, 19, 27, 29, 39, 42–47, 75, 86–87, 147, 151, 177, 200, 210, 244, 249, 251–55, 260; racial, 6, 23, 30, 55, 57, 147, 175n2, 176, 221; vigilante, 204; and whiteness, 31, 38, 43, 46. *See also* law; social justice; "truth, justice, and the American way"
Justice League of America (fictional team), 81, 174–75, 176, 177, 180–81, 183, 184, 187–88; and military-industrial complex, 178. *See also* Avengers, and state violence; superheroes, and national defense

Kamala Khan (character), 9
Karate Kid (character), 214, 221, 247
Kelly, Casey, 245–46, 251
Kennedy, John F., 176–77, 182, 187–88
*Kill Bill* (film, 2003), 248
Killer-Folk, the (characters), 49–52, 54; blackness and, 49–52. *See also* blackness, and animality
King Jr., Martin Luther, 57; whitewashing of, 143
Kiowa (indigenous people), 203–4
Kirby, Jack, 40, 47–49, 110, 116, 142–43, 146, 148, 154–55
Kree Empire (villains), 52–53, 218; and the origin of martial arts, 218
Kruse, Kevin M., 131
Krypton, 46, 98, 107, 114, 128, 262
Ku Klux Klan (KKK), 175, 179, 183, 185–86. *See also* racism

K'un-Lun, 213, 218, 222
*Kung Fu* (TV series, 1972), 212
Kutufam, Doreen, 253

Lady Shiva (character), 214, 215, 221
Lakota (indigenous people), 199, 208
*Last Samurai, The* (film, 2003), 231, 247
Latinx, xii–xiii, xv, 9, 109, 118, 215, 244; popular culture, xii; racial diversity and, 244; racialization of, 118–19; superheroes, xii–xiii, 9, 9n18, 215
law, xii, 23, 73, 74, 99, 147, 151, 244, 249; and colonialism, 4, 251; enforcement of, 28, 178; and lawlessness, 29; and order, 28, 259 (*see also* nonsense; racism); police and, 79; race and, xii, 4, 23, 33, 63, 98; social nature of, 86; superheroes and, 23, 178, 186; whiteness and, 28, 31, 38. *See* Jim Crow; race laws
*Lawrence of Arabia* (1962), 247
Legion of Superheroes, 183, 214
Lee, Bruce, 212, 215, 220–21
Lee, Stan, 40, 142–44, 146, 148, 153–55
Lei-Kung (character), 213, 218, 222
lesbians, xv, 163, 245. *See also* LGBTQ; sexuality; women
LGBTQ, xv, 143. *See also* sexuality
Lin Sun (character), 214, 221
Lipsitz, George, 238
Lorde, Audre, 163
Lotus Shinchuko (character), 215
Lowe, Lisa, 229–30
Luke Cage (character), 40, 42, 214, 217, 228
Lunella Lafayette (character), 39, 47–54, 47n29, 260; and blackness, 47–49; and post-race, 54; racialization of, 49, 51–52; and whiteness, 47–48, 52–54. *See also* Devil Dinosaur (character); *Moon Girl and Devil Dinosaur* (series, 2016)

Madame Mantis (character), 247
Magik (character), 66, 169
Magneto (character), 149, 150, 153–54, 164–65, 168; as communist, 142–43; compared to Malcolm X, 57, 143, 160
Malcolm X, 57, 179; vilification of, 143

male privilege, xiv, 5, 233, 245
*Man Called Horse, A* (film, 1976), 194, 208
Mandarin (character), 226
Mantis (character), 214, 221
Mantlo, Bill, 72–73, 75–76, 78, 81, 83, 87
*Mantoka* (series, 1940), 194
Manzar the Bright Arrow (character), 193, 199–200
Mariko Yashida (character), 226, 229–31, 234
martial arts, 3, 212–23; movies, 212, 215; whiteness and, 3, 213–14, 220–23; whitening of, 213, 222–23
Martian Manhunter, 174–76, 177–82, 183, 187–88; creation of, 177–78
Martin, Orion, 162
Martin, Trayvon, 6. *See also* whiteness, victims of
Marvel Comics, xii, 8, 10, 11, 21, 22, 25, 34, 40, 58, 60, 73, 104, 108, 110, 127, 128, 136, 144, 151n49, 153, 155, 158, 160, 161, 165, 166, 171, 175, 212, 214, 215, 216, 219, 220, 228, 247, 261
Marvel Universe, 28, 143n2, 160, 165, 166, 167, 218
*Marvelman* (series, 1982), 260
masculinity, 3, 8, 227, 255; as master narrative, 127, 129. *See also* black men; gay men; gender; white men
mass incarceration, 39, 74. *See also* racism
Master Kee (character), 215, 221
Master Khan (character), 216
*Master of Kung Fu* (series, 1973), 212, 219, 220, 221
McCarthy, Joseph, 149; McCarthyism, 148, 151
McDermott, Sinead, 176
McIntosh, Peggy, 5
Mekhala (character), 246–47
Melville, Herman, 43
men. *See* black men; gay men; gender; masculinity; white men
Mesmero (character), 150–51
Metropolis, 47, 90–95, 97–101
Milestone Media, 9, 90–91, 93–94, 97, 100–101
military-industrial complex, 180, 186. *See also* Justice League of America, and military-industrial complex

Miller, Frank, 73, 226, 228, 229, 230, 232–34, 240, 243. *See also* racism
minorities; lacking empathy with, 166; necessity of oppression, 166
Misty Knight (character), 214, 215
Moench, Doug, 220–21
"Mohican syndrome," 198–99
*Moon Girl and Devil Dinosaur* (series, 2016), 3, 39, 47–48, 54–55; race of creators, 41n14
Moreton-Robinson, Aileen, 62–63, 242
Morlocks (fictional group), 236, 240
Morris, Steve, 164
Morrison, Grant, 158–61, 162, 165, 250, 252, 254
Morrison, Toni, 1, 2, 5, 20, 24, 26–27, 31, 33, 38–39, 41n14, 43, 45–46, 49–50, 52, 78, 182
mutants (X-Men), 10, 128, 135–36, 142–55, 158–71; and apartheid, 160; as black, 159–60; as ethnic minority, 10, 10n20, 57–58; as Jewish, 142, 144, 152, 154–55; as Other, 143, 161; and white supremacy, 160, 161, 237
*Mystic Comics* (series, 1940), 194–95

Native Americans. *See* indigenous
Nazis, 19, 22, 24–26, 152n53, 239
Nelson, Scott Reynolds, 184
New Deal, the, 8, 177
New Frontier (policy), 177, 182, 188
*New Frontier, The*. See *DC: The New Frontier* (series, 2004)
New Mutants (superhero team), 59–79
New World, the, 38, 51, 108, 114, 119
New York City, 11, 74, 218, 236
Nightcrawler (character), 58, 228, 236, 240
Nightrunner (character), 251, 252–523
Nixon, Richard M., 73, 86, 150. *See also* racism
Nobody (character), 249
nonsense. *See* "reverse racism"; white genocide
Nordstrom, Georganne, 231
nostalgia, 136, 174–75, 176, 184–85, 188
Nova Romans (fictional civilization), 61–65, 67

O Sensei (character), 213–14, 217, 221
O'Cuana, Emmet, 254
Obama, Barack, 6, 19, 30, 168; and the X-Men (superhero team), 168–69
Oh, David, 253
Omi, Michael, 175
Orientalism, 218–20, 226–27, 229–31, 233–34, 247, 248–50, 252, 253–54, 255–56; eyes and, 220, 236, 239. *See also* Said, Edward

Paris Island, 91, 93–97, 101
passing. *See* whiteness, and passing
*Pawnee Bill* (series, 1951), 202–23
Pearson, Roberta A., 244
people of color and nonwhite people, xii, xv, 2, 4–5, 6n10, 9, 12, 20, 23, 25, 27–29, 27n27, 31, 48–49, 75, 81, 85–87, 95, 101, 106, 114, 118, 127–28, 132–34, 136, 138–40, 143, 160–61, 168, 175, 181n17, 183, 214, 215, 227, 231, 234–36, 243, 247, 255–56, 260, 263; Jewish Americans, 148n25. *See also* African American; black; ethnicity; indigenous; Latinx; Romani
*Playing in the Dark* (Morrison), 2, 5, 20, 25, 26, 31, 33, 38, 49, 50, 52, 78, 182
"playing Indian" (concept), 63–66, 67–68, 194, 196, 198, 205. *See also* redface
*Playing Indian* (Deloria), 59, 64, 68, 198n12, 203
police, 33, 44–45, 51, 66–67, 74–75, 79, 91, 170, 177–79, 214, 216, 244, 246–47, 259; brutality, 6, 29, 31; privatized, 30; as symbol of whiteness, 177–79; US as, 254
postcolonial(ism), 114, 169, 245
post-race, 6, 6n10, 7, 54, 72, 87, 128, 132–33, 164
*Power Man and Iron Fist* (series, 1978), 214, 217
Prats, Armando, 209
primitivism, 39–41, 48–50, 54, 247, 253–54
Punisher (character), 73, 228

queer, 83; and mutantcy, 57; superhero, 8; theory, 7; victims of discrimination, 25
Quesada, Joe, 165–68

race, 2, 4, 5, 7, 9, 13, 19–29; biology and, 2; comics and, 3; instability of, 198, 206 (*see also* whiteness, plasticity of); as power formation, 2, 3, 5, 7, 13; and racial shift, 61, 65; social construction of, 5. *See also* ethnicity; post-race; whiteness
race cognizance, 19–20, 22, 24–25, 27, 28, 30, 32–34
race laws, 6, 98. *See also* Jim Crow; law
racial bribe, the, 4, 181n17
racial fetishism, 166, 168–71. *See also* blackness, fetishization of
racial formation, 7, 162, 175, 175n2, 181n17, 188, 195
racial liberalism, 145–47, 148, 151, 153–55; limits of, 177, 182
racism, xv, 1–2, 6n10, 6n11, 7, 11, 24, 33, 54, 61, 63–64, 132–33, 148n25, 165n32, 166–67, 179, 205, 220, 260; antiblackness and, 32, 34, 150; anti-Semitism and, 148; in imagery, 220, 236–37; pseudo-science and, 54; white disavowals of, 132. *See also* aversive racism; Frank Miller's oeuvre; mass incarceration; white nationalism; white power; white supremacy; World War II (WWII), racist comics of
Rainmaker (character), 209
Raven Red (character), 252
Razack, Sherene, 169–70
Reagan, Ronald, 72–73; era of, 131–34; Reaganism, 72–73, 87, 134. *See also* racism
Reconstruction, 185–86
Red Wolf (character), 209
redface, 3, 193–210. *See also* blackface; white Indian
representational logics, 59, 59n8, 61–65, 69–70
"reverse racism," 204. *See also* nonsense; racism
Richard Dragon (character), 212–23, 247
*Richard Dragon, Kung Fu Fighter* (series, 1975), 214, 215, 216, 217, 219, 220, 221
Rift (character), 91–94, 96–97, 99–101
Rocket (character), 90, 94–95, 97, 99–101
Roediger, David R., 5, 6n10, 182
Romani, 25, 135–36; exoticization of, 135

*Ronin* (comic, 1983), 226, 240
Root, Deborah, 234

Said, Edward, 236, 245, 247–48
Salter, Colin, 181
Sam Wilson (character), 19, 22, 26–34, 259. *See also* Captain America (character); Falcon (character)
Sanderson, Peter, 236
savage(ry), 38, 40, 43–44, 52–53, 52n45, 63–65, 68, 78, 162, 169, 198–200, 203–4, 208, 249, 253–54
Scalphunter (character), 193, 203–5
Schueller, Malini Johar, 128
*Secret Empire* (series, 2017), 22, 24–25, 34
secret identity. *See* superhero(ine), and secret identity
*Shaman's Tears* (series, 1993), 208
Shang-Chi (character), 212, 220–21
Sheyahshe, Michael, 198–99
Shihan Matsuda (character), 246
Shingen Harada (character), 226, 229, 232–34
Shohat, Ella, 48
Shou-Lao the Undying (character), 218
Shu-Hu (character), 218
Shyminsky, Neil, 228, 238–39
Sienkiewicz, Bill, 65
Silverman, Kaja, 169
Simon Williams / Wonder Man (character), 129–30, 131, 134
Singer, Marc, 10, 128, 133, 183
Sioux (indigenous peoples), 199–200, 208, 252
skin color, xii, 146, 177; and blackness, 42, 93, 261; blue, 58, 236; green, 177–78; and indigeneity, 62–63, 69, 198, 204; and Latinx, xiii; light/dark binary, xii, 39–40, 46–47, 95, 236; and whiteness, 63, 162, 193, 199–200, 261
slave. *See* enslaved persons
slavery (racial), 4, 33, 42, 43, 52, 63, 98; and capitalism, 119n70. *See also* enslaved persons
social justice, 2, 6n11, 98; backlash against, 2, 2n3, 19
*Son of Tomahawk* (series, 1970), 208
Sons of the Dragon (fictional group), 214, 221

Southern Strategy, 150
speculative fiction, xiii–xv; "of Blackness," 11–12; as political strategy, xiv–xv; "the Whiteness of," 11–12
Spencer, Richard, 6. *See also* racism
Spider-Man, 10, 13, 76, 78, 82, 83, 113, 115, 118, 119, 222–23, 261; as black, 10
Spitzer, Leo, 176
Stam, Robert, 48
Static (character), 90, 95–97, 99–101
Steel (character), 90, 95, 100–101, 175
Steel Serpent (character), 222–23
stereotyping (of groups) 162, 166, 183, 198, 219, 226, 229, 239–40, 249. *See also* blackness, stereotyping of
Steve Rogers (character), 19–29, 25n18, 31–34, 193, 259
Storm (character), 9, 40, 52n45, 58, 150, 161, 228
*Straight Arrow* (series, 1950), 194
suburbia, 135. *See* whiteness, and suburbia
Sue, Derald Wing, 166–67
Superboy (character), 90, 92, 94, 99–102
superhero(ine), xviii, 2–4, 7–13, 20, 24–25, 28, 34, 39, 41–42, 46, 48, 51, 52n45, 54, 59–60, 73–74, 85, 87, 93, 95, 97–101, 103–6, 108, 111–20, 128, 130, 133–34, 136, 139–40, 142, 168, 174–78, 180–88, 193–200, 203, 205–6, 208–10, 214–15, 219, 222, 229–30, 234, 238, 242, 244, 247–48, 251, 255, 258–63; blackness and the (*see* black superhero); in Chicanx art, 103–20; of color (nonwhite), 39, 100, 128, 175, 260 (*see also* black superhero; ethnicity, and the superhero; Latinx, superheroes; race, and superhero comics); as conservative figure, 253; costumes, 42–43, 85, 93, 99, 106, 111, 116n58, 159, 178, 186, 197–98, 200, 206, 210, 223, 244, 249–50, 252–53, 255; as crimefighter, 8, 46, 128, 193–94 (*see also* law, superheroes and); disability and the, 8; gender and the, 2, 8, 205; genre, 10–13, 25, 31, 34, 47n29, 54, 84–85, 87, 87n58, 93, 100, 103, 115, 198, 260, 208, 229, 254, 260–63; history of, 2–4, 7–11, 38–39, 40n7, 108, 110, 176, 258–60; as imperialist fantasy, 87; indigenous, 193–97, 199–210 (*see also* indigenous/

indigeneity; white Indian, as superhero); as intellectual property, 22; and language, 203; and "minimal components," 244; as minority political group, 178; and national defense, 178; as paragon of white superiority, 3–4, 8–9, 21, 113, 128–30, 139, 195, 238, 259; queer, 8; race and the, 2, 9–10, 182–87; as racial allegory, 133; and secret identity, 13, 111, 145, 186, 193, 197, 200, 203, 206, 213, 227, 244, 259; studies, 3, 9, 11, 108; and tokenism, 183; as white ideological formation, 7, 13, 54, 186; whiteness and the, 2–3, 8–12, 18–19, 21–22, 34, 40, 54, 80–85, 90–92, 95, 98–99, 108, 114, 119–20, 128–30, 133, 136, 139, 175–76, 178, 183–84, 186, 194–95, 209, 216, 220, 222, 227, 234, 247, 255, 259–23

Superman (character), 2, 8, 11, 21, 44–47, 90–95, 97–101, 104–8, 110–16, 118–20, 174, 177, 178, 182, 183, 188, 259–61; as Clark Kent, 93, 98–99, 116n58; and ethnicity, 8; "going indian," 205; and whiteness, 11, 98–99

symbolic annihilation, 164, 204, 209, 220

Takaki, Ronald, 4, 144n11, 150n36
Talia Al Ghul (character), 244, 255
T'Challa (character), 40–41. *See also* Black Panther (character)
*Teenage Mutant Ninja Turtles* (series, 1984), 240
Thomas Hawkins (character), 206–7
Thomas, Roy, 149–50, 151–55
Thunderbird (character), 58; as copy of Hawkeye (character), 58; indigeneity of, 58–60, 58n5
Tierney, Sean M., 222, 234, 236, 248
Tobias Whale (character), 42–44, 55
tolerance, 132, 150, 153–54, 179, 243; in-, 149
*Tomahawk* (series, 1947), 195, 206
Tomasi, Peter J., 249
transmedia, 2, 127
Tribal Force (fictional team), 209
Trump, Donald J., 1, 2, 6, 6n11, 25; and white nationalism, 1, 2, 25. *See also* racism
Trushell, John M., 228

"truth, justice, and the American way," 45–46
*Truth: Red, White, and Black* (series, 2003), 20–22, 24, 34

Ultron (character), 127, 129–30
*Uncanny Avengers* (series, 2013), 163–64
*Uncanny X-Men* (series, 1978), 226, 228, 236
United Nations, 168
United States of America, xv, xviii, 1, 2, 4–6, 8, 11, 21–23, 26, 40n8, 45, 64, 68–69, 74, 85, 98–99, 104–6, 108, 145, 153–54, 169–70, 177–78, 181–84, 186, 197–98, 206–7, 214, 220, 244, 249, 252–54, 261; global hegemony and foreign policy, 113, 154, 178, 252–54, 261; identity and southern, 23, 28 (*see also* whiteness, and US South); military, 142, 145, 180; northern, 147; public culture of, 144
universalism, 153–54, 164
Uricchio, William, 244
USAgent (character), 27–28

vigilantes, 204; superheroes as, 178, 186, 251
villain(y), 33, 40n8, 41–42, 44, 46, 54, 73, 86, 91–92, 94, 111, 116, 120, 139–40, 142–43, 145–46, 153, 163, 168–69, 216, 220–21, 238, 244, 249, 258–60; -ization, 84; whiteness and, 92, 120. *See also* black (super)villain
violence, xv, 29, 104, 138–39, 159, 170, 184, 258, 263; civility and, 150, 150n44; and colonialism, 111–13; race and, 23–24, 43, 50, 63, 177, 186; of whiteness, 3, 12, 66–67, 118, 132, 177, 184, 186, 215
Vision (character), 127–40
*Vision, The* (series, 2015), 127, 136–40
*Vision and Scarlet Witch* (series, 1985), 127, 131–34
von Eeden, Trevor, 41, 41n14

Wakanda, 40–41, 169; as a black nation, 261
Wallace, George, 150. *See also* racism
Wanda Maximoff (character), 127, 130, 131–34, 138–39; Romani heritage and, 135–36

INDEX • 279

war, xv, 91, 164, 177, 180, 228, 249; against crime, 243, 254–55; atomic, 262; and genocide, 209; permanent war, xv; warfare state, xv. *See also* Cold War; World War Two (WWII)

War on Drugs, 72–74, 86

Washington, Booker T., 98

Wayne, John, 162

*Weapon X* (comic, 1991), 235

Weber, Max, 170

Wein, Len, 58–59

West, the, 2, 40–41 40n8, 106, 119, 159, 162, 165, 212, 230, 236, 239, 242, 245–51, 253–56, 260

*West Coast Avengers* (series, 1984), 134–36

Western (genre), 194–95, 195n6, 200, 202–4, 207n37, 209–10

Whitbrook, James, 164

white flight, 131–34

white genocide, 167–71. *See also* nonsense; racism

white heroism, xvi, 21, 38–39, 54, 80–84, 100, 114, 209, 220, 234–35, 245–46, 254, 259–60

white Indian, 193–200, 195n6, 202–10; as superhero, 193–95, 200, 203, 208–10. See also *Avatar* (2009); indigenous; Native American; redface

*White Indian* (series, 1953), 206–7, 206n34

white innocence, 24–25, 25n18, 27, 30, 33–34, 77–80, 186n34, 259. *See also* whiteness, as purity

white man's burden (concept), 76, 254, 261

white men (and masculinity), xv, 1, 7–9, 11, 25, 28, 53–55, 79, 83–86, 93, 98, 100, 128–40, 160–61, 177, 179, 194–95, 198, 200, 202–4, 213, 215, 217, 223, 229–30, 233–39, 242, 244–45, 249, 252–54, 258–59; as the superhero norm, 128–29, 140, 227

white nationalism, 1, 6, 25. *See also* white power; white supremacy

white people, xi, xv, 6n10, 7, 23–26, 48, 59–60, 75, 93, 128–29, 133–34, 143, 147, 159, 161, 163, 165–68, 171, 174, 177, 179–80, 183, 193, 203, 217, 221–22, 231, 247–48, 263; bodies of, 3, 12, 42, 87, 178, 195, 197, 206–7, 227, 238–39, 249, 254–55, 259; culture of, 60, 222; as a race, 5–6, 11, 23, 59, 61, 81, 178, 223; racialization of, 203, 205, 208. *See also* whiteness, as absence of race; whiteness, as racially unmarked

white power, 3, 21, 28, 32–34, 38, 166, 215. *See also* white nationalism; white supremacy

white privilege, xii–xv, 2, 5, 7, 13, 46, 72, 127, 132, 139, 140, 147, 154, 163, 198–99, 227–28, 230, 234, 236–39, 243–45, 248, 255–56. *See also* Batman (character); McIntosh, Peggy

white racial transmutation, 208

white savior, xi, 212, 247, 261. *See also* white heroism

white supremacy, xv, 1, 5–6, 13, 20, 22–24, 31, 34, 46–47, 67, 96, 132, 160, 165n32, 166–67, 169–70, 180, 194, 195, 205, 210, 217, 233–34, 245, 248, 251, 254, 255–56, 260. *See also* white nationalism; white power

White Tiger (character), 215; as first Latinx superhero, 215

white women (and femininity), 1, 48–49, 72, 75, 78–87, 127, 135, 138, 140, 166, 186, 207n37. *See also* black men, as a threat to white women; gender; women

*White Women, Race Matters* (Frankenberg), 5, 20, 23, 83

whiteness, xii–xiv, xvii–xviii, 2–7, 9, 11, 13, 19, 21–29, 27n27, 31–34, 38–39, 43, 46–49, 52, 54–55, 60–70, 72–87, 91, 95–101, 105, 118–20, 119n70, 128–34, 136–40, 144, 155, 159, 161, 175–76, 178–79, 181, 183–84, 187–88, 194–95, 197–200, 203–10, 213, 221–23, 227–29, 234–39, 242–46, 249, 255–56, 259–63; abolition of, xvii, 13; as absence of race, 161; and/as American identity and cultural norm, 20, 22–23, 26–27, 30, 38, 46, 49, 59, 77, 85–86, 104, 108, 128–30, 132–34, 137–39, 155, 161, 176, 177, 182–83, 238, 239, 242, 245, 255–56; as aspirational category, 252; in Australia, 181; and beauty, 78; in Canada, 181; and civilization, 43, 253; and class, 1–2, 4, 77, 95, 131–32, 176, 245; and colonialism, 6n11, 58–70, 119n70, 245, 249; definition of, 2; and discrimination, 128; difference from, xxi; dishabituate, xii; and domesticity (*see* domesticity, and whiteness); as embodied, 203, 206; and ethnic social mobility, 147 (*see also* blackness, urban associations with); exceptionalism, 242–43; eye color and, 193, 198, 199, 204, 205, 207, 208; and gender, 2; Greeks and, 8; habituation of, xi–xxi; hegemony of, 2, 3, 145, 149, 163, 170–71, 181, 195, 231, 234, 248, 251; history of, 8, 21; humanity of, 19–20, 128–31; ideologies of, xiv, xv, 1, 3, 43–44, 54–55, 63, 68, 163, 205, 263; and imperialism, xii, 6n11, 61, 87, 119n70, 254, 260; and indigeneity, 60–70; Irish and, 4; Italians and, 8; Jews and, 4, 8, 144–45, 146, 147, 148, 154–55, 181; and liberals, 148, 178; and the literary imagination, 20, 51–52 (see also *Playing in the Dark* (Morrison)); and "the majesty of Justice," 43; masculinity, 3, 8, 139; master narrative of, 4; as moral superiority, 242, 249; and multiculturalism, 100; nerds and, 47n29; normalization of, 3–4; "oxymoronic whiteness," 118–20; as parasitic, 197; and passing, xiii, 52, 98–99, 133–34, 136, 138–40, 143, 161, 165n32, 179–83, 187, 195, 201, 223; as performance, 127–40; plasticity of, 143–44, 155, 176, 178, 181, 183, 188, 194, 208, 222–23; popular culture and, 2, 108, 159; and possessive investment, 21, 23, 53–54, 68–70, 238, 248, 254; and possessive logics, 61–65; and procreation, 131; as purity, 76, 78–79, 81, 83–86, 238; and race, 2, 5, 7, 13, 28, 32, 59, 118–19, 131–33, 155; as racially unmarked or invisible, xi–xii, 3, 11–12, 20, 23–24, 32–34, 128, 161, 186, 227, 235, 240, 244–45; savagery of, 43, 66; and segregation, 131–33; and sexuality, 2; Slavs and, 4, 8; as social (and racial) formation, 5, 182, 188; and social control, 5, 12, 24, 28, 160–61, 181n17 (*see also* white supremacy); as social progress, 96; and suburbia, 57, 131–34, 137–40 (*see also* domesticity); subversion of, 4; as superpower, 12, 79, 83–84, 203, 214, 240, 254–56; and "truth, justice, and the American way," 45–46; and urbanism, 91, 95, 131–32; and the US South, 23; victims of, xviii. *See also* assimilation, into whiteness; ethnicity; race; race cognizance

whiteness studies, xvii–xviii, 2–7, 13, 26, 118–19; superheroes in, 10–11

whitewashing, 48, 222. *See also* comics, whiteness and flesh tone coloring in

Wild West, the, 202, 204

Winant, Howard, 175

Wolverine (character), 58, 162–63, 168, 247; appropriation of Japanese identity and, 227; and libertarianism, 228; as symbol of white supremacy, 239; whiteness and, 162, 227, 229, 234–39

*Wolverine* (series, 1982), 3, 226–40

women, xv; and motherhood, 48, 52, 62, 74, 79, 84, 131, 134–37, 146, 204, 214, 255. *See also* black women; gender; white women; women of color

women of color, xv; as threat to white masculinity, 135, 136, 138, 139, 140. *See also* black women

Wonder Woman, 21, 81, 104, 111, 113–14, 116, 174, 178, 187n35

World War Two (WWII), 22, 38–39, 194, 220, 226, 239, 251; racist comics of, 220, 226, 239; and superhero comics, 38–39, 174

"Worlds Collide" (event), 90–97, 99, 101

Wright, Richard, 5

Wu, William, 220

X-Men (series, 1963), 57–58, 142, 149, 151

X-Men (superhero team), 9, 10, 57–60, 183, 216, 227, 237; as black, 10; as Cold Warriors, 142; as outsiders, 228; and post-race ideology, 164; as privileged, 228; as victims of HIV/AIDS, 10; 160; whiteness of, 143, 161–63. *See also* mutants

"X-Men of Color" (art project), 162. *See also* Martin Orion; Wolverine

Yellow Claw (character), 220

Yü-Ti (character), 218

Zia, Helen, 227, 233

Zimmerman, George, 6. *See also* racism

NEW SUNS: RACE, GENDER, AND SEXUALITY IN THE SPECULATIVE
Susana M. Morris and Kinitra D. Brooks, Series Editors

Scholarly examinations of speculative fiction have been a burgeoning academic field for more than twenty-five years, but there has been a distinct lack of attention to how attending to nonhegemonic positionalities transforms our understanding of the speculative. New Suns: Race, Gender, and Sexuality in the Speculative addresses this oversight and promotes scholarship at the intersections of race, gender, sexuality, and the speculative, engaging interdisciplinary fields of research across literary, film, and cultural studies that examine multiple pasts, presents, and futures. Of particular interest are studies that offer new avenues into thinking about popular genre fictions and fan communities, including but not limited to the study of Afrofuturism, comics, ethnogothicism, ethnosurrealism, fantasy, film, futurity studies, gaming, horror, literature, science fiction, and visual studies. New Suns particularly encourages submissions that are written in a clear, accessible style that will be read both by scholars in the field as well as by nonspecialists.

*Unstable Masks: Whiteness and American Superhero Comics*
    EDITED BY SEAN GUYNES AND MARTIN LUND

*Afrofuturism Rising: The Literary Prehistory of a Movement*
    ISIAH LAVENDER III

*The Paradox of Blackness in African American Vampire Fiction*
    JERRY RAFIKI JENKINS

www.ingramcontent.com/pod-product-compliance
Lightning Source LLC
Chambersburg PA
CBHW030130240426
43672CB00005B/93